Design and Management of Service Processes

Keeping Customers for Life

Rohit Ramaswamy

ADDISON-WESLEY PUBLISHING COMPANY, INC.

Reading, Massachusetts · Menlo Park, California · New York · Don Mills, Ontario
Wokingham, England · Amsterdam · Bonn · Sydney · Singapore · Tokyo
Madrid · San Juan · Seoul · Milan · Mexico City · Taipei

Many of the designations used by manufacturers and sellers to distinguish their products are claimed as trademarks. Where those designations appear in this book and Addison-Wesley was aware of a trademark claim, the designations have been printed with initial capital letters.

The publisher offers discounts on this book when ordered in quantity for special sales. For more information, please contact:

Corporate & Professional Publishing Group
Addison-Wesley Publishing Company
One Jacob Way
Reading, Massachusetts 01867

Ramaswamy, Rohit, 1960–
    Design and management of service processes / Rohit Ramaswamy.
        p.   cm. — (Engineering process improvement series)
    Includes bibliographical references and index.
    ISBN 0-201-63383-3
    1. Customer services—Management.   2. Service industries—Quality control.
3. Production planning. 4. Total quality management.
I. Title.   II. Series.
HF5415.5.R35   1996
658.8'12—dc20   96–4344
                                                                           CIP

 AT&T

Copyright © 1996 by AT&T

0-201-63383-3
1 2 3 4 5 6 7 8 9-MA-99989796
First printing April 1996

STANDARD

WITHDRAWN

Design and Management of Service Processes

ENGINEERING PROCESS IMPROVEMENT SERIES

John W. Wesner, Ph.D., P.E., Consulting Editor

Lou Cohen, *Quality Function Deployment: How to Make QFD Work for You*

William Y. Fowlkes/Clyde M. Creveling, *Engineering Methods for Robust Product Design: Using Taguchi Methods® in Technology and Product Development*

Maureen S. Heaphy/Gregory F. Gruska, *The Malcolm Baldrige National Quality Award: A Yardstick for Quality Growth*

Jeanenne LaMarsh, *Changing the Way We Change: Gaining Control of Major Operational Change*

William J. Latzko/David M. Saunders, *Four Days with Dr. Deming: A Strategy for Modern Methods of Management*

Mary G. Leitnaker/Richard D. Sanders/Cheryl Hild, *The Power of Statistical Thinking: Improving Industrial Processes*

Rohit Ramaswamy, *Design and Management of Service Processes: Keeping Customers for Life*

Richard C. Randall, *Randall's Practical Guide to ISO 9000: Implementation, Registration, and Beyond*

Arthur R. Tenner/Irving J. DeToro, *Process Redesign: The Implementation Guide for Managers*

John W. Wesner/Jeffrey M. Hiatt/David C. Trimble, *Winning with Quality: Applying Quality Principles in Product Development*

ENGINEERING PROCESS IMPROVEMENT SERIES

Consulting Editor, John W. Wesner, Ph.D., P.E.

Global competitiveness is of paramount concern to the engineering community worldwide. As customers demand ever-higher levels of quality in their products and services, engineers must keep pace by continually improving their processes. For decades, American business and industry have focused their quality efforts on their end products rather than on the processes used in the day-to-day operations that create these products and services. Experts across the country now agree that focusing on continuous improvements of the core business and engineering processes within an organization will lead to the most meaningful, long-term improvements and production of the highest-quality products.

Whether your title is researcher, designer, developer, manufacturer, quality or business manager, process engineer, student, or coach, you are responsible for finding innovative, practical ways to improve your processes and products in order to be successful and remain world-class competitive. The **Engineering Process Improvement Series** takes you beyond the ideas and theories, focusing in on the practical information you can apply to your job for both short-term and long-term results. These publications offer current tools and methods and useful how-to advice. This advice comes from the top names in the field; each book is both written and reviewed by the leaders themselves, and each book has earned the stamp of approval of the series consulting editor, John W. Wesner.

Key innovations by industry leaders in process improvement include work in benchmarking, concurrent engineering, robust design, customer-to-customer cycles, process management, and engineering design. Books in this series will discuss these vital issues in ways that help engineers of all levels of experience become more productive and increase quality significantly.

All of the books in the series share a unique graphic cover design. Viewing the graphic blocks descending, you see random pieces coming together to build a solid structure, signifying the ongoing effort to improve processes and produce quality products most satisfying to the customer. If you view the graphic blocks moving upward, you see them breaking through barriers—just as engineers and companies today must break through traditional, defining roles to operate more effectively with concurrent systems. Our mission for this series is to provide the tools, methods, and practical examples to help you hurdle the obstacles, so that

v

you can perform simultaneous engineering and be successful at process and product improvement.

The series is divided into three categories:

Process Management and Improvement   This includes books that take larger views of the field, including major processes and the end-to-end process for new product development.

Improving Functional Processes   These are the specific functional processes that are combined to form the more inclusive processes covered in the first category.

Special Process Topics and Tools   These are methods and techniques that are used in support of improving the various processes covered in the first two categories.

CONTENTS

FOREWORD

During the 1980s, very effective quality methodologies were established which continually improved the value proposition for products being marketed to the public. Those firms which adopted the new methodologies grew and prospered. The methodologies were widely deployed . . . globally . . . and those producers who failed to adopt them generally lost much or all of their market share over the last decade. The values that were improved were, in varying dimensions, the quality and reliability of the delivered product; the cost (and by implication, price) of the product; and the speed with which the product could be brought to market.

The 1990s have brought similar, yet still developing methodologies to service industries . . . from fast food and retailers in the labor-intense service spectrum to software development and telecommunications in the high-technology services arena. Based on a deep understanding of customer value developed and proven in the late 1980s, service industries have begun to realize the importance of systematic service design to deliver high-quality, customer-delighting service.

At AT&T, being the service provider of choice drives our business. Success in that endeavor demands a process-based service design, development, and delivery approach—one which can deliver superior customer value that can be continually improved to defend and increase market share. Depending on market needs, this process-based approach has been employed to assure hassle-free operational service excellence, service speed and efficiency, and low service cost. These attributes are specifically identified and customized early in the service design process.

In this text, a leading service design expert at AT&T Bell Laboratories shares with the readers the fundamentals of a proven service design methodology. By understanding the service process approach, and implementing it vigorously and competently, you should gain a distinct advantage in achieving customer value and market share.

Ralph W. Wyndrum, Jr.
Director
Technology Realization Center
AT&T Laboratories

PREFACE

This book introduces readers to the details of a methodology for the design and management of processes used for delivering and maintaining service to customers. The procedures developed by companies for renting a car, checking in at a hotel or an airport, using an automatic teller machine at a bank, and reporting and resolving a problem with a customer's telephone service are all examples of such processes.

In recent years, several well-known practitioners in the field of engineering design such as the late Dr. Stuart Pugh and Dr. Don Clausing of MIT have written books about adopting a *total* approach to the design and development of products. The idea behind this approach is that product design does not merely consist of technology-specific engineering functions. An average customer who purchases and uses a product is less likely to care about the specific engineering method by which the product functions than about its ability to consistently and reliably satisfy the customer's performance expectations. This is not to say that the technical details of engineering design are not important. Clearly, the ability of a product to deliver consistent and reliable performance is correlated with the quality of the technology used in its design. However, an approach that *only* emphasizes the technical aspects of a design, without achieving a clear understanding of the customers' requirements for the product and the contexts in which it will be used, cannot be expected to deliver products that satisfy customers or are successful in the marketplace. A design methodology is therefore needed that integrates customer-focused, technology-independent methods such as Dr. Genichi Taguchi's quality engineering or Quality Function Deployment (QFD) with the traditional engineering design processes. Such a methodology is referred to as *total design*.

In summary, total design is a general approach that maintains a focus on the customer throughout the design process. It is intended to produce products or services whose primary objective is to satisfy, excite, or delight customers. This approach can be applied as successfully to the design of automobiles as to the development of processes for delivering telephone service to the customer. This book describes how the total design methodology can be applied to *services*.

In general, the design of a service involves three elements: the *features* to be offered by the service, the *layout* and *decor* of the facility where the service takes place, and the *processes* by which the service is delivered. All these elements may not be contained in every service. Many services (for example, package delivery or cleaning services) are not rendered in a designated facility. Some services (for example, an information hot line), may not contain a wide range of features. But every service consists of processes through which customers experience the service.

For any given service, the quality of the design of each of the above-mentioned elements influences the overall service quality experienced by a customer. While a new service is being developed, each element must therefore be carefully and systematically engineered, using the total design concept outlined above. In practice, however, this is not often the case. For many new services, features and facilities usually get planned, but the systematic design of processes tends to be ignored. The reason for this is that service features and facilities are tangible, material things, whose performance can be relatively easily defined in engineering terms. On the other hand, processes are less tangible, and their performance criteria are harder to define and measure. Many service managers therefore do not know how to approach the task of designing processes in a scientific manner. Processes are thrown together haphazardly with no information on how they are likely to perform or whether their performance meets the customers' needs.

As a result, even good services that have the potential for being successful in the market are held back by ineffective or poorly designed delivery or customer-service processes. Since a customer's contact with the organization is through these processes, poor performance leads to unhappy and dissatisfied customers and lost business. In many cases, much time and resources are spent after the service is implemented to repair and improve the processes. This time is doubly costly because it not only requires the expenditure of resources to correct past mistakes, but also takes away from time that can be far more productively spent in forward-looking strategic improvements. These situations can clearly be avoided if the processes are correctly designed before the service is implemented. This book has been written to help the reader achieve this objective. The book is a detailed, step-by-step guide that shows the reader how to create, evaluate, and implement service processes that will consistently satisfy customers by performing at levels that consistently exceed customers' expectations. A conceptual framework called the "Service Design and Management Model" directs the reader through the steps of the methodology. This model is described in Chapter 2. This model can be used to effectively design all elements of a service. In this book, the design of processes is emphasized, for the reasons previously mentioned.

This book complements the many books on service quality that have recently appeared[1] in the literature that illustrate how companies can use service quality as a difficult-to-copy strategic differentiator in the marketplace, and how an evaluation of the impact of service quality on the financial performance of the company can be used to plan and implement effective quality improvement initiatives. Many of these texts have a broad scope, and by using examples from different service in-

---

[1] References to relevant texts are provided in chapter footnotes and in a bibliography at the end of each chapter.

dustries, they describe the principles and philosophy of service quality management. This book has a narrower and more detailed focus and takes a practitioner or a student through the tools and methods required to transform these principles and philosophies to a successfully implemented service. A single case study is systematically developed through the chapters of the book to illustrate these tools and methods.[2]

The fundamental principle on which this book is based is that a service process that delivers a level of performance that consistently surpasses customers' expectations must be systematically designed and methodically managed. The first part of the book deals with the design aspects. Chapters 3 and 4 describe the use of QFD and experimental design to develop design specifications that are based on a detailed quantitative assessment of what customers desire from the service and how a deviation in peformance from this desired level affects their satisfaction with the service. Once the specifications are determined, a design solution that meets these specifications can be constructed. Several design solutions are available for each set of specifications, and it is necessary to compare these solutions and select the one that consistently delivers the highest performance level at an acceptable cost. Methods for design evaluation and selection are covered in Chapters 5, 6, and 7. After a design has been selected, it needs to be implemented. Guidelines for implementation are described in Chapter 8.

The rest of the book describes the management and improvement of the implemented design. The design specifications are also the natural standards against which the peformance of an implemented design can be monitored. Methods for measuring and analyzing process performance relative to the design standards are presented in Chapter 9. Ultimately, however, the true test for a successful service is whether it continues to satisfy customers. A service that performs well when compared with the design standards may still not be satisfying customers if their expectations have changed. Measures of service performance must therefore be continuously tested against measures of customer satisfaction. Satisfaction and its measurement are covered in Chapter 10.

In order for the service to remain competitive over time, its performance must be continuously improved. Since quality improvements require significant investments of time and money, it is important to carefully select only those improvement opportunities that produce the best returns measured in financial terms. This requires the ability to quantify the relationship between service performance and customer purchasing behavior. Methods for doing this are presented in Chapter 11.

As mentioned earlier, the methodology in this book is presented in the context of service processes, but the steps of the Service Design and Management Model can

---

[2]Throughout the book, the portions of the text that pertain to the case study are blocked between two horizontal lines to alert the reader that the example is being discussed.

be used for the design and management of the service features and facilities as well. In addition, the model can also used to *integrate* the design of these elements. The overall quality of a service depends not only on the design quality of the individual service elements, but also on the *interactions* between these elements. For example, the variety of furniture provided in a hotel room (features) and the process used for cleaning this furniture (process) are both individually important contributors to the quality of hotel service. However, taken together, the two elements may fail to satisfy customers if the cleaning process for a particular type of furniture takes so long as to inconvenience guests. A comprehensive methodology for designing services should therefore simultaneously consider the design of features, facilities, and processes of the service, and should explicitly include the impact of the interaction between these elements on the overall design performance. We refer to such a methodology as *integrated design* (do not confuse this with the *total design* principles mentioned previously, which refer to a customer-focused approach to design). The details of an integrated approach to service design are beyond the scope of this book, but we show how the Service Design and Management Model framework can be used to address this problem in Chapter 12.

The book is intended for managers who market and operate services, quality professionals involved in service improvements, and for use in college-level courses on service management. Readers who need to create new processes that do not currently exist will benefit by following the chapters of this book sequentially. Readers who manage existing services may which to read only selected sections of the book. Since the book presents a collection of tools and methods, all the techniques may not be required for all problems. Appropriate sections for different applications are presented in Chapter 2. However, the general approach adopted in this book of designing processes from customer-developed specifications and managing the processes with a focus on customer satisfaction is a good framework for all readers to follow. By adopting this framework, it becomes possible to develop services that distinguish themselves in the market through their superior quality.

ACKNOWLEDGMENTS

This book would still be no more than the glimmer of an idea in my head if it were not for a few special individuals whose support, encouragement, and insights were critical to ensuring the successful completion of this project.

Much of the material in this book crystallized through extensive discussions with colleagues at Bell Labs and AT&T Business Communication Services. Special thanks to Bobbi Bailey, Tom Bauer, S. Chandrashekhar, Shubhajit Chatterjee (of the University of Tennessee), Irv Dolobowsky, and Khalid Hafiz for sharing their experience and knowledge with me during the course of various conversations. Thanks also to Ralph Wyndrum, Luis Boza, and Mary Allen of the Process Engineering Center at AT&T Bell Labs for providing the organizational support that made the writing of this book possible.

The quality of this book was significantly enhanced by the detailed and insightful comments of the reviewers, some of whom met with me in person to provide constructive feedback about how to make this book better. Bill Feuss of AT&T Solutions and Tom Rood, Maureen Sammis, and Gene Speicher of AT&T Business Communication services provided invaluable assistance in aligning the material of this book to better meet the needs of practitioners. The comments of G. Lynn Shostack of Joyce International provided a strategic marketing perspective that helped to focus the context for this book. John Wesner of AT&T GBCS, the series consulting editor, suggested improvements to the structure and layout that would make the text most readable. Prof. David Collier of Ohio State University and Prof. Don Clausing of MIT also provided valuable comments about sections of the book. I am grateful to all of them.

Thanks also to Jennifer Joss and Tara Herries of Addison-Wesley Publishing Company for their patience, good cheer, efficiency, and encouragement during the writing process.

Finally, I owe the completion of this book to my parents, who provided the space for me to write the first half of the book when I was on extended leave to India; to Patty, who admirably balanced professional responsibilities with countless evenings and weekends of child care, and to Varun, age 2, whose astonishing accomplishments in the past year far surpass my own modest personal achievement.

Part

1

Introduction and Overview

Chapter

1

Designing Services— An Introduction

- *Competing through Service Quality—a Fictional Case Study*
- *Competing through Service Quality—Three Industry Examples*
- *Relationship between Products and Services*
- *Creating High-Quality Service—Service Design and Delivery*
- *Total Service Design*
- *Conclusion*

This book describes methods and tools for designing and managing services with an emphasis on service processes in the business context. By *service* we mean the business transactions that take place between a donor (service provider) and a receiver (customer) in order to produce an outcome that satisfies the customer. This definition applies both to industries that manufacture or assemble a physical product and to service industries whose only output is the result of the interaction. By *processes*, we mean the sequence of activities that are required to conduct the transactions (i.e., to deliver the service). By *design*, we mean a systematic analytical methodology to construct processes that will reliably deliver the expected outcome at a satisfactory level of quality and at a reasonable cost. By *management*, we mean the monitoring and improvement of designed processes to ensure continued high-quality performance over time.

The reader of the previous paragraph will no doubt find these definitions lacking in detail. Several questions come to mind, such as: Who are the donors and receivers of service? What is the nature of the business transaction? Who defines the sequence of activities to be performed? What is a satisfactory level of quality? Who decides what costs are reasonable? Finally: **Why do we care about service quality at all?**

The objective of this book is to systematically answer these questions. Before we address the details, let us first look at the question: "Why Service Quality?" We will introduce this topic with the following example about two hypothetical firms, named A and B.

1.1   COMPETING THROUGH SERVICE QUALITY— A FICTIONAL CASE STUDY

Introduction

A and B are two companies that manufacture similar kinds of home electronics equipment. Both firms market their products through department stores and direct order catalogs. Both companies offer a one-year warranty on their products, after which the customer can purchase a multiyear service plan. If some equipment needs servicing while under warranty, the customer can call a toll-free number for the location of the nearest local dealer. The piece to be serviced needs to be dropped off with the local dealer, who will repair it free of charge. After the warranty period expires, customers under a service plan need to send the equipment to regional service centers. The customer is responsible for the cost of shipping the product to the service center. The company bears the cost of return shipping.

Presently, both companies have similar market shares, so neither has a competitive edge in the market. The market strategy departments of both companies develop plans to increase their respective shares of the market. Company A's strategy is to be the first to enter the market with new models of its products. It assembles an engineering design team that is given the task of bringing out a new model every two years with enhanced features that use the latest developments in technology. The engineering design team will be helped by the marketing organization to determine the feature enhancements that are most important to customers. Prior to each new model introduction, the company plans to launch a large advertising campaign to inform its customers of the new features. By being known as the product development leader in the marketplace, Company A expects to create and maintain a strong competitive advantage over Company B.

Company B's market strategy team takes a different approach. The company's design engineers feel that they can copy many of Company A's design innovations within a few months. Company B decides to follow a strategy of increasing customer satisfaction by improving the quality of its service. Market research shows that most customers are not satisfied with either company's postpurchase service and maintenance options. Company B decides to concentrate on these service elements.

Company B's research shows that very few of its products require servicing within the first two years following purchase. The company can therefore afford to extend its warranty period without a significant investment in resources. Under Company B's "Super Service" banner, the warranty period on all products is increased to two years. Customers whose products fail within the warranty period will get an immediate replacement of the equipment at no charge. The replacement will be delivered to the customer by one of the company's service representatives, or by the local dealer in more remote locations.

Just before the end of the warranty period, the company offers to service the equipment at no charge. The equipment will be picked up by the company's representative and will be returned after servicing in two weeks. So as not to inconvenience the customer during this period, the company will temporarily replace the model to be serviced with an upgraded model. At the end of the two-week period, customers are asked to complete a marketing questionnaire about their perceptions of the upgraded model. They are then offered the opportunity to trade in their current model for the upgrade. Customers who choose to upgrade become members of the "Partners Club" that make them eligible to receive special service privileges.

At the end of the warranty period, customers who choose not to upgrade their equipment are offered the option of entering a two-year "Service Partnership" with the company for a fee. If the product fails within the duration of the partnership, it will be repaired and a replacement provided for the duration of the repair. If the product has not been serviced in the two years of the partnership, the company will perform "midlife servicing" of the product at the end of the fourth year of ownership. At this point, the customer will once again be offered the opportunity to trade in his or her current model for the upgrade, though at a lower trade-in value.

Let us break here and reexamine the strategies of each company. Each company has chosen a very different way of investing its strategic resources. Company A has chosen to compete on the basis of technical superiority. To this end, it has assembled an innovative team of engineers and scientists who can incorporate the latest technological advances into the product. Company B, on the other hand, has chosen to develop a product that is technologically competent, but may not be as sophisticated as that of Company A. Instead, it has chosen to spend its resources on developing the infrastructure for high-quality customer service.

At the end of five years, Company A's design team members feel as if they are on a treadmill that is going faster and faster, and they have to work harder and be more innovative just to remain in place. The company is still the technical leader, yet its customer base has begun to shrink. Company B, on the other hand, has seen an increase in market share on most of its product lines, even though it offers a more limited range of product features than its competitor. Customers who are satisfied with one of Company B's products often return to buy others. Company B has ensured a vital and growing market position for its future.

Lessons learned

What lessons can we learn from the story of Company B's success? What did Company B do differently from Company A? The answer to this question lies in understanding what Company A did *not* do. By concentrating on technological advantage, Company A neglected to pay attention to its most important constituent: *its customers.* The company's marketing strategy had a hit-or-miss approach. Every two years, new models of their products were introduced in the stores supported by an advertising campaign, but the company had no way of ensuring that customers would buy the new models. In some cases, the products were successful and sold well; in other cases, customers decided to make do with a perfectly serviceable older model. The company had no accurate method of ascertaining why certain products succeeded and others failed, since it did not have information about how customers used its products. Moreover, the company did not have a loyal customer base that it could rely on to continuously buy its products. In summary, its development effort was unfocused, leading to unpredictable market results.

By contrast, Company B designed a strategy that brought the company closer to its customers. This strategy consisted of two elements. First, the company created a marketing approach that actively motivated customers to upgrade their equipment. Since customers used the new models while the old equipment was being serviced, they had the opportunity to test the new features *in the context of their own applications,* which helped them to ascertain the suitability of an enhanced model for their needs. Customers were therefore able to accurately express their preferences and complaints about Company B's products, which was valuable information for future designs. Moreover, by studying the circumstances under which customers accepted or refused the offer to upgrade, Company B could also develop a more focused customer service strategy. This targeted approach to product development and marketing increased Company B's success in the marketplace.

Second, Company B's service strategy was executed *in a way that minimized inconvenience to customers.* Since the appliance was serviced without charge, and new appliances were substituted when the old ones were removed, customers were made to feel that Company B was aware of and sensitive to their needs. This helped to instill a feeling of trust toward the company in the customers' minds. They were therefore more likely to accept the company's suggestion to upgrade their equipment, and to purchase other equipment from the company. The feeling of partnership between the customers and the company was also encouraged by organizations such as the "Partner's Club." This further increased the loyalty that customers felt for the company.

In summary, Company B's *service-based competitive strategy* forged closer ties between the company and its customers. These ties helped to create a loyal customer base that continued to support the company's products in the marketplace.

Elements of a service-based competitive strategy

What does a service-based competitive strategy mean for Company B? This means that the company has made a commitment to increase its profitability by developing a reputation for excellence in its interactions with customers. This does not mean that the company employees go out and make friends with customers. Customers will not continue to purchase the firm's products simply because they like the sales representative. Instead, they will look for signs (such as timely and error-free service delivery, professional and knowledgeable employees, reliable and dependable service) that indicate to them that the company has done the hard work needed to design the service that meets their expectations. No amount of friendliness or pleasantness can take the place of this demonstration of competence.

Specifically, a company that successfully employs a service-based competitive strategy evokes the loyalty of its customers by doing the following:

1. Clearly understanding the service performance levels desired by customers
2. Committing to consistently and reliably meeting or exceeding these service levels
3. Spending the required time, effort and resources to develop the service infrastructure that can deliver this performance
4. Delivering the performance at a cost that allows the firm to remain profitable and satisfy its obligations to its stockholders

Let us now return to our example. What activities must be completed before Company B can implement its service-based strategy? The following activities are some of the most important:

- The processes for pickup and delivery of the equipment must be designed.
- Enough service centers must be available to service equipment, both immediately and in the future as the customer base expands.
- The necessary systems and databases to monitor purchases, track warranty expiration dates, and enter customer feedback must be developed.
- The sales representatives must be trained on the proper procedures for interacting with customers and for obtaining marketing information from them.
- The procedures for disposal or reuse of older models returned by customers must be arranged.

Need for a strategic service culture

The implementation of a service-based competitive strategy may necessitate significant changes in the way the company conducts its business. Such changes cannot take place without the commitment of all levels of management. Senior management has a very important role to play in ensuring the successful implementation of the strategy. As leaders of the company, high-level managers must not only initiate the changes, but must also support, champion, and finance their planning and implementation.

It is obvious that most companies try to satisfy customers. However, without an underlying strategy, the efforts may be inefficient and diffuse, and supporting data may not be available to test the impact of these efforts on customer satisfaction. A service-based competitive strategy should focus the efforts of the entire company on those activities that result in the greatest increase in satisfaction at relatively low costs. A firm in which a large portion of the employees exhibit this kind of emphasis can be referred to as having a *strategic service culture.* We use the word *strategic* to differentiate our definition from that of *service culture* found in many service quality texts. As used in these texts, service culture often acquires the connotation of a blind and subservient desire to satisfy all customers, irrespective of what it costs the firm to do so. A strategic service culture, on the other hand, is one that is sensitive to customers' service requirements, but also recognizes the need for the firm to remain profitable while satisfying these requirements. Firms with a strategic service culture should be driven to seek innovative design and improvement methods to satisfactory resolve these sometimes conflicting objectives.

Many service managers may find it easy to accept the notion of a service culture as a global corporate attitude that can be absorbed without effort. On the other hand, the idea of a strategic service culture is harder to envision, because it requires the organization to consciously balance the needs of the customers with those of the shareholders, and to continually make decisions to maintain this balance. For many companies, this may require a fundamental change in the company's way of thinking about itself, its customers, and its mission. Yet this change is critically important to ensuring the success of a service-based strategy.

Conclusion

The example presented in this section was hypothetical. The reader can legitimately argue that any position could be successfully demonstrated from this example, depending on how the story was concluded. Are there any real examples of companies that use a service-based strategy to differentiate themselves? We will review a few of these in the following section.

1.2   COMPETING THROUGH SERVICE QUALITY—THREE INDUSTRY EXAMPLES

IKEA—creating services through customer participation

Good service quality is a means of creating value for a customer. In a recent *Harvard Business Review* article, Normann and Ramirez (1993) state that in the volatile competitive environment of today, it is not enough for companies to merely worry about positioning themselves in the right place in the value chain, i.e., offering the right products or services to the right market segments. As more countries begin to compete in the international market, a company's market niche gets crowded very quickly, and its competitive advantage rapidly erodes. In order to stay in business, today's companies cannot passively offer products or services to customers. Instead, they must constantly look for innovative ways to better map their offerings to the requirements of their customers. This innovation cannot be carried out by the company in isolation, but requires the partnership of the company, its customers, and its suppliers. The traditional roles of the company as the manufacturer and deliverer of products, of the customer as the receiver of products, and of the supplier as the provider of raw materials are reconfigured into more flexible and mutually supportive roles in this partnership. This partnership has strategic value to the company because on one hand, it allows the company to be in tune with the evolving needs of its customers, and on the other, it can influence customer roles and the contexts of customer usage to create new demand for its products. Normann and Ramirez call this process the *co-production of value.*

IKEA, the Swedish home furnishing retailer, is an example of a successful implementer of this strategy. IKEA's commitment is to provide high-quality, low-cost furniture that customers can transport and assemble in their own homes. By removing the traditional responsibility of the manufacturer to assemble and transport the product, IKEA has been able to reduce the cost of its furniture. Some customers may perceive the necessity to assemble the furniture by themselves as a reduction in service. IKEA's service-based strategy counters this perception by making customers feel that they are active participants in several functions normally provided by the company, one of which is assembly. IKEA reinforces this relationship by providing the service infrastructure that is needed to support this participation. For example, customers visiting an IKEA store are provided with detailed catalogs, tape measures, and pen and paper to enable them to independently evaluate the suitability of the store's products for their homes. Furniture displays are grouped together by usage so that a customer can see how the pieces would fit in their homes. Clear information is provided on dimensions, materials, and price. Child-care facilities, children's entertainment, free strollers, and restaurants provide the support services that make shopping at IKEA with the family a feasible and enjoyable experience.

Like the fictional Company B, IKEA's strategy for differentiation is based on partnering with its customers to create a mutually beneficial set of services (information, displays, measuring materials, child care, etc.) that facilitates the task of buying furniture for the customers and allows the company to withdraw from labor-intensive and expensive support functions such as assembly and delivery. IKEA cannot hope to successfully implement this strategy by happenstance. Success can only be achieved through efforts to design, maintain, and improve the services provided to ensure that the customers' and the company's needs continue to be met over time.

Daiichi store—collecting strategic information through customer service

The second example is reported in an article by Stalk and Webber (1993) that presents the example of Daiichi, which is one of many home electronics stores in a consumer electronics shopping district of Tokyo. Most stores in the district display a dazzling array of home electronic items such as stereos, video recorders, watches, and cameras, as well as appliances such as refrigerators, washing machines, and air conditioners. Manufacturers dump their products in the stores in the district, with no specific targeting of customers. Customers randomly enter a store and purchase the items they need. As a result, except for the most popular items, retailers have no idea of the purchasing patterns of their customers and no way of generating repeat business.

The Daiichi store takes a different approach, somewhat similar to that adopted by the hypothetical Company B in the previous section. In order to initially attract customers, Daiichi offers two services to differentiate itself from other stores. First, it extends the traditional one-year warranty that most companies offer to three years. Second, it provides next-day delivery, compared to a week taken by the competition.

Once a customer makes a purchase, information about the purchase is recorded in the store's database. Just before the expiration of the warranty period, the store offers to send a technician to the customer's home to check the purchased item. As a courtesy, the technician also offers to check any other appliances in the home during the visit, whether or not the appliance was purchased at Daiichi.

When the technicians return to the store, they fill out a report on the models and ages of all appliances in the house they just visited. This information is entered into a database which can be accessed at the store. Shortly after the visit, the customer is called by a store salesperson and invited to visit the store to look at new products that can replace the old models in the customer's home. As a result of this policy, Daiichi sees 70% return business, compared to 20% for its competitors.

What is the secret of Daiichi's success? Clearly, the store cannot hope to compete on the basis of product variety, since every store in the district carries the same items. As in the case of IKEA, Daiichi uses its service processes to build mutually beneficial relationships with its customers. This makes customers feel that the store is taking an interest in them, and keeps them returning for future purchases. At the same time, the relationship between the technician and the customer allows the store to gain valuable information about customer purchases that is used for targeting future sales opportunities. As in the previous example, both the customer and the store benefit from this partnership.

AT&T Universal Card—creating a service-based differentiation strategy

The third example is that of AT&T's exceedingly successful Universal Card. AT&T launched the card in 1990 to maintain its name recognition by linking its calling card with a commonly recognizable Visa credit card. Prior to 1990, AT&T had never been in the credit card business, and so had the opportunity to design the service from scratch. Using the Malcolm Baldrige National Quality Award criteria as a template, AT&T designed the service right from the beginning with the customer in mind. As described in Gale (1994), AT&T's Universal Card Services is designed to excel on eight customer satisfiers. Each satisfier is further subdivided into categories of attributes.

AT&T's Universal Card strategy to differentiate itself from its competitors followed two principles:

1. Positioning the card in the market so that customers would accept the card.

2. Delivering the promised service so that customers would keep and use the card.

1. *Positioning:* AT&T designed a service package that provided value to customers. The company offered a free Universal card to all its calling-card customers. In addition, users of the card could make telephone calls at a 10% discount from regular calling-card rates. Moreover, the interest rate charged for the card went up and down with the prime rate. AT&T therefore positioned its card in a way that made it attractive for customers to initially acquire the card.

2. *Delivery:* This involved ensuring that the service commitments are met consistently, and paying attention to the following commitments:

- Defining a customer-driven service strategy that clearly understands customers' service requirements and expectations.

- Identifying service performance standards and tolerances that customers expect the service to meet.

- Developing a successful service delivery process where every service encounter is satisfactory to the customer.

- Constructing relationships with customers to better serve their future needs.

By paying close attention to the design of the core service product and its delivery, AT&T created a phenomenal success that earned it the Malcolm Baldrige award in 1992.

Summary

Let us examine the principles that are common to these three companies that have chosen a service-based competitive strategy. We see that such companies do the following:

- Involve customers actively in the delivery of the service

- Design service offerings in partnerships with customers

- Develop long-term personal relationships with customers that build trust

- Design processes that consistently and reliably meet customers' performance expectations

- Provide individualized service that satisfies customers one at a time

- Provide this service at a cost that keeps the company profitable

These principles require the simultaneous satisfaction of contrasting objectives. Business partnerships between the company and customers to define service requirements must be balanced with personal relationships that build mutual confidence and trust. Processes should be designed to deliver predictable and reliable outcomes, but at the same time should provide individualized and personal service. The challenge of developing a service-based strategy is to successfully achieve this balance between the tangible and reproducible aspects of the service and the intangible and individual aspects. This requires an integration of the firm's *service design* with its *service delivery*. We will describe these concepts in more detail in Section 1.4.

1.3 RELATIONSHIP BETWEEN PRODUCTS AND SERVICES

The traditional view of industry tends to differentiate between product and service firms. Product industries are commonly understood to be those that produce physical products such as cars or television sets. Service firms are those that create "soft" outputs such as a restaurant meal or an airline passage.

This differentiation has sometimes resulted in managerial misconceptions about both products and services. On one hand, it has created the belief that the only determinants of product quality are engineering attributes such as the number of features offered or the absence of manufacturing defects. On the other hand, it has relegated services to the category of unmeasurable, uncontrollable phenomena whose presence can only be experienced in some emotional way. Moreover, as mentioned before, it has created the impression that the primary objective of service firms should be to do what it takes to serve customers, with profitability being a secondary consideration. Clearly, these are extreme positions.

As the examples described previously indicate, black-and-white distinctions between products and services are not meaningful in practice. It is more accurate to think in terms of "productlike" or physical attributes and "servicelike" or experiential attributes. The output of most industries is a mixture of these attributes. The precise nature of the mix depends on the particular industry. For example, expensive durable goods almost always have supporting services of selling, repair, and maintenance. Inexpensive goods such as pencils may not have extensive support services, but a customer service telephone number that can be used to call the manufacturer with questions or complaints may be available. Conversely, some service industries such as restaurants have associated physical products (the meal) whose quality is an integral part of the service experience.

We can therefore visualize companies occupying various positions along a continuum from product to service attributes. One end of this continuum is the *tangible* end with product-related attributes. The other end is the *intangible* end related to service attributes. Different companies occupy various positions on this continuum. Close to the tangible end are the *core product* companies such as pencil manufacturers. Further along are the companies that have a *core product with supporting services* such as automobile manufacturers. Closer to the services end are *core services with supporting products* such as a banking service with an ATM or a restaurant. Finally, *core services* with limited product support occupy the intangible service end.

What does this continuum imply from the perspective of designing a product or service? The important fact to remember is that customers make no distinction between the product and service aspects of an organization. Customers view the outputs of a company as a package, and their satisfaction is determined by the total performance of the elements of this package. In the case of IKEA, for example, customers would not visit the store if it could not provide high-quality, low-cost furniture (product). However, customers would be unwilling to transport and assemble their own furniture if the company did not provide the services to facilitate these functions. Therefore, it is not possible to conceptually distinguish between product and service attributes. In this book, we use the word "product" generically to refer to the physical attributes (such as the features offered) of a service, and the word "service" to refer to the nonphysical aspects.

1.4 CREATING HIGH-QUALITY SERVICE—SERVICE DESIGN AND DELIVERY

Let us return to the examples of successful companies described in Section 1.2. What have we learned from these examples? We see that companies delivering high-quality service are able to accomplish two objectives simultaneously. First, they are able to meet their service commitments reliably and consistently. Second, they are able to create an individual approach based on personal interaction. In other words, they are able to integrate a good **service design** with effective **service delivery.**

Design and delivery are the foundations on which the edifice of service is constructed. *Service design* refers to the elements that are planned into the service. The features offered by the service, the nature of facilities where the service is provided, and the processes through which the service is delivered are all part of the design. The quality of the design determines the ability of the service to effectively and efficiently supply the performance level expected by the customers. The design, therefore, is an indicator of the **stability and reproducibility** of the service performance.

Service delivery refers to the manner in which the service is offered to the customer during a service encounter. Unlike the design, whose quality can be measured against commonly established standards, the perceived quality of the delivery depends on the specific nature of the interaction between the service provider and the customer, the mutual roles played by each, the customer's prior experiences with the service, the customer's mood and stress level, and other intangible factors. The delivery, therefore, is an indicator of the **individuality and heterogeneity** of the service encounter.

These two components of service quality are shown in Figure 1.1.

Service design

Customers' requirements for what is needed from the service and the performance standards that the service needs to satisfy form the specifications for the design. The design consists of four related components. *Service product design* refers to the design of the physical attributes of the service. The meal served at a restaurant, subscription options for home cable television service, or the banking transactions that are available through an automatic teller machine are examples of such attributes. Since providing these attributes may involve the assembly of raw materials or developing software, the design of these attributes is analogous to designing a physical product.

Service facility design refers to the design of the physical layout of the facilities where the service is delivered—for example, a restaurant interior or a car rental of-

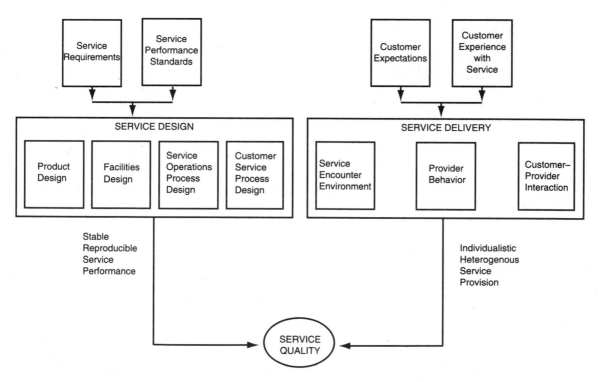

Figure 1.1   Design and delivery components of service quality

fice. Customers' perceptions of the quality of the service are influenced by attributes such as the cleanliness, spaciousness, lighting, and layout of the environment where the service takes place. In addition to these "front room" (i.e., visible to the customer) facilities, back-room facilities (invisible to the customer) such as a restaurant kitchen or an airport baggage handling building also need to be designed. The efficiency of service operations depends on the configuration of these facilities.

Service operations process design refers to the activities that are needed to deliver or maintain a service. Examples are the steps needed to rent a car (collect license, collect credit card, validate payment option, check car availability, print contract, obtain customer signature, deliver car keys and contract), or to deliver a meal to a customer. The activities that make up the operations processes are those required for the service to deliver its output. By contrast, the activities comprising the *customer service process design* pertain to the interactions between the customer and the service provider. For example, in the car rental example described above, in addition to the operational steps, the representative may greet the customer on arrival, refer to him by name, ask him for his preference of cars, and bid him farewell on departure. The customer service and service operations activities together make up the car rental process. The quality of the service experience depends on the performance of both types of activities. These activities therefore need to be designed together.

Service delivery

Service design overlaps with service delivery in the execution of the service and in the environment in which the service encounter takes place. A good design will ensure that the customer contact employees are adequately trained and enough guidelines have been provided to them so that their interactions with each customer will produce a predictable level of performance. Similarly, if service is provided in a designated facility, the design will ensure that the facility is clean, well-lit, and comfortable. However, as Figure 1.1 shows, each service encounter brings with it new customers, with their own experience and expectations. The perceived performance of the service, or the perceived attributes of the service delivery environment, can therefore be influenced by the particular circumstance of the service encounter. The challenge faced by a service manager is to contain the extent of variability in the delivery of the service so that the performance levels of the processes are generally predictable, but still maintain the flexibility to deal with special cases and individual situations. This can be done by designing the routine transactions to take place smoothly, effortlessly, and predictably. This frees the service provider to concentrate on abnormal situations, fulfill special requests, and deliver that extra level of personalized service that may be needed to satisfy the occasional customer.

In conclusion, a high-quality service that satisfies customers can only be achieved by the creative blending of two fundamentally dissimilar components. It requires the integration of the generic with the individual, the expected with the spontaneous, the tangible with the intangible. Neither good design nor good delivery alone is adequate, although, depending on the service situation, one or the other component may be the predominant determinant of customer satisfaction.

For example, customers who conduct bank transactions using automatic teller machines (ATMs) expect all machines to be relatively similar and offer the same set of services. Over the years, the design of ATMs and the services offered by most machines have achieved a broad similarity to meet this need. On the other hand, customers hiring a professional service provider to meet a personal or a business need (such as a private investigator or a consultant) expect the delivered service to be customized to meet that particular need. In this case, the service provider may design a general approach to tackle a class of problems, but the customers' satisfaction will depend primarily on the delivery of the service.

Need for service design

The examples described above represent two extremes of the design/delivery spectrum. Most companies fall in between these extremes, with both a design and a delivery component required to provide high-quality service. Unfortunately, the importance of design is rarely emphasized in the vast body of literature on service quality. Instead of focusing on the millions of customers served satisfactorily and without incident, the literature often concentrates on the heroic efforts made by a single employee to provide out-of-the-ordinary service during a special and unique service encounter. This creates the general impression that good service consists largely of spontaneous good deeds performed by exceptional employees. One tends to forget that these efforts are possible only if the products and processes have been designed so that the hundreds of thousands of average service encounters can be processed satisfactorily without intervention. It is important to remember that the greatest everyday impact of effective service delivery is to add to the quality of services that already function well. In exceptional cases, special attention paid to delivery may be used to resolve problems with service performance. However, over time, no amount of effort at delivery can make up for failures in design.

Service managers have not paid much attention to planned and systematic service design. Most often, services are put together haphazardly, relying on a mixture of judgment and past experience. In a recent paper, de Brentani (1993) studied the approach used to develop new services in the financial sector. In her opinion, ". . . companies tend to use a hit-and-miss approach when planning new services where: ideas are generated and defined in a haphazard fashion, limited customer research is carried out prior to planning the design, service designs often lack creativity and precision and do not incorporate the appropriate technology, testing for possible fail points is rarely done, and market launch is often characterized by trial and error." Managers compensate for the absence of a well-designed service by trying to please the customers through ad hoc activities, and by constantly tinkering with their processes to make them more effective. These are clearly expensive methods and are not competitive in the long run.

The preceding discussion established the importance of a good design for providing high-quality service. But what constitutes a good design? We answer this question in the following section. Let us begin by looking at three examples of not-so-good designs.

1.5 TOTAL SERVICE DESIGN

Example 1—Magazine subscription process: In a bid to attract new customers, a magazine offers a subscription plan with bonus gifts and lower rates. Current subscribers to the magazine are also eligible to enroll in the new plan. Customers are given a toll-free number to subscribe. Current subscribers who call this number are informed that they must cancel their current subscription and resubscribe under the new plan. However, in order to cancel, the customers are required to call another telephone number. They can then call back the original number to enroll. Clearly, this design inconveniences established subscribers.

Example 2—Purchasing movie tickets: A suburban multiple-hall movie theater complex has several ticket windows. A single queue is maintained in the parking lot in front of the windows. Individuals proceed from the head of the queue to the next available window. The company acquires a theater complex in the downtown area of a city, and implements the same process for purchasing tickets. In this case, however, a single queue stretches out to the street, disrupts traffic, and is difficult to control.

Example 3—Automating a bank's customer service process: To reduce cost, a bank replaces its telephone customer service operators with an automated menu leading to recorded messages. Many of the bank's customers are suspicious of technology and enjoy the personal interaction with the customer service representatives. Despite attempts to make the design user friendly, customers are unwilling to listen to the recordings and express dissatisfaction with the new process.

How are these three examples similar? Clearly, they are all examples of designs that did not work. But the similarity ends there. Let us examine the reasons for the failure of each design.

In the first example, there is a *technical flaw* in the design, since current subscribers have to perform several operations where one would have sufficed. The creators of this process did not consider options for integrating the enrollment and cancellation functions. This is an example of a defective design. In the second example, the design itself is technically sound but is *not appropriate for the circumstances* in which it is to be used. The queuing process appropriate for a theater complex in a suburban mall does not work when it is transferred to a downtown location. In the third example, customers do not want the bank to switch to an automated customer service system. The system may be intrinsically well designed, but it *does not meet the needs of its customers,* and therefore remains unused.

Let us return to the question we asked at the beginning of the section: "What constitutes a good service design?" From the three examples presented above, it is clear that a design cannot be judged only on its technical capability. A perfectly good technical design that meets all specifications can fail if it is not applied in the right context or if it does not meet the needs of its customers.

Total and partial design methodology

The point that even a technically well designed service can fail *in the marketplace* has also been made by the pioneers of engineering design methodology such as Clausing (1994) and Pugh (1991). These authors contend that the technical design principles based on mathematics and physics taught in university engineering courses address only part of the overall design problem. They refer to these technical aspects as *partial design*. By contrast, a real design exercise involves the complex interactions of a variety of technical and nontechnical factors that affect the quality of the design. In order to design a product that can be competitive in the market, it is imperative to employ a methodology that integrates the engineering aspects of the design with the marketing and management principles that are required to ensure the commercial viability of the product. Such a methodology is referred to as *total design*. In Pugh's words, total design is "a multidisciplinary iterative process that takes an idea or market need forward into a successful product."

Five principles need to be followed in order to adopt a total design methodology:

Principle 1: Involve the customer in all stages of the design process.

Principle 2: Derive the specifications of the design from the customers and not from previous designs or internal organizational criteria.

Principle 3: Derive the technical aspects of the design from these customer-provided specifications. In other words, the technology should be a derivative of the customer needs and not the other way around.

Principle 4: Design the service using a multifunctional team with representatives from all relevant organizations.

Principle 5: Test the design in the marketplace, and not in the laboratory. A successful design should not only be one that creatively applies the latest technology, but should also be one that customers like, purchase, and use.

Implementing a total design methodology for service processes

The objective of this book is to develop a total design methodology for services. As shown in Figure 1.1, this requires the design of the service product, the service facility (if one exists), the operations processes, and the customer service processes. The methodology described in this book is applicable to the design of all these components. However, in this book, we present the methodology in the context of the *processes* through which the customer experiences the service. This is because the processes are the least tangible components of a service, and their design is often not systematically approached. Yet, in some cases, these processes may be the only point of contact between the customers and the service, and their performance may have a significant impact on customer satisfaction. It is therefore important to design them with care.

Much of the work in service process design is due to G. Lynn Shostack. In a *Harvard Business Review* article entitled "Designing services that deliver," (Shostack, 1984), Shostack presents an analytical tool for process design and documentation called *service blueprinting*. Blueprinting is a graphical technique for documenting processes that displays process functions above and below the "line of visibility" to the customer. It therefore helps a process manager to identify potential failure points in the process, assists in the tracking of activities whose failures affect customers, and, with the assignment of time and cost for each function or process, allows the calculation of profitability and process efficiency. In the first part of this book, we extend this work to describe methods for the definition of customer-focused design specifications, and the generation, evaluation, and selection of design concepts that are inputs for the detailed technical design represented in the service blueprint.

In the second part of the book, we turn our attention to process management. Even the best designs need to be regularly monitored to ensure that their performance continues to be stable and acceptable to the customers. The design specifications serve as natural standards against which the performance of the processes can be measured. In the latter half of the book, we describe methods for measuring, analyzing, and reporting process performance, and for identifying process improvement opportunities that ensures the continued success of the service in the market.

The application of a total design methodology to service process design results in services that not only are technically sound, but also truly reflect customer needs and usage contexts. The successful implementation of this methodology requires teamwork and commitment from all organizations that are involved with selling, delivering, maintaining, or managing the service. Design can no longer be considered a problem for the operations organizations and selling a problem for marketing. It is unacceptable for the marketing managers to promise anything the customer wants and let the "nuts-and-bolts" guy in operations figure out the technical details. It is as unacceptable for the service operations managers to follow the philosophy of "let's build what we like and let the marketing guys figure our how to sell it." Indeed, the design activities are now the joint responsibility of a multidisciplinary design team consisting of members from operations, marketing, front-end sales, customer service, engineering, and all other relevant organizations. The team should be supported by continuous input and feedback from customers. Members from all appropriate technical and nontechnical organizations should be committed members of the core team and should participate in all design decisions.

Service processes designed using these principles are easier to operate, are cheaper and more strategically focused, satisfy the customers better, and, in general, contribute to a firm's profitability much more than processes constructed with no planning. Moreover, traditional Total Quality Management (TQM) and process improvement efforts are no longer just shots in the dark with various managers implementing their pet projects. Instead, process improvement becomes a focused, strategic effort conducted to fine-tune deviations from the design or to incorporate changes in customer expectations and needs into the process. Most TQM efforts falter and die because of lack of direction, failure to achieve perceptible financial gains for the firm, and lack of management support. Combined with a strong design approach, continuous process improvement initiatives can be a strong driving force in ensuring the long-term competitiveness of a company in the marketplace.

1.6 CONCLUSION

Summary

The following are the main points covered in this chapter. The section in which each point is discussed is listed in parentheses.

- A service-based strategy that builds a long-term relationship with customers gives a company a market advantage that is difficult for competitors to replicate. (1.1)

- Competing on service quality requires companies to develop the service infrastructure (processes) needed to continuously and reliably provide high-quality service. (1.1)

- Companies that deliver high-quality service need to balance consistent and reliable delivery with individualized attention to customers. (1.2)

- No rigid distinction can be made between "product" industries and "service" industries; the outputs of most companies have both product and service attributes in different combinations. (1.3)

- Service quality depends on both the design and the delivery of the service; the design refers to aspects of the service that can be planned, while the delivery is the unique characteristic of each service encounter. (1.4)

- Service design involves the design of the service product (features), the service facilities, the operational process activities, and the customer service process activities. (1.4)

- No amount of effort at service delivery can correct deterioration in service quality that occurs because of poor service design. (1.4)

- A good technical design may still fail in the marketplace if it does not meet the needs of the customers. (1.5)

- A successful service needs a total design approach, which is a multidisciplinary activity encompassing both the business and technical aspects of the design. (1.5)

- To implement a total design approach, the customer must be involved in all stages of the design process, and design specifications must be based on customer requirements. (1.5)

Chapter
2

The Service Design And Management Model— A Methodological Overview

- *Basic concepts: vacation planning example*
- *The service design and management model*
- *Overview of model stages*
- *Organization of chapters*
- *Using this book to manage and improve existing services*
- *Introducing the "Service Edge" restaurant*
- *Conclusion*

Before we embark on the specifics of our mission, it would first be useful to see where we want to go and how to get there. This chapter presents the conceptual framework for the methodology that is described in subsequent chapters of this book. The framework itself is a systematic approach that is not unique to services; the concepts can be applied to any design problem. However, the design and management issues involved, and the methods and activities needed to implement the framework, depend on the particular application.

In this chapter, we describe an overview of the activities required to apply the framework to design and manage services, with an emphasis on service processes. In Section 2.1, we illustrate the concepts of our approach using a common household example. This approach is formalized in eight stages of the Service Process Design and Management Model, which we present in Section 2.2. An outline of the activities involved in each stage of the model is presented in Section 2.3. In Section 2.4, we describe the organization and the contents of the remaining chapters of this book. Readers who are designing, implementing, and managing processes for a service from scratch should read all the chapters sequentially. Readers interested in implementing already designed processes, or in measuring and stabilizing the performance of existing services may only need to read some chapters. In Section 2.5, we describe different ways in which the chapters of the book may be packaged to address the needs of different readers. In Section 2.6, we introduce the case study, the "Service Edge" restaurant, which will be used throughout the book to illustrate our methodology. Section 2.7 is a summary of this chapter.

2.1 BASIC CONCEPTS: VACATION PLANNING EXAMPLE

Description

Consider a family (which is a good example of a multifunctional team with all associated teamwork challenges) planning an annual winter vacation. Since the family lives in a cold climate, the members desire to travel to a *warm* destination *near a beach*. These are the family's vacation *needs*.

Clearly, there are many destinations that satisfy these needs. Also, *warm* and *near* are nontechnical terms subject to different interpretations. In order to select a suitable destination, the family needs to develop criteria to evaluate the various available choices. These criteria, or *attributes,* should be quantifiable characteristics of the destination that can measure the extent to which a given destination meets the family's vacation needs. Moreover, the family should agree on *standards* which are the performance values for the attributes that will satisfy the family. Only those destinations that meet or exceed the specifications should be considered as possible choices for a vacation.

What could be some possible standards for the family's vacation destination? Let us first consider the attributes that characterize the two needs: *warm* and *near a beach*. An attribute that measures the extent of warmth is the *minimum temperature* at the destination. Similarly, an attribute that measures the extent of proximity to the beach is the *number of blocks from the farthest hotel to the beach*.

Let us now set acceptable standards for these attributes. Suppose the family desires the vacation destination to have a minimum temperature of 70 degrees Fahrenheit, and the farthest hotel to be no more than two blocks from the beach. These are the *desired standards*.

It may not always be possible to find a vacation destination that meets all the desired standards. The family may have to compromise on the performance of one or more of the attributes. For any attribute, the extent of compromise will be based on the family's tolerance for a deviation in performance from the desired standards for that attribute. For example, the family members may feel that they are not willing to compromise on the temperature of their vacation destination, but an additional walk of two blocks to the beach is not a problem. Based on these considerations, the family may settle on *acceptable* standards for the attribute that are different from the desired standards. An example of such standards for the

Table 2.1 Example of specifications for vacation destination

Need	Attribute	Acceptable Standard	Gap from desired
Warmth	Temperature	Greater than 70 degrees	0 degrees
Proximity to beach	No. of blocks to beach	Less than 6 blocks	4 blocks

temperature and distance attributes are shown in Table 2.1. The gap from the desired standard is also shown in this table. The reader can see that the gap is larger for the distance than for the temperature attribute. As indicated in Table 2.1, the attribute and standards together form the *specifications* for the destination.

After the standards are established, the family generates vacation ideas that are evaluated against the standards. Initially, the ideas are restricted to broad categories, called *concepts.* For example, two concepts may be the following:

1. Vacation at an island resort.

2. Take a cruise that makes daily stops at island beaches.

Since a cruise does not offer the continuous proximity to the beach required by the second need, suppose the family decides to select the first concept, i.e., a vacation at an island resort. Clearly, a large number of island resorts are available, and the next task is to select the particular resort at which the family will vacation. This task requires the *detailed, technical analysis* of each candidate resort to evaluate their performance against the standards. For each resort, this is done by examining brochures, obtaining weather reports, interviewing others who have visited the resort to obtain their opinions, and so on. In addition to the information about the general, or average, conditions, the family should also obtain information about the *variability* of the conditions that may affect the performance standards (for example, how likely is it to rain, do the close beaches get shut down, is there a limit on the number of people who can enter the closest beaches, etc.).

As the result of this technical analysis, suppose the family selects a resort whose average minimum temperature is 72 degrees and where the hotels are no more than five blocks from the beach, and which is available at a price that is acceptable. The family then travels to this resort. This represents the *implementation* of the vacation plan.

After a few days at the resort, suppose it begins to rain and the minimum temperature drops below 70 degrees. Moreover, suppose that five blocks to the beach turns out to be a longer walk than was expected. This indicates the following:

1. The destination does not meet the standards for the warmth attribute.

2. While the destination meets the specifications for the distance attribute, the family's acceptable performance standards have changed, and a distance of five blocks from the beach is no longer acceptable.

Both these situations result in dissatisfaction, and give rise to *opportunities for improvement*. As a result, the family decides to move to another resort on a neighboring island with different weather patterns and closer beach access. This represents an *improvement plan*.

Key steps followed in selecting and visiting a vacation destination

The following were the key steps followed during the *design, implementation,* and *improvement* of the family's vacation plans:

A. *Needs* for the vacation destination were identified ("warm and near a beach").

B. *Attributes* that measured whether a destination could meet these requirements were defined ("minimum temperature and the number of blocks between the beach and hotel").

C. *Standards* for judging destinations on these attributes were established ("minimum temperature of at least 70 degrees and six blocks or less between the beach and the hotel").

D. Vacation *concepts* were generated and selected ("island resort or cruise").

E. An island destination was selected based on *detailed technical analysis*.

F. The family *implemented* the plan and traveled to the destination.

G. The *standards were not met or acceptable standards had changed* ("minimum temperature was less than 70 degrees and five blocks were too far").

H. *Dissatisfaction* gave rise to *opportunities for improvement*.

I. The family selected an *improved site* ("with better weather and closer beach access").

These nine steps form the core of the design and management methodology that is presented in this book. These events are generalized into eight stages of the **Service Design and Management Model** shown in Figure 2.1. The contents of the remaining chapters in this book are presented in the context of this model. Let us describe this model in greater detail.

2.2 THE SERVICE DESIGN AND MANAGEMENT MODEL

The model consists of eight stages from the conception through the life cycle of the service. Each stage of the model is not a single activity, but must be viewed as a

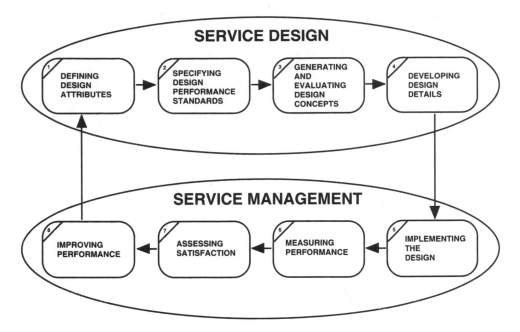

Figure 2.1 The service design and management model

phase with several activities taking place sequentially or simultaneously through the life cycle of the service. The end of the life cycle is when the market conditions, the competitors, the technology, or the customer base change to the extent that the existing processes are obsolete and new designs are needed. The design process is then started afresh.

This does not imply that new design activity should only be begun at the end of the life of a service. Rather, the design of new processes should be an ongoing activity, and new designs should be phased in smoothly before the old designs lose their effectiveness. It is too late to introduce new designs after customers complain or switch to the competition's service. The development and introduction of new services and enhanced processes should be an integral part of the service management strategy of the firm.

Mapping the model stages to the vacation planning example

How do the eight stages of Figure 2.1 compare with the steps of the vacation planning example? *Stage 1* encompasses the first two steps (A and B). In this stage, the needs of the customers for the service are obtained, and the attributes of the service that are needed to satisfy these desires are defined. *Stage 2*, in which performance standards for the attributes are specified, is analogous to step C. *Stages 3 and 4*, which deal with the generation, evaluation, and selection of design concepts and detailed alternatives, correspond to steps D and E. Implementation of the selected design is addressed in *Stage 5*, corresponding to step F. *Stages 6 and 7* parallel steps G and H. In Stage 6, the performance of the designed processes is compared to the standards, and action is taken to stabilize this performance, if required. Over time, some processes may no longer perform at the level predicted by the design, or the performance level desired by customers may change. A service whose performance meets the standards can now fail to satisfy customers. The impact of performance on customer satisfaction is evaluated in Stage 7. Poorly performing processes are candidates for improvement or redesign. The most cost-effective improvement activities are selected and implemented in *Stage 8*. This stage corresponds to Step I.

2.3   OVERVIEW OF MODEL STAGES

Stage 1: Defining design attributes

STAGE 1 ACTIVITIES

- Identify the key customers of the service.
- Determine the needs that customers expect the service to fulfill.
- Prioritize the needs in order of importance.
- Specify the attributes required by a service that meets these needs.
- Create quantitative measures for design attributes.
- Establish the relationships between needs and attributes.
- Determine the most important attributes.

An accurate understanding of the needs of the customers is critical to the success of the design. Services that are designed without a clear understanding of customer expectations will fail in the marketplace. The needs must reflect the voice of the customer, and they must be a personal, nontechnical statement of the what the customer expects from the service. These needs should be obtained through face-to-face communication with the customer.

After the needs are collected and prioritized, the nontechnical statements of the customers should be translated into the design attributes for the service. These attributes specify the technical elements that the service must contain to satisfy the needs. For example, consider the following need expressed by a restaurant customer: "I should not feel hungry after completing my meal." To fulfill this desire, the restaurant should ensure that enough food is served to assuage the customer's hunger. "Food quantity" is an attribute that satisfies this need.

Design attributes should be quantifiable, so that the effectiveness of a design in satisfying a need can be objectively evaluated. For example, food quantity can be measured in weight units such as ounces or pounds. Not all attributes have such well-defined scales. Consider an attribute such as "degree of professionalism" that measures the attitude of a service provider. This attribute may be quantified by creating a scale that uses the judgments of experts.

One or more design attributes should be defined for each important need. An attribute may also satisfy more than one need. The association between a need and an attribute is measured by the degree of correlation between them. The technique of *Quality Function Deployment* (QFD) uses a matrix called the *House of Quality* to represent the needs, the attributes, and their associations. The needs are listed as rows of this matrix. A column is created for each attribute. Correlations between the needs and the attributes are represented in the cells of the matrix using numerical weights or special symbols. The most important attributes, which are those that are strongly correlated with the largest number of needs, are identified from the matrix. The quality of the design is judged by the performance of the service on these attributes. QFD is described in detail in Chapter 3.

Stage 2: Specifying performance standards

STAGE 2 ACTIVITIES

- Identify the customers' desired performance level for each attribute.
- Analyze the performance of the competitors.
- Determine the relationship between performance and satisfaction.
- Specify design performance standards for each attribute.

In this stage, we specify the *design performance standards* that each attribute should be designed to satisfy. As far as possible, these standards should match the standards *desired* by the customers. However, technological constraints or expense may make it impossible to design a service that meets these standards. In this case, the design standards should be a compromise between the desired standards and the *minimum acceptable standards* that match the service provided by the competitors.

What analysis is needed to specify where exactly to set the design standard for each attribute? The answer depends on the relationship between performance and satisfaction for each attribute. Clearly, customers are most satisfied when the performance meets the desired standards. If small deviations in performance from the desired level for an attribute cause large decreases in satisfaction, then the design standards should clearly be set as close to the desired standards as possible. On the other hand, if customers display a greater degree of tolerance for performance deviations from the desired level, then the design standards can be set closer to the minimum acceptable level.

Estimating the performance/satisfaction relationship for each attribute is therefore an important step for defining design standards. This is done using a method called *conjoint analysis*. In this method, customers are asked to rate their overall satisfaction with the service when experiencing hypothetical combinations of the design attributes at various prespecified performance levels. The slope of the relationship between performance and satisfaction for each attribute is then extracted from these ratings using regression. These techniques are described in Chapter 4.

Stage 3: Generating and evaluating design concepts

STAGE 3 ACTIVITIES

- Define the key functions needed to provide the service.

- Assemble these functions into processes.

- Document these processes using flow charts.

- Create alternate design concepts for the service.

- Evaluate and select a concept for detailed design.

We now begin to design the service based on the attributes and performance standards developed in stages 1 and 2. At this stage, the system-level structure of the service is developed. The activities that need to be performed to deliver the service are defined at a high level using a visual flow diagramming technique called *FAST* (*Functional Analysis System Technique*). In this technique, each function is represented as a block described by a verb–noun combination. *Enter order into system* is an example of such a function. Each block is connected to other function boxes to the right and left. The boxes to the right of a given activity answer the question "Why is this activity performed?", while those on the left answer the question "How is it performed?" The activities therefore increase in detail from right to left. This technique is described in Chapter 5.

After the activities are identified, processes are constructed by placing the relevant activities in sequential order. At this stage, it is enough to define the boundaries of each process and the interactions between them in order to obtain an overall view of the service. As far as possible, all processes must begin and end with the customer. The processes should be documented using flow diagrams that represent how the processes interact to provide the service. *Service blueprinting* is a visual flow-charting technique that shows the interactions between customers and process activities. This technique is also described in Chapter 5.

Once the overall structure of the service is defined, system-level design solutions are created. These solutions, called *concepts,* are innovative design ideas. The emphasis of a concept generation exercise, which is conducted through a group effort such as brainstorming, should be on creating as many innovative solutions as possible without consideration of their feasibility. As many as a hundred concepts may be generated in the initial phase. When this phase is completed, the group discusses the concepts, and irrelevant or infeasible concepts are discarded. A small number of concepts (about 8–10) are retained for further evaluation. The procedure developed by Stuart Pugh (1991) is a useful tool for evaluating and selecting concepts. The method is designed to create a genuine understanding of the concepts through discussion during the course of the evaluation process to ensure that the final concept selected is carefully thought out and well understood. The Pugh method is also described in detail in Chapter 5.

Stage 4: Developing design details

STAGE 4 ACTIVITIES

- Partition concept into process-level design components.
- Generate design alternatives for each component.
- Predict performance of each design alternative.
- Evaluate and select alternatives for each component.
- Evaluate and select design for implementation.
- Test performance of overall service design.
- Make any necessary modifications to the design.
- Specify detailed functional requirements.

In this stage, each process outlined in Stage 3 is designed in detail in conformance with the selected concept. The design specifications from stages 1 and 2 are translated to the process level to establish the performance requirements for each process. Design alternatives are generated and evaluated for each process, and the alternatives that meet the performance standards are selected. The functions associated with each process are developed in detail.

Many different alternatives exist for designing the details of a service that matches the concept. Each alternative is a technology or mix of technologies by which the service can be provided. Based on the limitations of the technology, the performance that can be delivered by each alternative will vary, as will the implementation and operating costs. The objective of the detailed design stage is therefore to select the design alternative that delivers the highest level of performance at an acceptable cost.

This highest level of performance of a design alternative is not necessarily obvious. The reason for this is that the performance of an alternative depends on the *operating characteristics* under which the design operates. For example, the time taken to deliver a meal to a restaurant customer will depend on the number of orders in the queue, and therefore on the arrival rate of customers into the restaurant. At the very least, therefore, we require an acceptable design alternative to meet the performance standards over the entire range of operating characteristics in which the design is expected to operate. This calls for some measure of the *stability* of the performance of the design alternative. Clearly, a design that is less sensitive to the operating characteristics has a greater likelihood of meeting the performance requirements over a wide range of conditions. Such designs are called *robust*, and they are preferable.

In this stage, several alternatives are created for each process into which the overall service is partitioned. The performance of each design alternative is evaluated on all the attributes that pertain to the alternative. For each attribute, the *average*, or *base*, performance of each alternative is first predicted under the range of operating characteristics that the service is likely to encounter in practice. This is done by specifying *performance functions* that represent the relationship between the average performance of the attribute and the operating characteristics. The alternatives whose average performance meets the design standards over the range of operating characteristics are compared on the basis of cost and on the ease of implementation of the design. The alternatives that are most robust and meet the cost criteria are then selected for further analysis.

The next stage of analysis tests the sensitivity of the selected design alternatives to random variability. All services are subject to variability due to unpredictable environmental causes, and a design alternative whose performance is robust with respect to the operating characteristics on the average may still be sensitive to random variability. Clearly, therefore, the design alternative that is selected for implementation not only should meet the standards on the average, but should also have little performance spread around this average.

The robustness of each candidate design alternative to random variability in performance is tested by *simulating* the service and predicting the performance of the alternative. The effect of variability is captured in the simulation by specifying *probability distributions* for the performance of each alternative. The results of the simulation help to identify potential *failure points* for each design alternative.

From the simulation results and the performance functions, modifications may need to be made to each design alternative to reduce its performance variability. Based on these modifications, a design alternative whose performance is stable, reliable, and predictable across a range of operating characteristics and random environmental conditions should emerge. This is the design that should be selected for implementation.

Detailed design is the topic of Chapter 6 and 7. Simulation methods are described in Chapter 7.

Stage 5: Implementing the design

STAGE 5 ACTIVITIES

- Develop implementation project plan

- Develop a service construction plan

- Develop a pilot and testing plan

- Develop a communications plan

- Develop a rollout and transition plan

- Develop a service management plan

- Implement all the plans

The activities of this stage ensure that the design is implemented successfully. Often, carefully planned designs fail because the transition from existing to future service cannot be executed seamlessly. As a result, many temporary "fixes" and interim solutions need to be deployed during the transition. These solutions cannot be easily dismantled when the new designs are finally implemented. The overall integrity of the design is therefore compromised. In order to minimize the extent and duration of disruption, a carefully thought-out, detailed set of plans must be developed for the implementation.

The activities in this stage involve the development and implementation of six plans:

- Overall project plan
- Service construction plan

- Piloting and testing plan
- Communications plan
- Rollout and transition plan
- Service management plan

The *overall project plan* is the blueprint for the entire implementation project. It identifies the leaders of the overall project, and the time frames by which the major components of the implementation need to be completed. The *service construction plan* refers to the actual assembly of the service and involves the purchase of hardware, the development of software, the documentation of procedures and training materials, and the completion of the other details that are required to make the new service operation. Once the service is constructed, it needs to be tested to ensure that it can function effectively when completed deployed. The *piloting and testing plan* lays out the guidelines for testing. The *communications plan* spells out the medium, the schedule, and the personnel by which the details of the implementation of the new service and the changes arising from the deployment of the service are conveyed to employees and customers. The *rollout and transition plan* describes the sequence and schedule of deployment of the new service across various work locations or organizations.

Finally, the *service management plan* details how the service will be managed, monitored, and improved after the deployment is complete. These activities are carried out by the *service management team,* whose structure and roles should be identified before the new design is implemented. The service management team should be convened and ready to take over the service on the first day of operations, to ensure that the new service is effectively managed right from the start. Often, the service management team is only assembled several months after the service is in operation, or only in response to a problem or a crisis. By this time, it is too late to make strategic or forward-looking improvements to the service, and all the energies of the service management team are taken up in fixing the parts of the services that do not work. The development and implementation of a service management plan can forestall this eventuality.

Details of implementation planning are presented in Chapter 8.

Stage 6: Measuring performance

STAGE 6 ACTIVITIES

- Select key attributes to be analyzed
- Measure performance of attributes relative to standards

- Measure capability of attributes
- Measure efficiency of key processes
- Develop reporting and analysis procedures
- Identify attributes whose performance does not meet standards
- Analyze the root cause of poor performance
- Perform any corrective action, if necessary

Processes that are designed by carefully following the activities of the previous stages have the capability to meet or exceed their design performance standards. However, inefficiencies in implementation, inadequate training, negligence and boredom, or unexpected changes in the process inputs can cause the performance of the process to deteriorate over time. The activities during this stage involve monitoring the performance of the designed service relative to the standards, and taking corrective action to improve or stabilize the service, if necessary.

Three sets of measures are used to monitor the performance of the service in this stage:

1. *Effectiveness metrics*, which measure the performance of the service relative to the standards and are indicators of overall effectiveness of the service.

2. *Capability metrics*, which are the averages and standard deviations of performance and of key internal process activities. Even if the performance of a process currently meets the design standards, a deterioration or an increase in variability of the performance of important activities may provide an early warning of future problems.

3. *Efficiency metrics*, such as operating costs and resource utilization levels.

In order to effectively monitor the performance of the service, it is critically important to have current and accurate information on these metrics. To make this information available quickly and easily where it is needed, reporting and analysis plans must be developed that detail how the data will be collected, how they will be processed, and how the results will be analyzed and presented. Once these plans are implemented, the service management team should regularly examine the analysis results to ensure that the performance of all key attributes is stable, and that the operational costs are under control. Any observed patterns of deviations must be analyzed in greater detail, and corrected if necessary.

The activities of this stage are described in detail in Chapter 9.

Stage 7: Assessing satisfaction

STAGE 7 ACTIVITIES

- Measure customers' satisfaction with performance of service
- Measure satisfaction relative to customers' expectations
- Measure satisfaction relative to the competition.
- Validate these results against those from Stage 2

In Stage 2, design standards were specified using performance/satisfaction functions that were developed from customers' satisfaction ratings of hypothetical service profiles. If these ratings were perfectly accurate, and customers' needs and competitors' behavior remained stable, then we could guarantee that a service that reliably met the performance standards would consistently deliver the degree of satisfaction predicted by the performance/satisfaction functions.

In reality, this is not the case. Customers' expectations of the service may change after they experience it in operation. Customers' needs may change over time. Competitors may improve the quality of their service, creating a new minimally acceptable performance level. In these cases, the satisfaction of customers with the service may change even if the service continues to meet the design standards. The satisfaction therefore has to be regularly monitored over time.

Satisfaction is defined in the service quality literature as a *disconfirmation* between expectations and perceptions of quality. If the perceived quality matches or exceeds the expectations, the customer is satisfied; if not, dissatisfaction results. There are three approaches to measuring satisfaction:

- On an absolute scale (for example, from 1 to 6)
- Relative to expectations (for example, *much better than expected*)
- Relative to competitors (for example, *much better than competitor X*)

The absolute scale is most effective when measuring the satisfaction levels of a *homogeneous* population that has roughly the same overall expectation level. Otherwise, it is not possible to determine whether a given rating is due to the effect of expectations (i.e., a person with low expectations is satisfied with a poorly performing service) or due to a real perception of quality (i.e., a high satisfaction score is really indicative of good quality). As a result, it is not possible to easily compare satisfaction scores across individuals.

Measures relative to expectations and relative to competitors are generally better than absolute scales. Measures relative to expectations have a longer-term focus and can be used to design customer-delighting services in the future. Measures relative to the competition have a shorter term focus and can be used to plan responses to changes in competitors' performance.

Whatever the measure used, the actual satisfaction level is measured and is compared to the predicted satisfaction in this stage. Similarity between the actual and the predicted measures is an indication that the performance of the service does satisfy customers as expected, and improvements should be directed toward strategic activities that help the firm maintain a competitive edge in the market. These activities may involve improving the performance of the processes on attributes where the initial design standards were lower than what the customers desired, or delighting the customers by improving the service beyond their expectations. On the other hand, a discrepancy between the actual and predicted satisfaction values indicates that a correction of the design may be necessary. Service improvement efforts should be focused in this direction.

Details about satisfaction measurement are presented further in Chapter 10.

Stage 8: Improving performance

STAGE 8 ACTIVITIES

- Estimate relationship between financial objectives and overall satisfaction
- Set strategic satisfaction targets
- Estimate relationship between satisfaction and attribute performance
- Select one or more attributes for improvement, and set targets
- Estimate relationship between service-level and process-level attributes
- Select process-level improvement alternatives
- Evaluate the benefits and costs of different improvement alternatives
- Select and implement optimal process improvement initiatives

---

Many choices for improvement present themselves during the lifetime of the service. Some of these may be reactive, involving corrections to the design to align the processes more closely with customers' service requirements. Others may be strategic, focusing on enhancing the firm's competitive edge through exceptional service quality. In this stage the improvement opportunities that yield the greatest returns are selected for implementation.

The activities of this stage involve the development of three relationships:

1. The relationship between strategic financial objectives (e.g., market share) and overall satisfaction

2. The relationship between overall satisfaction and service-level attribute performance

3. The relationship between service-level and process-level performance

From these relationships, the service management team identifies the process improvements that are needed to achieve a strategic revenue or market share objective.

Each process improvement effort also involves a cost. All improvement activities require the investment of time and money. The benefits associated with achieving increased revenue or market share must be compared to the costs of the improvement efforts. A *sensitivity analysis* must be performed to evaluate the costs and benefits of various partial improvement efforts. The amount of improvement that results in the greatest net benefits should be implemented.

The activities of this stage are described in more detail in Chapter 11.

Summary of service design and management model

The main point to be realized from the model of Figure 2.1 is that the design and management stages are two sides of the same coin. Processes that are haphazardly assembled without a careful design approach or proper performance standards will perform unpredictably and will not effectively meet customers' service requirements. Even the best management efforts applied to a poor design will invariably be directed toward stabilizing and controlling the process performance, which is an ineffective use of management resources. On the other hand, without proper management and monitoring, even the best design will fail to satisfy customers over time. Both design and management activities are needed to plan, deliver, and maintain a successful high-quality service.

It must also be emphasized that though the stages of Figure 2.1 are represented sequentially, activities in different stages can take place simultaneously. For example, measurement, monitoring, and improvement of processes (Stages 6, 7, and 8) should take place continually throughout the service life cycle. Also, some stages may be repeated several times during the execution of the model. For example, while evaluating design concepts in Stage 3, it may become necessary to understand some concepts in detail. In this case, it may be necessary to iterate several times between Stages 3 and 4 until a satisfactory design is obtained. The model should therefore be treated as a guideline rather than as a rigid description of mandatory activities. Depending on the service and process characteristics, some steps may be performed out of sequence, repeated, or omitted altogether.

2.4   ORGANIZATION OF CHAPTERS

We now summarize the organization of material in the book. This book consists of the following three parts:

Part 1—Introduction and Overview

Part 2—Design

Part 3—Management and Improvement

This chapter concludes Part 1. Chapters 3 through 7 make up Part 2 of the book. In Chapter 3, we describe how the House of Quality matrix can be used for assessing customer needs, defining design attributes, and specifying the relationship between the needs and attributes. In Chapter 4, we discuss various methods for estimating the performance/satisfaction relationship and show how these relationships can be used in conjunction with competitor benchmarks to set design standards for the attributes. In Chapter 5, we construct FAST diagrams and high-level process flowcharts from the design attributes, and present the Pugh technique for evaluating design concepts. Detailed process design is the topic of Chapter 6, and we translate service performance standards into process and activity level specifications. In Chapter 7, we describe the use of performance functions to evaluate design alternatives and to select a design that meets the performance standards over the entire range of operating characteristics. Uncertainty is also introduced into the evaluation of design performance in Chapter 7, and we describe the use of simulation methods to determine the robustness of the designed service and to identify points of potential failure.

Part 3 of the book encompasses Chapters 8 through 12. Design implementation issues are presented in Chapter 8, and we touch upon some aspects of the planning required to successfully introduce new processes. In Chapter 9, we demonstrate how the effectiveness and efficiency of the designed processes can be measured, and how the results can be reported and analyzed. Chapters 10 and 11 deal with process improvement. In Chapter 10, we describe the assessment of customer satisfaction with process performance. In Chapter 11, we present methods for analyzing the relationship between process performance and profitability, and show how optimal improvement strategies can be selected. Finally, Chapter 12 is a brief summary and review of future steps.

For easy reference, the model stages and the chapter where each topic is presented are shown in Table 2.2. A more detailed summary table that lists the activities in each stage is presented in the summary section (Section 2.7) at the end of this chapter.

Table 2.2   Summary of chapter contents

Chapter	Stage	Contents
3	1	Customer needs assessment
4	2	Benchmarks and design standards
5	3	Concept generation and selection
6	4	Detailed functional design
7	4	Reducing design variability
8	5	Design implementation
9	6	Performance measurement and stabilization
10	7	Customer satisfaction measurement
11	8	Strategic service improvements

2.5   USING THIS BOOK TO MANAGE AND IMPROVE EXISTING SERVICES

Readers who need to design, implement, manage, and improve a new service will benefit by sequentially following Chapters 3 through 11 of this book. Since new services are not designed from scratch very often, most readers of this book are more likely to need tools for managing services currently in operation. The methodology described in this book can also be used for such services. The following examples list some common requirements for existing services and the chapters in the book that address them.

Setting customer-focused performance standards for existing services

If a systematic procedure has not been followed for designing a service, then customer-focused performance standards may not exist for the service. The material in Chapters 10, 11, 3, and 4 can be used to set performance standards for existing services. The steps to be followed are these:

- Measure overall satisfaction and the performance of key attributes (Chapter 10)
- Correlate overall satisfaction with attribute performances (Chapter 11)

- Determine the attributes whose performances have the largest impact on satisfaction (Chapter 11)

- Validate these attributes by interviewing customers (Chapter 3)

- Determine how competitors perform on the key attributes (Chapter 4)

- Set (or reset) performance standards for these attributes (Chapter 4)

The difference between an existing service and a new service is that actual historical measurements of satisfaction and performance are available for an existing service. The attributes of the existing service that are most important to customers can be directly inferred from these measurements by using the regression methods presented in Chapter 11. QFD can then be used to validate the results of the regression, and to collect new needs.

Similarly, the slope of the satisfaction/performance relationship for each attribute can be directly obtained from historical data. The slope is simply the parameter estimate for the attribute obtained from the regression model that links overall satisfaction with the attribute performance. There is no need to use the conjoint analysis method using hypothetical service profiles (described in Chapter 4) in this case.

Evaluating performance variability and sizing/staffing requirements for existing services

Service managers who need to estimate the number of resources that are required to operate a service typically base their estimates on average load levels, with some adjustment for peak and off-peak periods. If the service is subject to a wide range of operating conditions, these approximate methods may lead to inefficient staffing plans. A more accurate method for estimating sizing requirements is to quantitatively predict the impact of operating characteristics on the average performance and performance variability of the service. The simulation methods described in Chapter 7 can be used to do this. The steps to be followed are these:

- Develop an accurate simulation model for the existing service

- Use historical data to specify the performance functions and parameters of the distributions

- Run the model under the range of expected operating characteristics

- Predict the performance of the service in this range

The output of the simulation model can be used to create a performance profile over the operating range. This profile can be easily translated into a sizing profile if the resource capacity is known. The sizing profile predicts the optimal staffing levels throughout the operating range. This information gives a service manager flexibility in managing resources.

Developing process metrics for existing services

If effectiveness, capability, and efficiency metrics do not exist for a service in operation, then it is clearly not possible to determine whether the service performance is stable, whether resources are being used effectively, or whether the service is capable of meeting customer requirements. The approach described in Chapter 9 for developing service performance measures and for analyzing the performance for newly designed services is applicable for existing services as well.

Designing processes for existing services

Clear and methodical documentation of process functions and procedures is needed for managing a service in an effective and systematic manner. Process documentation is useful for training new employees, for identifying bottlenecks or failure points, or for determining the causes of employee overwork or stress. In Chapters 5 and 6, we show how the FAST technique and service blueprinting can be used to generate and represent the functions of the processes of a new service to the required level of detail. The same approach can be applied for documenting the processes of existing services.

Organizational structure for the management of existing services

Service management is a team activity, and the team needs to include members who represent the right functions and who have the authority to make the decisions that are needed to manage and improve the service. Very often, services are managed by an ad hoc operational team that has neither the time nor the power to make strategic decisions about the future of the service. In Chapter 8, we present some guidelines for the structure and responsibilities of a service management team, and describe how the members of this team differ from the personnel responsible for the day-to-day management of the service. These guidelines can also be used for setting up a service management team for an existing service.

2.6   INTRODUCING THE "SERVICE EDGE" RESTAURANT

Background

A restaurant owner who operates a chain of fine restaurants in several metropolitan areas decides to open a new establishment in the business district of a busy commercial city. The restaurant will be open seven evenings a week, and will serve lunch on weekdays. The intention is to market the restaurant as a comfortable and convenient dining location for business travelers and as a choice location for a "special evening out" for casual diners. This dual target market requires the restaurant to be sensitive to the convenience and reliability needs of the business diners as well as to the intimate and personalized service needs of diners who are looking for a memorable experience.[1]

---

[1] Throughout the book, we use two horizontal lines to block the portions of the text in which the Service Edge restaurant example is discussed to help delineate these sections to the reader.

Competitors' profiles

There are several restaurants within a few blocks of the proposed restaurant that are targeted at the same market segment. Initial market research shows that of these, three restaurants can be considered to be the closest competitors. Their profiles are described below:

1. *Vive La France:* This is a restaurant that serves French and European cuisine, and currently has approximately a 25% share of the target market. Average entree prices range from $20 to $25. The restaurant mainly attracts casual diners who are celebrating special events such as birthdays or anniversaries. The restaurant is known for the responsiveness of its employees, and a very attentive waiter is usually constantly at the side of the diners, advising them on the choice of food or wine. The atmosphere is considered formal and somewhat unfriendly by American standards. There is a perception that meal delivery is a little slow. Food quality is rated very high. Food portions are considered small.

2. *Downtown Steakhouse:* This restaurant has a market share of approximately 20% and serves steaks and seafood. Average entree prices range from $15 to $20. The restaurant attracts a fairly large business clientele and a number of families dining with their children, or attending group celebrations such as family reunions. The restaurant is known for its friendly and cheerful waiters and markets itself with the friendly service slogan "welcome to the family barbecue." The atmosphere is considered informal and very casual. Food quality is rated very high. Food portions are very large. The meal delivery interval is considered about average.

3. *Sarah's Seafood House:* This restaurant also has a market share of approximately 20% of the target market. The restaurant serves seafood and some European dishes. Average entree prices are in the $17 to $22 range. The restaurant attracts mostly business customers. The restaurant is known for the use of technology that reduces the meal delivery time. The food is therefore delivered reliably and quickly, which is an important requirement for business diners. Food quality is rated very high. Food portions are average. The atmosphere is considered about average as well.

The profiles of the key competitors are summarized in Table 2.3. Table 2.4 summarizes the customer segment and estimated customer satisfaction ratings (on a scale of 1–7) for each restaurant for the previous quarter.

Business strategy

It is clear that from Table 2.3 that all three restaurants are rated excellent on food quality. Also, the prices charged by each restaurant are within five dollars of each other, and the customer segments that visit the restaurant are insensitive to price variations in this range.

Table 2.3   Profiles of competitors of Service Edge restaurant

Restaurant	Price	Cuisine	Food quality	Promptness of service	Personal attention
Vive La France	$20–25	European	Excellent	Slow	Responsive
Downtown Steakhouse	$15–20	Steak/ seafood	Excellent	Average	Friendly
Sally's Sea-food House	$17–22	Seafood/ European	Excellent	Fast	Average

It appears from this data that it would be difficult for a new restaurant to differentiate itself from its competition on the basis of food quality or on price. However, there is a difference in the perceived level of promptness and attention offered by each restaurant. Table 2.3 shows that on these attributes, each restaurant is rated higher than the other restaurants in the market on its particular specialty, but rates lower on other attributes. For example, the service at Vive La France is perceived to be very responsive to customers' needs, but slow. On the other hand, Sarah's Seafood provides quick and reliable service, but is perceived to be average on the personal attention attributes.

On the basis of this information, the restaurant owner estimates that it would be possible to enter this market by differentiating on *customer service*. She surmises that if technology can be creatively used to deliver quick and reliable service, but at the same time the waiters can be trained to deliver high-quality (but not overbearing) personal attention, the new restaurant can compensate for the perceived limitations of the competition. If properly designed, managed, and marketed, customer service can be used as a strategy to attract the competitor's customers.

In pursuance of this strategy, the restaurant is named *Service Edge*. Publicity notices for the restaurant claim that the restaurant operates at the "cutting edge of service quality." The objective is to design the food, facilities, and services of the

Table 2.4   Customer segments and satisfaction rating for each restaurant

Restaurant	Customers	Satisfaction ratings
Vive La France	Couples/small groups of casual diners	6.25
Downtown Steakhouse	Business/large groups and families	6.20
Sally's Seafood House	Business	6.18

restaurant at a level that would result in an average satisfaction rating of 6.5, which is 0.25 units higher than that of the closest competitor. The strategic mission is to capture and sustain a market share of about 40%. This share would be made up not only of customers drawn from the three main competitors, but also of new diners attracted by the restaurant's name and quality.

Design approach

The restaurant owner realizes that in order to achieve the strategic objective outlined above, the restaurant needs to provide a food and service package that delivers an unforgettable dining experience. Since the competition is fierce, there is not much opportunity to correct mistakes and bring back customers who have been dissatisfied once because of a poor service offering. The package therefore needs to be designed correctly the first time. The owner believes that this can only be achieved by approaching the design process systematically, using quantitative data and analysis wherever possible.

The owner assembles a team of the most skilled and motivated employees from her other restaurants. This team is given the task of designing the food, facilities, and service operations for the new restaurant that will make it justify its name. This team, referred to as the *design team*, is empowered to make all decisions about the design of the service.

The design team consists of representatives from all major restaurant functions, and is instructed to remain together until the completion of all design activities. Each member has been chosen to combine a specialization in a particular function with a broad knowledge of several other functions, lending a diversity of backgrounds and experiences to the team. Moreover, the team is nonhierarchical, with a mix of management and nonmanagement employees. The design team is responsible for: (1) specifying the requirements of the design; (2) evaluating and selecting a design concept; and (3) supervising the implementation of the design. Each design team member is also the member of several functional teams that are responsible for carrying out the detailed design of the selected concept.

How we use this example

In the first half of the book, we use the activities of the design team as a running example to illustrate the service design methodology. As we proceed through the first four stages of the service design and management model, we systematically describe the steps that are needed to design the customer service processes of the Service Edge restaurant. In the second half of the book, the design team gives way to a service management team whose objective is to monitor, manage, and improve the implemented service. We use the designed processes of the Service Edge restaurant to demonstrate how this is done as we proceed through the last four stages of the service design and management model.

A restaurant example has been selected because all readers are familiar with this service experience and can therefore personally relate to the activities involved. We have attempted to develop the example as realistically as possible, but the case study is not intended to be a perfect portrayal of the details of restaurant operations. Readers with a background in managing restaurants are requested to suspend judgment about the authenticity of the descriptions, and to concentrate instead on the concepts illustrated by the example.

2.7 CONCLUSION

Table 2.5   Summary of model steps and activities

Stage	Stage description	Activities	Chapter
1	Defining design attributes	Identify the key customers of the service	3
		Determine the needs that customers expect the service to fulfill	
		Prioritize the needs in order of importance	
		Specify the attributes required by a service that meets these needs	
		Create quantitative measures for design attributes	
		Establish the relationships between needs and attributes	
		Determine the most important attributes	
2	Specify performance standards	Identify the customers' desired performance level for each attribute	4
		Analyze the performance of the competitors	
		Determine the relationship between performance and satisfaction	
		Specify performance standards for each attribute	

(continued)

Stage	Stage description	Activities	Chapter
3	Generating and evaluating design concepts	Define the key functions needed to provide the service	5
		Assemble these functions into processes	
		Document these processes using flow charts	
		Create alternate design concepts for the service	
		Evaluate and select a concept for detailed design	
4	Developing design details	Partition concept into process-level design components	6, 7
		Generate design alternatives for each component	
		Predict performance of each design alternative	
		Evaluate and select alternatives for each component	
		Evaluate and select design for implementation	
		Test performance of overall service design	
		Make any necessary modifications to the design	
		Specify detailed functional requirements	
5	Implementing the design	Develop an implementation project plan	8
		Develop a service construction plan	
		Develop a pilot and testing plan	
		Develop a communications plan	
		Develop a rollout and transition plan	
		Develop a service management plan	
		Implement all the plans	

(continued)

Stage	Stage description	Activities	Chapter
6	Measuring performance	Select key attributes to be analyzed	9
		Measure performance of attributes relative to standards	
		Measure capability of attributes	
		Measure efficiency of key processes	
		Develop reporting and analysis procedures	
		Identify attributes whose performance does not meet standards	
		Perform any corrective action, if necessary	
7	Assessing satisfaction	Measure customers' satisfaction with performance of service	10
		Measure satisfaction relative customers' expectations	
		Measure satisfaction relative to the competition	
		Validate these results against those from Stage 2	
8	Improving performance	Estimate relationship between financial objectives and satisfaction	11
		Set strategic satisfaction targets	
		Estimate relationship between satisfaction and attribute performance	
		Select one or more attributes for improvement, and set targets	
		Estimate relationship between service and process-level attributes	

Part

2

Design

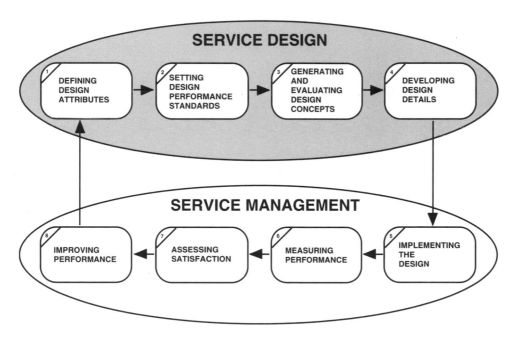

Chapter

3

Developing Design Specifications—Part 1: Defining Design Attributes

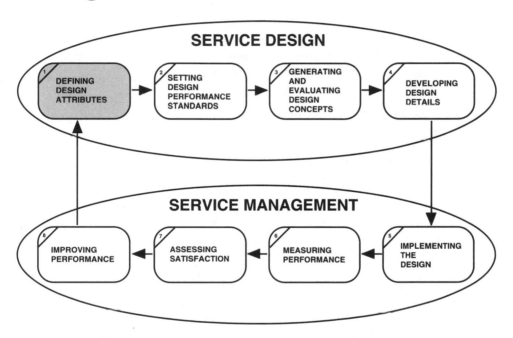

- *Introduction to Quality Function Deployment*
- *Understanding Customer Needs—HOQ Room 1*
- *Generating Design Characteristics—HOQ Rooms 2 and 3*
- *Determining Importance of Attributes—HOQ Rooms 6 and 7*
- *Conclusion*

With this chapter, we begin our journey through the operational details of the design methodology. The focus of this chapter and the next is on the first two stages of the service design and management model introduced in Chapter 2. The material in these two chapters describes the development of specifications for the design of the service. These specifications answer the following questions:

1. What characteristics should be used to evaluate the design of the service?

2. What is the expected performance level of these characteristics?

In this chapter, we address the first question. The second question is covered in Chapter 4. The framework for our presentation in these two chapters is the Quality Function Deployment (QFD) methodology, which is introduced in Section 3.1. In Section 3.2, we describe methods for obtaining and documenting customer needs. Sections 3.3 and 3.4 describe the translation of these needs into the design characteristics and the selection of the most important characteristics. The terms "design characteristics," "design attributes," "technical characteristics," and "technical attributes" are used interchangeably in this chapter. These attributes and their associated performance requirements constitute the "design specifications" for the service. Section 3.5 is a chapter summary.

3.1 INTRODUCTION TO QUALITY FUNCTION DEPLOYMENT

Quality Function Deployment (QFD) is a systematic matrix-based visual approach for designing quality products and services. QFD is based on the Total Quality Management (TQM) philosophy that high-quality products and services distinguish themselves by adhering to quality standards in all activities throughout their life cycle. The specification of quality requirements and the deployment of quality for such products and services begins as early as possible in the life cycle. Moreover, the quality requirements are obtained directly from the customers.

The successful deployment of quality in a product or service therefore requires the following three ingredients: (1) a structured method for defining quality standards early in the design process; (2) a system for incorporating these standards into the design; and (3) a technique for propagating the designed quality through the life cycle of the product or service. The QFD methodology supports all three requirements. The technique uses a series of interconnected matrices which establish the quality relationships between higher-level (i.e., product- or service-level) design activities and their associated lower-level (i.e., subprocess, subsystem, or function) activities. The higher-level matrices assist in planning the design concept; the lower-level matrices assist in detailed design and post-implementation monitoring and improvement of the service. The design standards that are established in the earlier matrices are carried through to the later matrices.

The House of Quality

The best-known matrix is the first in the QFD hierarchy. This matrix, referred to as the *House of Quality (HOQ)*, is used to translate customer needs into service design

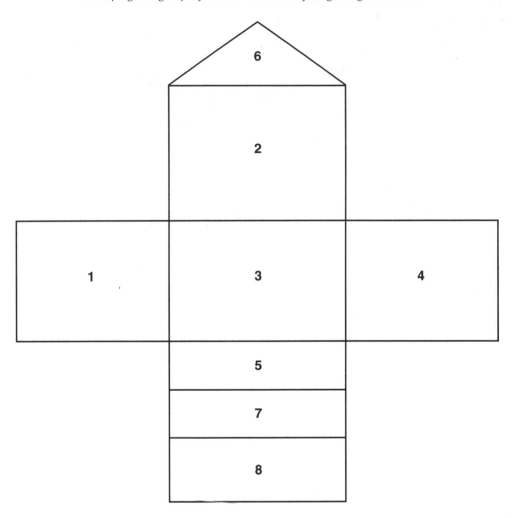

Figure 3.1 The "House of Quality" matrix

characteristics. This term was popularized by Hauser and Clausing (1988) in their seminal *Harvard Business Review* paper of the same name. A schematic of the matrix is shown in Figure 3.1. As can be seen, the matrix consists of eight rooms, one of which is a roof that gives the matrix its name.

Customer needs in the verbatim form of the "voice of the customer" and a rating of their importance are collected in room 1. Room 2 contains the "voice of the design team" and lists the characteristics that the design must have to satisfy the needs. Room 3 is the relationship matrix where the associations between the design characteristics and the needs are represented. Benchmarking is carried out in room 4 to

obtain customers' views about the extent to which their needs are met by competing services. The counterpart to this is the technical benchmarking in room 5,
where the design team evaluates the quality of the performance of the competitors' designs. In room 6, the roof, correlations between the design characteristics
are identified which indicate potential design conflicts or opportunities for reinforcement. In room 7, the importance of each characteristic is calculated from the
needs importance data in room 1 and the associations in room 3. This information
helps the team to identify the characteristics that satisfy the most needs. Finally,
the performance standards for the service are listed in room 8.

Hierarchy of QFD matrices

Different conventions exist in the QFD literature for representing the hierarchy of
matrices. Figure 3.2 shows the most common convention (referred to as the American Supplier Institute [ASI] model or the Clausing model; see Clausing, 1994),
customized for service design. The matrix labeled 1 is the HOQ matrix described
above. The service requirements obtained from customers are translated into design characteristics and service performance targets in this matrix. The design

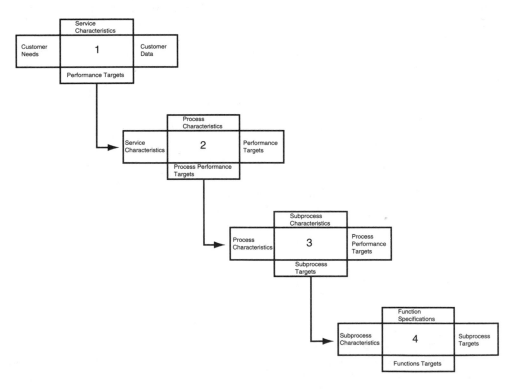

Figure 3.2   Hierarchy of QFD matrices for service design

characteristics are the inputs to the matrix labeled 2, which we call the *service/process matrix* in this book. In this matrix, the service design attributes are partitioned into process design attributes and associated process performance targets. In matrix 3, called the *process/subprocess matrix*, we go to the next level of detail and translate the process performance characteristics into the design requirements for the subprocesses that make up the process. These requirements are also the standards to which the service operations should be managed after the design is implemented. Finally, the design requirements for the individual functions are specified in matrix 4, called the *subprocess/function matrix.* Detailed specifications for hardware, software, documentation, training, etc., to meet the subprocess performance requirements are entered in this matrix. By linking the output of each matrix to the input of the following matrix, the hierarchy of Figure 3.2 allows the voice of the customer to drive the design of the service down to the most detailed level.

In this chapter, we will describe how to construct rooms 1, 2, 3, and 6 of the House of Quality in detail using the "Service Edge" restaurant case study introduced previously. The remaining HOQ rooms are covered in Chapter 4. The contents of the service/process and the process/subprocess matrices for the restaurant example are described in Chapter 6. The subprocess/function matrix is presented in Chapter 7.

3.2   IDENTIFYING CUSTOMER NEEDS—HOQ ROOM 1

Characteristics of needs

Since the needs represent the voice of the customer, they must be a personal, non-technical statement of what the customers expect from the service. The manner in which the needs are documented should retain the directness and nuance of the customer expressions. Sometimes, customers may express needs that are actually their perceived solutions to the design problem. In such cases, the team must question the customer further to extract the need that underlies the solution. For example, suppose a restaurant customer states a need for "many daily specials." Questioning may reveal that this is the customer's proposed solution for the need "wide choice of food." The design team may decide that an expanded menu, weekly theme cuisine, or the ability to order from the menu of a sister restaurant are better methods for meeting this need than daily specials. The team should be careful not to lock itself into premature design solutions. This impedes its ability to consider different and creative design alternatives.

Types of needs

All needs are not created equal, and the resolution of all needs does not have the same impact on customer satisfaction. This concept is very well represented by the

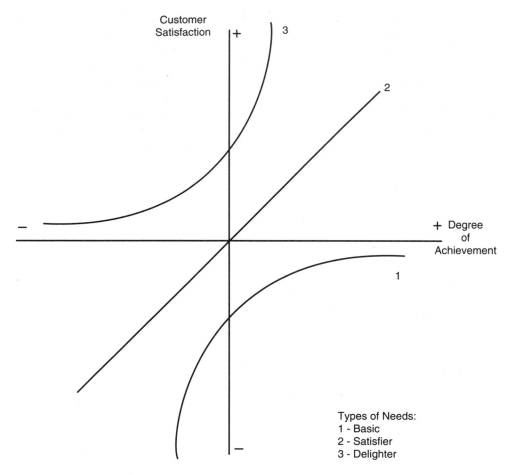

Figure 3.3 The Kano model of customer needs

well-known model shown in Figure 3.3 and attributed to Noriaki Kano.[1] The horizontal axis in this figure shows the extent to which customers' expectations are achieved. The vertical axis shows the customer satisfaction associated with this achievement.

Three types of needs are identified in this model. The first type, depicted by curve 1, defines the *basic expectations* that customers have about a service. As the level of achievement of these expectations increases (as we move from left to right along

---

[1] Though the Kano model is widely quoted by authors, a reference to the paper is rarely provided. The following reference is from Lou Cohen's QFD text (Cohen, 1995): Kano, N., N. Seraku, F. Takahashi, and S. Tsuji (1984). "Attractive Quality and Must-Be Quality," *Hinshitsu* **14**, (2), Japan Society for Quality Control. The author has not seen the paper, but, according to Lou Cohen, an English translation by Glenn Mazur exists for this paper.

the horizontal axis), customers barely begin to be satisfied. On the other hand, the absence of attributes that satisfy these needs causes a quick and nonlinear deterioration into dissatisfaction. This is because customers take these needs for granted, and assume that attributes will be provided to satisfy these needs. The availability of a nonsmoking area in a fine restaurant is an example of such a need.

The second type of need is represented by curve 2. The achievement of these needs increases customer satisfaction, but only at a linear rate. Most needs stated by the customer fall into this category. For example, most customers will respond positively if the amount of time they have to wait for a table at a restaurant is reduced. However, a reduction of five minutes in waiting time on an average twenty-minute wait is unlikely to leave the customer screaming in delight. Clearly, the design team must try to reach as high an achievement level as possible for these needs so that the highest possible degree of satisfaction is provided, but the returns in terms of customer satisfaction may not be spectacular. Over time, as the needs in this category are fulfilled by more and more service providers, they will move into the basic category.

The satisfaction of the type of need represented by curve 3 has the potential for producing large returns for little effort. Customers either do not have a conscious knowledge of these needs, or they fall into the category of "Wouldn't it be great if someday . . . ?" They may not therefore be verbally expressed in a QFD needs assessment interview. A service design that does not fulfill them will still satisfy the customer; however, a company that manages to address these needs even partially will experience a nonlinear increase in customer satisfaction. An example of such a need is the provision of baby-sitting facilities at fine restaurants. Once again, over time, some of these needs will migrate to other categories.

The preceding discussion illustrates four points. First, all basic needs have to be fulfilled, irrespective of whether they are requested or not. Second, the design team must pay careful attention to verbatim customer statements to accurately capture all linear satisfiers. Third, the design team should make an effort to identify or create delighters, since it is through their satisfaction that real service differentiation can be created. Fourth, any advantage gained by delighting customers only holds temporarily until the competition catches up. Continuous innovation is necessary in order to maintain an edge.

Methods for obtaining needs

Four methods are commonly used for obtaining needs:

1. Surveys and market research

2. Group interviews

3. One-on-one interviews

4. Observation

The obvious advantage of surveys and quantitative market research data is that a large amount of information can be collected from customers with relatively little effort. For example, before starting the QFD process, the restaurant owner can use survey results from restaurants in other cities to identify the most important determinants of customer satisfaction. The disadvantage of survey data is that they do not directly capture the customer's voice. Customers only answer the questions that are posed to them in the surveys, or evaluate only the attributes provided to them by the designers. In some cases, the designers may only ask questions that reflect their beliefs of what the customers need. Therefore, survey data should not be used as a substitute for detailed conversations with customers. However, survey data, if available, is a valuable source of background information and should be analyzed before customers are interviewed. Answers to open-ended questions are especially useful. This information helps to direct and focus future interviews.

Group and one-on-one interviews typically last from one to two hours. About thirty hours of interviewing has been shown to be adequate to obtain up to 90% of the needs (Griffin and Hauser, 1993). Interviews are usually conducted by more than one person so that several transcripts of the customers' statements exist. Interviewers attempt to record these statements in the customers' words as faithfully as possible. Some probing of the initial answers may be necessary to get to the underlying need, and multiple interviewers can adopt different questioning approaches that elicit needs more effectively. However, the number of interviewers should not be so large as to intimidate the customer. Typically two interviewers suffice, with a third person as a scribe, if necessary.

Customers are interviewed in a focus group or individually. Focus groups have been preferred because it is thought that the group dynamics will result in a greater number of needs being expressed in a shorter time. Griffin and Hauser found that approximately the same number of needs was generated by two one-on-one interviews as by a single two-hour group interview, and no group synergy effects were found. Depending on the application, the less expensive option can therefore be implemented.

Observation of a customer's interaction with a service is a good method for identifying unstated needs and for understanding the motivation behind the need statements. This is because this method gives us information about the behavior of customers *in the context of the service experience.* We are able to observe the immediate, emotional reaction of customers to the quality of the service rather than the more distant, rational responses obtained from an interview session.

For example, consider customers at an airport rental car return site, waiting for a bus to take them to their terminals. What are their facial expressions? Are they nervous, bored, or relaxed? How often do they look at their watches? Are they all huddled in the only dry corner or lit space? Are they sitting on their luggage since no seating is available? How do they approach the bus when it arrives? These and other observations provide the team with needs that may not always be stated during interviews. Over a span of fifteen years, Citibank collected data for designing its ATM service and service locations by filming encounters in a prototype environment and paying close attention to details such as what customers did with their umbrellas on a rainy day.[2]

The ideas generated as a result of these observations should be documented by the team and validated with customers. Since the observations are made when customers are using the service, it is useful, at least initially, to validate the ideas in the same context. For the car rental example above, this involves spending a few minutes discussing the ideas with customers as they wait for the bus or as they travel to the airport. To ensure that the customers' reaction to the ideas is not influenced by the immediacy of the situation, the most promising ideas should also be discussed in focus group sessions or interviews. If the responses continue to be positive, the needs and any solutions to address them should be added to the QFD matrix.

Grouping needs

It is not uncommon for a qualified group to extract two or three hundred needs from thirty hours of interviewing. These will be at various levels of detail, and they may include the same need statement with multiple wordings. This is too large a set to work with. The list of needs should be reduced by combining duplicates, discarding ambiguous or incomplete statements, and grouping very detailed statements into higher-level categories. The target should be to reduce the list to about thirty needs categorized into two or three levels.

The initial cleaning of the data is done by the design team. Subsequent organization can either be done by the team members or by the customers. If done by the team, the categorization is achieved by group consensus using affinity diagrams (or K-J diagrams, named after their inventor Jiro Kawakita). In this approach, each team member is given a number of cards, each of which carries a need. Team members take a card from their pile in turn, discuss its contents, and place it in another pile where cards bearing similar needs are stacked. When all the cards have been placed in piles, the team organizes each pile into several levels of detail. The highest levels categorize the needs into abstract groups, while the lower levels contain the more detailed, operational statements. Three levels are commonly used, and a fourth level may be added if appropriate. The team iterates through this procedure several times, adjusting the categories as necessary. The objective is to achieve consensus among the team members. Each group of needs is labeled, either by using an appropriate lower-level need or by the team generating a label that suitably

---

[2] The author thanks G. Lynn Shostack for providing this example while reviewing the manuscript.

describes the group. In a slightly different approach, described by Wesner *et al* (1995), the design team writes down all needs on adhesive notes and mounts the notes on a wall or board. Working silently and simultaneously, the team moves the adhesive notes around on the board, placing each note with other notes that belong together. No discussion is allowed at this stage. After all the notes are grouped, the team members discuss the groups and assign headings to them. Any regrouping needed for clarity and precision is done at this stage. The reader is also referred to Brassard (1989) for more information on affinity diagrams.

When the affinity diagrams are created by customers, each customer is given a set of cards, each with a need. The customers are asked to sort the cards into similar piles, and choose a card from the pile that best represents the pile as a label. Griffin and Hauser (1993) argue that this method is better because it represents the customer's viewpoint and doesn't introduce the biases of the design team. However, the teamwork that is necessary to generate affinity diagrams and the emphasis on a consensus is a valuable experience for the team that helps in later steps of the process. Either method is acceptable, and both may be used if time and resources permit.

Restaurant example

Some examples of customer needs for the Service Edge restaurant are presented in Table 3.1. The order of presentation is arbitrary and should not be taken to represent any prioritization of the needs. Notice that the needs are documented in simple, verbal terms. As far as possible items should be documented directly in the customer's words (such as "make me feel at home" or "get what was ordered"). Some of the needs may sound trivial. For example, the item "food tastes good" is tautological; one would hardly expect customers to say that they expect the food to taste bad. However, in this case, the need must be understood in the *context* of the service being designed. Clearly, a guest who pays $50 for a meal at the Service Edge restaurant will have a very different expectation of how the food should taste than a customer who pays $1.99 for a hamburger at the local fast food outlet. Therefore, even a seemingly trivial need has a very specific design implication. In the case of the need "tasty food," the design team should investigate exactly what "good-tasting food" means to potential restaurant customers. This can be done through more detailed interviews, by providing sample meals to test customers in a prototype setting, and by benchmarking the quality of food provided by competing restaurants. This investigation should lead to a clear understanding of the specific unstated needs that are collapsed into the high-level statement "Food tastes good." Design attributes should then be developed to meet these unstated needs.

Using affinity diagrams, the team groups the needs of Table 3.1 into three levels shown in Table 3.2. As we see in later chapters, not all design activities need data at the most detailed level. Having the data available at various levels will allow the team to easily access the data view most appropriate for the activity.

Table 3.1   List of customer needs for restaurant service

1 Food tastes good	20 Can order quickly
2 Unusual items on menu	21 Know how long a wait for table
3 Hot soup, cold ice cream	22 Food is healthy
4 Feel full after the meal	23 Menu items easy to understand
5 Don't feel overfull after meal	24 Prompt delivery after ordering
6 Food looks appetizing	25 Get what was ordered
7 Food courses arrive on table at right time	26 Get the correct bill
8 Don't feel hungry one hour after meal	27 Billed as soon as meal is over
9 Clean restrooms	28 Shouldn't feel rushed out of restaurant
10 Clean tables	29 Make me feel at home
11 Clean plates and silverware	30 Order additional items quickly
12 Clean, well-dressed employees	31 Errors and problems quickly resolved
13 Lights not too bright	32 Errors and problems satisfactorily resolved
14 Lights not too dim	33 Staff willing to answer questions
15 Shouldn't feel crowded in space	34 Waiter should be patient while ordering
16 Don't want noisy atmosphere	35 Greeted immediately on being seated
17 Want smoke-free atmosphere	36 Fill water glass promptly without asking
18 Wide choice of food	37 Polite, friendly staff
19 Enough time to read menu	38 Short wait for table

Table 3.2 First-, second- and third-level needs for Service Edge restaurant example

First-level need	Second-level need	Third-level need
Satisfying food	Tasty food	Food tastes good Balance of flavors Hot soup, cold ice cream Food looks appetizing Food is healthy
	Enough food	Feel full after meal Don't feel overfull after meal Don't feel hungry one hour after meal
	A lot of variety	Wide choice of food Unusual items on menu
Clean and attractive surroundings	Clean facilities	Clean restrooms Clean tables Clean plates and silverware Clean, well-dressed employees
	Comfortable atmosphere	Lights not too bright Lights not too dim Shouldn't feel crowded in space Don't want noisy atmosphere Smoke-free atmosphere
Good service	Friendly and knowledgeable staff	Make me feel at home Staff willing to answer questions Polite, friendly staff Waiter should be patient while ordering Menu items easy to understand Shouldn't feel rushed out of restaurant Fill water glass promptly without asking Enough time to read menu
	Quick and correct service	Short wait for table Know how long a wait for table Can order quickly Greeted immediately on being seated Prompt delivery after ordering Get what was ordered Order additional items quickly Food courses arrive on table at right time

(continued)

First-level need	Second-level need	Third-level need
	Accurate billing	Get the correct bill
		Billed as soon as meal is over
	Problems and complaints addressed effectively	Problems quickly resolved
		Problems satisfactorily resolved

The following *first-level needs* are shown in Table 3.2:

- Satisfying food

- Clean and attractive surroundings

- Good service

The *second-level needs* explain the first-level needs and aggregate the verbatim customer statements into categories. The *third-level needs* are mostly the verbatims from Table 3.1, after some cleaning up to remove ambiguities, duplicates, etc. Most QFD applications do not partition the data beyond four levels.

3.3 GENERATING DESIGN CHARACTERISTICS—HOQ ROOMS 2 AND 3

Representation of design attributes

Let us now move to room 2 of the House of Quality. In this room, we define the design attributes (also referred to as design characteristics, or quality characteristics) for the service. These attributes specify the way in which the design team expects to satisfy the customer needs. The attributes can be represented in several ways. The preferable representation is one that is *solution independent*. In this case the attribute for a given need is expressed as a *quantifiable characteristic* that can measure the extent to which a design solution meets the need. For an example of this representation, consider the third-level need "Short wait for table" in Table 3.2. A quantifiable characteristic corresponding to this need could be "Interval between guest arrival and seating (in minutes)." There are many ways in which the design team can affect customers' waiting time. For example, they can control the *capacity* (number of seats) at the restaurant. Another way would be to control *throughput* (the number of guests dining per hour). We refer to each of these solutions as a *design*. Clearly, the quantifiable design attribute described above can be used to test the ability of each design to satisfy the need. This representation of the attribute is therefore independent of the design solution.

In some cases, especially when QFD is used to improve the performance of an existing design, the design attribute may be represented as a service or process

64   *Design and Management of Service Processes*

feature, rather than as a quantitative characteristic. For example, the attribute associated with the need "Short wait for table" could be "Increase restaurant capacity." In this case, the design decision has already been made—the attribute merely documents the activity that has to be performed to satisfy the need. The advantage of this representation is that it is very specific and easily understood. Clearly, the disadvantage is that it does not allow design solutions to be evaluated. The reader is referred to the text by Cohen (1995) for more details on these representations. In this book, since our example deals with the creation of a new service, we will represent the design attributes as solution-free quantitative characteristics. We will build processes and functions around these characteristics using the FAST technique in Chapter 5.

In summary, a successful definition of design attributes is a balance between abstraction (which can pertain to multiple solutions) and specificity (which can pertain to a single or a few solutions). Abstraction should not give way to generality, and specificity to inflexibility. The team must avoid getting overwhelmed by detail, but at the same time must define the attributes to a level where they are easily understood. The team must therefore use a systematic procedure for defining the attributes.

Either a "top-down" or a "bottom-up" approach will work, as long as it is consistently followed. In the top-down approach, we first start with defining higher-level attribute categories that satisfy the first- and second-level needs. These categories are expanded to the required degree of detail as necessary. In the bottom-up approach, attributes are first defined to address the most detailed level of needs. The attributes are subsequently aggregated into categories using affinity diagrams. There is little difference between the two approaches, except that the top-down approach is easier to control because only the required amount of detail is considered at any time. In any case, either approach will require some iteration between higher and lower levels of detail. We will now demonstrate the generation of attributes using the top-down approach for the needs from Table 3.2.

Generating design characteristics—restaurant example

The team begins by asking the question: *What characteristics of the restaurant service will satisfy the first- and second-level customer requirements in Table 3.2?* To answer this question, the team should consider not only the needs but the broader context of the conditions in which the restaurant operates, the kinds of customers that are targeted, the service provided by the competitors, the functions that need to be performed to provide the service, and the nature of the service to be provided (e.g., high-contact, personalized attention). Based on these considerations, all the possible service attributes that the team members can generate should be enumerated. At this stage, it is enough to define the characteristics broadly; details can be incorporated later. The immediate focus should be on completeness rather than on precision.

Table 3.3 Design attributes from first- and second-level needs

Need	Characteristic
Satisfying food ■ Tasty food ■ Enough food ■ A lot of variety	Taste Nutrition Smell Appearance Temperature Quantity Variety
Clean and attractive surroundings ■ Clean facilities ■ Comfortable atmosphere	Cleanliness Lighting Layout Interior decoration Entertainment
Good service ■ Friendly and knowledgeable employees ■ Quick and correct service ■ Accurate billing ■ Problems and complaints addressed effectively	Friendliness of employees Waiter responsiveness Order-taking patience Knowledge of employees Promptness of service Accuracy of service Problem resolution effectiveness

An example of characteristics that may be obtained from the needs of Table 3.2 is shown in Table 3.3. It is important that the team have a clear common understanding of what each characteristic means. This is especially important for those characteristics that are broadly interpretable such as "nutrition" or "responsiveness." The team should discuss and clarify vague terms and agree on a common set of definitions. These definitions should be documented and be made available to team members for future reference. For example, the design characteristics associated with the first-level need "good service" are listed in the second column of Table 3.3. These characteristics may be defined as shown in Table 3.4.

Verifying completeness of attributes

The next step is to verify that the attributes generated by the team adequately cover the needs. This is done by completing the relationship matrix (HOQ room 3) in which the attributes are correlated with the second-level needs. Table 3.5 shows the matrix for the attributes from Table 3.3. As in the case of needs, the affinity diagram technique can be used to group the attributes and remove redundancies and duplications. In Table 3.5, the characteristics from Table 3.3 have been grouped into three attribute categories: *Food design, Facilities design,* and *Customer*

Table 3.4   Definition of design characteristics for good service

Friendliness: Providing personal, courteous, and cheerful service that makes customers feel comfortable in the restaurant. Not overbearing or inappropriately intimate.

Responsiveness: Responding to customer requests quickly and efficiently, being flexible to handle special service requests, and anticipating and fulfilling needs even before customers ask for service.

Patience: Giving customers the time they need to make their choices, and being willing to answer any questions they may have about the restaurant, menu, or service.

Knowledge: Having the right information about the contents and availability of menu items, bar items, and daily specials.

Promptness: Servicing customers quickly and without delay. This is distinguished from responsiveness by the kind of request. Promptness is a measure of the effectiveness of standard processes; responsiveness is the ability to deal with spontaneous or nonstandard requests.

Accuracy: Giving customers what they request without errors.

Problem resolution effectiveness: Solving any problems that arise quickly and professionally in a manner that does not result in customer dissatisfaction. Providing appropriate apologies or compensation commensurate with the situation. Ensuring that the right person is available to address the problem.

service design. These categories correspond to the three service components described in Chapter 1 (see Figure 1.1), i.e., service product, service facility, and service processes. Since the emphasis of this book is on the application of design methodology to service processes, our exposition of the Service Edge restaurant example in this book will only concentrate on the attributes of the "Customer Service Design" category, though the methodology of this book can be used for designing the other attribute categories and their interactions.

In Table 3.5, a solid circle represents a strong association between a need and an attribute, an empty circle depicts a moderate association, and a triangle a weak association. For example, customers' need for tasty food is satisfied strongly by the degree of taste of the food, moderately by the smell of the meal, and weakly by the nutritional value (caloric content) and appearance. Another common convention represents a strong association by two concentric circles. A strong association is usually assigned a weight of 9 units, a moderate association 3 units, and a weak association 1 unit. Any other weighting scheme that is appropriate can also be used.

Table 3.5   Relationship matrix for second level needs

WHATs vs. HOWs Legend		
Strong	●	9
Moderate	○	3
Weak	△	1

	FOOD DESIGN	Degree of taste	Degree of smell	Degree of nutrition	Quanity of food	Degree of attractiveness of food presentation	Food variety	FACILITIES DESIGN	Degree of cleanliness	Degree of lighting	Entertainment provided?	Restaurant decor	Restaurant layout	CUSTOMER SERVICE DESIGN	Promptness of service	Accuracy of service	Degree of friendliness	Degree of responsiveness	Degree of patience	Extent of knowledge	Degree of problem resolution effectiveness
SATISFYING FOOD																					
Tasty food		●	○	△		△															
Enough food					●																
Lot of variety							●														
CLEAN AND SATISFYING SURROUNDINGS																					
Clean facilities									●												
Comfortable atmosphere									●	○	●	○									
FOOD SERVICE																					
Friendly and knowledgeable employees																	●	●	●	●	
Quick and correct service															●	○					
Accurate billing																●	●	●			
Problems and complaints addressed effectively																		○		○	●

Four criteria are used in evaluating Table 3.5. The first is *completeness*, where we verify that all needs are matched by at least one design attribute. If an empty row exists in the matrix, then the appropriate attributes corresponding to that need must be included. The second criterion, which we can call *strength of association*, verifies that we have identified at least one attribute that is strongly associated with each need. This may not be so crucial at lower levels where the needs are more specific, but is important at this level. The third criterion, *breadth of coverage*, is a measure of the richness of the design. It may be possible to satisfy all needs with a single attribute. Such a design lacks flexibility and does not give much opportunity for seeking innovative solutions. This criterion seeks to verify that we have defined approximately as many design characteristics as there are needs, i.e., that the filled circles fall approximately along the diagonal of the relationship matrix. Once again, this criterion may not be critical at lower levels of detail where one attribute may satisfy several needs, but at this level, this criterion provides a yardstick for the breadth of the design space. Finally, the fourth criterion, *density of coverage*, verifies whether too many cells are not populated. A case can always be made for relating every attribute to every need, but doing so would draw attention away from the few important relationships that should shape the design. The rule of thumb is that no more than one-third to one-half of the cells of the matrix should be filled.

Specifying attributes in quantitative terms

When the team is satisfied that the higher-level design attributes are completely defined, the relationship matrix can be expanded to the next level of detail. For the Service Edge restaurant, this is shown in Table 3.6, where we present the relationship matrix for the third-level needs and the attributes of the "Customer Service Design" category of Table 3.5. The seven attributes of Table 3.5 belonging to this category have been expanded to fourteen attributes in Table 3.6. Each attribute has been assigned to one of four operational groups: *(1) meal service; (2) seating, ordering, and delivery; (3) billing and payment;* and *(4) trouble resolution.* We will design processes for each of these groups in Chapters 5, 6, and 7.

Compared to Table 3.5, the attributes of Table 3.6 are expressed in more specific quantitative terms. Promptness attributes have been replaced by appropriate time intervals and accuracy by the percentage of correct orders or bills. However, the ability to quantify is not the same as the ability to measure. Even if all the attributes can be expressed in quantitative terms, it may not be possible to collect data regularly on these attributes without disrupting or delaying the process. The need for quantification therefore needs to be balanced by the ease of measurement and testing.

Attributes related to continuous quantities such as time, weight, and rate of defects can be quantified relatively easily because they can be measured on natural scales. Not all attributes have such well-defined scales. Attributes such as politeness, friendliness, patience, or knowledge in Table 3.6 are intangible variables whose degree of performance cannot be measured on an obvious continuous scale. For these attributes, we need to create arbitrary scales that take on discrete values. Since there is no commonly understood definition for each of these values (for example, there is no universal standard for "excellent level of responsiveness"), the performance level implied by each scale value must be clearly defined when the scale is created and must be commonly understood by the users of the scale. We will now illustrate how scales for these attributes can be created.

Quantifying intangible design attributes

The first step to quantifying intangible attributes is to look for measurable or observable features that can be used to describe the performance of the attribute. These elements are obtained from the following sources:

- Third- or fourth-level needs that are associated with the attribute

- Opinions of experts

- The design team's judgment

An experiment is then conducted in which a team of experienced raters (e.g., customers who are familiar with similar services) is asked to rate scenarios where the attribute elements perform at various predetermined levels. The scenarios can be

Table 3.6   Relationship matrix for third-level needs for "Good Service"

WHATs vs. HOWs Legend	Symbol	Value
Strong	●	9
Moderate	O	3
Weak	△	1

Need	Importance Rating of Need	SERVICE DELIVERY	Degree of patience	Degree of responsiveness	Degree of knowledge	Degree of friendliness	SEATING, ORDERING, AND MEAL DELIVERY	Time between arrival and seating	Time between seating and menu delivery	Time between menu delivery and order-taking	Time between ordering and meal delivery	Percent of meals delivered as ordered	BILLING AND PAYMENT	Time between meal completion and bill delivery	Percent of bills produced without errors	Time between bill delivery and transaction completion	TROUBLE RESOLUTION	Promptness in problem resolution	Effectiveness in problem resolution
Friendly and knowledgeable staff																			
Staff willing to answer questions	4		●		O	△													
Polite, friendly staff	5					●													
Waiter should be patient while ordering	2		●			△													
Menu items explained	3		O	△	●														
Enough time to read menu	2		△							●									
Fill water glass promptly without asking	3			●															
Shouldn't feel rushed out of restaurant	3					●										O			
Quick and correct service																			
Short wait for table	3							●											
Know how long a wait for table	4			O				O											
Can order quickly	4								●	●									
Greeted immediately on being seated	3					O		●											
Prompt delivery after ordering	5										●								
Get what was ordered	4											●							
Order additional items quickly	3			●						O									
Food courses arrive on table at right time	3										●								
Accurate billing																			
Get the correct bill	5														●				
Billed as soon as meal is over	3													●		O			
Problems and complaints handled effectively																			
Problems quickly resolved	3			O														●	
Problems satisfactorily resolved	5			O															●
Absolute Importance			65.0	81.0	51.0	87.0		39.0	63.0	63.0	72.0	36.0		27.0	45.0	18.0		27.0	45.0
Percent Importance			9.0	11.3	7.1	12.1		5.4	8.8	8.8	10.0	5.0		3.8	6.3	2.5		3.8	6.3

presented to them in different ways. If real experiments are used, the raters may be asked to experience a prototype of the service. For example, consider an experiment to evaluate the politeness of hotel reception staff. Suppose the politeness is determined by the performance of the following two elements:

1. Receptionist greets guests by name

2. Receptionist asks guests how they are

As part of the experiment, several scenarios are created with varying performance levels for each of these elements. Consider the following three scenarios:

Scenario 1: The receptionist says: "Good evening, Ms. Visitor. How are you today?"

Scenario 2: The receptionist says: "Good evening, Ms. Visitor."

Scenario 3: The receptionist says nothing at all.

Clearly, the first scenario represents high performance on both elements, the second only addresses the first element, and the third addresses neither element.

The receptionist is asked to follow one of these scenarios for each simulated interaction. The experiment is repeated multiple times so that each rater can experience all the scenarios. After each interaction, the rater is asked to rate the quality of the interaction on a quantitative (e.g., 1 to 5) or a qualitative (e.g., poor, good, excellent) scale.

In another approach, the group may be shown a videotape of a series of receptionist/guest interactions and be asked to rate each situation. An approach that combines an experiment with a survey may also be used. A small number of customers may be asked to participate in the experiment to develop the scale. The scale may be validated by sending out a survey to a larger sample where the experimental scenarios are described in words.

After the experiment is complete, each rater should have provided a rating value of each scenario. If the raters represent a fairly homogeneous group, with relatively similar expectations for the service, each rater's evaluation of a particular scenario should be approximately the same. In other words, the distribution of ratings for each scenario should be expected to have a well-defined mode (most common rating) and a small deviation around the mode. For example, suppose thirty customers are asked to evaluate the performance of Scenario 2 above on a scale of 1 to 5. This scenario represents average performance since the receptionist addresses only one of the two elements of performance (greeting guests by name). We should therefore expect most raters to assign a rating of 3 to this scenario.

This expectation is realized in the distribution shown in Figure 3.4 (a). In this figure, 80% of the ratings are between 2 and 4, with a clear majority having a value of 3. The modal value (3) can be chosen as the aggregate rating for this scenario in

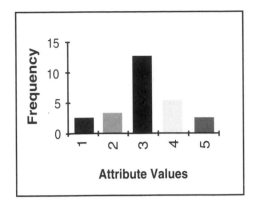 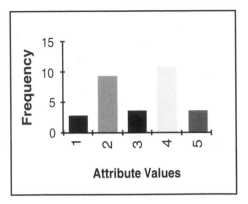

Figure 3.4: Distributions of ratings for Scenario 2 (average hotel staff politeness)

this case, though additional investigation may be warranted if a significantly different rating is given by a particularly trusted or experienced rater. Figure 3.4 (b) shows a different situation. In this case, the ratings follow a bimodal distribution with approximately an equal number of customers selecting two rating values. Two market segments with different performance expectations may be present in the data. A single aggregate rating for this scenario cannot be chosen from this data without additional analysis.

Quantifying intangible attributes for the Service Edge restaurant

Tables 3.7. and 3.8 show two examples of scales for measuring intangible attributes for the Service Edge restaurant. Table 3.7 shows eleven elements describing the attribute *degree of friendliness* in Table 3.6. The performance levels of these elements corresponding to three scale values of the attribute ("Excellent," "Good," and "Below Average") are shown in the table.

In Table 3.8, ratings for ten scenarios of the attribute "degree of problem resolution effectiveness" are presented, rated on a scale from 1 (abysmal) to 10 (extraordinary). Two elements describe this attribute: (a) who resolves the problem and (b) nature of compensation provided. "Appropriate compensation" refers to free meal, free desserts, a gift coupon for a future visit, or other items offered to the customer by the restaurant management.

3.4 DETERMINING IMPORTANCE OF ATTRIBUTES—HOQ ROOMS 6 AND 7

After completing HOQ rooms 1, 2, and 3, the team should turn its attention to rooms 6 and 7. In room 7, the importance of each attribute is calculated to select the critical few that the design should emphasize. In room 6, the correlations between these attributes are specified to identify the extent of reinforcement or conflict that needs to be considered in the design.

Table 3.7   Various levels of "degree of friendliness" attribute

Characteristic	Scenario 1	Scenario 2	Scenario 3
When greeted by host	Immediately	Few minutes	Not greeted
Where greeted by waiter	Waiting area	Table	Not greeted
Escorted to table by	Host	Waiter	No escort
Waiter checks if table is acceptable	Yes	No	No
Waiter uses polite language	Yes	Yes	Yes
Greeted by manager	Yes	No	No
Waiter/host/manager remember your previous visit	Yes	No	No
Waiter stops by to say a few words during meal	Yes	Yes	No
Waiter says good-bye when you leave restaurant	Yes	Yes	No
Host says good-bye when you leave restaurant	Yes	Yes	No
Host/waiter escorts you to door	Yes	No	No
Degree of friendliness rating	**Excellent**	**Good**	**Below average**

Calculating attribute importances

While completing room 1, customers are asked to rate the importance of each need, usually on the following scale: 1—Not important; 2—Below average importance; 3—Average importance; 4—Above average importance; 5—Extremely important. In Table 3.6, the importance of each need for the Service Edge restaurant is listed under the column heading "importance rating of need." These importance ratings and the associations from the relationship matrix are used to calculate the importance of each attribute.

The importance of an attribute is calculated by multiplying the customer importance rating for each need that is associated with the attribute by the appropriate association strength (i.e., 1, 3, or 9) from the relationship matrix and summing up the products. For example, consider the first attribute column "degree of patience" in Table 3.6. This attribute is strongly associated with "willing to answer questions" with an importance rating of 4 and "patient while ordering" with importance of 2. It is also moderately associated with "menu items need to be explained" and weakly with "enough time to read menu," with importance ratings 3 and 2, respectively. The total importance score for this attribute is therefore $(4 \times 9) + (2 \times 9) + (3 \times 3) + (2 \times 1) = 65$. This score is shown at the bottom of Table 3.6 under the row

Table 3.8 Various levels of "effectiveness of problem resolution" attribute

Scenario	Attribute element performance	Scale value
1	Problem resolved by waiter, appropriate compensation provided	10
2	Problem resolved by manager, appropriate compensation provided	9
3	Problem resolved by waiter, apology provided	8
4	Problem resolved by manager, apology provided	7
5	Problem resolved by waiter, no apology provided	6
6	Problem resolved by manager, no apology provided	5
7	Problem not resolved, appropriate compensation provided	4
8	Problem not resolved, apology provided	3
9	Problem not resolved, no apology provided	2
10	No one available to report problem	1

heading "importance of needs." The percent importance row normalizes each score as a percentage of the total.

Since the importance of an attribute is calculated by multiplying customer importances and association weights, those attributes that address a larger number of needs will be more important. If key design attributes for the service are selected based on importance, *coverage of needs* is emphasized over *importance of needs*. In other words, this choice rule will favor an attribute that addresses several needs of moderate importance over an attribute that addresses a single need of high importance. The team must ensure that the attributes selected from such a choice rule do not unwittingly leave an important customer need unfulfilled, or if they do, that this is a conscious decision of the design team. In some cases—for example, where some needs relate to safety considerations—a decision rule based on maximizing coverage may not be appropriate. A rule such as "Choose all attributes that address needs with an importance rating of 5 or 4" may be more suitable in such cases.

Also, since the number of needs addressed by an attribute increases the importance of that attribute, the results may be skewed by differences in the degree of knowledge or effort of the team members. For example, if the team pays more attention to some attribute categories than to others, the categories that have received greater attention will appear to be more important, only because they have been defined in greater detail. This reduces the calculation of attribute importances to a meaningless manipulation of numbers. These kinds of imbalances must be avoided. The team must make several iterations through the first three rooms and qualitatively understand the implication of each cell assignment. Arithmetic calculations should be carried out only after this understanding has been achieved.

In Table 3.9, we show the attributes from Table 3.6 sorted in decreasing order of importance. The first nine attributes of this table account for 80% of the importance scores. In later chapters, our service design will therefore focus on only these attributes.

Correlation between design characteristics (HOQ room 6)

Room 6 of the House of Quality is the triangular matrix that forms the roof of the house. This matrix shows the interactions between pairs of design attributes. These interactions may be positive and reinforce each other, or they may be negative and necessitate trade-offs. Attributes with positive correlations can be designed, marketed, and operated as a common concept. For example, if the degrees of patience, friendliness, and responsiveness are positively correlated, then a common design solution operationalized by a single training package can be implemented for these attributes. Also, these attributes can be part of a common customer service strategy that can be marketed under a single banner. On the other hand, attributes that are negatively correlated require design trade-offs that must

Table 3.9 Customer service attributes sorted in decreasing order of importance

	Degree of friendliness	Degree of responsiveness	Time between ordering and meal delivery	Degree of patience	Time between seating and menu delivery	Time between menu delivery and order-taking	Degree of knowledge	Percent of bills produced without errors	Effectiveness in problem resolution	Time between arrival and seating	Percent of meals delivered as ordered	Time between meal completion and bill delivery	Promptness in problem resolution	Time between bill delivery and transaction completion
Absolute Importance	87.0	81.0	72.0	65.0	63.0	63.0	51.0	45.0	45.0	39.0	36.0	27.0	27.0	18.0
Percent Importance	12.1	11.3	10.0	9.0	8.8	8.8	7.1	6.3	6.3	5.4	5.0	3.8	3.8	2.5

be carefully considered. For example, the patience and promptness attributes are negatively correlated, since customers want waiters to give them all the time they need and answer all their questions, but at the same time want their menus and their food to be delivered promptly without delay. The solution to this problem is not to tell the customer: "Well, we can satisfy one attribute or the other—just tell us which." Instead, the design team should seek the possibility of innovative solutions that satisfy both attributes to the greatest possible extent.

3.5 CONCLUSION

Summary

A summary of the topics presented in this chapter is presented below. The section in the chapter where a particular topic is covered is indicated in parentheses.

Introduction to QFD (3.1)

- Best-known matrix called "House of Quality."

- Clausing/ASI QFD model uses four matrices.

- The QFD model can be used to develop detailed functional specifications driven by customer needs.

Identifying customer needs (HOQ room 1) (3.2)

- Needs must be personal, nontechnical statements of customers' expectations.

- Needs can be characterized as basic expectations, linear satisfiers, and delighters.

- Basic expectations and satisfiers must be provided by the design; delighters should be provided if possible.

- Needs can be collected by surveys, interviews, or observations.

- Needs must be grouped into three or four levels using affinity diagrams.

Generating design characteristics (HOQ room 2) (3.3)

- Design characteristics can be represented as quantitative measures or as features.

- A successful definition of design characteristics balances abstraction and specificity.

- Either a top-down or a bottom-up approach can be used for defining design attributes.

- Intangible attributes must be clearly defined and commonly understood.

Establishing relationships between needs and attributes (3.3)

- Relationships between needs and attributes are specified by the relationship matrix.

- Completeness, strength of association, breadth of coverage, and density of coverage indicate whether all needs are adequately and succinctly covered by attributes.

Creating quantitative measures for design attributes (3.4)

- All attributes may not have obvious measurement scales.

- Intangible attributes are measured by creating arbitrary scales.

- Scales are created by consensus of experienced raters.

- The performance associated with each scale value should be clearly documented and understood.

Determining attribute importance (3.4)

- Importance of needs is rated on a scale of 1 to 5.

- Attribute importance is calculated by the product of the need importance and association strength.

- Attribute importance formula emphasizes coverage of needs over importance of needs.

Correlation between design characteristics (HOQ room 6) (3.4)

- Correlation between attributes is represented in the roof of QFD matrix.

- Attributes with positive correlations can be designed together.

- Trade-offs between attributes with negative correlations must be considered.

Suggested Reading

The following four texts are recommended for further reading on QFD. This is not an exhaustive list, but a collection that provides a good overview of different aspects of the topic. Some of these texts have already been referenced in this chapter.

Akao, Yoji, Editor-in-Chief (1990). *Quality Function Deployment: Integrating Customer Requirements into Product Design,* translated by Glenn H. Mazur and Japan Business Consultants, Ltd. Productivity Press, Cambridge, MA. Difficult reading, but provides valuable insights into the philosophy of QFD.

Cohen, Lou (1995). *Quality Function Deployment: How to Make QFD Work for You.* Addison-Wesley, Reading, MA. A highly readable, detailed practical guide.

Bicknell, Barbara A., and Kris D. Bicknell (1995). *The Road Map to Repeatable Success: Using QFD to Implement Change.* CRC Press, Boca Raton, FL. Shows how QFD integrates with other well-known quality approaches such as Robust Design, Continuous Improvement, Business Process Reengineering, and Concurrent Engineering.

Clausing, Don P. (1994). *Total Quality Development: A Step-by-Step Guide to World-Class Concurrent Engineering.* ASME Press, New York. Chapter 3 of this book provides an excellent step-by-step overview.

4

Developing Design Specifications—Part 2: Setting Design Performance Standards

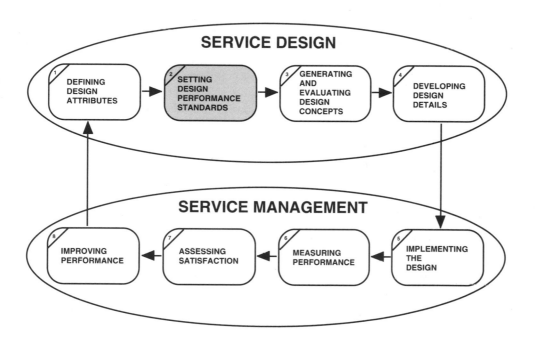

- *Design performance standards*
- *Measuring the desired performance level*
- *Customer and technical benchmarks—HOQ rooms 4 and 5*
- *The performance/satisfaction function*
- *Setting design performance standards—HOQ room 8*
- *Estimating the performance/satisfaction relationship*

- *Experimental designs with attributes at two levels*
- *Analyzing profiles with attributes at three levels*
- *Conclusion*

In Chapter 3, we covered the first part of the methodology for developing the specifications for the design of services. The collection and organization of customer requirements, and the definition, prioritization, and selection of quantitative design attributes to satisfy these requirements were described. This information was entered into rooms 1, 2, 3, 6, and 7 of the House of Quality. In this chapter, we continue the development of design specifications, and complete the remaining rooms (4, 5, and 8) of the QFD matrix.

4.1   DESIGN PERFORMANCE STANDARDS

In Chapter 3, we showed how the needs from room 1 of the House of Quality matrix could be translated into quantifiable design attributes that are listed in room 2. For example, the need *quick food delivery* for the Service Edge restaurant can be translated into the attribute *number of minutes between ordering and meal delivery*. This attribute, called the *meal delivery interval*, is one of the characteristics that need to be considered when designing the meal delivery process for the restaurant.

How do we design the meal delivery process? We describe the approach in detail in Chapters 6 and 7. The design team generates different *design alternatives* for the process, which represent different ways in which a meal order is prepared to be delivered the customer. For example, the design alternative may reflect different cooking methods, different use of ingredients (fresh vs. frozen), and different kitchen technologies. Each alternative will result in a different value for the meal delivery interval. To select an alternative, the design team must evaluate the performance of each alternative. The alternative with the best performance is selected for implementation.

How do we identify the alternative with best performance? Clearly, some method is needed of comparing the alternatives. We need a yardstick against which we can evaluate the performance of different designs. This yardstick is the *design performance standard*. A performance standard should be defined for each design attribute. For example, for the meal delivery process, the design standard will be a specific value of the meal delivery interval. But what should this value be? Should it be 7 minutes, or 8 minutes, or 10 minutes? What analysis is needed to make this determination? We address this question in this chapter.

Specifying design standards

Let us begin by considering an *upper* and a *lower* bound for the standard. Clearly, a service performs at the upper bound (*best value*) for an attribute when it meets or exceeds the performance expectations of the customers. The *performance level desired by customers* therefore represents the high end for the standard. For example, for the meal delivery interval of the Service Edge restaurant, suppose that customers require their meal to be delivered about 10 minutes (and not much later and not much sooner) after they place their order. We refer to this as the *desired standard*. If possible, the design should be developed to meet this standard.

A rough lower bound (i.e., *minimum acceptable value*) for the design standard of an attribute can be determined from *benchmarks* of the performance of some important competitors on that attribute. In order to remain competitive, the firm must offer a service level in the vicinity of that provided by key competitors. For example, suppose the main competitor of the Service Edge restaurant guarantees to serve a meal in approximately 15 minutes. Obviously, the design team cannot select a design alternative that produces a meal delivery interval of 20 minutes.

We have established that the design standard for the meal delivery interval of the Service Edge restaurant example should desirably be close to 10 minutes, and cannot be greater than 15 minutes. But should it be 11 or 12 or 13 or 14 minutes? For any attribute, the exact value of the design standard depends on the interaction between two factors:

1. the relationship between the performance and satisfaction for the attribute, and

2. the cost or technology requirements for designing a service that delivers a given performance level.

The *relationship between performance and satisfaction* specifies the extent to which satisfaction degrades as the performance moves away from the desired value. Customer satisfaction is maximized when the performance of an attribute is at its desired level, and is lower when the performance is not. However, the amount of deterioration depends on the attribute. For some attributes, the loss in satisfaction between the desired and the minimum acceptable performance levels may be small. These attributes can be designed to perform close to the lower bound. For other attributes, the satisfaction may deteriorate sharply as the performance moves away from the desired value. These attributes should be designed to perform close to the upper bound.

The *cost or technology availability* places a constraint on the design performance. Clearly, if it were possible to easily and cheaply satisfy the desired standards, all designs would do so for all attributes. However, it may be too expensive, or too difficult, for a firm to design a service that performs at the desired standard for all attributes and still remains profitable. Firms therefore need to trade off the gains in satisfaction resulting from superior performance with the costs of achieving the performance.

The task of specifying the exact performance standards for the attributes of a design therefore requires the solution of a complex optimization problem that achieves the maximum satisfaction subject to the constraints of cost or technology. Moreover, this problem is *design dependent*, since the technology used and associated costs may vary by the design. We do not attempt to solve this problem in this chapter. At this stage, we do not even have a design, so we do not have any estimates of the costs. All we do in this chapter is to describe a systematic approach to specify a set of *design-independent performance guidelines*. These guidelines represent the design team's initial estimates of how well *any* design should perform in order to produce a required level of satisfaction.

These estimates are based on some common-sense heuristics. For example, as mentioned above, irrespective of the design, we should try and maintain a performance level close to the desired value for those attributes for which small deviations in performance result in large deviations in satisfaction. Similarly, attributes that are more important should be designed with more care (i.e., with a closer eye to the desired performance level) than attributes that are less important. We use these rules to define a set of performance standards for the attributes of the design that will meet any desired customer satisfaction level. These standards are good initial yardsticks for the team to use to evaluate design alternatives, and can be fine-tuned once a design is selected.

The reason for presenting a systematic methodology for setting design performance standards is that very often design teams have no real basis for evaluating the quality of a design until after it is deployed. Standards are developed arbitrarily, if at all, with no link to customers' needs, and no ability to predict the satisfaction that will result from a design that adheres to these standards. As a result, service designs often need a lot of adjustment before they finally work right. The methods described in this chapter may not produce optimal standards, but will result in values that provide a reasonable and logical initial guess. Processes designed to meet these standards are guaranteed to be at least in the range of performance desired by customers. The task of final adjustment to the design performance then becomes much easier.

In summary, in order to set the design performance standard for an attribute, information about the following factors is required:

1. A knowledge of the customers' desired performance level for the attribute.

2. Benchmarks of key competitors' performance of the attribute.

3. Relationship between overall satisfaction and the performance of the attribute (referred to as the performance/satisfaction function).

4. The importance of the attribute.

We will describe these factors in greater detail in the following sections. This chapter is divided into two major parts. In the first part, consisting of Sections 4.2 through 4.5, we present an approach for setting the standards. In the second part, consisting of Sections 4.6 through 4.8, we describe statistical methods for estimating the satisfaction/performance relationship using experimental design. Each part is self-contained and can be read separately.

The desired standard is described in Section 4.2, competitor benchmarks obtained from customers and from the design team in Section 4.3, and the performance/satisfaction function in Section 4.4. In Section 4.5, we present a step-by-step procedure for setting the performance standards for the attributes of a service. Estimation methods for the specification of the performance/satisfaction function using experimental design are described in Sections 4.6, 4.7, and 4.8. Section 4.9 is a chapter summary.

4.2   MEASURING THE DESIRED PERFORMANCE LEVEL

Desired and ideal performance levels

As mentioned earlier, the *desired* standard for an attribute indicates the customers' expectations for the performance of the attribute, based on their prior experience with similar services and a realistic assessment of their needs. Customers are completely satisfied if the attribute performs at the desired level; they are delighted if the process performs better. Performance that is poorer than the desired level provides less satisfaction.

For some attributes, we can think of a natural optimal performance level at which a perfect service would perform. For example, an attribute such as a defect rate has an optimal value of zero. Similarly, the degree of responsiveness has a theoretically unlimited optimal value. These optimal values may not be cost-effective to immediately attain in practice, but represent the direction in which the design should be improved over time. We refer to this level as the *ideal* performance level.

The gap between the ideal and desired performance level depends on the attribute and on the application. In situations where process errors affect safety (such as the method for maintaining aircraft components), the desired and ideal performance levels may be identical, and any deviation from perfect performance (zero defects) will cause an unacceptable loss in satisfaction. In the terminology of the Kano model (see Chapter 3), the service must perform at the ideal performance level to satisfy the basic need for personal safety. In cases where defects are not life-threatening, performance approaching the ideal level may be a delighter, but customers will be satisfied by a service that meets a less stringent performance standard. In such cases, the desired and ideal performance level may be different. The service can then be designed to meet or exceed the desired performance level, and improved to approach the ideal level.

Measuring the desired performance level for an attribute

How can we obtain data on the desired standards for each design attribute? For some easily quantifiable attributes such as time intervals, estimates of the desired performance may be obtained directly from the customers. For many other attributes, this may not be possible. This is because the design attributes are the voice of the design team and represent the translation of customer needs into the technical characteristics of the design. The desired performance standards for each attribute should therefore be expressed in technical terms, which may be different from the way in which customers view service performance. For example, customers who require a reliable telephone service will usually be unable to express this need in terms of a failure rate. They are more likely to state something like "I want to call service maintenance very rarely," and the design team has to quantify "very rarely."

Sometimes, the design team may be able to obtain quantitative information from customers by careful questioning in follow-up interviews. For example, an interviewer may ask a customer: "In your opinion, what is an acceptable number of times to call service maintenance in a year?" Another approach would be to ask the customer to respond to a multiple choice question such as:

> *I would consider my telephone service reliable if I called service maintenance:*
> *(a) At most once every three months*
> *(b) At most once every six months*
> *(c) At most once every year*
> *(d) At most once every two years*
> *(e) At most once every five years.*

While this approach may provide accurate quantitative answers for some attributes, the hypothetical nature of the question makes it difficult for respondents to distinguish between desired and ideal service levels. Customers may be generally satisfied with the reliability of a service that requires maintenance once every couple of years. However, in response to the above question, they are more likely to state that they expect to call maintenance only once every five years. This is because, in the absence of a realistic or comparative context, there is no reason to expect a less than ideal service performance level.

For this reason, it is more accurate to estimate the desired performance level indirectly. This is done by examining the extent to which the performance of similar services in the market satisfies customers' needs. This information for this analysis is available in the customer and technical benchmarks collected in rooms 4 and 5 of the House of Quality. We will now describe these benchmarks and how they can be used to estimate the desired performance standards.

4.3   CUSTOMER AND TECHNICAL BENCHMARKS—HOQ ROOMS 4 AND 5

Collecting customer and technical benchmark data

Customer benchmarks are entered into room 4 of the House of Quality matrix. They measure the customers' perceptions of the effectiveness of the service provided by the competition. Customers are asked to rate their perceptions of the ability of competitors' services to satisfy each need listed in room 1. A scale of 1 to 5 is typically used, with the following levels: 1—poor; 2—below average; 3—average; 4—above average; 5—excellent. Either second- or third-level needs can be used for this evaluation, depending on the degree of detail required and the amount of effort entailed. If available, these benchmarks can be supplemented with published market research data from trade publications.

The selection of competitors for benchmarking is an important consideration. An average service provider in the market may not be a good candidate for comparison because they may not provide best-in-class data. Some good choices are market share leaders, competitors generally known in the industry for their service quality, or service providers who have implemented innovative technology or service concepts. The overall customer benchmark is obtained by aggregating the evaluations of a number of individual respondents who have experienced, or are familiar with, the service provided by the competition. The ratings should have relatively little variability if the customer segment is fairly homogeneous. If a significant amount of variability exists, a more precise definition of needs or a more careful segmentation may be needed.

The technical benchmarks are the design team's professional assessment of the *technical* performance of the competition on each of the design attributes. The technical benchmarks are listed in room 5 of the House of Quality, and are measured in the technical units appropriate for each attribute.

Estimating the desired performance level from benchmark data

The correlation between the technical and customer benchmarks can be used to infer the desired performance level for attributes for which this information is not directly available. To see how this can be done, let's consider an example of a design attribute of the Service Edge restaurant. Table 4.1 is a subset of Table 3.6 where three needs are shown with a single attribute "time between menu delivery and order-taking" associated with these needs. Customer and technical benchmarks are shown for two competing restaurants labeled 1 and 2. From the customers' perspective, their needs are better satisfied by restaurant 2 than by restaurant 1 because restaurant 2 is rated higher on the more important needs (ordering quickly and ordering additional items quickly). Therefore, we can infer that restaurant 2's ordering interval of 5 minutes is closer to the customers' desired performance level than restaurant 1's interval of 10 minutes.

However, Table 4.1 also shows that restaurant 2's order interval of 5 minutes only receives an average rating in its ability to give customers enough time to read the menu. Even the 10-minute interval provided by restaurant 1 only receives an above-average rating. We can therefore infer that some customers would prefer more than 10 minutes to read the menu. However, since the need to order quickly is more important than the time needed to read the menu, we can deduce that the

Table 4.1   Customer and technical benchmarks

WHATs vs. HOWs Legend		Customer Importance	Time between menu delivery and order-taking	Customer benchmark 1	Customer benchmark 2
Strong	● 9				
Moderate	○ 3				
Weak	△ 1				
Enough time to read menu		2	●	4	3
Can order quickly		4	●	2	5
Order additional items quickly		3	○	2	5
Technical benchmark 1			10 minutes		
Technical benchmark 2			5 minutes		

order-taking interval should be closer to 5 minutes than to 10. From these data, the desired performance level can therefore be estimated to be about *6 minutes*.

Consistency between customer and technical benchmarks

Since the customer benchmarks and the technical benchmarks are evaluations of the same service from different perspectives, it is desirable that they be consistent. This means that if the design team feels that a service performs well on a particular attribute, we also expect that the customers will indicate that the service satisfies the needs associated with the attribute. A discrepancy between the two evaluations indicates a mismatch between the perspectives of the customers and those of the design team. Several reasons are possible for this mismatch. The first possibility is that the technical measures are accurate, but customers' perceptions are not. For instance, customers at a restaurant may perceive the meal service to be slow even if the technical performance indicates that this is not the case. This perception may be created if staff appear to be idle when the restaurant is not crowded, or if a lot of activity does not appear to be going on in the kitchen. In this case, the problem is not with the design, but with its implementation. Some relatively simple operational changes (such as a large clock that is easily visible to customers) will help to correct these perceptions. The second possibility could be that the customers' perceptions are correct, but the design team's measurements are not accurate. The benchmarking tests may not provide the right information about the competitors' performance. In this case, the methods used for measuring the technical performance need to be re-evaluated. The third possibility could be an erroneous association between the needs and the attribute. If the needs are not truly associated with the attribute, then we cannot expect a correlation between the technical performance of the attribute and the perception of fulfillment of needs. Room 3 must be revisited and the entries in the relationship matrix verified.

In general, any perceived discrepancy between the customer benchmarks and the technical benchmarks should be a warning signal to the design team that the design attributes may not be accurately capturing customer needs. This should lead to a re-evaluation of customer perceptions, performance measurements, and attribute definitions. Through discussions with customers, the team must seek to understand the reason for the inconsistencies and the steps that must be taken to remove them.

4.4   THE PERFORMANCE/SATISFACTION FUNCTION

As mentioned previously, the acceptable gap between the desired standard and the design standard depends on the degradation in customer satisfaction that the design team is willing to tolerate. The extent of dissatisfaction arising from a unit deterioration in performance depends on the relationship between performance and satisfaction. For example, in the case of an attribute that affects safety, small deviations from the desired performance level will result in a large deterioration in satisfaction. For noncritical attributes, the extent of acceptable deviation will be larger. The relationship between performance and satisfaction is given by the performance/satisfaction function.

The performance/satisfaction function for the design attribute "time between menu delivery and order-taking" of the Service Edge restaurant is shown in Figure 4.1. Recall from the previous section (Table 4.1) that the desired performance level for this attribute was estimated to be 6 minutes. Satisfaction is at its maximum value of 100% when the interval has this value. Suppose the design team is willing to tolerate a maximum satisfaction degradation of 10% from this value. This is

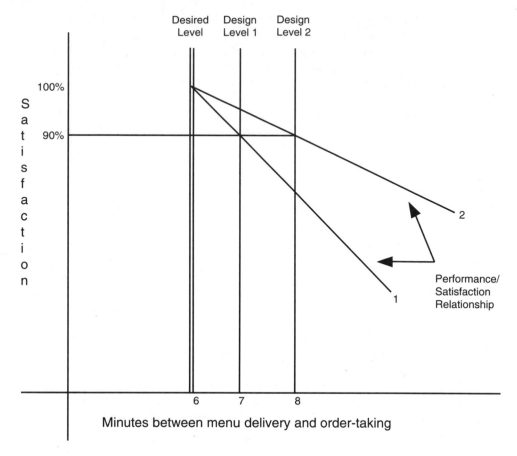

Figure 4.1 The performance/satisfaction function for the order-taking interval attribute

indicated by the point marked 90% in Figure 4.1. The deviation in performance from the desired standard that corresponds to this 10% degradation in satisfaction depends on the *slope* of the performance/satisfaction function. If the function has a steep slope as indicated by the line marked 1, any order-taking interval greater than 7 minutes will result in a satisfaction deterioration that is greater than 10% and is therefore not acceptable. The design performance standard for this attribute should therefore be set at 7 minutes or less. If the function has a shallower slope, as indicated by the line marked 2, a design standard of up to 8 minutes is acceptable.

Functional forms for the performance/satisfaction function

Many functional forms are possible for the performance/satisfaction relationship, some of which are presented in Figure 4.2. In figure 4.2 (i), the satisfaction remains constant for deviations of performance until a threshold T. Beyond this threshold, the satisfaction deteriorates sharply. The design standard can be set anywhere be-

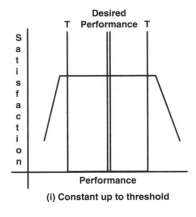

(i) Constant up to threshold

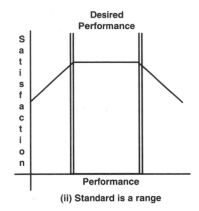

(ii) Standard is a range

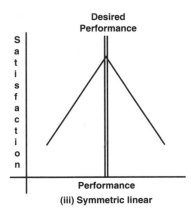

(iii) Symmetric linear

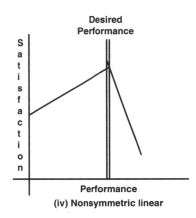

(iv) Nonsymmetric linear

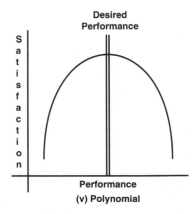

(v) Polynomial

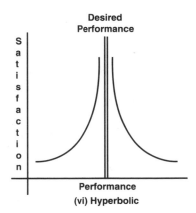

(vi) Hyperbolic

Figure 4.2 Different functional forms for the performance/satisfaction functions

tween the desired performance and the threshold, since no gain in satisfaction is obtained by being closer to the desired performance level. This function is applicable to services where customers are sensitive to attributes other than service quality, such as price. If the price is low enough, customers may accept poor service because they still feel that they are receiving adequate service for their money. If the performance drops to the extent that the low price cannot make up for it, satisfaction begins to deteriorate. However, this is an unstable situation. Clearly, the tendency of all service providers will be to deliver a performance level at the threshold. However, any service provider who is able to deliver a marginally better level of service at the same price can cause the threshold to shift, and can capture a large portion of the market while the competitors adjust their performance to meet the new threshold. The threshold will therefore gravitate toward the desired performance level over time.

Figure 4.2 (ii) looks similar, but represents a different situation. In this figure, the desired service itself is expressed as a range, because the customer cannot qualitatively differentiate performance levels within this range. Therefore, for a given attribute, all firms whose performance falls within this range will provide equal satisfaction. For example, consider the attribute "time between ordering and meal delivery" for the Service Edge restaurant in Table 3.6. Suppose customers perceive 10 minutes or less for this interval as "too short," 15 minutes or more as "too long," and 10–15 minutes as "acceptable." Any interval between 10 and 15 minutes will equally satisfy customers because they are truly indifferent to any delivery time that is within this range. There is no instability in this situation.

In the models illustrated in Figures 4.2 (iii) to (vi), a deviation in performance from the desired level results in a loss of satisfaction. Figure 4.2 (iii) shows a linear relationship similar to that of Figure 4.1. The rate of deterioration is the same on both sides of the standard. The relationship in Figure 4.2 (iv) is also linear, but the line is steeper on one side of the standard than on the other, resulting in an asymmetrical rate of loss. This occurs when customers are less dissatisfied by deviations on one side of the desired performance than on the other. Consider the interval between the order and delivery of a restaurant meal. Customers do not want the meal either to be delivered too early or too late, but may be more dissatisfied when a meal arrives late than when it arrives early. Figure 4.2 (v) illustrates a nonlinear polynomial relationship. If the polynomial is of degree 2, then this function is similar to the "Quality Loss Function" concept used by Taguchi's quality engineering methodology.[1]

Finally, Figure 4.2 (vi) depicts a hyperbolic function. In this figure, the rate of deterioration of satisfaction is larger closer to the standard than further away from it. This kind of situation arises when the purpose of the service vanishes as we move

---

[1] For a nontechnical overview of Quality Loss Functions and Taguchi's quality philosophy, see Kacker (1985).

further away from the standard. An example is the temperature at which ice cream is served at a restaurant. The ice cream has the right consistency if the temperature is at the desired standard. Small deviations from the standard cause a large amount of dissatisfaction because the consistency is close, but not perfect. At large deviations from the standard, the ice cream is either soupy or a block of ice, and a few degrees more or less is not going to make a difference. At this point further deviation is not going to affect an already low level of satisfaction.

We will now describe how the desired standards, the benchmarks, and the performance/satisfaction function can be used to set performance standards for the attributes of a service.

4.5   SETTING DESIGN PERFORMANCE STANDARDS—HOQ ROOM 8

The procedure involves the following steps:

Step 1: Specify the minimum acceptable satisfaction threshold.

Step 2: Rank attributes in order of decreasing slope of the performance/satisfaction function.

Step 3: Rank attributes in order of importance.

Step 4: Set design performance levels for each attribute.

Step 5: Predict the overall satisfaction from the attribute performance levels set in Step 4.

Step 6: Determine whether the predicted satisfaction is higher than the minimum acceptable threshold.

Step 7: If it is not, tighten the performance of some attributes, or drop some less important ones.

Description of steps

Step 1: Specify the minimum acceptable satisfaction threshold: The minimum acceptable satisfaction threshold is the base level of customer satisfaction that is needed for the firm to maintain the required market share or revenue. Every design should perform at a level that meets or exceeds this threshold. This threshold is based on customers' satisfaction with competitors' service, and on the strategic service objectives of the firm.

Step 2: Rank attributes in order of decreasing slope of the performance/satisfaction function: The attributes with the steepest slopes are the ones whose performance must be as close as possible to the desired standard.

Step 3: Rank attributes in order of importance: The service should be designed to perform closer to the desired value for the more important attributes than for the less important ones.

Step 4: Set design performance levels for each attribute: Use the following guidelines:

1. The performance level should be set at or close to the desired level for *more important* attributes with a *steep slope* of the performance/satisfaction function. These are the attributes that have to be provided in the design and have to perform as close as possible to the desired levels. Set these values as close as the current technology can feasibly provide.

2. The performance level should be set at or close to the minimum acceptable levels (benchmarks) for the *less important* attributes with a *shallow slope.* These are the attributes with the most flexibility.

3. The performance level of the remaining attributes should be set at intermediate values. The performance of attributes whose performance/satisfaction function has a steeper slope should be set closer to their desired standards.

Step 5: Predict the overall satisfaction from the attribute performance levels set in Step 4: From the performance/satisfaction function for each attribute, the *loss* in satisfaction arising from the specified performance level in Step 4 can be calculated. There is no loss if the performance level is at the desired standard; the further the design standard is from the desired level, the greater the loss. The losses for each attribute are summed to produce the overall satisfaction loss.

Step 6: Determine whether the predicted satisfaction is higher than the minimum acceptable threshold: The predicted satisfaction is calculated from the overall satisfaction loss computed in Step 5. For example, if the maximum achievable satisfaction rating is 7 points, and the overall loss is 0.3, the predicted satisfaction is $7 - 0.3 = 6.7$. This value is compared to the threshold.

Step 7: If it is not, tighten the performance of some attributes, or drop some less important ones: If the satisfaction level does not meet the threshold, then the performance standards for some attributes may have to be brought closer to their desired levels. If this is not feasible for any attribute because of perceived cost or technology constraints, then the team may consider excluding some of the less important attributes in the design, especially if the slopes of their performance/satisfaction functions are steep. If this relaxes some technological constraints and reduces costs, there may be some additional flexibility to tighten the standards of the more important attributes. Some trial and error may be necessary before an acceptable solution is obtained.

In summary, there is no formulaic procedure that can be routinely followed to set the design standards for the attributes of the service. Some judgment and experience, as well as an understanding of the market, the competition, and the constraints, are necessary. The design team should work together to set the standards, and should reach consensus through discussion. The standards are entered into room 8 of the House of Quality matrix (see Figure 3.1, Chapter 3).

Let us now see how this approach can be used to set design standards for the Service Edge restaurant example.

Setting the performance standards for the Service Edge restaurant attributes

Table 4.2 shows the desired performance level for the nine important design attributes presented in Table 3.9. The performance of the discrete attributes are measured on the following 6-point scale: *poor, below average, average, good, excellent,* and *exceptional.*

Table 4.2 also shows the technical benchmarks against the three competitions to the Service Edge restaurant described in Chapter 2 (Section 2.6). The reader will recall that they are (a) *Vive La France,* a French restaurant known for the responsiveness of its employees; (b) *Downtown Steakhouse,* which markets itself with the friendly service slogan "welcome to the family barbecue"; and (c) *Sarah's Seafood House,* which uses technology to increase throughput and reduce service delivery time.

As can be seen from Table 4.2, each restaurant meets the desired performance for the attributes associated with its specialty. The technical benchmarks indicate that the meal service processes of Vive La France are designed for exceptional responsiveness, those of the Steakhouse for exceptional friendliness, and those of the seafood restaurant for prompt delivery. None of the restaurants meet the desired level of service on all attributes.

Let us now follow the steps outlined above to set design standards for the restaurant.

Step 1: Specify the minimum acceptable satisfaction threshold: Consistent with the business strategy described in Chapter 2 (Section 2.6), the design team sets a minimum acceptable threshold satisfaction rating of 6.5 points or higher on a 7-point scale. This is significantly higher than the competitors' ratings shown in Table 2.4.

Step 2: Rank attributes in order of decreasing slope of the performance/satisfaction function: Through discussions, the team determines that all attributes except for two can be set at the desired standard. The two exceptions are the *meal delivery interval* and *billing accuracy.* The performance/satisfaction functions for these attributes are shown in Figures 4.3 and 4.4, respectively.

Since the functions are nonlinear, they do not have a constant slope. The slope varies depending on the performance level of the attribute. Figures 4.5 (a) and 4.5 (b) show the slopes of the meal delivery interval and the billing accuracy

Table 4.2   Desired service, technical benchmarks, and design standards—restaurant example

	Degree of patience	Degree of responsiveness	Degree of knowledge	Degree of friendliness	Time between seating and menu delivery	Time between menu delivery and order-taking	Time between ordering and meal delivery	Percent of bills produced without errors	Effectiveness in problem resolution
Desired Performance	Exceptional	Exceptional	Exceptional	Exceptional	< 5 minutes	< 5 minutes	10 minutes	> 95%	Excellent
TECHNICAL BENCHMARKS									
Vive la France	Good	Exceptional	Excellent	Good	< 5 minutes	< 10 minutes	15 minutes	> 90%	Excellent
Downtown Steakhouse	Excellent	Excellent	Excellent	Exceptional	< 5 minutes	< 8 minutes	15 minutes	> 90%	Good
Sarah's Seafood House	Good	Good	Good	Good	< 5 minutes	< 5 minutes	10.5 minutes	> 92%	Good
Design Standards	Exceptional	Exceptional	Exceptional	Exceptional	< 5 minutes	< 5 minutes	> 10 & < 11.5	90%	Excellent
Direction of Improvement					<↓	<↓	|<↓	↗	↗

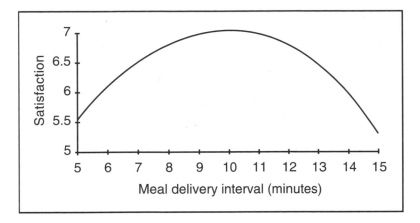

Figure 4.3 Performance/satisfaction function for the meal
delivery interval

attribute, respectively. It is evident that the meal delivery interval has the steeper slope across the entire performance range. This is also evident from the relatively flat performance/satisfaction relationship for the billing accuracy attribute shown in Figure 4.4.

Step 3: Rank attributes in order of importance: The attributes of the Service Edge restaurant ranked in decreasing order of importance were shown in Table 3.9. Once again, we will only concern ourselves with the meal delivery and the billing accuracy intervals, since these are the only two that are not expected to meet the desired standards. The meal delivery interval is significantly more important than the billing accuracy.

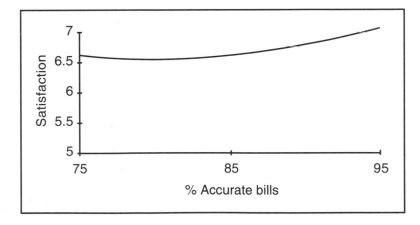

Figure 4.4 Performance/satisfaction function for billing
accuracy

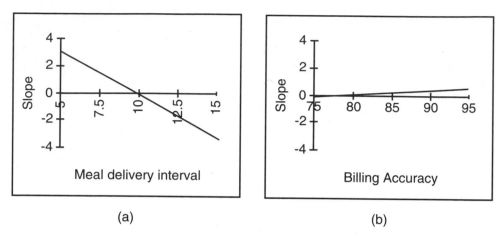

Figure 4.5 Slopes of performance/satisfaction functions

Step 4: Set design performance levels for each attribute: All attributes are set at their desired standards, except the *meal delivery interval* and the *billing accuracy* attributes. Since billing accuracy is a less important attribute and has a relatively flat performance/satisfaction function, it is enough to set the performance level for this attribute at the same level as the average competitor, even though this level does not meet that desired by the customers. The performance level is therefore set to match that of Vive la France and Downtown Steakhouse (90%). Sarah's Seafood House has a marginally better performance level, but the gain in satisfaction as a result of achieving that level is not considered worth the expense involved.

The meal delivery interval is a much more important attribute. The desired standard is 10 minutes in this case. Sarah's Seafood House comes closest to this value, delivering a meal between 10 and 10.5 minutes. The other two competitors cannot deliver a meal in less than 15 minutes. The Service Edge restaurant design team decides that since the strategic design objective is to concentrate on delivering world class customer service, the restaurant does not need to exactly match the delivery interval of Sarah's Seafood House. However, the design must come close to this interval, and must surpass the intervals of the other two competitors. It therefore decides to set the standard for this interval at 11.5 minutes. This means that the design should deliver a meal between 10 (the desired value) and 11.5 minutes.

Step 5: Predict the overall satisfaction from the attribute performance levels set in Step 4: From Figure 4.3, the overall satisfaction associated with a meal delivery interval performance of 11.5 minutes is 6.75. The *loss* in satisfaction is therefore 0.25 units. From Figure 4.4, the satisfaction associated with a billing accuracy of 90% is 6.9. The loss in satisfaction is therefore 0.1 units. The total satisfaction loss is therefore 0.35 units.

Step 6: Determine whether the predicted satisfaction is higher than the minimum acceptable threshold: From Step 5, the total satisfaction loss was 0.35 units. The predicted satisfaction is therefore $7 - 0.35 = 6.65$. Since the satisfaction threshold is 6.5, the predicted satisfaction is higher than the threshold. The design standards are entered in room 8 of the House of Quality. This is shown in Table 4.2.

The arrows in the "direction of improvement" row in Table 4.2 indicate whether the value of the attribute has to increase or decrease for an improvement in performance. Arrows without a bar represent the possibility of unbounded improvement to the largest or smallest possible value. The arrows with a bar represent bounded improvement to a specified nominal value.

In all our discussion so far, we have assumed that the performance satisfaction function is known to the design team. But how do we estimate this function? It is desirable to estimate this function as accurately as possible, since the results from this function affect the accuracy of the design standards. In the rest of this chapter, we will show several empirical approaches to estimating these functions. We will start with the case of a single attribute, and proceed to the estimation of these functions for all attributes simultaneously.

4.6   ESTIMATING THE PERFORMANCE/SATISFACTION RELATIONSHIP

Estimating the performance/satisfaction relationship for a single attribute

How do we estimate the performance/satisfaction relationship for a single design attribute? One approach would be to ask a group of customers to rate their overall satisfaction with the service at various levels of performance of a *single attribute*. The words *overall satisfaction* are important. The customers are not asked: *How satisfied are you with the performance of attribute X?*, but rather: *How does the performance of attribute X affect your satisfaction with the service?*

Clearly, the overall satisfaction is a function of *all* attributes, and not only of the one under consideration. How can we isolate the effects of a single attribute? We do this by assuming that when we consider a particular attribute, all the other attributes perform at their respective desired standards. Therefore, when the attribute under consideration also performs at the desired level, the highest possible overall satisfaction rating is obtained. Deviations from this satisfaction value arise when the attribute fails to perform at the desired standard.

For an example of this approach, consider the attribute "time between menu delivery and order-taking," for the Service Edge restaurant, with a desired standard of 6 minutes. Ten customers are asked to rate their overall hypothetical satisfaction (on a scale from 1 to 7) with the restaurant service for various values of this interval from 1 to 9 minutes. The scale is anchored by specifying a satisfaction rating of 7.0 (the highest value) when this interval meets the desired standard of 6 minutes.

Table 4.3   Aggregate satisfaction ratings for order-taking interval

Minutes between menu delivery and order-taking	Minimum satisfaction rating	Maximum satisfaction rating	Average satisfaction rating	Median satisfaction rating
1	1.4	3.1	2.3	2.2
2	1.3	6.6	3.1	2.6
3	4.4	5.4	4.8	4.8
4	5.7	6.2	6.0	5.9
5	5.9	6.4	6.2	6.2
6	7.0	7.0	7.0	7.0
7	1.6	5.5	3.3	3.2
8	1.0	4.3	1.9	1.4
9	1.0	2.9	1.7	1.5

The aggregate ratings obtained from the ten customers for each value of the interval is shown in Table 4.3.

The data from Table 4.3 are used to plot the performance/satisfaction relationship for this attribute in Figure 4.6. The x-axis represents various performance levels of the attribute, while the y-axis represents the overall satisfaction rating. The three graphs in Figure 4.6 represent the minimum, maximum, and average ratings from Table 4.3 for each value of the order-taking interval.

The advantage of considering each attribute separately is that the rating task itself is easy, though it may rapidly become tedious if data is being collected on a number of attributes. Therefore, data points can be collected to trace the performance/satisfaction relationship for each attribute over its entire range of performance. Moreover, no statistical knowledge is required to implement the survey or interpret the results.

Disadvantages of the single-attribute approach

The simplicity of the single attribute approach can lead to misleading results. There are two reasons for this.

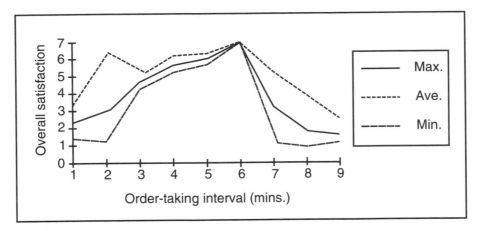

Figure 4.6   Performance/satisfaction relationship for the Service Edge order-taking interval

First, recall that the approach requires the rater to evaluate the change in overall satisfaction as the result of a change in the performance of a single attribute, with the performance of all other attributes remaining constant. In practice, customers estimate their overall satisfaction with the service by considering trade-offs in the performance of several attributes at a time. It is not usually possible to accurately rate changes in overall satisfaction as a result of changes in performance of a single attribute. The satisfaction scores assigned to each performance level of the attribute are likely to be biased. A rating method that requires customers to evaluate "bundles" of attributes at various performance levels will produce a more accurate satisfaction score.

Second, even if the satisfaction ratings are accurate, the performance/satisfaction function for each attribute is calibrated under the assumption that all remaining attributes operate at the desired standards. This calibration may not be valid if this assumption is not true. For example, consider the following two attributes from Table 3.6 for the Service Edge restaurant: "percent bills produced without error" and "effectiveness of problem resolution." Suppose most of the problems that need special attention are due to inaccurate bills. Also suppose that the restaurant improves the problem resolution process so that its effectiveness of problem resolution increases from a low to a high level. This naturally causes an increase in satisfaction. However, the *amount* of increase in satisfaction will depend on the *extent* of the billing accuracy problem. This is shown in Figure 4.7. If only 20% of the bills are accurate, then most customers have a problem, and the problems' effective resolution will cause a large increase in customer satisfaction. However, if 95% of the bills are accurate, then the improvement in problem resolution effectiveness will not cause the same increase in satisfaction. The performance/satisfaction relationship for problem resolution effectiveness therefore depends on the level of performance of billing accuracy attribute. This effect is called an *interaction* between

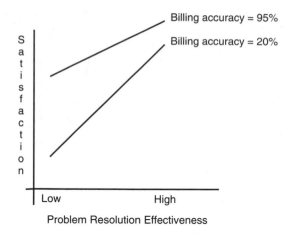

Figure 4.7 Increase in satisfaction depends
on billing accuracy level

billing accuracy and problem resolution. The effect of interactions cannot be estimated when only one attribute is considered at a time. An approach that considers both attributes at various performance levels is needed.

In summary, the single-variable method can be used to provide some exploratory insights about the functional form of the performance/satisfaction relationship. These insights can be used to develop an approach in which all the design attributes are varied at the same time. In this approach, raters are asked to evaluate their overall satisfaction with a collection of attributes performing at carefully pre-selected levels. The performance/satisfaction relationships for all attributes are simultaneously estimated. In marketing, this methodology is called *conjoint analysis*. An overview of conjoint analysis and its applications is provided by Green and Srinivasan (1978); an update can be found in Green and Srinivasan (1990).

We will now illustrate how conjoint analysis can be used for estimating performance/satisfaction relationships.

Estimating the performance/satisfaction relationship for all attributes—conjoint method

In this approach, customers are asked to rate their satisfaction with a number of *service profiles* that are made up of combinations of the design attributes at various *prespecified discrete performance levels*. Each profile represents a single combination of attributes. For each profile, customers are asked to rate their overall satisfaction with the service when the attributes perform at the level specified in the profile. The objective of conjoint analysis is to use the ratings of several profiles to decompose the overall satisfaction ratings into individual performance/satisfaction relationships for each attribute.

Table 4.4 Sample design for four restaurant attributes

Profile number	Degree of friendliness	Time between seating and order-taking (minutes)	Percent of bills produced without error (percent)	Effectiveness in problem resolution
1	Average	5	95	Excellent
2	Excellent	10	75	Good
3	Average	5	95	Good
4	Excellent	10	75	Excellent

The set of profiles to be rated by customers is referred to as a *design* (do not confuse this with the design attributes for the service!). Table 4.4 show a sample design consisting of four profiles for four attributes of the Service Edge restaurant. Designs cannot be created arbitrarily, but must be carefully assembled following certain specific rules described later in this chapter. These rules are part of a statistical methodology called *experimental design,* which has a long and rich history in many diverse fields. It is beyond the scope of this text to describe anything but its most rudimentary aspects. For readers interested in more detail, we will provide references to several texts in the bibliography at the end of this chapter.

The first step in the development of experimental designs is to select the number of discrete performance values, or *levels,* of each attribute to be considered in the design. This selection affects the number of profiles in the design, since each design consists of a combination of attributes performing at various levels. For example, recall that nine performance values of the order-taking interval (1 to 9 minutes) were used for charting its performance/satisfaction function in Figure 4.6. If nine values each of four attributes were combined into profiles such as the ones shown in Table 4.4, and all profiles were included in the design, the total number of profiles to be rated would be 9^4, or 6561! This is clearly an unacceptably large number. To avoid errors arising from rater fatigue, the number of profiles to be rated should be kept to a small and manageable number. Typically, most designs use two, three, or at most four performance levels of each attribute. The appropriate number of levels for each attribute will be different and must be chosen carefully. Let us see how this can be done.

Selecting the number of levels for each attribute

As mentioned above, a level denotes a discrete performance value of an attribute, selected from the range of anticipated performance for the attribute. This range can be based on the design team's judgment or on evaluations of the performance of competitors, and it should include the desired performance level. For example, consider the order-taking interval for the Service Edge restaurant discussed above. The desired standard is 6 minutes. Suppose a study of the key competitors reveals that customers are used to experiencing intervals as short as 3 minutes, and as long as 10 minutes. These form the endpoints of the range.

For a given attribute, the number of appropriate levels depends on the following:

1. The shape of the performance/satisfaction function.

2. The extent of the range of performance for the attribute.

Consider an attribute for which the functional form for the performance/satisfaction relationship is a straight line over the range of performance. These are attributes whose performance level either increases or decreases over the range. An example is the function, shown in Figure 4.8, for the Service Edge restaurant attribute *percent of bills accurately produced*. The desired performance standard for the attribute is at 95% billing accuracy, at which the highest level of satisfaction is obtained. The lowest anticipated performance level is at 75% accuracy. The function is linear between these values.

Suppose we wish to estimate this function from ratings of satisfaction at various performance values. How many performance values are needed? Clearly, two will suffice. To ensure that the raters of the profiles can distinguish between the two values, it seems reasonable to select these values at either end of the range (i.e., at accuracy values of 75% and 95%). Therefore, for a performance/satisfaction function that increases or decreases linearly within a range, *two levels* of the attribute, selected at the *extremes* of the range, are adequate for determining the function. In some cases, if the possible range of performance is large (for example, if the billing

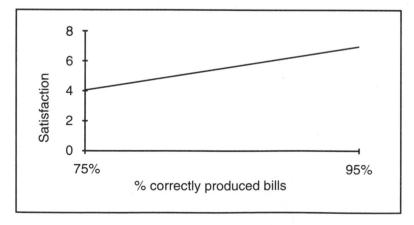

Figure 4.8 Linear performance/satisfaction function for billing accuracy attribute

accuracy can vary from 20 to 95%), a third intermediate value may be chosen to better anchor the scale.

Now consider the performance/satisfaction function for an attribute such as the order-taking interval shown in Figure 4.9. For this attribute, the highest satisfaction occurs at a performance level in the middle of the range. The center point in Figure 4.9 corresponds to the desired performance level, and the two endpoints represent lower levels of performance. This function cannot be completely represented with only two attribute levels, because two data points are not enough to depict the shape of the function on both sides of the desired performance level. At least one more data point is needed to capture the shape of the function. Therefore, *three* levels are appropriate for this attribute: one at each endpoint, and one in the middle.

More than two levels are also needed to represent nonlinear relationships. Three levels of the order-taking interval can be used to define a quadratic performance/satisfaction function for the order-taking interval, as shown in Figure 4.10. In this figure, the discontinuous lines of Figure 4.9 have been replaced with a smooth curve.

A quadratic function is called a polynomial of degree 2 since it involves a squared term. At least three levels are required to completely define this function. More levels are needed for fitting higher-degree polynomials. In general, the number of levels needed is one more than the degree of the polynomial representing the performance/satisfaction function.

Let us summarize the guidelines for selecting the appropriate number of levels for an attribute:

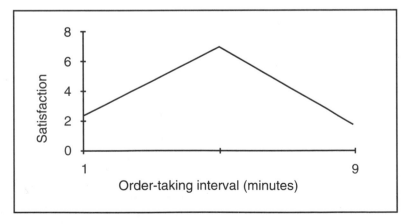

Figure 4.9 Linear performance/satisfaction relationship for the order-taking interval

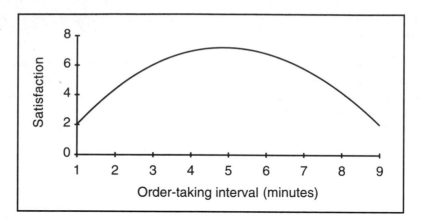

Figure 4.10 Quadratic performance/satisfaction relationship for
attribute at three levels

- A realistic performance range that includes the desired performance level for the attribute is determined by judgment or from industry benchmarks.

- The shape of the performance/satisfaction function is determined, from a single-variable analysis or from experience.

- Two levels are adequate for attributes with a linear function whose desired standard is at either extreme of the range; the extreme points are chosen as the two levels in this case.

- An additional level representing the middle of the range may be useful if the range is very broad.

- Three levels are needed if the desired standard falls in the center of the range; in this case, two levels are selected at the extreme points, and the third at the desired standard.

- More than two levels are needed if the performance/satisfaction function is nonlinear.

- At least three levels are needed to specify a quadratic function.

- In general, the number of data points needed is one more than the degree of the polynomial representing the function.

Once the number of levels of each attribute is known, the design can be created, and the ratings of the profiles that make up the design can be analyzed. We will now show how this is done. We will start with attributes at two levels and move on to attributes at three levels.

4.7 EXPERIMENTAL DESIGNS WITH ATTRIBUTES AT TWO LEVELS

In this section, we will first describe the rules for combining two-level attributes into designs. We will then show how the satisfaction ratings obtained from these designs can be used to estimate the performance/satisfaction function.

Creating designs

Let us begin with an example. Consider the four attributes for the Service Edge restaurant shown in Table 4.5, each of which assumes two performance levels. The desired standard for each attribute is indicated with an asterisk.

Notice that the attributes are both discrete and continuous, and that they are measured on different scales. In order to be able to compare the effect of the performance of different attributes on overall satisfaction, it would be convenient to represent them on the same scale. This is achieved by *coding*. By this, we mean that for each attribute, we replace the measured values of the low and high performance levels by a code. The same code is used for representing the low and high levels for all attributes.

Any convenient coding convention can be used. For example, the low performance level of each attribute can be assigned a value of 0, and the high level a value of 1. In the designs supporting the quality engineering methodology of Taguchi, the low value is coded as 1 and the high value as 2 (Phadke, 1985). In engineering convention, the low value of each attribute is coded as −1 and the high value as +1. This convention is convenient for the regression analysis methods that we present later in this chapter. We will therefore employ this convention in this book.

How can we create a design with the four restaurant attributes of Table 4.5? Clearly, the most obvious design would be one that includes all possible combina-

Table 4.5 Values of two levels of restaurant attributes

Attribute	*Low value (code = −1)*	*High value (code = +1)*
Menu delivery promptness	1 minutes(*)	5 minutes
Degree of friendliness	Average	Excellent(*)
Billing accuracy	75%	95%(*)
Problem resolution effectiveness	Average	Excellent(*)

Table 4.6 Full factorial design for four restaurant attributes

Profile number	Degree of friendliness	Menu delivery promptness	Billing accuracy	Problem resolution
1	−1	−1	−1	−1
2	−1	−1	−1	1
3	−1	−1	1	−1
4	−1	−1	1	1
5	−1	1	−1	−1
6	−1	1	−1	1
7	−1	1	1	−1
8	−1	1	1	1
9	1	−1	−1	−1
10	1	−1	−1	1
11	1	−1	1	−1
12	1	−1	1	1
13	1	1	−1	−1
14	1	1	−1	1
15	1	1	1	−1
16	1	1	1	1

tions of the four attributes. This design has $2^4 = 16$ service profiles and is shown in Table 4.6 with the attribute levels represented by their coded values.

The design shown in Table 4.6 is called a *full factorial design,* since all combinations of the four attributes are considered. This design is referred to in experimental design terminology as $L_{16}(2^{15})$, where the 16 denotes the number of profiles that each customer has to rate and the 2 refers to the number of levels per attribute.

In order to explain the number 15, let us examine Table 4.6 further. For each customer, sixteen satisfaction ratings can be obtained from the design. How many of these ratings are needed to estimate the performance/satisfaction function for each attribute of the design?

Each attribute has two performance values: a low value coded −1, and a high value coded +1. Recall from the previous section that an attribute at two levels implies a linear relationship between satisfaction and performance. Clearly, a satisfaction rating associated with the −1 value and one associated with the +1 value is enough to specify the relationship between satisfaction and performance for this attribute. For example, consider an attribute whose satisfaction rating at the low performance level is 4.8 and at the high performance level is 7.3. The performance/satisfaction function for this attribute can be determined by joining the points (−1, 4.8) and (+1, 7.3) as shown in Figure 4.11.

The above example shows that the ratings from two profiles are enough to determine the performance/satisfaction relationship for each attribute in Table 4.6. Let us formalize this concept in mathematical terms. A straight line is characterized by a *slope*, which is a measure of the steepness of the line, and an *intercept*, which is a measure of the point at which the line intersects the y axis.[2] One data point is needed to determine the slope, and one to determine the intercept. A total of two ratings, one at each performance value of the attribute, is therefore needed to completely specify the line.

Since the L_{16} design is made up of four attributes, and each attribute has a linear satisfaction/performance function, a maximum of eight profiles is needed to determine all four functions. However, in practice, it is enough to estimate a single composite intercept for all four attributes.[3] Therefore, five profiles (four for the slopes and one for the intercept) are enough to determine the satisfaction/performance functions for four attributes. Since sixteen ratings are available, the L_{16} design can be used to estimate linear satisfaction/performance relationships for as many as fifteen independent attributes (i.e., one intercept and fifteen slopes). This is the meaning of the number fifteen in the design nomenclature.

We have seen that only five ratings are required to estimate the functions for the four attributes of Table 4.5. In practice, therefore, we do not need to subject the raters to the task of evaluating sixteen profiles for four attributes. It is enough to consider a design that has fewer profiles than the full factorial design described above. Such a design involves only a fraction of the full design and is called a *fractional* factorial design. We will now examine the details of such a design.

---

[2] A linear function can be written as $Y = a + bX$, where a is the intercept and b the slope.

[3] The model is written as $S = a + b_1X_1 + b_2X_2 + b_3X_3 + b_4X_4$, where S is the satisfaction and X_1, X_2, X_3, X_4 are the performance values of the four attributes. We therefore need to estimate the common intercept a and the four slopes b_1, b_2, b_3, b_4.

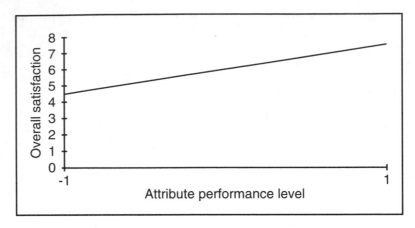

Figure 4.11 Linear performance/satisfaction function requires two satisfaction ratings

Fractional factorial designs

How can we select an appropriate fraction? Clearly, for four attributes, we only need a 5/16th fraction, i.e., 5 profiles out of the 16 in Table 4.6. But how do we decide which profiles to select? To understand this, we must look once again at the properties of the full design. Notice that the design in Table 4.6 is *balanced*. This implies that in each column the low and high values appear an equal number of times (eight times each). In addition, all *combinations* of values of two or more attributes also appear an equal number of times. For example, for any two attributes, the combinations HH, HL, LH, and LL appear four times each, while a combination of three attributes such as HHL appears twice. Such a design is called *orthogonal*.

Orthogonality is an attractive property for a design because it ensures that an attribute is evaluated an equal number of times at each performance level. Intuitively, this implies that the data are available at the same amount of detail throughout the performance range of each attribute and that all attributes are treated equally. Therefore, we should only select those fractional designs that are orthogonal.

It is not possible to generate a balanced 5/16th fraction for the L_{16} design of Table 4.6, but it is possible to create an orthogonal design with eight profiles, referred to as the L_8 (2^7) design. One version of this design is formed from rows 1, 4, 6, 7, 10, 11, 13, and 16 of Table 4.6 and is shown in Table 4.7. The reader can verify that this design is balanced.

We will now describe how the performance/satisfaction function can be estimated for each attribute from the design of Table 4.7. There are two estimation methods. The first, called the *direct method*, requires no statistical knowledge, but becomes cumbersome when the number of attributes and the number of levels increases.

Table 4.7   Eight-profile fractional factorial design for four restaurant attributes

Profile number	Degree of friendliness	Menu delivery promptness	Billing accuracy	Problem resolution effectiveness
1	−1	−1	−1	−1
2	1	−1	−1	1
3	−1	1	−1	1
4	1	1	−1	−1
5	−1	−1	1	1
6	1	−1	1	−1
7	−1	1	1	−1
8	1	1	1	1

The second method, called the *regression method*, is more flexible, but requires some statistical sophistication. We will describe only the direct method in this section. The regression method is presented in the following section.

Estimating the performance/satisfaction function—direct method

We will illustrate this method by an example using the design of Table 4.7. For this example, we created fictitious but realistic satisfaction ratings for ten customer evaluations of the profiles of this design. We assumed that each customer rated all profiles on a seven-point scale. We therefore generated a total of $(10 \times 8) = 80$ data points, with 10 for each profile. We then averaged these ten ratings to create one average satisfaction rating for each profile. The results are shown in Table 4.8. Note that all attributes in the last profile perform at the desired level, and that the associated satisfaction is assigned a perfect score. This helps to anchor the scale.

Readers interested in a real example of the use of conjoint analysis to evaluate restaurant attributes are referred to a paper by Dubé *et al* (1994). In this paper, the authors compare seven restaurant service attributes measured at two levels each. The data for this study were obtained from 127 customers who dined at an upscale restaurant during the course of a week.

Recall from the previous section that for four attributes, all the functions can be specified by calculating four slopes and one common intercept. For this design, the

Table 4.8 Average satisfaction ratings for two-level design

Profile number	Degree of friendliness	Menu delivery promptness	Billing accuracy	Problem resolution effectiveness	Average satisfaction rating
1	Average	5 minutes	75%	Average	2.8
2	Excellent	5 minutes	75%	Excellent	3.9
3	Average	1 minute	75%	Average	3.5
4	Excellent	1 minute	75%	Excellent	5.6
5	Average	5 minutes	95%	Excellent	3.2
6	Excellent	5 minutes	95%	Average	5.0
7	Average	1 minute	95%	Average	4.7
8	Excellent	1 minute	95%	Excellent	7.0

intercept can be calculated by averaging the average satisfaction ratings in Table 4.8. This gives a value of 4.47 for the intercept. The objective is to now estimate the slope of the linear satisfaction/performance relationship for each attribute.

The slope of a straight line is calculated by dividing the change in the y values for a given change in the x values by the change in the x values. For example, in Figure 4.12, the y value changes from 10 to 0 when the x value changes from 0 to 5. The (negative) slope of the line is therefore $(0 - 10)/(5 - 0) = -2$.

This formula can be used for calculating the slope for each attribute in Table 4.8. For example, consider the attribute "degree of friendliness." The *average* satisfaction rating when friendliness is at the *low* level (coded as −1) is calculated by averaging the ratings for profiles 1, 3, 5, and 7 in Table 4.8. Its value is $(2.8 + 3.5 + 3.2 + 4.7)/4 = 3.55$. Similarly, the average satisfaction rating for the *high* levels of friendliness (coded as +1), calculated by averaging the ratings for rows 2, 4, 6, and 8 in Table 4.8 is $(3.9 + 5.6 + 5 + 7) = 5.375$. Therefore the satisfaction (y-value) changes by $(5.375 - 3.55) = 1.825$ units for a change in the performance of the friendliness attribute (x-value) by 2 units from −1 to +1. The slope of the satisfaction/performance function for the degree of friendliness attribute is therefore $1.825/2 = 0.9125$. The slopes for the other attribute categories can be calculated similarly. Table 4.9 shows the results. The slope for promptness is negative because lower values of this attribute provide more satisfaction than higher values.

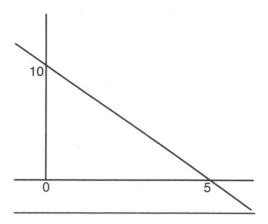

Figure 4.12 Calculating the slope of a
straight line

From the data in Table 4.9, the complete performance/satisfaction relationship for the four attributes can be written as follows (see footnote 3) :

$$Satisfaction = 4.47 + 0.9 * Friendliness - 0.75 * Promptness + 0.5 * Accuracy + 0.05 * Problem\ resolution\ effectiveness \qquad (4.1)$$

Recalibrating the model

When all the attributes perform at their desired levels (+1 for friendliness, accuracy, and problem resolution effectiveness, and −1 for promptness), the satisfaction rating is 4.47 + 0.9 + 0.75 + 0.5 + 0.05 = 6.67. Why is the rating not a perfect 7? This is because Equation 4.1 is estimated from empirical data, and the difference results from random variability in customers' ratings. Since the intercept is common for all attributes, its exact value does not matter as long as all attributes are compared from the same base. If it is felt that a score of 7 when all the attributes perform at the design value is easier to understand and interpret, then Equation 4.1 can be adjusted by adding (7 − 6.67) = 0.33 to the intercept term, increasing the value of this term to 4.8. This recalibrates the model without affecting the results.

Developing performance/satisfaction relationships

For each attribute in Equation 4.1, performance/satisfaction relationships can be developed by substituting appropriate coded values for the perfomance of other attributes. For example, suppose we want to determine the performance/satisfaction function for the attribute *degree of friendliness* when the other attributes are performing at their desired levels. We substitute the coded values of these levels

Table 4.9 Slope of performance/satisfaction function for each restaurant attribute

Attribute	Average satisfaction rating at low value (1)	Average satisfaction rating at high value (2)	Difference in average satisfaction rating (3) = (2)−(1)	Change in attribute performance (4)	Attribute slope (3)/(4)
Friendliness	3.6	5.4	1.8	2	0.9
Promptness	5.2	3.7	−1.5	2	−0.75
Accuracy	4.0	5.0	1.0	2	0.50
Resolution	4.4	4.5	0.1	2	0.05

(−1 for promptness, +1 for accuracy and problem resolution effectiveness, respectively), and determine the following relationship between satisfaction and the degree of friendliness:

$$Satisfaction = 6.1 + 0.9* Friendliness \qquad (4.2)$$

Equation 4.2 is the performance/satisfaction relationship for the friendliness attribute. The functions for the other attributes are calculated similarly. Figure 4.13 shows the performance satisfaction relationships for each attribute, assuming that the other attributes remain at their desired level.

Interpreting the slopes

What do the slopes tell us about the customers' tolerance for the deviation of the performance of each attribute from its desired value? The largest change in satisfaction takes place as the degree of friendliness changes from average to excellent [Figure 4.13 (a)]. The smallest change in satisfaction occurs with problem resolution effectiveness. From the design perspective, this implies that even if there is a large gap between the desired and the design standards for the effectiveness of problem resolution, the satisfaction will not be affected by a large amount. On the other hand, the service should be designed to perform as close to the desired performance as possible for the degree of friendliness attribute. The other attributes fall in between.

For the continuous attributes such as menu delivery interval or billing accuracy, satisfaction varies linearly between the two extreme values. We can therefore meaningfully talk about the satisfaction associated with an intermediate perfor-

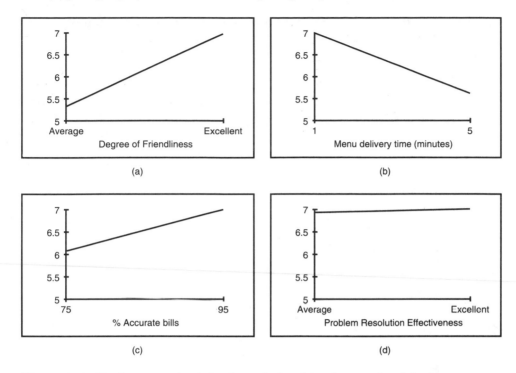

Figure 4.13   Performance/satisfaction relationships for two-level design
attributes

mance of the attribute (e.g., 80% accuracy). For the discrete attributes such as
friendliness or problem resolution (i.e., those that can only take values such as
"good" or "excellent," but no values in between), the continuous linear function of
Figure 4.13 is a useful guideline, but judgment must be used to interpret the satisfaction rating at intermediate scale values.

In this section, we showed how designs could be created, analyzed, and interpreted for attributes at two levels. We extend this presentation to designs with attributes at three levels in the following section.

4.8   ANALYZING PROFILES WITH ATTRIBUTES AT THREE LEVELS

Creating designs with attributes at three levels

As described in Section 4.5, in addition to the extreme values, we choose a third
data point in the middle of the performance range for attributes that need to be
evaluated at *three* levels. For each attribute at three levels, *three* pieces of information are needed to specify the performance/satisfaction function, rather than the

two pieces (slope and intercept) that we obtained from the two-level model. For a quadratic function, this second piece of information is a quadratic term,[4] as shown in footnote 4. Quadratic functions are meaningful only for continuous attributes, such as promptness or accuracy. For attributes such as attitude and problem resolution effectiveness that do not have an obvious continuous scale, we separately estimate the change in satisfaction as we move from the low to the medium level of the attribute, and from the medium to the high level. This requires the estimation of *two* slopes for each attribute. Clearly, three pieces of information (one intercept and two slopes) are needed for such attributes as well.

To illustrate our discussion in this section, let us once again consider four attributes of the Service Edge restaurant. The low, high, and mid-values of the attributes are shown in Table 4.10. A full factorial design for four attributes at three levels each requires $3^4 = 81$ profiles. As before, if we estimate a composite intercept for all attributes, and two parameters for each attribute (as mentioned above, the quadratic term for the continuous attributes, and two slopes for the discrete ones), we only need only $2 \times 4 + 1 = 9$ data points. We therefore need a fractional design that has at least nine profiles.

A three-level fractional design

The $L_9(3^4)$ design is a three-level orthogonal fractional design. Following the naming convention described in the previous section, we can see that this design has nine profiles of three levels each and can be used to estimate the slopes of the performance/satisfaction relationship of at most four attributes. This design therefore suits our purposes perfectly. This design is shown in Table 4.11, with the coded values for the attributes. In the three-level case, the low level assumes a coded value of -1, the mid-level a value of 0, and the high level a value of +1. The reader should verify that the design shown in Table 4.11 is orthogonal.

Higher-level and mixed designs

Many two-, three-, four-, and higher-level designs have been tabulated in the literature. Moreover, mixed-level designs are available for analyzing combinations of attributes that are measured at different levels. The reader is referred to experimental design textbooks such as Grove and Davis (1992) and Taguchi and Wu (1979).

Estimating the performance/satisfaction relationship—regression method

Recall that the slope of the performance/satisfaction relationship using the direct method was calculated by subtracting the satisfaction at the high performance

---

[4]A quadratic function can be mathematically written as $y = a + bx + cx^2$. In addition to the intercept a and the linear slope b, we need to estimate the value of the parameter c. This parameter is a measure of the curvature of the function; if $c = 0$, the quadratic function becomes linear.

Table 4.10   Values of three levels of restaurant attributes

Attribute	Low value	Medium value	High value
Meal delivery promptness	5 minutes	10 minutes(*)	15 minutes
Degree of friendliness	Average	Good	Excellent(*)
Billing accuracy	75%	85%	95%(*)
Problem resolution	Average	Good	Excellent(*)

level from the satisfaction at the low performance level. The same method can be used for attributes at three levels if the relationship between satisfaction and performance is piecewise linear, as in Figure 4.7. In this case, *two* slopes can be calculated: one for the difference between the medium and low performance levels, and the other for the difference between the high and medium levels.

As the number of attributes and the number of levels increases, this rapidly becomes tedious and impractical. We therefore need an approach where the intercept

Table 4.11   Three-level fractional design for restaurant attributes

Profile number	Degree of friendliness	Promptness of meal delivery	Billing accuracy	Problem resolution effectiveness
1	−1	−1	−1	−1
2	−1	0	0	0
3	−1	1	1	1
4	0	−1	0	1
5	0	0	1	−1
6	0	1	−1	0
7	1	−1	1	0
8	1	0	−1	1
9	1	1	0	−1

and the slopes of all attributes are calculated simultaneously. The regression method allows us to do this. In this method, overall satisfaction is expressed as a function of the performance of the attributes, in a form similar to that shown in Equation 4.1. The parameters of the function are estimated using Ordinary Least Squares (OLS) regression. For the fundamentals of regression, the reader is referred to any standard statistics or econometrics textbook (for example, Pindyck and Rubinfeld, 1981).

We will demonstrate the regression method using the design shown in Table 4.11. In order to keep the example simple, we will only use two attributes: *billing accuracy* and *promptness of meal delivery.* As in the two-level case, we generated fictitious data for ten customer ratings of each profile in the design of Table 4.11, giving us $10 \times 9 = 90$ data points. If the customers are relatively homogeneous, these 90 points can be pooled and a single model can be estimated using all the data. On the other hand, if the data span a diverse population from different market segments, a separate model can be estimated from the nine data points available for each individual.

In this example, we estimate a pooled model with 90 data points. We also assume that for both variables, the shape of the performance/satisfaction function identified from exploratory studies justifies a *quadratic* model in footnote 4. The model to be estimated is shown in Equation 4.3:

$$Satisfaction = Intercept + a1 * Promptness + a2 * Promptness^2 + b1 * Accuracy + b2 * Accuracy^2 \tag{4.3}$$

In Equation 4.3, the variables *promptness* and *accuracy* are the linear independent variables. For each data point, these variables are represented by the coded value (-1, 0, or 1) of the appropriate attribute from the service profile. For example, from the first profile in Table 4.11, it can be seen that the linear term for promptness will take the value −1, and so will the linear term for accuracy. From the second profile, these terms will take the value (0,0). The values of these terms for the other profiles can be similarly obtained from Table 4.11. Clearly, the same set of nine independent variables will be repeated ten times in the data set, once for each customer.

The independent variables $promptness^2$ and $accuracy^2$ are the quadratic independent variables. We saw above that the linear variables could be represented by their coded values. How do we represent the quadratic terms? Under the coding convention we have used in this book $(-1, 0, 1)$, the regression method gives the right results if the quadratic terms are represented as squares of the linear terms. This means that, for the first profile, the quadratic term for promptness will have the value $(-1 \times -1) = 1$, and the term for accuracy will also have the same value.

For the second profile, both quadratic terms will have the value $(0 \times 0) = 0$. The reason why this rule works is complicated, and we will not address it in this book. Instead, we will present it here as an operational rule, and refer the reader to Grove and Davis (1992) for more details.

The dependent variable in the model is the satisfaction rating. One rating is available for each customer and each profile. The *intercept* and the terms *a1, a2, b1,* and *b2* are the parameters that need to be estimated.

Analyzing the results of the regression model

The parameter values estimated for the linear and quadratic terms of Equation 4.3 are presented in Table 4.12. The model was estimated using the regression feature of a common spreadsheet program. From the entries in this table, the relationship between satisfaction and promptness and billing accuracy can be written as follows:

$$Satisfaction = 6.69 - 0.12 * Promptness - 1.57 * Promptness^2 + 0.18 * Accuracy + 0.13 * Accuracy^2 \qquad (4.4)$$

The intercept term in Equation 4.4 has been recalibrated to predict a satisfaction rating of 7 when promptness and accuracy are at their desired coded values (0 and 1, respectively).

Developing quadratic performance/satisfaction relationships

For each attribute, the quadratic performance/satisfaction relationship can be determined by the same method used for the linear functions in the previous section. We substitute the coded value of the desired performance level for all attributes other than the one whose function is being defined. For example, the relationship

Table 4.12 Parameter values for linear and quadratic terms of Equation 4.1

Parameter	Estimate
a1	−0.12
a2	−1.57
b1	0.18
b2	0.13

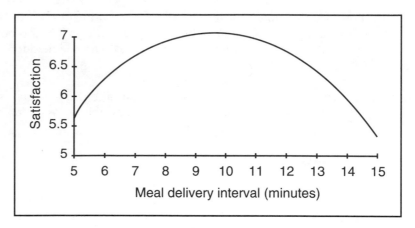

Figure 4.14   Performance/satisfaction function for meal delivery
interval (same as Figure 4.3)

between satisfaction and promptness is determined by substituting the desired
performance level of billing accuracy (+1) in Equation 4.4. This leads to the function presented in Equation 4.5, which is graphed in Figure 4.14. The reader will recall that we used this performance/satisfaction function in Section 4.5 to
demonstrate how to set design standards for the meal delivery interval of the Service Edge restaurant.

$$Satisfaction = 7 - 0.12*Promptness - 1.57*Promptness^2$$ (4.5)

Similarly, when promptness is at the desired performance level of 0 (10 minutes),
the relationship between satisfaction and accuracy is:

$$Satisfaction = 6.69 + 0.18 * Accuracy + 0.13 * Accuracy^2$$ (4.6)

This function is shown in Figure 4.15.

Other specifications for the performance/satisfaction relationship

The greatest advantage of the regression method is that it provides us the flexibility to easily model different functional forms for the relationship between satisfaction and performance. For example, linear relationships can be modeled by

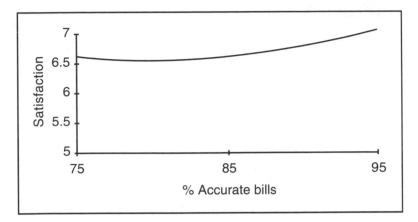

Figure 4.15   Performance/satisfaction function for billing
accuracy (same as Figure 4.4)

omitting the quadratic term from the regression equation. Functions that have two
linear functions over the performance range (see Figure 4.9 for an example) can be
represented by including two terms in the regression equation for each attribute.
One term is applicable for the range from the low to the medium performance
level, and the second term for the range from the medium to the high performance
level. An example of this specification is presented in DeSarbo *et al* (1994).

The regression model can also be used to estimate *interactions* between the attributes. As shown in Figure 4.7, an interaction between two attributes implies that
the slope of the performance/satisfaction function for one attribute depends on
the performance level of the other. In the regression model, interactions are specified as *products* of the independent variables. For example, the interaction between
promptness and accuracy can be represented by the term *promptness*accuracy* in
Equation 4.3. Under the $(-1, 0, 1)$ coding convention, the interaction terms are represented as the product of the coded values of the linear terms in the regression
equation. For example, in the first profile in Table 4.11, both accuracy and promptness take the value of -1. The interaction between these variables is represented
by the product of their coded values (i.e., $-1 \times -1) = 1$.

Our coverage of experimental design topics in this book has necessarily been very
brief. Our objective in this chapter was to give the reader an introduction to the
methods that can be used to estimate the performance/satisfaction relationship
for an attribute. Readers wishing to apply these techniques to their own services
may require a more detailed exposition of the theory and practice of experimental
design. We direct this reader to the references mentioned in the bibliography at the
end of this book.

4.9 CONCLUSION

Summary

A step-by-step summary of the topics covered in this chapter is presented below. The section in the chapter where a particular topic is covered is indicated in parentheses.

Design performance standards (4.1)

- Design performance standards are yardsticks for evaluating design alternatives.

- Performance level desired by customers is the upper bound for standards.

- Performance of competitors is the minimum acceptable lower bound.

- Exact value of standard depends on performance/satisfaction relationship.

- Standards are design-independent performance guidelines.

Factors affecting design performance standards for an attribute (4.1)

- Knowledge of customers' desired performance level.

- Benchmarks of key competitors' performance of the attribute.

- Performance/satisfaction relationship.

- Attribute importance.

Desired and ideal performance level (4.2)

- Desired standard indicates customers' expectations for the performance of the attribute.

- Ideal level is the natural optimal performance level at which a perfect service performs.

- Desired and ideal performance levels may be different.

- Desired performance level may sometimes be obtained by direct questioning.

- In other cases, the desired performance level may be indirectly extracted through benchmarks.

Customer and technical benchmarks—HOQ rooms 4 and 5 (4.3)

- Customer benchmarks measure perceptions of competitors' effectiveness in satisfying needs.

- Either second- or third-level needs can be used.

- Choice of competitor should be market leader or distinguished firm.
- Customer benchmarks are listed in room 4 of House of Quality.
- Technical benchmarks measure design team's perceptions of competitors' performance.
- Technical benchmarks are listed in room 5 of House of Quality.
- Customer and technical benchmarks are used together to infer desired performance level.
- Discrepancies between benchmarks indicate mismatch between perceptions and measures.

Performance/satisfaction function (4.4)

- Measures relationship between performance and satisfaction.
- Can have many functional forms.
- Slope of function indicates customers' tolerance for deviations from desired performance.

Setting design performance standards (HOQ room 8) (4.5)

- Specify minimum acceptable threshold.
- Rank attributes in order of decreasing slope of performance/satisfaction function.
- Rank attributes in order of importance.
- Using the slope and importance as guidelines, set design performance levels for each attribute.
- Predict overall satisfaction from specified attribute performance levels.
- Determine whether predicted satisfaction is higher than the threshold.
- If not, tighten performance of some attributes, and drop less important ones.

Estimating the performance/satisfaction relationship for a single attribute (4.6)

- Measure change of overall satisfaction with performance levels of attribute.
- Assume that all other attributes are at desired levels.
- Not an accurate method for estimating the performance/satisfaction function.
- Use for exploratory data analysis.

Estimating the performance/satisfaction relationship for all attributes (4.6)

◆ Customers are asked to rate their satisfaction with service profiles.

◆ These are made up of combinations of attributes at prespecified discrete levels.

◆ Conjoint analysis is used to decompose the overall ratings into individual relationships.

Selecting the number of levels for conjoint analysis (4.6)

◆ Select a realistic performance range.

◆ Estimate the shape of the performance/satisfaction function.

◆ Two levels are adequate for linear function.

◆ More than two levels needed for nonlinear functions.

◆ At least three levels needed for quadratic function.

Two level designs (4.7)

◆ Attribute scales are equalized through coding.

◆ Low value is scored −1, high value is scored +1.

◆ Full factorial designs consider all combinations of attributes.

◆ Fractional designs consider fewer combinations and are easier to rate.

◆ Fractional designs should maintain orthogonality, i.e., balance.

◆ Performance/satisfaction functions are estimated by regression using coded values.

◆ Parameter values are function slopes.

Three-level designs (4.8)

◆ An additional level is specified in the middle of the range.

◆ Values are coded −1, 0, 1.

◆ Quadratic terms are represented by squares of coded values of each attribute.

◆ Piecewise linear functions and interactions can also be estimated.

Suggested Readings

The following six texts are recommended for further reading on experimental design and Taguchi methods. This is not an exhaustive list, but a collection that provides a good overview of different aspects of the topic. Some of these texts have already been referenced in this chapter.

Grove, D. M., and T. P. Davis (1992). *Engineering, Quality, and Experimental Design,* John Wiley and Sons, New York. Very well written, comprehensive guide to experimental design that discusses both classical experimental design and Taguchi methods. Also places the role of experimental design in the framework of quality and variability reduction. Very highly recommended.

Condra, L. W. (1993). *Reliability Improvement with Design of Experiments,* Marcel Dekker, New York. Basic, but rather simplistic, introduction to design of experiments and analysis of experimental results. Presents design of experiments within the quality framework.

Barker, T. B. (1994). *Quality by Experimental Design.* Marcel Dekker, New York. Contains detailed, step-by-step instructions on how to set up various types of experiments. Good reference text.

Hicks, C. R. (1993). *Fundamental Concepts in the Design of Experiments,* 4th edition. Saunders College Publishing, New York. Presents a broad range of topics in experimental design. More detailed statistical approach than the texts mentioned above.

Peace, G. S. (1993). *Taguchi Methods.* Addison-Wesley, Reading, MA. A practitioner's book that simply and clearly lays out how to design, conduct, and carry out experiments in Taguchi's Quality Engineering framework.

Fowlkes, W. Y., and C. M. Creveling (1995). *Engineering Methods for Robust Design: Using Taguchi Methods in Technology and Product Development,* Addison-Wesley, Reading, MA. A detailed, somewhat technical text that shows the use of Taguchi methods in product design.

Chapter

5

Generating and Evaluating Design Concepts

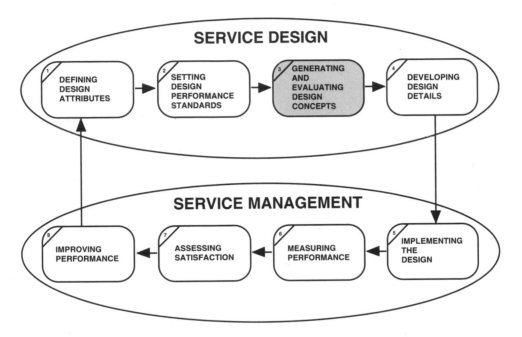

- *Functional Analysis*
- *Defining and Documenting Processes*
- *Concept Generation*
- *Evaluating and Selecting Concepts—Description of the Pugh Method*
- *Using the Pugh Method to Evaluate Restaurant Concepts*
- *Conclusion*

In this chapter, we describe stage 3 of the service design and management model, in which we give shape to the service described by the design specifications. The activities of this stage are shown in Figure 5.1.

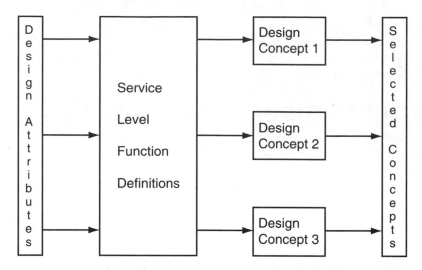

Figure 5.1   From specifications to concept selection—stage 3 activities

In this stage, the design specifications identified in Stage 2 are used to define the generic functions by which the service will be delivered. In this chapter, we show how these functions can be assembled into processes, how process boundaries can be established, and how the interactions between the processes can be specified. We then create global service designs, called *concepts,* each of which represents an innovative strategy for delivering the service. We evaluate these concepts using a semiquantitative comparison procedure. Each pass through the procedure results in the creation of enhanced concepts that adopt the best features of the previous set. Several passes through the procedure enable the creation of the best overall concept for the design of the service. The individual processes and activities of the selected concept are then designed in detail. Methods for detailed design are described in Chapters 6 and 7.

In Section 5.1 we describe the FAST (functional analysis system technique) approach for determining the key functions that need to be performed to deliver a service. The steps for assembling these functions into processes and flow-charting methods for documenting these processes are presented in Section 5.2. In Sections 5.3 and 5.4, we describe methods for the generation, evaluation, and selection of design concepts. In Section 5.5, we show how these methods can be applied to select a concept for the Service Edge restaurant. Section 5.6 is a chapter summary and suggested readings.

5.1 FUNCTIONAL ANALYSIS

Functional analysis is a method for identifying the activities that must be completed in order to deliver the service. FAST (functional analysis system technique)

is a useful tool for visually representing these activities and the relationships between them. In this technique, the functions are represented by boxes arranged in a horizontal tree structure. The root of the tree is at the extreme right of the diagram and is a high-level description of the service. Detail is successively added as we expand the tree leftwards through the diagram. For any given function box ("X") in the diagram, the function to its immediate right answers the question *"Why is function X performed?"* and the functions to its immediate left answer the question *"How is function X performed?"* (i.e., what activities are required to perform this function?). Starting from the root, the FAST diagram is constructed layer-by-layer by successively answering a series of "how" and "why" questions.

The best method of demonstrating the FAST technique is through an example. Figure 5.2 shows the first stage of the FAST diagram for the Service Edge restaurant.

To begin Figure 5.2, we begin with the "why" question: *"Why do we need to design the features, facilities, and service of the Service Edge restaurant?"* The answer to this question is the overall service objective: "Satisfy customers through a complete dining experience." This objective is written on a piece of paper that is pinned or pasted to a board. The team then asks the "how" question: *"How can we satisfy customers with a complete dining experience?"* The answer can be found from the design attributes in the QFD matrix. The first-level attributes from Table 3.3 are a good

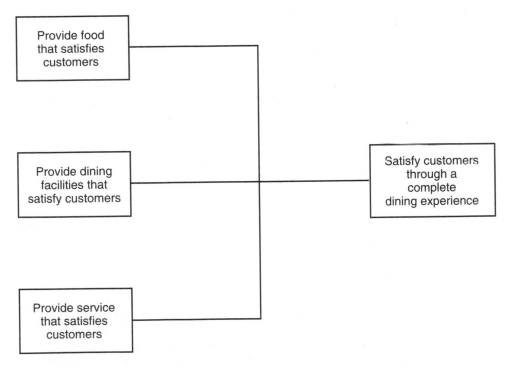

Figure 5.2 FAST diagram for Service Edge restaurant—first level

starting point. Each of the three functions to the left of Figure 5.2 (e.g., "provide food that satisfies customers") is a verb–noun combination of one of the three attribute categories "Food design," "Facilities design," and "Customer service design." Since the functions are at the same level of detail, they are positioned one below the other.

It can be seen from Figure 5.2 that the FAST diagram is a natural extension to the House of Quality matrix. The functions listed in the diagram are obtained from the columns of the HOQ matrix. The FAST diagram represents these functions in a logical sequence that displays their interactions. Clausing (1994) considers all techniques used for product design and development and for the deployment of a consistent set of specifications through all levels of the design (such as QFD, functional analysis, failure mode analysis, robust design, and concept selection) to be part of a common interlinked methodological framework. Sontow (Sontow and Clausing, 1993) refers to this framework as *extended enhanced QFD*.

After the functions of the service have been identified at the level shown in Figure 5.2, they must be expanded to the next level of detail. Let us consider the function "Provide service that satisfies customers" from Figure 5.2. The team asks the question: "How to provide service?" The second-level attributes from the columns of the House of Quality matrix in Table 3.5 can be used to answer this question. As before, these attributes are translated into verb–noun combinations and posted on the board to the left of the "provide service" block. This is shown in Figure 5.3.

Once the diagram is complete, the team reviews the entire chart to check for inconsistencies or gaps. The pieces of paper on the board are moved around at the suggestion of team members until a consensus is reached that all activities have been accurately listed at the required level of detail. If some activities are identified that are not covered by the design attributes, room 2 of the House of Quality should be revisited. It may be possible that some attributes are defined too broadly in the QFD matrix, or that the FAST diagram is too detailed. However, it could also be that some attributes have been omitted from the House of Quality. The team should also watch out for situations where the functions do not cover all attributes. In this case, it may be possible that the functions in the FAST diagram have been defined too broadly. More detail should be added to the diagram if required.

5.2   DEFINING AND DOCUMENTING PROCESSES

Process definition

Processes are created by assembling the functions in the FAST diagram into the temporal sequence in which the activities are performed. Each process should be a collection of activities that can logically be designed or managed as a single entity. Each process must take an input from the customer and produce an output that is visible to the customer. The construction of processes that do not have a customer

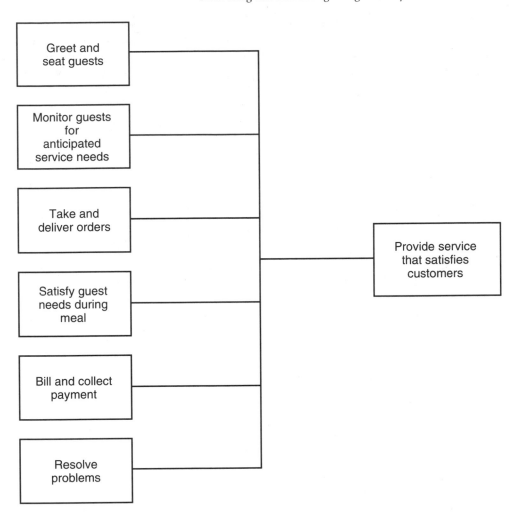

Figure 5.3 FAST diagram for Service Edge restaurant—second level

at the input and output ends should be avoided. The reason for this is that it is difficult to evaluate the impact of the quality of such processes on the customer. As a result, the designs that are selected for such processes may not optimally satisfy customers' needs. In cases where a logical sequence of functions appears internally within the operations of the service, the design team must try to incorporate these functions within a larger process that faces the customer.

For example, suppose the design performance standard (see Chapter 4) specifies that the attribute "meal delivery interval" (the interval between a customer ordering a meal and its delivery) at the Service Edge restaurant should not be greater than or less than 10 minutes. This interval is influenced by the activities required to prepare the meal in the kitchen, referred to as the "food assembly process." Consider two designs for the food assembly process, one of which takes 3 minutes and the second 5 minutes. Which design is better? Without further information, our natural tendency might be to select the design with the shorter assembly time, since this increases the efficiency of kitchen operations. But this choice is unacceptable if it results in a total meal delivery time that is less than 10 minutes, since customers may be left with the perception that the service is too rushed for them to enjoy the dining experience. In this case, the satisfaction/efficiency trade-offs for the food assembly process cannot be evaluated in isolation without considering the broader context of the meal delivery interval.

There is no limit to the amount of detail in which a process can be defined. At the concept generation stage, it is enough to identify only the beginning and end points of each process and the interactions between them. Other levels are appropriate for other applications. For example, a description of overall restaurant operations may not even include the individual processes, but may characterize them as broad categories. On the other hand, for detailed process design (described in Chapters 6 and 7), each process needs to be broken down into its constituent tasks. The team must be careful to document the process to the level of detail that is most appropriate. Too little detail results in loss of information, while too much creates confusion and may obscure the main process steps. Also, all the steps of the process should be represented at the same level of detail. If levels are mixed, more importance may be attributed to the processes whose appearance of complexity is merely an artifact of representation.

Operational and customer service activities

Processes consist of two types of activities: the *operational activities,* which are the steps that are needed to deliver the service to the customer, and the *customer service activities,* which reflect the personal interactions between the customer and the service provider during the course of service delivery. For example, consider the operational and customer service activities involved in taking a restaurant customer's order. The operational activities include the tasks that are needed to collect the order information from customers, note this information, and transmit it to the kitchen for the preparation of the meal. The quality of these activities is measured by attributes such as the promptness and accuracy with which they are performed. The customer service activities focus on the attitude of the waiter when the order is taken, the waiter's professionalism and knowledge of the items on the menu, how comfortable the customers feel while interacting with the waiter, and so on. The quality of these activities is measured by attributes such as the friendliness, responsiveness, and patience of the waiter when taking the order. These attributes are characteristics of *people,* not processes, but through careful design, procedures can be developed that deliver a reliable level of performance on these attributes as well. For example, customers are as likely to be turned off by waiters who are excessively familiar as they are by waiters who are rude. Adequate training can help to develop approaches for interacting with customers in a manner that is both personally appealing and professional.

In many process design efforts, the largest amount of effort goes into designing the operational activities because the attributes of these activities can be easily quantified or measured. As described above, the operational activities and the customer service activities *together* influence the quality of the service. A service whose operations are carefully planned will not satisfy customers if the service is delivered by untrained or unprofessional service providers. The design team should therefore pay careful attention to the design of both sets of activities.

Once all processes have been defined, the design team must ensure that all the functions of the FAST diagram have been assigned to processes, and that no gaps exist in the process definitions. If gaps exist, the team must return to the diagram to investigate the functions between which gaps are present and must define any additional functions that may be missing. In addition, for each process, the team must clearly define the process boundaries, specify the inputs and outputs at the boundaries, and establish procedures for the transfer of information at the process interfaces. Finally, the sequence of process functions must be visually displayed in a process flow chart.

Defining processes for the Service Edge restaurant

Table 5.1 shows the processes created from the service functions for the Service Edge restaurant presented in the FAST diagram of Figure 5.3. The reader should verify that each succeeding process in Table 5.1 begins where the preceding process ends, leaving no gaps in the process definitions. Notice also that each process begins and ends with the customer. And finally, even if it is not explicitly shown in Table 5.1, the reader should always keep in mind that each process consists of both service operations and customer service activities. The attributes of both types of activities should be included in the process design.

Process flow-charting

Processes are documented by drawing flow charts that indicate how the process functions are connected to each other. Figure 5.4 shows a flow chart of the processes listed in Table 5.1. Some of the processes in Table 5.1 are aggregated into a single box in Figure 5.4. For each process, the customer service and the service operations activities are represented separately to emphasize the fact that the process design should include both sets of activities.

An expanded segment of Figure 5.4 is shown in Figure 5.5 to illustrate the interaction between the service operations and customer service activities. The *meal service* and *problem resolution* processes and their inputs and outputs are shown in Figure 5.5. The *meal service process* refers to the activities required to fulfill service needs during the meal. Both service operations and customer service activities are

Table 5.1 Processes for restaurant service

Process name	Begins	Ends
Greeting and seating	Customer arrives	Customer is seated
Menu delivery	Customer is seated	Customer receives menu
Order-taking	Customer receives menu	Customer orders meal
Meal delivery	Customer orders meal	Customer receives meal
Meal service	Customer is seated	Customer leaves table
Billing	Customer requests bill	Customer receives bill
Payment collection	Customer receives bill	Customer pays
Bill settlement	Customer pays	Bill is settled
Leavetaking	Customer leaves table	Customer departs
Problem resolution	Customer has problem	Problem is resolved

important for this process. The service operations activities pertain to the completion of service requests. As shown in Figure 5.5, the input to these activities is a service need; the output is the completed request. Some of these requests may be expressed by the guests, such as a request for extra bread. Others may be anticipated and fulfilled by the waiter, such as filling an empty water glass. The quality of these activities is judged by the efficiency and accuracy of the service provided.

The customer service activities of the meal service process pertain to the *response* provided by the waiter while satisfying the need. The input to these activities is a customer response, which could be a question, a greeting, a request, a warning, a complaint, or any other interaction with the waiter. The output to these activities is the waiter response, measured by attributes such as serving style, body and verbal language used, politeness and professionalism, and breadth of knowledge.

The relationship between the service operations and customer service activities is also shown through the interaction between the meal service and problem resolution processes in Figure 5.5. If there is a service problem, the problem resolution process is initiated. First, the *recording* of the problem is communicated through the customer service activities. The problem is resolved through a set of service operations activities. Finally, the *communication* of the solution takes place once again through the customer service activities.

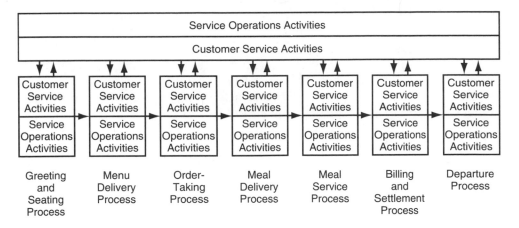

Figure 5.4 Flow chart of processes for restaurant service

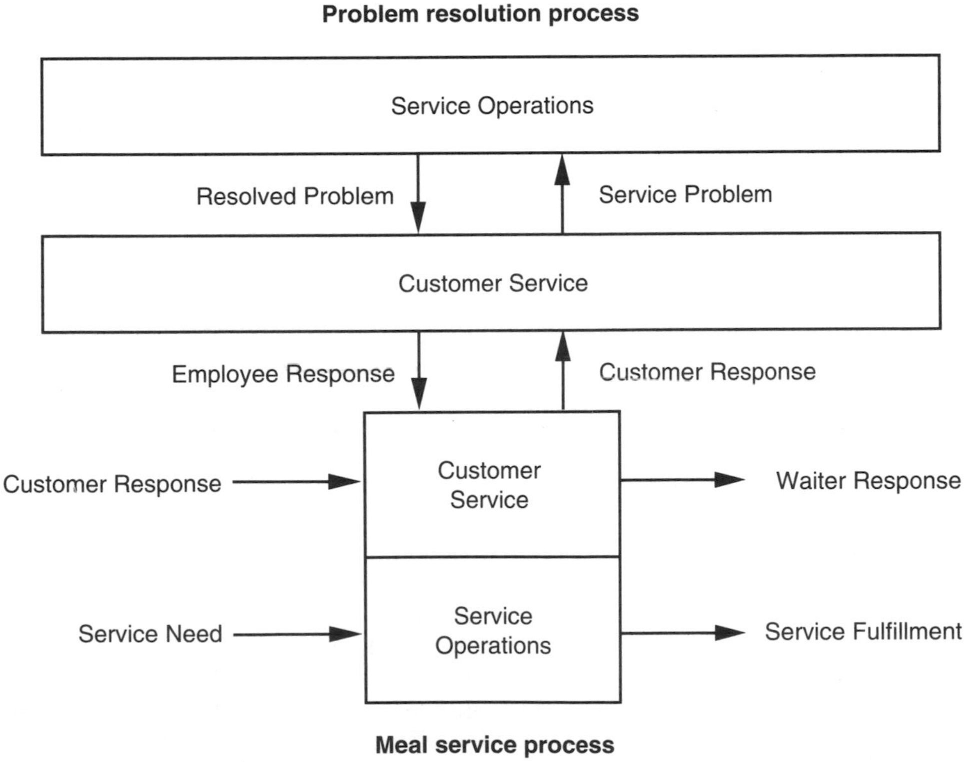

Problem resolution process

Service Operations

Resolved Problem ↓   Service Problem ↑

Customer Service

Employee Response ↓   Customer Response ↑

Customer Response → Customer Service → Waiter Response

Service Need → Service Operations → Service Fulfillment

Meal service process

Figure 5.5 Details of the meal service and problem resolution process (from Figure 5.4)

The customer's satisfaction with the customer service activities is determined by how seriously the complaint is taken, and the manner in which the solution to the problem is conveyed. The output of these activities is therefore the *employees' response* to the problem. The satisfaction with the service operations activities is determined by how the problem is resolved. The *solution to the problem* is the output of these activities. Clearly, both types of activities together influence the customer's perception of the quality of the process.

Diagrams such as Figures 5.4 and 5.5 are useful for presenting an overall system-level view of the processes that affect restaurant service. The limitation of such diagrams is that they do not clearly indicate the interaction between the customers and the process. The extent to which the process activities are visible to customers is not clear from Figure 5.5. A flow-charting convention called *service blueprinting* provides a means to explicitly include the customer in the process diagram.

Service blueprinting

Service blueprinting is a process analysis methodology developed by G. Lynn Shostack. In a *Harvard Business Review* article (Shostack, 1984), Shostack described the need to apply a nonsubjective quantifiable framework to design service processes. Shostack developed a flow chart (called the blueprint) to systematize the description, documentation, and analysis of service processes. The blueprint structures the process activities on either side of a customer "line of visibility." The activities above the line are visible to the customer; those below the line are back-room activities that are necessary to complete the service operation but that the customer does not see. By explicitly depicting the interactions between the process and the customer, the blueprint makes it possible to easily identify the critical process points where customer service can be affected.

An example of a flow chart using the blueprinting convention is shown in Figure 5.6 for the meal delivery process. Step 6 is visible to the customer, as is the last step of the order-taking process ("take customer order"), also shown in Figure 5.6. These steps involve both customer service and service operations activities, as shown in Figure 5.6.

The link between steps 5 and 6 in Figure 5.6 indicates a point in the process at which the output of the internal workings of a process becomes visible to the customer. Strong impressions of the quality of the service are formed at these moments, since customers compare the perceived quality of the process outputs with their expectations of a personal, satisfying service experience. These points present opportunities for delighting customers through exceptional service. At the same time, they also carry the risk of disappointing or dissatisfying the customer by delivering a service outcome that does not match the expectations. Special care should therefore be taken to design and manage these links to minimize the risk of service failure at these points. These points are referred to in the literature as *moments of truth*.

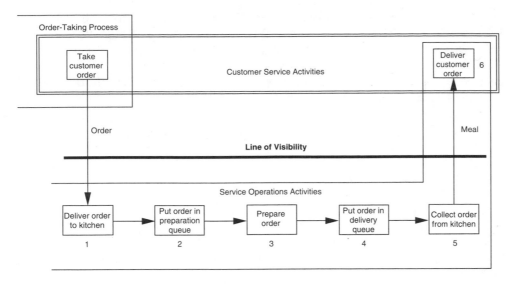

Figure 5.6   Process blueprint for meal delivery processes

Whatever the flow-charting convention used, it must be borne in mind that the process flow diagram is basically a visual representation of the main activities of the process. While it is important to be as accurate and detailed as possible when drawing the flow chart, the team must not become so involved in capturing every possible process nuance that the production of the chart becomes an end in itself. Excessive time spent in ensuring that every detail of the charting convention is adhered to takes away from time that can be valuably spent in thinking about the design. The team should strive to achieve a quick consensus on the major aspects of the diagram and move on to the next stage. Additional detail can be incorporated later if necessary.

5.3   CONCEPT GENERATION

Consider the different ways in which a monthly credit card bill can be delivered to a customer. The customer may call a telephone number to ascertain the payment due. A paper bill may be mailed to the customer. The customer may call a remote computer and download or print the bill. The bill may be mailed to the customer on floppy disk or CD-ROM. Each of these methods is a design solution for the bill production process. We refer to each solution as a *concept*.

Concept generation is a service-level activity whose objective is to develop innovative design solutions for the service features, facilities, and processes. A high-level view of the entire service should be maintained during this activity so that solutions that take the interactions between these service components into account can be generated. The concepts should pay equal attention to all components of the service. It is not uncommon for a design team to develop concepts that use state-of-the-art technology to offer new service features, but to ignore the enhancement of processes through which these features can be offered. This may result in the new services being deployed using old processes that are not capable of meeting the new delivery requirements. Dissatisfaction with the delivery of the service may manifest itself as dissatisfaction with the service itself, mitigating the impact of the new technology on the customers.

The emphasis during concept generation should be to create as many innovative ideas for the service as possible. No cost, feasibility, or implementability constraint should be placed on the design team members during the initial creation of ideas, since this may restrict the free flow of ideas and prevent the consideration of truly innovative options. A new concept that initially appears infeasible may turn out to work with a few modifications. Only when the creative input of all team members is exhausted should the ideas be evaluated for implementability.

Brainstorming

The success of a concept generation exercise depends on the ability of the team to focus on the design problem, but at the same time allow the free and unrestricted flow of ideas. This necessitates a disciplined approach to the discussion. The brainstorming technique developed by Osborn (1957) has been successfully used for concept generation. Osborn defined brainstorming as a "technique by which a group attempts to find a solution for a specific problem by amassing all the ideas spontaneously contributed by its members." Brainstorming allows ideas generated by a group to trigger new ideas in an individual's mind. Team members sit in a room and spontaneously express ideas about solutions to the design problem. A moderator or facilitator is appointed to reiterate the problem criteria if the discussion becomes random or unfocused. The facilitator also establishes ground rules for the conduct of the team members and ensures that these are adhered to during the session. All ideas are noted on a flip chart or blackboard that is in full view of everyone in the room. In the first few rounds, the team may choose to go around the room giving each member in turn the opportunity to present ideas. Random creation of ideas may ensue in the following rounds. All ideas, however irrelevant or outrageous, are documented without judgment. A far-fetched idea thrown in during a lull in the discussion can serve as a trigger for a fresh spate of concepts.

Brainstorming is most effective when the problem to be addressed is clearly stated. All members of the team should have a common understanding of the problem to be addressed before the general discussion begins. Before the session starts, the team should review the QFD data to reaffirm a consensus on the needs, design specifications, and benchmark data. The FAST diagrams and process flow charts should also be examined to achieve a common overview of the problem at hand. However, no requirement should be placed to generate ideas based only on the data. Instead, the data should primarily be used as a guideline to help team members to focus on the problem.

Methods for generating ideas

Apart from spontaneous flashes of brilliance, three methods are typically used by team members to generate new ideas:

1. Transference

2. Enhancement

3. Analogy

All three methods are based on the principle that solutions to similar problems can serve as a source of ideas for the problem at hand. In *transference*, a design solution used for one application is directly transferred to another. For example, suppose a videotape-based training method is found to be effective for training restaurant managers. The same technique may be adopted for training waiters as well. The obvious advantage of this approach is that the solution has already been tested in another application. The disadvantage is that it may encourage trying to fit existing solutions to all problems, without considering new or innovative options.

Enhancement refers to the modification of an existing solution to adapt it to the current problem. A combination of several solutions may also be considered. For example, suppose a competing restaurant uses a scenario-based on-the-job training method for its staff. The team may consider a training program that includes both scenario-based and videotape-based components.

Analogy is a broader version of the above two methods, where solutions to analogous problems in other industries are used to generate concepts. One example is a virtual reality–based "restaurant simulator" analogous to a flight simulator for employee training. Another example is a usage-based incentive program analogous to the frequent-flier miles scheme adopted by airlines to reward loyal customers.

Reducing the number of solutions

The end of the first brainstorming session should generate a large and varied selection of concepts. A good session can produce a hundred or more ideas. The team performs an initial evaluation of the concepts and rejects those that are irrelevant or far-fetched. Half to two-thirds of the concepts are rejected at this stage. The remaining concepts are analyzed further to assess whether they can be consolidated, combined, or enhanced to create a set of feasible options. A second elimination follows, reducing the number of concepts to ten or less. These remaining concepts should be analyzed in greater detail.

At this stage, Pugh (1991) recommends individual brainstorming by team members to construct the details of these concepts. The originator of the idea, or a subset of team members, may be assigned to examine each concept. The purpose of this examination is to ensure that the concept is really capable of producing a design that meets the service requirements. The concept should be compared against the following:

- A summary of the market segmentation studies listing characteristics of targeted customers.
- Verbatim statements of the five most important needs.
- The five most important design attributes.
- The three most critical features.
- System view (high-level) flow diagram of the major processes to be designed.

Other activities, such as literature research or visits to other industries to inspect the operation of analogous designs, may be scheduled at this point as well. When the examination of all concepts is complete, the entire design team spends as much time as necessary in discussions, presentations, and research until all team members feel comfortable that they have enough information to understand the principles of performance of each concept. It is important to ensure that all team members have a common level of understanding of the concepts, since differences in knowledge between team members will affect the evaluation procedure. The next step is to evaluate the concepts. This procedure is described in the following section.

Concept generation is often the most neglected activity in the service design methodology. It is a rare design team that gives this activity the importance and time that it deserves. The reason for this is that this step makes the most demands for creative participation from team members. Individuals with a lot of everyday job responsibilities feel pressured to generate quick design solutions and consider concept generation to be an excessive drain on their time. A commonly followed approach is to rehash old design solutions and force the current problem to fit to these solutions. Sometimes, senior management gives in to this way of thinking as well, preferring "tried and true" methods to new solutions.

It should be clear to the reader by now that while fitting old solutions to new problems may be appropriate in some cases, this should not be seen as a "quick-fix" approach applicable in all cases. Good process designs that satisfy customers and conform to specifications require thought and planning. It may not be necessary to generate and evaluate new concepts for every planned enhancement to the design. A basic concept may be maintained with modifications through several design cycles. However, the decision to retain, modify, or enhance an existing design should be made after careful consideration of all possible options, and should not be automatically assumed to be the only practical decision when a new service needs to be designed in a short time. In many cases, the extra time spent in discussion and evaluation is more than compensated by the reliability of the ensuing design.

5.4 EVALUATING AND SELECTING CONCEPTS— DESCRIPTION OF THE PUGH METHOD

In this section we describe the method developed by Professor Stuart Pugh (Pugh, 1991) for evaluating design concepts. Pugh developed the approach for product design. Here we demonstrate its use for evaluating service concepts.

The characteristic of the Pugh method that makes it superior to other techniques is that a clear qualitative understanding of the concepts is required for a successful application. The usual method for evaluating discrete alternatives is to assign quantitative ratings to each alternative on several weighted criteria. The overall rating for each alternative is calculated by summing the weighted score for each criterion. The alternative with the highest overall rating is selected for implementation.

The problem with such an approach is that it can degenerate into a meaningless exercise in numerical manipulation. Time that should be spent in developing an understanding of the qualitative differences between the concepts may actually be spent in arguing about what ratings to assign to each alternative. There may also be the tendency to view the final rating scores as absolute because they are the output of a "mathematical" procedure. This limits the opportunity to create even better design solutions by combining the best aspects of several alternatives. The Pugh method discourages these tendencies.

Evaluation matrix

A matrix called the *evaluation matrix* is used to compare the concepts. An illustration of this matrix is shown in Figure 5.7. The *criteria for evaluation* make up the *rows* of the matrix. The concepts are compared on both performance and cost criteria. The performance criteria are usually the design attributes from the columns of the QFD matrix, or some subset of these that represents the key performance dimensions along which the concepts can be differentiated. The cost criteria must include implementation, transition, and training costs, hardware and software acquisition and implementation costs, and the costs of operating and maintaining the service. Other nonfinancial criteria, such as probability of success, difficulty of implementation, and compatibility with existing designs, may also be used for comparing the concepts. Five performance criteria and two cost criteria are shown in Figure 5.7.

The *concepts to be evaluated* are listed as the *columns* of the evaluation matrix. Five concepts are shown in Figure 5.7.

Selecting a baseline concept

One of the concepts is chosen as a *baseline* or a *datum*. Concept 1 is chosen as the baseline in Figure 5.7. The performances of the remaining concepts on the evaluation criteria are compared to the baseline. The choice of the concept that is to be

Concept Selection Legend	Concept 1	Concept 2	Concept 3	Concept 4	Concept 5
Better + Same S Worse –					
Performance Criterion 1		+	S	S	+
Performance Criterion 2		S	+	S	+
Performance Criterion 3		S	+	–	S
Performance Criterion 4		+	S	–	S
Performance Criterion 5		–	+	+	+
Cost 1		S	–	S	+
Cost 2		S	S	+	+
Sum of positives		2	3	2	5
Sum of negatives		1	1	2	
Sum of sames		4	3	3	2

Figure 5.7 Example of a Pugh concept evaluation matrix

used as a baseline is important because it can influence the evaluation of the remaining concepts. The least attractive concept should be avoided, because all remaining concepts will look better, and trade-off between concepts may not be difficult. For the same reason, the most attractive concept should be avoided. A concept that is better than average, but not the best, is a good first choice. Another approach is to create a concept that performs as well as the best competitor on each criterion, using the technical benchmarks from room 5 of the House of Quality matrix (see Chapter 4). The remaining concepts are then compared to this "ideal best competitor."

On subsequent passes through the evaluation procedure, the best concept from the previous iteration is typically used as the baseline. This gives the opportunity to discuss the merits and drawbacks of the other concepts relative to the current best solution, and to confirm the validity of the initial ratings.

Comparing concepts

As shown in Figure 5.7, for each concept and criterion, the appropriate matrix cell is filled with one of the following three symbols: +, −, or S. A + indicates that the concept is judged to be better than the baseline for the criterion. Similarly, an S indicates parity between the concept and the baseline and a − implies that the baseline is superior to the concept.

Analyzing results

When the evaluation is complete, the matrix with the concept definitions and ratings should be prominently displayed so that it is visible to the entire team. The total number of +, −, and S ratings for each concept are computed and listed in rows at the bottom of the evaluation matrix. These totals are maintained separately so that the composite positive, negative, and neutral aspects of each concept can be analyzed independently, as shown in Figure 5.7.

The team then discusses the score received by each concept. Concepts with the smallest number of negative scores are first considered. The team analyzes the reasons for the negative ratings, and investigates whether it is possible to modify the concept to reverse these ratings without affecting the positives. If this is possible, the modified concepts are added to the matrix. Subsequently, the weaker concepts are also examined to determine the opportunities for redesign. If no such opportunities exist, the inferior solutions are dropped from the matrix. A new baseline (the best concept from the previous iteration, as mentioned above) is then chosen, and the modified concepts are re-evaluated against this baseline. Several iterations of this process will leave only the strongest concepts remaining.

Sometimes teams compute an overall rating for each concept by assigning each + a value of 1, each − a value of −1, and each S a value of 0. This is not a good practice and should be avoided. Judgments based on the overall ratings do not provide the insights necessary to improve the designs. Two concepts with the same overall total can result in very different designs. For example, consider two concepts evaluated on eight criteria. Suppose the first concept rates better than the baseline on five criteria and worse on three. The overall rating for this concept is 2 ($5 \times +1 + 3 \times -1$). Suppose also that the second concept rates the same as the baseline on six criteria and better on two. This concept also has an overall rating of 2 ($6 \times 0 + 2 \times 1$). Clearly, the two concepts do not demonstrate the same level of performance. The first concept will be significantly better than the second if its performance on the three negative criteria is improved. These are the kinds of trade-offs that should be considered by the team.

Occasionally, one or two concepts will stand out as clearly better than the rest and will stay that way throughout the evaluation. In such cases, obviously any metric of comparison will indicate the superiority of these concepts. But in most cases, better designs can be created by combining or improving existing concepts. These insights are lost if only overall scores are considered.

Summary of method

The following are the main steps involved in the evaluation and selection of a design concept:

1. List concepts as evaluation matrix columns

2. Select criteria for evaluation

3. List criteria as matrix rows

4. Select baseline concept

5. Evaluate concepts against baseline

6. Total the +, −, and S ratings for each concept

7. Identify opportunities to remove negatives

8. Identify opportunities to accentuate positives

9. Create improved concepts

10. Remove weak concepts from the matrix

11. Rerun matrix with new concepts and a new baseline

12. Repeat as often as necessary until a superior concept is found.

For further details on the use of this technique, the reader is referred to the descriptions in Pugh (1991) and Clausing (1994). We will now demonstrate the application of this technique to evaluate design concepts for the Service Edge restaurant.

5.5   USING THE PUGH METHOD TO EVALUATE RESTAURANT CONCEPTS

We demonstrate the Pugh approach for evaluating seven hypothetical concepts for delivering service at the Service Edge restaurant. We have selected a set of diverse concepts on purpose to be able to better illustrate the application of the methodology. Each concept addresses one or both of the following service objectives:

1. Provide quick, accurate service

2. Deliver responsive, individualized service

Each concept reflects different ways in which technology, staffing, restaurant layout, food preparation methods, and training are used to meet these objectives. Each concept affects one or more of the processes listed in Table 5.1. The concepts are described below.

Description of restaurant concepts

Concept 1—customer database: The objective of this concept is to provide high-quality customer service by developing a database for recording customer information. On their first visit to the restaurant, guests are assigned a "valued customer number" and are asked to complete a questionnaire about their food and service expectations, special likes or dislikes, dietary restrictions, etc., in return for a free appetizer or dessert. This information is entered into the database. After each visit, the items ordered, positive or negative comments about the service, any problems encountered with the service, and other relevant data are input into the system. On each visit, the customers are asked for their numbers by the host as they enter the restaurant. Before a guest is seated, the waiter assigned to the table receives a summary of the customer profile, with any special instructions on how to treat the guest. This makes it possible to offer personal service to each customer.

Concept 2—dedicated waiter: This concept is designed to blend personalized attention with prompt service. Under this concept, one waiter is assigned to an average of only two tables. The restaurant layout is designed so that the waiter station is close to the tables without being obtrusive. Waiters can observe diners and anticipate their needs, and customers can easily locate their waiters for service requests. The proximity and availability of the waiter makes it possible to provide personal service quickly and efficiently.

Concept 3—customer interaction training: This concept requires the restaurant employees to undergo special training to have a better appreciation of customers' unstated emotional expectations of how they should be treated. The objective of this training is to reduce the distance between the employees and guests and to assist the employees in providing genuinely friendly and professional service.

Concept 4—food expertise: The objective of this concept is to make each waiter an expert on the food served in the restaurant. Waiters receive training in the history and geography of menu items, ingredients used, and cooking techniques. Before every shift, waiters receive a briefing from the kitchen staff about the day's specials and how they are made. Waiters are also encouraged to inquire about the dietary or taste preferences of their guests and to suggest menu variations that better satisfy these preferences.

Concept 5—waiter-operated POS system: This concept emphasizes the promptness of meal delivery by the development of a POS (point of sale) system. This system consists of a terminal at the waiter station into which the customer orders can be entered. The system instantaneously transmits the order to the kitchen. Based on the number and type of pending orders, it automatically assigns the order to the cook with the shortest predicted wait. When the order is completed, the kitchen sends a signal that is transmitted to the terminal from which the order was entered. The system can deliver meals to any desired degree of promptness by adjusting the scheduling algorithm.

Concept 6—frozen ingredients: Prompt meal delivery can be achieved either by an effective system for delivering orders to the kitchen as in concept 5 or by a quick method of meal preparation. This concept controls the food preparation time by using as many frozen ingredients as possible. The menu is designed to enable quick preparation by assembling already prepared frozen components.

Concept 7—customer-operated POS system: This is a variation of concept 5 in which the POS system is operated by the customer. The menu appears on a terminal at the customer's table along with detailed explanations of the items. Diners make their selections on the terminal, which then transmits the requests to the kitchen. When the meal is ready, a signal appears on the terminal at the waiter station assigned to the table and the waiter delivers the food. Additional requests may also be made through the POS system.

The concepts are summarized in Table 5.2.

Setting up the evaluation matrix

The concept evaluation matrix is shown in Table 5.3. The concepts are listed as the columns of this matrix. Each concept should be clearly identifiable and distinguishable from the others. The team should use a word or short phrase that describes each concept succinctly and uniquely. If possible, the team should create

Table 5.2 Summary of concepts for restaurant service

Concept number	Concept	Service objective affected
1	Customer database	Personal attention
2	Dedicated waiter	Personal attention
3	Customer interaction training	Personal attention
4	Food expertise	Personal attention
5	Waiter-operated POS	Quick service
6	Frozen ingredients	Quick service
7	Customer-operated POS	Quick service

Table 5.3 Concept evaluation example—first run

Concept Selection Legend	Concept 1 – Customer database	Concept 2 – Dedicated waiter	Concept 3 – Customer Interaction training	Concept 4 – Food expertise	Concept 5 – Waiter-operated POS	Concept 6 – Frozen ingredients	Concept 7 – Customer-operated POS	Importance ratings
Better + / Same S / Worse –								
Degree of friendliness	S	S	+	S	S		–	12
Degree of responsiveness	+	+	S	S	S		–	11
Promptness of meal delivery	–	–	–	S	S		S	10
Degree of patience	S	+	S	S	S		+	9
Promptness of menu delivery	S	+	S	S	S		+	9
Promptness of order-taking	S	+	S	–	S		+	9
Degree of knowledge	+	S	S	+	S		+	7
Problem resolution effectiveness	+	S	S	S	S		–	6
Implementation cost	–	S	S	S	–		–	9
Operating cost	S	+	+	+	S		S	9
Sum of positives	3.0	5.0	2.0	2.0			4.0	
Sum of negatives	2.0	1.0	1.0	1.0	1.0		4.0	
Sum of sames	5.0	4.0	7.0	7.0	9.0		2.0	
Weighted sum of positives	24.0	47.0	21.0	16.0			34.0	
Weighted sum of negatives	19.0	10.0	10.0	9.0	9.0		38.0	

icons that pictorially depict the central idea behind each concept. Each icon should be a unique visual identifier for the concept, and should clearly distinguish the concepts from the others in the evaluation matrix.

The criteria for comparison are chosen from the important design attributes (Table 3.9). Only those attributes that can be used to differentiate between the concepts are chosen. For example, none of the concepts has any effect on the accuracy of billing. This attribute is therefore not included as a criterion. Conversely, the team should also make sure that all relevant criteria that are affected by a concept are included in the evaluation matrix. For the purposes of this example, we compare the concepts only on the design attributes that relate to the processes used to deliver service at the restaurant. However, a concept such as concept 6 (use of frozen ingredients) will influence some food design attributes as well, because the necessity of using only frozen ingredients restricts the menu variety that can be offered and affects the taste of the food. In a real life application of this methodology, these attributes must also be included as criteria in the evaluation matrix.

Two cost criteria are considered. *Implementation cost* refers to the initial cost of setting up, developing, and deploying the concept. *Operating cost* refers to the cost of operating, maintaining, and updating the design after implementation.

A relatively neutral concept should be selected as the baseline so that the strong and weak concepts stand out by comparison. It is also helpful to choose a concept that is simple to understand and similar to current operations or the operations of a competitor. Concept 6 (frozen ingredients) is commonly used in restaurants to increase the efficiency of kitchen operations. This is therefore chosen as the baseline.

The evaluation of each concept relative to the baseline is shown in the matrix cells in Figure 5.3. For an illustration of how the evaluation is performed, consider concept 1. Let us start with the performance criteria. The objective of the customer database is to provide the restaurant with information on customer likes and dislikes, ordering patterns, and special requests so as to be more responsive to their needs. The team feels that this concept will provide a *higher degree of responsiveness, more knowledge about the customer's eating preferences, and more information for effectively resolving problems* than the baseline. A rating of + is therefore given to these criteria. Neither concept 1 nor the baseline affect *friendliness, patience,* or *the promptness of menu delivery and order-taking* in any special way, so the performance of concept 1 along these criteria is rated the same as the baseline. Finally, the emphasis of the baseline is to *reduce the meal delivery time by streamlining the food preparation process.* Concept 1 has no such emphasis, and therefore receives a relative negative rating on this criterion.

For the two cost criteria, the design team feels that the hardware, software, development, training, and implementation costs of the customer database will be *higher* than the cost of the equipment required to maintain frozen ingredients. Concept 1 therefore receives a relative negative rating on this criterion. However, the team also feels that once the database is in place, it will cost the *same* to operate and maintain as the equipment in the baseline option. The concept is therefore rated on par with the baseline on this criterion.

The other concepts are similarly evaluated.

Analyzing results

The +, −, and S ratings for each concept are totaled separately. The results are shown at the bottom of Table 5.3. Both unweighted totals and totals weighted by the importance of the criteria are calculated. The importance weights for the performance attributes are the attribute importance weights calculated in room 7 of the HOQ matrix (see Table 3.9). The importances for the cost criteria were selected by the team using judgement.

From Table 5.3, we can see that concept 2 has the smallest negative total and the largest positive total. This is followed by concept 1. Both these concepts are rated inferior to the baseline in their ability to deliver meals quickly. In addition, concept 1 has higher implementation costs than the baseline. The design team feels that these costs may be justified if the design can be modified to deliver quick service as well. Also, concepts 1 and 2 are designed to provide responsive service, but the designs do not place any special emphasis on the attitude and demeanor of the waiters. Enhancing this aspect will lead to even better designs.

Concept 7 has the largest positive total, but is perceived to be inferior in the friendliness and responsiveness attributes, since no interaction with waiters takes place. Moreover, it has a higher implementation cost than the baseline. Once again, the team feels that the additional costs may be justified if a personalized service component is added to this design.

Creating new concepts

Based on the analysis of the data from the first run, the team creates the following new concepts:

Concept A: This is a blend of concept 1 and concept 3. The customer database improves the responsiveness of service, and at the same time employees are trained to improve their interaction with customers.

Concept B: This is a blend of concepts 2, 3, and 4. The dedicated waiters improve service responsiveness. They are also trained to be friendly and professional and to improve their knowledge of the menu.

Concept C: This adds a personal attention component to concept 7. When the guest enters an order into the terminal, the order is transmitted to the appropriate waiter station. The waiter confirms the order with the customer before sending it to the kitchen and is available for service requests during the meal. This interaction between the customer and the waiter creates the human interface missing from the original concept.

Combinations of existing concepts do not always generate better concepts. The team must be careful to ensure that the positive aspects of existing concepts are not reversed by the new concept. Consider the following concept:

Concept D: This concept is intended to improve the quickness of meal delivery for concept 1 by blending it with concept 6 (which uses frozen ingredients to speed up the meal preparation time). Such a concept would restrict menu items to those that could be prepared using frozen ingredients. While the speed of delivery may be enhanced, this concept counteracts the fundamental principle of the customer database in concept 1, which is intended to improve flexibility in meeting customers' requirements. Restricting the menu items curtails this flexibility. In this case, the combined concept is clearly not an enhancement.

Evaluating the new concepts

A new evaluation matrix is created to compare the enhanced concepts A, B, and C listed above. These concepts are compared to a new baseline, which is the best concept from the previous run (concept 2). The results are shown in Table 5.4.

Selecting a concept

From Table 5.4, we can see that all the new concepts cost the same. They are all more expensive to implement than the baseline, but have the same operating costs. On the performance side, concepts B and C have the smallest number of negative ratings. Concept A has a larger number of positive ratings, but also a larger negative number.

Also, concepts B and C have identical totals. The lack of a clearly superior concept in this run indicates that at least one additional run of the procedure is needed before a concept can be selected for detailed design. Concepts B and C represent very different design solutions. Concept B emphasizes responsiveness by adding more employees and better training, while concept C focuses on quick and responsive delivery through the use of technology. Even though the team estimates that both concepts will cost the same, the implementation and management implications of each design may be very different. Before the next run of the evaluation matrix, the team should gain an understanding of these implications by analyzing the designs in greater detail. This will entail iterating between the concept evaluation and the detailed design stages (stages 3 and 4) until a greater understanding of the details of each design is obtained.

In the following run, these details should be added as additional criteria to the evaluation matrix. Also, any other possible enhancements to the concepts should be included in this run. For example, a hybrid design that is a blend of concepts A, B, and C may reflect the optimal use of both technology and people. The evalua-

Table 5.4 Concept evaluation example—second run

Concept Selection Legend Better + Same S Worse –	Concept 2 – dedicated waiter	Concept A – customer database with training	Concept B – dedicated waiter with training	Concept C – customer-operated POS with waiter support	Importance ratings
Degree of friendliness		+	+	S	12
Degree of responsiveness		S	S	S	11
Promptness of meal delivery		S	S	+	10
Degree of patience		–	S	S	9
Promptness of menu delivery		–	S	S	9
Promptness of order taking		–	S	S	9
Degree of knowledge		+	+	+	7
Problem resolution effectiveness		+	S	S	6
Implementation cost		–	–	–	9
Operating cost		S	S	S	9
Sum of positives		3.0	2.0	2.0	
Sum of negatives		4.0	1.0	1.0	
Sum of sames		3.0	7.0	7.0	

tion procedure should then be repeated with the new criteria and concepts until a single alternative remains.

As the design process proceeds, the design will continue to evolve and will be continuously refined. At some point, it may become necessary to revisit the evaluation procedure to confirm the validity of the overall design approach or to compare lower-level design concepts. It must be remembered that there is always room for reconsideration at the design stage, and modifications that are feasible at this point become difficult or impossible after the design is implemented. The team should therefore make the effort to discuss, analyze, and improve the concepts as many times as is necessary to develop an innovative, yet well-planned and implementable design.

5.6 CONCLUSION

Summary

The following is a summary of the topics described in this chapter. The section in the chapter where a particular topic is covered is indicated in parentheses.

Functional analysis (5.1)

- FAST diagram represents sequence of functions needed to deliver service.
- Service functions identified from columns of QFD matrix.
- Why function is performed is depicted by boxes to the right of each function.
- How function is performed is depicted by boxes to the left of each function.
- FAST diagram can be represented at various levels of detail.

Step 2—Define processes from functions (5.2)

- Processes connect FAST diagram functions in temporal sequence.
- Processes should connect to customers at either or at both ends.
- Process definition should proceed from less detail to more detail.

Process documentation (5.2)

- Processes should be documented through textual descriptions or process flow charts.
- High-level flow charts depict interaction between processes.
- Flow charts can be expanded to any desired level of detail.
- Blueprinting convention can be used to illustrate process–customer interactions.

Operational and customer service activities (5.2)

- ◆ Operational activities reflect the steps needed to deliver the service.

- ◆ Customer service activities reflect the personal interactions between customer and service provider.

- ◆ The quality of both activities *together* influences the quality of the design.

Generating design concepts (5.3)

- ◆ Concepts are high-level views of the service.

- ◆ Initial set of concepts are generated by group brainstorming.

- ◆ Final set of concepts are selected by individual brainstorming.

Concept evaluation using the Pugh method (5.4 and 5.5)

- ◆ Describe and understand concepts.

- ◆ Select cost and performance evaluation criteria.

- ◆ Select baseline concept.

- ◆ Compare concepts to baseline on better (+), worse (−), same (S) scale.

- ◆ Discuss results and generate superior concepts.

- ◆ Continue evaluation until no more improvements are possible.

- ◆ Select concept for detailed design.

Suggested Reading

The following texts are recommended for further reading on the topics covered in this chapter. This is not an exhaustive list, but a collection that provides a good overview of different aspects of the topic. Some of these texts have already been referenced in this chapter.

Clausing, Don P. (1994). *Total Quality Development: A Step-by-Step Guide to World-Class Concurrent Engineering*. ASME Press, New York. Chapter 3 of this book provides an excellent overview of the Pugh method.

Pugh, S. (1991). *Total Design: Integrated Methods for Successful Product Engineering*. Addison-Wesley Publishing Company, Reading, MA. Dr. Pugh's book is an excellent introduction to customer-focused product design. Many of these concepts are also applicable for service design. Concept selection is covered in Chapter 4.

Cross, Nigel (1989). *Engineering Design Methods*. John Wiley and Sons. Simple and clear introduction to the design process. Chapters 7 and 8 describe some alternative methods for concept generation and evaluation that have not been covered in this book.

Chapter

6

Performing Detailed Process Design—Part 1: Generating Design Alternatives

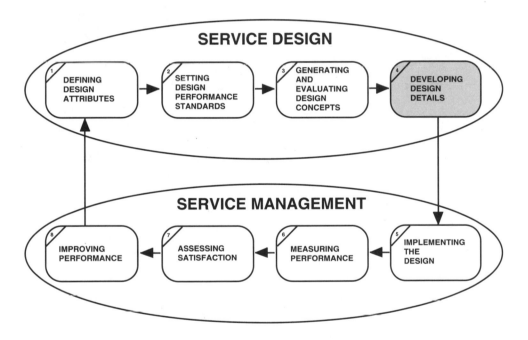

- *Partitioning the Design Concept*
- *Generating Design Alternatives*
- *Predicting Design Alternative Performance*
- *Performance Functions*
- *Specifying Variability using Distributions*
- *Properties of a Good Design*
- *Conclusion*

The selection of a design concept marks the end of stage 3 of the service design and management model. The concept provided a broad, qualitative view of the technology and the method of operation of the new design. In this chapter, we begin stage 4 of the model, where the details of the design corresponding to the selected concept are developed. The concept concentrated on the *components* of the design and answered the following question: "Of the many ways by which we can provide the service, which is the most innovative way in which we can satisfy our customers' requirements?" The detailed design stage concentrates on the *performance* of the design and on the following question: "How should we select the components of the design specified by the concept (e.g., process steps, systems, service features, personnel) whose *combined* performance will meet the design performance standards?" An innovative concept is a product of integrated, holistic, system-level thinking. A successful design occurs when this concept can be *partitioned* into tangible constituent elements that are constructed so that, *together*, they can achieve both the innovative intent and the performance expectations of the service.

Difference between concept design and detailed design

A lot of work is involved in designing a service that works right. From the many options of technology, process configurations, employee skill levels, and feature alternatives, the team has to select the few that can collectively cohere into an acceptable working service. This requires team members to use their knowledge, experience, and intuition to test various design combinations until they converge on a suitable one. The outcome of the detailed design stage is a *blueprint* that details how the service will be delivered and maintained through its life, and what level of performance we can expect from each component of the service. Some of the elements specified by the blueprint include the following:

- The functions that need to be performed for each process

- Who performs these functions (system, internal employees, external organization, managers)

- The manner in which these functions are performed (for example, automatic, manual triggered by exceptions, manual triggered by schedules)

- The average performance of each function or group of functions (subprocesses) that can be expected under normal operating conditions

- The variability of the performance characteristics of each function or group of functions (subprocesses) that can be expected under normal operating conditions

- Features that require special treatment, and the nature of that treatment

- The performance requirements of systems supporting the service

- The data that needs to be collected or retrieved to perform each function or subprocess

The detailed design may not precisely specify the particular brand of hardware or the name of the software package or the organizational job functions required to deliver the service. These decisions are usually made during the design implementation stage (Stage 5 in the service design and management model), discussed in Chapter 8. But the detailed design will spell out the number of systems that need to be used, their interactions with process functions, the data they need to collect and store, and their anticipated performance. The implementation team can use this information to select the specific product that will meet these requirements.

Let us look at an example to illustrate the differences among the *concept*, the *detailed design*, and the *implementation*. Consider a customer service inquiry process needed to answer two types of questions: (a) general information about the service and (b) questions about a customer's bill. The concept for the design of this process may be

> *One stop shopping—the customer should be able to get answers to both types of questions from a single telephone number.*

The detailed design may specify the following:

> *The general information calls will be processed by a customer service representative. The billing inquires will be processed by a specialist. An automated call distributor will send the calls to the appropriate person based on customer input. Under normal call volumes, no customer should wait for more than four rings before the telephone is picked up. Information to answer both types of questions will be stored in a common database.*

The implementation team may decide:

> *Customer inquiries will be processed in four regional centers, each with the same telephone number. Information for all regions will be stored in a centralized database using product X, and will be accessible to all regions. In each center, the service representatives and billing specialists, who have the same job classifications, will be seated in the same room.*

This example shows how the ideas embodied in the concept are transformed into an operational service as we move from stage 3 to stage 5 in the service design and management model. Even though these stages are represented sequentially in the model, the process is often iterative in practice with refinements made to the concept as the design unfolds, or modifications made to the design to facilitate its implementation. Moreover, the distinctions between the concept, design, and implementation are not rigid, and some parts of the design may be developed in detail during the concept selection, or some implementation decisions may be made during the detailed design. The important point to keep in mind is not where each stage begins and ends but rather the following:

> **A successful design process requires a *systematic* approach that starts with the creation of an idea and achieves fruition through the addition of successive layers of detail.**

Our objective in this chapter and the next is to give the reader a taste of this approach.

Detailed design activities

The activities required to develop a detailed design were first presented in Chapter 2 (Table 2.5). We repeat them below:

Activity 1: Partition concept into process-level design components.

Activity 2: Generate design alternatives for each component.

Activity 3: Predict performance of each design alternative.

Activity 4: Evaluate and select alternative for each component.

Activity 5: Test performance of overall service design assembled from selected alternatives.

Activity 6: Make any necessary modifications to the design.

Activity 7: Specify detailed functional performance requirements.

These activities are applicable for the design of all elements of the service, i.e., the features, facilities, and processes. In keeping with the rest of this book, we focus here on the design of service processes and use the Service Edge restaurant example to illustrate the concepts.

Let us briefly examine each activity. In the first activity, the design concept, which is a system-level view of the service, is broken down into manageable design units, or components. The performance standards for the overall design are also partitioned into component-level requirements. In the second activity, several designs for each component are developed. In the third activity, we predict the average performance and the variability in performance of each of these designs. The fourth activity involves comparing the performance of these designs and selecting a few candidate designs for more detailed analysis. In the fifth and sixth activities, the selected design components are assembled to create one or more designs for the overall service. Each of these designs is tested, either through experiments or by simulation, and the results are compared against the performance standards. Modifications to the design are made where necessary, and the testing and improvement activities are continued until a single implementable design solution is obtained. The detailed specifications that are needed to construct the service based on this design are developed in the final activity.

These seven activities are covered in this chapter and in the next. Activities 1, 2, and 3 (partitioning the design concept, generating design alternatives, and predicting the performance of these alternatives) are covered in this chapter. In Section 6.1, we illustrate how the service-level design specifications can be translated to the component level, and how common design elements across components can be identified. The generation of design alternatives is discussed in Section 6.2. In Section 6.3, we describe how the environment, the operational characteristics, the design, and random variability interact to affect the performance of the design. In

Section 6.4, we show how performance functions can be used to predict the average performance of design alternatives, and in Section 6.5, we illustrate the use of distributions to model variability. In Section 6.6, we present two critical properties of a good design: capability and robustness. The evaluation, testing, and selection of designs (activities 4, 5, 6, and 7), covered in the following chapter, are based on these properties. Section 6.7 is a summary of this chapter.

6.1 PARTITIONING THE DESIGN CONCEPT—DETAILED DESIGN ACTIVITY 1

The concept is a system-level view of the service; it explains how the different parts of the design fit together. It is very difficult to keep this entire picture in mind and work on the design details at the same time. Therefore, the concept needs to be broken into smaller and more manageable units. This is called *partitioning*.

Partitioning the design dimensions of the Service Edge restaurant

Let us look at some examples of how the design dimensions of the Service Edge restaurant can be partitioned. We refer the reader back to Figure 5.2 (Section 5.1), where the FAST diagram for the restaurant service shows three functions: food, dining facilities, and service. This is a first-level partition, but is too broad for the purposes of detailed design. Each of these functions needs to be partitioned further. For example, the food can be partitioned into the category of *menu items* (appetizers, soups, salads, main vegetarian items, main poultry items, main seafood items, main meat items, desserts, etc.). Facilities can be partitioned by *functional areas* (foyer, main dining hall, waiter station, kitchen, store rooms, bathrooms, etc.). We already showed how the service dimension can be partitioned in Chapter 5. The FAST diagram of Figure 5.3 (Section 5.1), repeated in Figure 6.1, lists the functions that are needed to provide the service. As shown in Section 5.2 (see Table 5.1), each function in Figure 6.1 can be represented by one or more processes. The overall service design requirements for the Service Edge restaurant can therefore be partitioned into a set of *process design requirements*. The detailed design is then performed at the process level.

Steps for partitioning a service-level concept to the process level

Four steps are required:

1. Converting the service-level attributes to the process level
2. Converting the service-level design performance standards to the process level
3. Documenting the detailed process functions
4. Identifying common design elements

We will now describe each step in detail, using the example of the Service Edge restaurant.

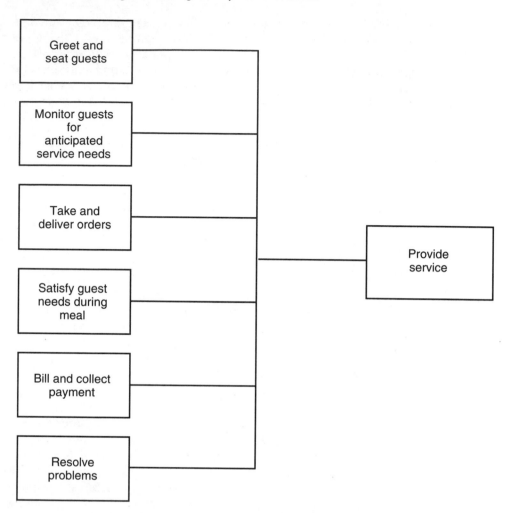

Figure 6.1   FAST diagram for Service Edge restaurant service (repeat of Figure 5.3)

Translating service-level design attributes to the process level

In our discussion on QFD in Chapter 3, we stated that one of the key characteristics of the QFD methodology was its ability to propagate quality specifications through successively detailed stages of the design. As shown in Figure 3.2, this can be accomplished by passing information through a hierarchy of QFD matrices. In Chapters 3 and 4, we presented the House of Quality, which is the first matrix in this hierarchy. We now present the second matrix, which we refer to as the *service/process* matrix. In this matrix, the design specifications for the service from the columns of the House of Quality are partitioned into specifications for each individual process. The *service design attributes,* which are the *columns* of the House of

Quality, are the *rows* of the service/process matrix. The *process attributes* and process performance requirements are the *columns* of this matrix.

Let us examine how service requirements can be translated to the process level for the Service Edge restaurant. The service/process matrix for the restaurant is shown in Table 6.1. The rows of this matrix are the nine most important attributes identified from the House of Quality matrix (see Table 3.9). The columns of the ma-

Table 6.1   The service/process matrix for the Service Edge restaurant

WHATs vs. HOWs Legend		
Strong	●	9
Moderate	○	3
Weak	△	1

PROCESS	Degree of friendliness of greeting / greeting	Degree of friendliness of meal service / meal service	Degree of responsiveness of meal service / meal service	Degree of friendliness of leavetaking / leave taking	Time between seating and menu delivery / menu delivery	Time between menu delivery and order-taking / order-taking	Degree of knowledge about menu / order-taking	Degree of order-taking patience / order-taking	Time between ordering and meal delivery / meal delivery	Percent of bills produced without error / billing	Percent of bills settled without error / payment collection	Degree of effectiveness in problem resolution / problem resolution
Degree of friendliness	●	●		●								
Degree of responsiveness			●									
Time between ordering and meal delivery									●			
Degree of patience								●				
Time between seating and menu delivery					●							
Time between menu delivery and order-taking						●						
Degree of knowledge							●					
Percent of bills produced without errors										●	●	
Effectiveness in problem resolution												

trix are these same attributes, but partitioned across the restaurant processes defined in Chapter 5 (Table 5.1). The cells of the matrix show the associations between the service and the process-level attributes. Attributes such as the degree of friendliness affect several processes, and so are partitioned into three process attributes (degree of friendliness of greeting, degree of friendliness of meal service, and degree of friendliness of leavetaking). On the other hand, attributes such as the meal delivery interval influence only a single process and are therefore translated unchanged from the row to the column of Table 6.1.

Translating service-level design standards to the process level

The second step is to translate the service-level design performance requirements to the process level. Table 6.2 shows the design performance standards for the nine most important service attributes. Recall that these standards were set in Chapter 4 (see Section 4.5) from the desired standards, the technical benchmarks, and the performance/satisfaction functions.

The design standards from Table 6.2 are translated to the process level in Table 6.3. There are three ways in which the service performance standards are translated into process performance requirements. In the first case, service design attributes pertain to a single process. The process standard is therefore identical to the service standard. An example of this is the attribute "time between seating and menu delivery," which is only applicable to the menu delivery process. The standard is "less than 5 minutes" in both Tables 6.2 and 6.3.

In the second case, the performance of an attribute may affect the quality of more than one process, but the performance standard cannot be partitioned across these processes. "Degree of friendliness" is an attribute of this type. As shown in Table 6.2, the standard for the service is to achieve an "exceptional" rating on this attribute. The friendliness attribute pertains to three processes: greeting, meal service, and leavetaking. Clearly, the "exceptional" rating cannot be divided among these processes. The standard for each process is the same as the standard for the service.

In the third case, the service-level performance requirement for a service attribute can be distributed among the constituent processes. An example is "billing accuracy." Table 6.2 shows that the performance standard for this attribute is 85%. This implies that at the most 15 out of every 100 bills can be inaccurate. Errors in either the billing (bill creation and delivery) or the payment collection (payment processing and change return) processes can contribute to inaccurate bills. The performance of these processes together must meet the service standard. Therefore, each process must individually perform better than the service performance requirement. If we partition the fifteen allowable errors equally between the two processes, we can allow a maximum of seven errors for each process. The performance standard for each of these processes is therefore 92–93%. If both processes

Table 6.2   Design performance standards for the Service Edge restaurant attributes

	Service design standards
Degree of friendliness	Exceptional
Degree of responsiveness	Exceptional
Time between ordering and meal delivery	>10 and <11.5 mins.
Degree of patience	Exceptional
Time between seating and menu delivery	< 5 mins.
Time between menu delivery and order-taking	< 5 mins.
Degree of knowledge	Exceptional
Percent of bills produced without errors	85%
Effectiveness in problem resolution	Excellent

perform to this standard, the billing accuracy will meet the overall service standard of 85%. Other partitions will produce different performance standards for each process. For example, suppose it is known from experience that twice as many errors occur in billing as in payment collection. In this case, we can partition the allowable fifteen errors into a maximum of ten errors for billing and five for payment collection. The process performance standards would then be 90% for billing and 95% for payment collection.

Table 6.3 Conversion of service design standards to the process level

	CUSTOMER SERVICE	Degree of friendliness of greeting	Degree of friendliness of meal service	Degree of responsiveness of meal service	Degree of friendliness of leavetaking	SERVICE OPERATIONS	Time between seating and menu delivery	Time between menu delivery and order-taking	Degree of knowledge about menu	Degree of order-taking patience	Time between ordering and meal delivery	Percent of bills produced without error	Percent of bills settled without error	PROBLEM RESOLUTION	Degree of effectiveness in problem resolution
PROCESS		greeting	meal service	meal service	leavetaking		menu delivery	order-taking	order-taking	order-taking	menu delivery	payment collection	bill settlement		problem resolution
Process design standard		Exceptional	Exceptional	Exceptional	Exceptional		< 5 minutes	< 5 minutes	Exceptional	Exceptional	> 10 & < 11.5	> 92%	> 92%		Excellent

Documenting detailed process functions

Once the process attributes and the process-level design standards have been identified, the next stage is to determine the relevant activities for each process. In the concept generation stage, it is enough to define processes by their beginning and end points (see Table 5.1, for example). In this stage, each process needs to be expanded into its constituent subprocesses and functions. Let us see how this can be done.

We start with the FAST diagram of Figure 6.1. Each block in this diagram represents one or more processes. Each block is now expanded leftward to the required level of detail by answering the question: "How is the process performed?" For example, consider the block "Take and deliver orders" in Figure 6.2. The answer to the question "How are orders taken?" identifies the activities that make up the order-taking process. Similarly, the answer to the question "How is a meal order delivered to the customer?" will provide a list of the meal-delivery process activities.

Once the expanded FAST diagram is completed to the required level of detail, it is straightforward to draw process flow charts showing the process activities. When outlining the processes, the team should attempt to achieve the most parsimonious configuration of process functions that is needed to produce the required output. By this, we mean that the process should contain the smallest possible number of steps and should reflect the most important functions that are needed to convert the input to the output. Non–value-adding activities, such as multiple verification or validation steps, should be avoided. The team should avoid constructing a separate process for every possible type of process input. Two or three process types are usually adequate in most cases to account for a large part of the inputs. Error avoidance should be emphasized over error checking and correction. Steps that check for errors should be built in as early as possible in the process. The team's objective should be to produce the simplest and most efficient process designs that are supported by the design concept. At this stage, the team still has a lot of flexibility to analyze, discuss, and simplify processes. As the design gets closer to implementation, it becomes successively more difficult to incorporate fundamental changes. After implementation, it is almost impossible to make large changes without incurring significant expense. Careful planning at this stage will go a long way toward preventing expensive modifications in the future.

Documenting the functions of the Service Edge restaurant order-taking process

Figure 6.2 shows the flow chart of the order-taking process for the Service Edge restaurant using the service blueprint convention (see Section 5.2). The number 2 enclosed in the box represents a loop in the process. The line of visibility is shown between the points marked **L**. All points above this line are visible to the customer. Another useful convention is to indicate the person or organization responsible for each function on the flow chart. This helps to establish the function owners who will be part of the service management team when the service is in operation. This topic is discussed in detail in Chapter 8. At this stage, the owner of most functions is generically listed as "system." As the design evolves through detailed design into implementation, the name of the specific system component (e.g., computer program or human operator) that is responsible for each function will be added to the chart.

A more detailed breakdown of the individual functions may be needed for preparing operating procedures or training documents. An example of the detailed

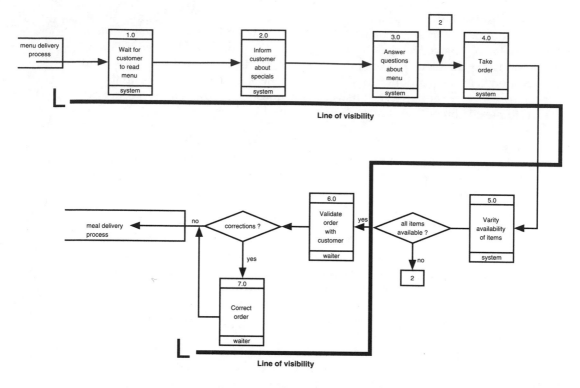

Figure 6.2   Process activities for the order-taking process

breakdown of the validation activity (activity 6) of Figure 6.2 is shown in Figure 6.3. For flow charts at different levels of detail, it is good practice to use a numbering scheme for the function boxes that indicates how the lower- and higher-level functions fit together. The reader should note how the function numbers in Figures 6.2 and 6.3 are related.

Verifying completeness of process descriptions

After the flow diagrams for all the processes have been documented, the team should verify their completeness to ensure that no important activity has been excluded and that all functions are represented at the appropriate level of detail. For each flow diagram, the following questions should be considered:

- What are the process inputs? Have all inputs been represented?
- Are there different kinds of inputs into the process?
- Do the process activities differ by kind of input?
- Are there any intermediate inputs or outputs?

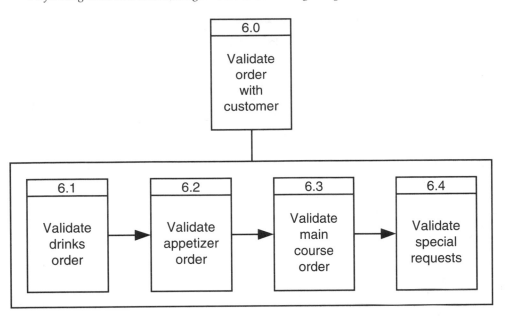

Figure 6.3: Detailed functional description of validation activity

- Have all the steps that are needed to convert the inputs into the outputs been defined?
- Are there activities from other processes that should be documented?
- Are there any activities that are performed only when some condition is met?
- Are there any loops in the process? Have they been represented?
- Are all functions at the same level of detail? Is this level adequate?
- Are there any functions that need to be broken down further?
- Is the function numbering complete and accurate?
- Is the correspondence between the high- and low-level functions complete and accurate?

Identifying common design elements

The fact that the detailed design of a service takes place at the process level does not mean that each process should be designed independently in a vacuum. One or more processes may share common components that may be advantageous to design together. These common components are called *subsystems* and represent naturally occurring similarities between processes.

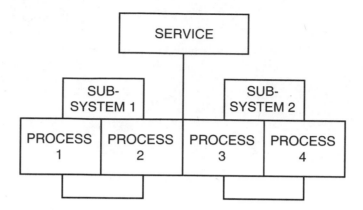

Figure 6.4 Creating subsystems from processes

The relationship between processes and subsystems is shown in Figure 6.4. In this figure, the service is decomposed into four processes named 1, 2, 3, and 4. Parts of processes 1 and 2 can be designed jointly as subsystem 1. Similarly, parts of processes 3 and 4 can be designed jointly as subsystem 2. The remaining parts of each process are designed separately.

Typically, the subsystems are designed first. The individual processes are designed subsequently and should complement the subsystem designs. It may be necessary to iterate until a satisfactory match is obtained between the common and individual designs. The objective should be to seek the blend of common and individual elements that produces the most effective design.

Opportunities for common designs

The extent to which commonality between processes can be exploited depends both on the service being designed and on the concept. Some natural opportunities for common designs across process boundaries occur in the following situations:

- Functions of different processes share common resources (for example, a customer service representative who handles both installation and problem resolution requests)

- Several processes use a common database through a common interface

- Multiple processes have similar functions (for example, data entry)

- Processes have similar design attributes and may benefit from a common design approach

- Processes have customer interfaces which need a common "look and feel" across the entire service

The order in which the components of a service are designed depends on the extent of commonality between the components. Components with greatest commonality are designed first, followed by components with successively fewer commonalities. In Table 6.4, we classify the extent of commonality into four levels. At the first level, process components across the entire service share similar elements. For example, the amount and type of data needed to operate all processes may be stored on a common hardware platform for the entire service. The second level of commonality is similar to the situation represented in Figure 6.4. Some process functions may be similar, which makes it possible to integrate the design of these functions. An example is a single training manual for all employees working similar types of functions for different processes.

At the third level, the designs may not be identical across processes, but are customized versions of a similar underlying design. An example of this would be screen layouts or menus that look the same across several processes, but whose menu items are customized to each process. Finally, at the fourth level there is little or no commonality, and the processes must be designed separately.

When partitioning the service, the team should identify potential situations where subsystems with commonality levels 1, 2, and 3 may exist. Level 1 subsystems should be designed first, at least in outline, followed by level 2 and level 3 subsystems. Individual processes should be designed last. The design of each subsystem or process should be constrained and guided by the designs of the subsystems of which it is a part, and which have already been designed. Several iterations between the common and independent designs will be necessary before a good match can be obtained.

Identifying subsystems for the Service Edge restaurant service design

Let us identify some of the main sub-systems for the Service Edge restaurant service design. At the end of Chapter 5 (see Table 5.4), we evaluated three concepts entitled A, B, and C for designing the service element of the Service Edge restau-

Table 6.4 Levels of commonality between process components

Commonality level	Description
1	Components common to all processes
2	Components common to some processes
3	Customized version of common design approach
4	No commonality: independent design required

rant. We will select *concept C* to illustrate the detailed design methodology in this book. In this chapter, and in subsequent ones, we will continue to develop the design example using this concept.

This concept is called a *customer-operated point-of-sale system with waiter support*. It involves a computer terminal placed at each table in the restaurant that displays the menu with a detailed description of the menu items. Customers input their choices into the terminal at their respective tables. The choices appear on a terminal at the waiter station. The waiter confirms the order and sends it to the kitchen, where it is automatically scheduled for preparation. When the meal is ready, a signal appears on the terminal at the waiter station, and the meal is delivered to the customer.

Four subsystems can be identified for this concept. The first two affect the menu-delivery, order-taking, and meal-delivery processes. Since these processes are all supported by the POS system, this concept requires that these processes be linked by a single system supported by a common hardware and software platform. However, the display screens on the customers' terminals and on the waiter stations may be different. The concept therefore provides the opportunity for a design with level 2 (common hardware and software across some processes) and level 3 (same design, different screens) commonality.

The third subsystem (with level 2 commonality) is evident from the service/process matrix of Table 6.2. This involves the friendliness attribute, which relates to the customer service activities of three processes: greeting, meal service, and leavetaking. A single design solution (training programs, documentation, or employee recruitment procedures) can be implemented for incorporating this attribute for all these processes.

The fourth subsystem integrates the design of the bill production and the bill settlement process (See Table 5.1). Recall that the bill production process involves tallying the bill and presenting a check to the customer. The bill settlement process involves collecting the customer's payment, registering it, and returning change. Both these processes can be affected by computational errors. To reduce the number of errors, suppose a verification procedure is designed into these processes that prompts the cashier to confirm the accuracy of the input. The same procedure can be developed for both the bill production and settlement processes, except that the procedure may be customized to the specific activities of each process. This subsystem therefore has a level 3 commonality.

Table 6.5 summarizes the four examples discussed above. The service attributes impacted by the common designs are also shown in this table.

After the service is partitioned into its constituent processes and the important subsystems are defined, the next step is to generate different design alternatives for these subsystems and processes. This is described in the following section. The same approach can be used for developing design alternatives for both subsys-

Table 6.5   Subsystems for Service Edge restaurant

Processes	Commonality level	Subsystems	Attributes affected
Menu delivery Order-taking Meal delivery	2	Common hardware and software	Promptness
Menu delivery Order-taking Meal delivery	3	Common screen layout design with different screen menus	Promptness Knowledge Patience
Greeting Meal service Leavetaking	2	Common procedures for ensuring friendliness	Friendliness
Bill payment Bill settlement	3	Common approach for verifying accuracy customized to process	Accuracy

tems and processes. For clarity of presentation, we will illustrate the approach using the example of a single process.

6.2   GENERATING DESIGN ALTERNATIVES—DETAILED DESIGN ACTIVITY 2

Consider a service company that is designing a process for effectively responding to customer complaints. The design team evaluates several concepts and decides that the most effective response can be provided by a design in which the complaint is directly sent to the person responsible for resolving the problem. In this way, the customer is able to interact with the person who can directly solve the problem, and if the problem is serious, the organization can immediately implement any process changes necessary to avoid a similar problem in the future.

In how many ways can this concept be put into practice? Clearly, many different designs can be conceived for this process, each involving a specific method of transmitting the customer complaint to the appropriate individual. For example, one method is to set up a central complaint number that the customer calls. Based on the nature of the complaint, the customer is transferred to the right person. The customer does not need to hang up and make another call. In another approach, the person who receives the complaint may record a detailed description of the complaint. This ensures that the complaint is completely and accurately documented at its source, without customers having to tell their stories twice. The complaint is immediately transmitted by electronic mail to the person who will respond to this complaint, and the name and telephone number of this person is given to the customer. A third alternative is to hand the customer a complaint form and a postage-paid envelope addressed directly to the individual who has the authority to respond to the complaint.

Each method described above is a *design alternative* for the process. Each alternative is in conformance with the design concept, but has different performance and cost implications and may have different impacts on customer satisfaction. For example, the telephone call may produce instant resolution, but may not be suitable if the persons responsible for resolving the problem are busy and customers cannot speak directly to them. The e-mail solution ensures that the customer has an opportunity to accurately record the problem, but adds another contact point to the process, since the person who takes the complaint is not the same person who resolves it. The letter provides direct access to the right person, but is clearly slower than the other two designs. In order to select the best design alternative, each alternative must be evaluated on its ability to meet the process performance requirements specified in the service/process matrix. The evaluation of design alternatives is discussed in the following chapter (Section 7.1). In this section, we focus on how the design alternatives can be created.

Steps for creating design alternatives

This requires the following steps:

A. Identify the appropriate design units.

B. Specify performance requirements for each design unit.

C. Identify the constraints placed on each design unit by previously designed subsystems.

D. Identify the key dimensions that influence the performance of each design unit.

E. Create design alternatives for each dimension.

Instead of qualitatively describing these steps, it is easier to illustrate their application using an example. In the previous section (Figures 6.2 and 6.3), we presented the activities of the order-taking process of the Service Edge restaurant in detail. We will continue to use this process to demonstrate our approach in this section.

Generating design alternatives for the Service Edge restaurant order-taking process

A. Identify the appropriate design units

Design alternatives can be created for a whole process, for a subprocess, or even at the level of an individual function. The appropriate level depends on the process, and on the number and type of activities involved. Designing an entire process is appropriate when a process consists of only a few activities that can all be supported by a single technology. Subprocess- or function-level designs should be developed if there are *transitions* in a process. A change from one type of activity to another, a change of function ownership, or a front-room activity giving way to a back-room activity are examples of transitions. In this case, each function or subprocess between the transition points can be treated as an independent design unit.

The seven activities of the Service Edge restaurant order-taking process can be segmented into the three subprocesses shown in Table 6.6. The beginning and end of these subprocesses are natural transition points, since the type of activity performed changes at these points. The *menu reading and ordering* subprocess begins when the menu appears on the screen and ends when all items are ordered. The *availability verification* subprocess begins when the ordering is complete, and ends when the system verifies that all items are available and the order is transmitted to the waiter. The *order validation* subprocess begins when the waiter receives the order, and ends when the order is sent to the kitchen. We will now generate design alternatives for each of these subprocesses.

B. Specify performance requirements for each design unit

The service/process matrix of Table 6.1 was used to partition the service performance standards into performance requirements for each *process*. Since the design unit for the order-taking process is a *subprocess,* we need to establish the relationship between the performance of each subprocess and the overall process performance. This is done using the *process/subprocess* matrix, which is the third matrix in the hierarchy of QFD matrices shown in Figure 3.2. Table 6.7 shows this matrix for the order-taking process. The three performance attributes for the order-taking process (from the columns of the service/process matrix) are the rows of this matrix. The attributes of the three subprocesses from Table 6.6 are the columns. It can be seen from the table that the timeliness of order-taking (which we call *promptness*) is influenced by all three subprocesses. The *knowledge* about the menu items refers to the extent of information that customers can access about the history and ingredients of the dishes on the menu; this is only pertinent to the menu reading

Table 6.6 Subprocesses for the Service Edge order-taking process

Subprocesses	*Activity numbers (from Figure 6.2)*
Menu reading and ordering	1, 2, 3, 4 Feedback 2
Availability verification	5
Order validation and correction	6, 7

Table 6.7   Process/subprocess matrix for the order-taking process

WHATs vs. HOWs Legend		
Strong	●	9
Moderate	○	3
Weak	△	1

Subprocess	Time taken to read menu — Menu reading and ordering	Time taken to enter order — Menu reading and ordering	Time available to browse menu — Menu reading and ordering	Amount of explanation of menu items — Menu reading and ordering	Time to verify order availability — Availability verification	Time to validate customer order — Order validation
Time between menu delivery and order-taking	●	●	○		●	●
Degree of knowledge about menu				●		
Degree of patience while taking order			●			

and ordering subprocess. Similarly, the *patience* reflects the time that customers have to read the menu; clearly, this pertains to the menu reading and ordering subprocess as well.

C. Identify the constraints placed on each design unit by previously designed subsystems

The design alternatives generated for the process should be compatible with the concept requirements and the preliminary design of the subsystems with which the process shares common components. Recall from Table 6.5 that the order-taking process shares two common components with the menu delivery and meal delivery processes: common hardware and software, and common screen layouts with different screen menus. As far as possible, the design alternatives that are created for the order-taking process should be compatible with this predetermined common infrastructure. If the subsystem designs are so constraining that it is not possible to generate any design alternatives for the process, then it may become necessary to modify these designs. This sort of iterative procedure is very important for producing designs that are well integrated and efficient across the entire service.

D. Identify the key dimensions that influence the performance of each design unit

Design dimensions are the process or subprocess characteristics that can be manipulated to influence the performance of the design. Each specific manipulation produces a design alternative. For example, in the complaint resolution process described earlier this section, the method by which the complaint is transmitted to the appropriate person is the design dimension. Each individual method (telephone, e-mail, letter) described above is a design alternative.

For another example, consider the design of a check-out process at a supermarket. Suppose that the concept requires that the design should let customers know that they are being charged for each item only once as their purchases are being rung through the cash register. One way in which this can be achieved is to design the register or bar-code reader so that it makes a sound as an item is being charged. "Sound of bar code reader" is the design dimension for this example. The volume, pitch, and duration of sound or the technology used to produce the sound are the design alternatives for this dimension.

Let us identify the design dimensions for each subprocess of the order-taking process, beginning with the menu-reading subprocess. From Table 6.7, we can see that the performance of this subprocess affects all three attributes (promptness, patience, and knowledge). What design characteristic of this subprocess influences its performance? Since the menu is read from a terminal placed on each table, the *menu display screen format* is clearly one such characteristic, which affects the promptness and knowledge attributes of the subprocess. For example, a more compact display will shorten the time taken to read the menu and to complete the order, and so will increase the order-taking promptness. However, an excessively compact display may not be able to present a large amount of information about the menu, and so may reduce the customers' perception of the amount of knowledge about the menu items contained in the system.

Another design dimension for this subprocess is the amount of time given to the customer to read the menu before being prompted for an input (called the *menu display interval*). This dimension affects the promptness and patience attributes. A shorter reading time will positively influence the order-taking promptness, but will have a negative impact on the customers' perception of the degree of patience of the order-taking system. In an extreme case, a system that beeps every 30 seconds asking for an input can cause considerable annoyance.

Design dimensions for the availability verification and the order validation subprocesses can be identified in a similar manner. These dimensions represent the methods by which availability verification and order validation is carried out. In all, four dimensions were identified for the order-taking process. These are summarized in Table 6.8.

E. Create design alternatives for each dimension

Design alternatives are created by enumerating different ways in which the design dimensions identified above can be manipulated while remaining within the constraints imposed by the concept and the other subsystem designs. For the order-taking process, nine design alternatives encompassing the four subprocesses in Table 6.6 can be generated. They are shown in Table 6.9. It can be seen from this table that these alternatives can be segmented as follows:

1. Three alternatives for the screen display format dimension
2. Two alternatives for the menu display interval dimension
3. Two alternatives for the availability verification dimension
4. Two alternatives for the validation procedure dimension

For the screen display dimension, the alternatives, referred to as SD1, SD2, and SD3, represent varying levels of detail in menu presentation. The first display alternative (SD1) is the most detailed and takes the greatest time to read, but also displays the greatest amount of information about the menu items. The second display alternative (SD2) is the most compact, but also carries the least information. The third display alternative (SD3) falls in between.

Table 6.8   Design dimensions for order-taking subprocess

Design dimension	Subprocess	Affected attribute
Screen display format	Menu reading and ordering	Promptness, knowledge
Menu display interval	Menu reading and ordering	Promptness, patience
Availability verification procedure	Availability verification	Promptness
Validation method	Order validation and correction	Promptness

Two alternatives are generated for each of the remaining dimensions. The two alternatives for the menu display intervals, labeled DD1 and DD2, are a short interval (of 2 minutes) and a long interval (of 4 minutes). Two availability verification methods are considered. The first (AV1) checks the availability of each item as it is ordered. This takes more time than alternative AV2, where all items are checked together after the ordering is complete. The two order validation alternatives (VP1 and VP2) reflect trade-offs between delaying a few orders for a long time and delaying all orders for a relatively shorter time. Under alternative VP1, the order is sent to the kitchen before it is validated. This speeds up the overall order-taking interval for an average order, but incorrect orders need to be corrected at the kitchen, and this considerably increases the delivery time associated with these orders. Under alternative VP2, all orders are validated before they go to the kitchen. This holds up all orders until a waiter is available to validate the order, but any mistakes are corrected before the orders reach the kitchen. As a result, we minimize the risk of seriously dissatisfying some customers.

The nine design alternatives for the four subprocesses create a total of $3 \times 2 \times 2 \times 2$ = 24 possible designs for the order-taking process. All designs are not likely to be feasible, and not all feasible designs may meet the performance standards. To identify the designs that are potential candidates for implementation, we first need to predict the performance of each design alternative. This is described in Section 6.3.

Managing the alternative generation process

Unlike concept generation, which was best performed as a group effort involving the entire team, the activity of creating design alternatives can benefit most from the experiences and areas of expertise of individual team members. The design team is often broken up into subteams for this task. Each subteam consists of functional experts in its particular area of responsibility. Each major process usually has its own subteam. For example, the subteam designing the meal delivery process for the Service Edge restaurant may consist of waiters, managers, cooking staff, and kitchen preparation staff. Each process subteam should work simultaneously, meeting regularly or as often as is needed. The amount of interaction required between the subteams depends on the degree of commonality between the processes involved. Subteams designing processes that are closely associated with each other should obviously work together more than those designing independent and unrelated components. For example, a subteam designing the friendliness training requirements for the meal service process should interact closely with the teams responsible for designing similar requirements for the greeting and leavetaking processes. In cases where service-level commonalities exist, or where several processes contain identical elements, a single subteam may be assembled to design these elements. The design team as a whole needs to perform an overall supervisory and coordinating role in order to ensure that the efforts of each subteam are integrated. Design teams under time constraints sometimes hand over the process design tasks entirely to subteams that do not communicate with each

Table 6.9 Design alternatives for the order-taking subprocess

Design dimension	No.	Description of alternative
Screen display	SD1	One menu item displayed per page, with a detailed description of item on the page
	SD2	All items displayed on one page with item descriptions on a separate help screen
	SD3	Appetizers, entrees, desserts, and beverages on separate pages, with a brief description of items following each entry
Menu display interval	DD1	Two-minute wait before prompting for input
	DD2	Four-minute wait before prompting for input
Availability verification	AV1	Verification of availability of each item is done immediately after ordering the item
	AV2	Verification of availability is done once for all items after the order is completed
Validation procedure	VP1	Waiter sends order to kitchen immediately on receipt of order; any corrections are sent subsequently after validation with customer
	VP2	Waiter holds order until validation is complete; all corrections are made before the order is sent to the kitchen

other. Often, this results in disparate process designs that need to be reconciled. Sometimes this reconciliation consists of artificial and inefficient "workarounds" that degrade the overall performance of the service.

In summary, the careful management of the detailed design process and an open team structure that facilitates communication between the members are critical ingredients for developing a robust, well-integrated design and for ensuring that the different parts of the design come together on time. We cannot cover this important topic in this book at the level of detail required to do it justice. Instead, we refer the reader to the texts on concurrent engineering and the management of design projects presented in the suggested reading section at the end of this chapter, and in a similar section following Chapter 8.

6.3 PREDICTING DESIGN ALTERNATIVE PERFORMANCE— DETAILED DESIGN ACTIVITY 3

Note to the reader: The concepts introduced in this section form the basis of a methodology for evaluating and selecting design solutions whose performance reliably meets the design specifications. The reader is advised to read this section carefully and clearly understand the concepts before moving further.

It is useful to begin by reviewing what has been said so far in this chapter. Earlier in this chapter, we showed how the service-level attributes and performance requirements could be partitioned into process-level design requirements. We also showed how process functions and subprocesses could be documented in detail, and how design alternatives could be generated for these functions and subprocesses. The next step is to predict the performance of these alternatives and compare the performance of each alternative against the design performance standards. The methodology for doing this is the topic of the remainder of this chapter and most of Chapter 7.

We will introduce the concepts of this section through an example. Suppose we wish to exactly predict an air passenger's travel time from New York to Boston. Let us define this time as the interval from the moment the boarding is announced at New York to the moment the passenger steps into the terminal at Boston. Is it possible to estimate a single value of travel time that will be true for every passenger on every flight? Obviously not. The travel time from New York to Boston depends on a variety of factors that will influence the travel times experienced by passengers. To understand what these factors might be, let us partition the travel time into the following segments:

- Boarding time
- Taxi time before take-off
- Flight time
- Taxi time after landing
- Disembarkation time

The *boarding time* is the time taken from when the boarding is announced to when all passengers are seated. Clearly, this time depends on the number of seats in the aircraft and the number of passengers boarding the aircraft. The *taxi time before take-off* depends on the departure gate, time of departure, and the number of other flights scheduled to depart around that time. The *flight time* depends on the aircraft type, wind velocity, wind direction, route followed, weather conditions, and congestion at the destination airport. The *taxi time after landing* depends on the arrival gate and ground congestion at the airport. The *disembarkation time* depends on the number of passengers in the aircraft and the row in which the passenger is seated.

Table 6.10   Factors affecting travel time from New York to Boston

Factor	Category
Aircraft capacity	Design factor
Number of passengers on flight	Operating characteristic
Departure gate	Design factor
Departure time	Design factor
Other departing flights	Environmental condition
Weather	Environmental condition
Congestion at arriving airport	Environmental condition
Row in which passenger is seated	Design factor

The factors affecting travel time can be divided into three categories (summarized in Table 6.10: **operating characteristics, environmental conditions,** and **design factors**.

Operating characteristics refers to the nature, volume, type, and mix of inputs that affect the day-to-day performance of a service. In the flight example, the number of passengers (segmented by first class and coach passengers, or by children, adults, and passengers needing special attention) is an operating characteristic that influences the embarkation and disembarkation time.

Environmental conditions refers to the characteristics of the surroundings in which the service operates that influence the performance of the service. In the flight example, congestion at airports, wind velocity and direction, weather conditions, etc., are all environmental conditions that affect the travel time.

Design factors are characteristics that affect the performance of a service because of the way in which the service is designed or operated. The number of seats in the aircraft, the type of aircraft, the schedule of the flight, and the row in which the passenger is seated are all design factors that influence the travel time from New York to Boston. Each design alternative is characterized by a set of design factors.

The travel time for a passenger from New York to Boston depends on the particular values of the factors shown in Table 6.10, and on how the three factor groups interact. Predicting the performance of a design alternative is not an easy task. To make an accurate prediction, we need to clearly understand the impact of each of the factors on the performance of the design. We will now illustrate this with a general model.

Relationship between the factors affecting design performance

The relationships among the three factor categories mentioned above and their impact on the performance of a design are shown in Figure 6.5. We will proceed systematically through the figure to illustrate the different linkages using the travel time prediction example introduced above.

Let us start with the upper half of Figure 6.5. Suppose we wish to predict the *boarding time* (i.e., the total time taken for all passengers to board the aircraft) for all passengers on a flight from New York to Boston at 6 A.M. on a Monday. In general, we can assume that this time is a function of the number of passengers on the flight. What causes passengers to fly from New York to Boston on this flight? Clearly, the demand for the flight is influenced by the *environmental conditions*. These conditions are factors that generate or inhibit demand for the flight. The number of meetings scheduled in Boston, the timing of these meetings, the distances of the pool of potential passengers from the airport, and the weather are examples of these conditions.

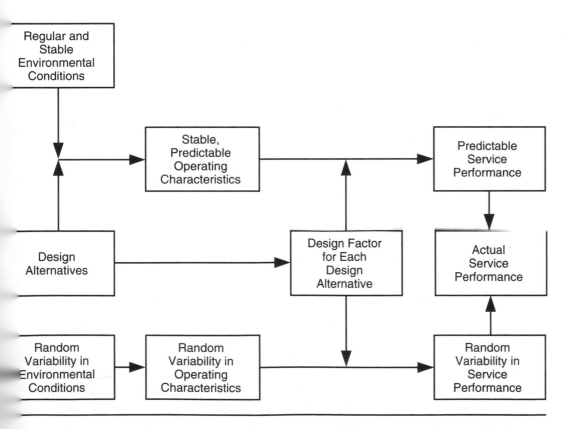

Figure 6.5   Relationship between factors affecting design performance

In addition to these environmental conditions, the airline can also manipulate the demand for the flight by the choice of design alternative. For example, in the interests of reducing the overall boarding time and getting under way quickly, the airline may seek to discourage families (or leisure travelers) from the 6 A.M. flight by giving them lower fares on later flights. This strategy would affect the *mix* of business and leisure passengers on the 6 A.M. flight. Another design alternative is the size and type of aircraft which would affect the number of passengers who can reserve a seat. For example, the airline can limit the number of passengers who travel on the flight by selecting a small aircraft for the route.

The number of passengers, their mix, the training levels of gate employees, etc., that are affected by the environmental conditions or by the choice of design alternatives are the *operating characteristics* of the service. Suppose the environmental conditions are regular and stable every week, as shown in the top half of Figure 6.5. Then the operating characteristics are predictable and stable as well. This means that we could expect the same number and mix of passengers on the flight every Monday morning, that the passengers would be similar and have the same amount of luggage, and that the same ground staff would service the aircraft. Therefore, we should be able to predict the boarding time of passengers on every flight with precision for any value of the operating characteristics.

How can we do this? Figure 6.5 shows that two factors affect the block *predictable service performance*. They are the *operating characteristics* described above, and the *design factors* that characterize the performance of the design alternative. Consider the design alternative *type of aircraft flying the route*. For each aircraft type, the capacity of the aircraft, the number of aisles, the number of doors, the number of rows, etc., are the design factors. If we know the operating characteristics and the design factors for each alternative, we can estimate the amount of time it will take all passengers to board. For example, suppose there are 100 business passengers and no families or leisure travelers on every flight. Clearly, an aircraft with a capacity of 90 passengers will have very different boarding times for these 100 passengers (10 passengers will have a very long boarding time as they wait for the next flight) than an aircraft with a capacity of 125 passengers. Similarly, an aircraft with two aisles will have a different boarding rate than an aircraft with a single aisle. In this way, once we know the operating characteristics, we can predict the boarding time for any design alternative and its associated set of design factors.

If the stable and repeatable conditions shown in the top half of Figure 6.5 were the only factors that affected the boarding time, then the actual, observed boarding time on every flight would be the same and exactly equal to its predicted value. Clearly, in practice, this is not the case. Every Monday morning is not precisely the same. The reasons for this are found in the bottom half of Figure 6.5. There is *random variability* in the environmental conditions from day to day. Many factors could contribute to this variability. Bad weather during the previous evening may have delayed many passengers. There may have been a special event that brought a lot of passengers to New York over the weekend. The airline may be training flight attendants. A rock band may be boarding the flight on that day with a large quantity of musical equipment.

This random variability in the environmental conditions will cause unpredictable variations in operating characteristics. For example, the number of passengers on the flight may be different from 100. The mix of passengers may be different. The time taken to process each passenger may be different. This will result in variability in the actual boarding time from flight to flight. In the presence of random variability, therefore, the predictable component of boarding time is only an *average*, or *base*, value that we could *expect* on a given 6 A.M. flight. The actual boarding time for any given flight will be different from this time.

As far as possible, the design team must attempt to minimize the effect of random variability by developing design alternatives whose performance is not influenced by the bottom half of Figure 6.5. For example, suppose the airline selected an aircraft with a capacity of 120 passengers to meet the average demand of 100 passengers. If it is known that random variability can cause the number of passengers to be as high as 140, the airline may choose to select an aircraft with a capacity of 150 passengers to ensure that no passengers get left behind.

It is also desirable to select a design that is relatively insensitive to variation in the operating characteristics that may result from cyclical, seasonal, or long-term changes in the environmental conditions that impact these characteristics. For example, if the weekday average demand is 120 passengers, and the weekend demand is 100 passengers, the airline may select a 150 seat aircraft as a design that performs adequately in both situations. A design whose performance is not significantly affected by random variability or by variations in the operating characteristics is called *robust*. We will describe design robustness in greater detail later in this chapter.

Before moving forward, let us summarize the main points of our discussion so far. What have we learned about predicting the performance of a design? The following are some key points:

1. The performance of a service design depends on the operating characteristics, environmental conditions, and the design factors.

2. The actual performance has two components: a *base*, or *average*, component, that is predictable, and a *random* component that is not.

3. The average performance can be predicted from a knowledge of the average operating characteristics and the design factors.

4. The random component of performance introduces unpredictable variability to the average service performance.

5. The random component is the result of unpredictable changes in the environment that cause variability in the operating characteristics, and of variability in the performance of the design alternative under consideration.

6. The detailed design process should attempt to select and develop designs that are less sensitive to variation in the operating characteristics and in the environmental conditions. Such designs are called *robust*.

These concepts are important, and in order to ensure that the reader understands them completely, we will illustrate them again through another example.

Predicting the cycle time of an order shipping process

Consider a process designed to ship ordered items to customers. Suppose we need to predict the time taken to ship an order to the customer. This is called the *shipping cycle time*.

What are the factors that affect the value of the shipping cycle time? As mentioned in the previous example, the cycle time can be affected by:

- the values of the operating characteristics
- random variability

What operating characteristics influence the shipping cycle time? Clearly, it is reasonable to assume that, for a fixed number of employees in the shipping office (which is a design factor), the cycle time will increase as the number of orders arriving per day (the *order arrival rate*) increases. This is because the backlogs will increase as more and more work comes in.

Suppose data on the order arrival rate are collected for a number of days. Suppose also that a few orders on each day are tracked, and that the shipping cycle time for these orders is calculated. The results are plotted in Figure 6.6. It can be seen that

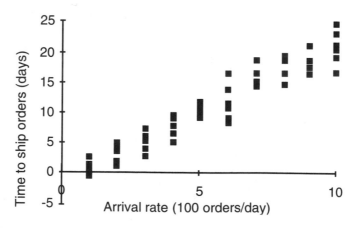

Figure 6.6   Average shipping cycle time and random variability

the line in the figure slopes upward. The shipping cycle time is therefore influenced by the order arrival rate.

What about random variability? The effect of random variability on the shipping cycle time is also shown in Figure 6.6. This variability could occur due to environmental factors such as the shipping shift's fatigue levels, unscheduled absences, and a variety of other unpredictable factors. The effect of this variability is shown by the "scatter" in Figure 6.6. For each value of order arrival rate, the shipping cycle time cannot be predicted precisely. Several values of cycle time exist for each value of the order arrival rate.

The range of cycle time values when 500 orders arrive each day is shown in Table 6.11. The cycle times are split into two parts: an average or predictable part, which is the same for each order at the arrival rate of 500 orders/day, and a random part, which is different for each order. As a result, the total cycle time is different for each order. We can see from the table that if the random variability is zero, then the actual cycle time for *every* order will be the same and equal to the average cycle time.

Steps for predicting performance of design alternatives

From the two examples above, we can conclude that predicting the performance of a design alternative requires the following steps:

1. The environmental conditions under which the design will operate must be defined.

2. The impact of these conditions on the operating characteristics of the alternative must be determined.

Table 6.11   Random variability in shipping cycle time for 500 orders/day

Arrival rate (orders/day)	Average cycle time (days)	Random variability (days)	Actual cycle time (days)
500	9.45	−1.02	8.43
500	9.45	−0.60	8.95
500	9.45	−0.01	9.44
500	9.45	−0.60	8.95
500	9.45	1.46	10.91
500	9.45	0.56	10.01

3. The impact of the design alternative on the operating characteristics must be understood.

4. The relationship between the operating characteristics and average performance for the alternative must be estimated.

5. The effect of random variability on performance must be estimated.

We will continue to discuss these steps in detail in this chapter and the next. We will first describe the prediction of average performance, and then the estimation of variability.

6.4 PERFORMANCE FUNCTIONS—DETAILED DESIGN ACTIVITY 3

In the examples presented above, we showed how operating characteristics, such as the number and mix of passengers or the arrival rate of orders, and design factors, such as aircraft type, influence the performance of a design. Table 6.12 shows some examples of other common factors that affect design performance. In this section, we describe how the impact of factors affecting the average performance of a design can be systematically represented using *performance functions*.

Table 6.12   Characteristics affecting design performance

Characteristic	*Example*
Weight	The unloading time of baggage from an airport conveyor belt will increase with the average weight of the packages
Distance	Delivery time of hand-delivered packages increases with travel distance
Quality	The level of completeness of orders entered into a service provisioning system determines the provisioning interval
Experience	The average experience level of personnel at an order-by-phone service affects the accuracy of the orders
Exceptions	An increase in the number of requests for special meals increases the meal delivery time

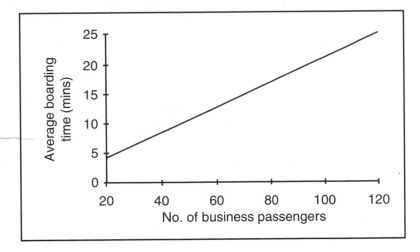

Figure 6.7 (a) Linear performance function for boarding time

Examples of performance functions

For examples of performance functions, let us return to our favorite flight from New York to Boston and consider the factors affecting the average time taken for all passengers to board the aircraft. Figures 6.7 (a), (b), and (c) show the impact of boarding time as a result of three factors:

(a) the number of business passengers boarding the flight;

(b) the number of families with children on the flight;

(c) aircraft type.

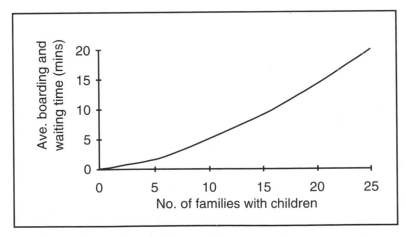

Figure 6.7 (b) Nonlinear performance function for boarding times

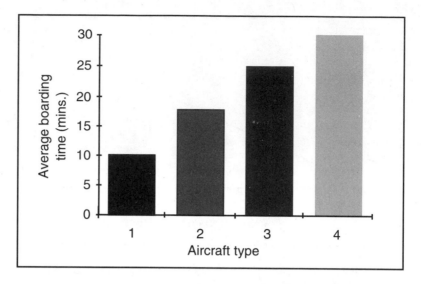

Figure 6.7 (c)   Discrete performance function for boarding time

Performance functions can take different functional forms and can be continuous or discrete. A linear form is shown in Figure 6.7 (a). The boarding time increases linearly with the number of business passengers boarding the flight.

Figure 6.7 (b) is an example of a nonlinear performance function. This function shows the relationship between average time taken to board the aircraft and the number of families with children. As the number of families increases, boarding becomes more chaotic. The amount of time taken increases nonlinearly.

Finally, Figure 6.7 (c) shows a discrete performance function for the relationship between aircraft type and boarding time. A specific aircraft type implies a specific boarding time.

Units of measurement

When specifying performance functions, care must be taken to ensure that the operating characteristics affecting performance are measured in the appropriate units. The performance of two subprocesses of the same process may depend on the *same* operating characteristics, but be *measured in different units*. For example, consider a process for ordering items from a mail-order catalog by telephone. Suppose the process consists of two steps. In the first step, the customer calls a toll-free number to place an order. The order is taken at a centralized customer service facility. This facility processes the order, and based on the zip code of the customer's delivery location, sends a shipping request to the warehouse nearest the customer. The warehouse packages and ships the ordered items to the customer.

Suppose the performance of the overall process is measured by the average time between the receipt of an order and the delivery of the items to the customer. This interval is made up of the following two parts: (a) the time taken by the order processing center to send a shipping request to the warehouse and (b) the time taken by the warehouse to ship the order to the customer. The time taken for each part depends on the *volume of work* experienced by the company. However, the units in which the volume is measured should be different for each part of the process. The shipping request requires the transmittal of a complete order to the warehouse, and therefore the time taken is a function of the *number of orders* arriving at the order processing center, irrespective of the number of items in each order. However, since the warehouse has to procure and package each item, the time taken for shipping also depends on the *number of items* in each order. The volume of work for the order processing center should therefore be measured by the *number of customers placing orders;* for the warehouse, it should be measured by the *total number of items requested*. For the order processing center, fifty orders with one item on each order will take longer to process than a single order with fifty items; for the warehouse, both cases will result in approximately the same amount of work.

Guidelines for developing performance functions

For each design alternative, one performance function should be defined for each operating characteristic that impacts performance. This may seem like an impossible task, since in any practical design example, there is likely to be a large number of design performance attributes for each alternative, and multiple factors that affect each attribute. For example, if there are three design alternatives with ten attributes, each of which are affected by five major factors, we have 150 performance functions to estimate.

In practice, it is not so hard. The definition of performance functions is not usually an exact science; it is a mixture of experience and judgment. It is not necessary to specify every performance function precisely to the last degree of detail. The following guidelines may be used to select the few important functions that are usually the only ones which need to be defined.

(a) Select only those factors that are relevant to the design alternatives: It is not necessary to determine performance functions for every factor that affects the design. The design alternatives typically vary only on a few key factors. It is enough to specify performance functions for these factors, and assume that the others remain constant across all alternatives.

(b) Understand causal links between factors: All factors do not affect the performance of an attribute directly. Some do so through other factors. The causal links between the various factors must be understood. Only the factors that affect performance directly should be included in the performance function. As shown in Figure 6.5, environmental conditions do not affect the performance of the design directly, but do so through the operating characteristics. The performance functions should only specify the relationships between performance and the operating characteristics.

(c) Select only unusual or complex relationships for defining performance functions: Performance functions only need to be explicitly specified when the relationship between a design or operating factor and performance is discontinuous, nonlinear, or unusual in some other way. For example, if it is known that the boarding rate into an aircraft is 20 passengers per minute, then we don't need to establish a formal performance function to determine the total boarding time for a given number of passengers waiting to board. In this case, the boarding time can be easily obtained by simple multiplication.

(d) Simplify the specification of the performance function using judgment: The team should only aim for a general representation of how the performance of each design alternative is affected by the most important operating characteristics and design factors. Often it is enough to specify the shape of the function, with some estimates of maximum and minimum values. Some other important points are those at which the performance function changes slope or makes a transition to the next discrete level. Once these points are estimated, the rest of the function may be approximated.

For a new design, performance functions may be estimated by observing the performance of similar services. In cases where the service being designed is similar to an existing one, but operates in a different environment, the data required may be obtained by careful extrapolation of the functions for the existing service. If no analogous processes exist, the function may be specified directly using experience and expert judgment.

If these guidelines are followed, then it is possible to reduce the 150 potential performance functions mentioned above to as few as ten. These few functions clearly delineate the most important factors, and how they affect each design alternative. These functions can then be used to evaluate the average performance of a design alternative under different operating characteristics. In Chapter 7 (Section 7.1), we show how performance functions are used to compare the performance of the Service Edge restaurant order-taking process design alternatives shown in Table 6.9.

6.5   SPECIFYING VARIABILITY USING DISTRIBUTIONS— DETAILED DESIGN ACTIVITY 3

Performance functions allow us to predict the average or base service performance levels as a function of operating characteristics. *Distributions* are used to specify random variations from these levels. Roughly speaking, a distribution is a function that links a value of a variable with the probability of attaining the value. For example, consider the shipping cycle time example shown in Table 6.11. Suppose experience or measurements may show that for the arrival rate of 500 orders/day, cycle times between 9 and 9.5 days are the most common, with about 25% of the orders being shipped in this time. This is followed by cycle times between 8.5 and 9 days and 9.5 and 10 days for 20% of the orders. Other intervals occur less frequently. This information is presented graphically in Figure 6.8.

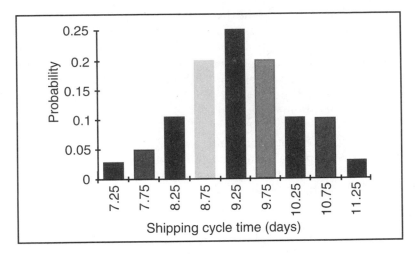

Figure 6.8   Distribution of shipping cycle time at an arrival rate of 500 orders/day

Figure 6.8 is called the *distribution* of shipping cycle times, and shows the spread of cycle times when the arrival rate is 500 orders/day. For example, we know that the cycle times cannot be less that 7 days or greater than 11.5 days. We know that cycle times between 8.5 and 9 days are four times more likely than cycle times between 7.5 and 8 days. We know that 85% of the orders are shipped between 8 and 10.5 days. The distribution therefore gives us a measure of the amount of variability in the data.

It is tedious and time-consuming to develop a distribution for each performance function using the method described above. It is easier to approximate Figure 6.8 with a standard distribution whose statistical properties are well known. Since the distribution is symmetric, the well-known *normal distribution* can serve as a good approximation in this case.

The normal distribution is a generic family of curves. In order to use this distribution for the particular application shown in Figure 6.8, we need to provide measures that can help to identify a particular normal curve from the family. These measures, called *parameters*, specify the center point, shape, and spread of the particular curve that fits our data. A normal distribution is characterized by two parameters: its mean (or center point), and its standard deviation (which is a measure of its spread). From Figure 6.8, we know that the average cycle time is 9.25 days. We also know that all the cycle times lie between 7 and 11.5 days. A property of the normal distribution is that over 99% of all data on a normal curve lies within three standard deviations from the average. If we assume that the cycle time data is normally distributed with a mean of 9.25 days and a standard deviation of 0.75 days, then over 99% of our data will lie between $(9.25 - 3 \times 0.75) = 7$ and $(9.5 + 3 \times 0.75) = 11.5$ days. This replicates our observations from Figure 6.8 very closely.

By making an assumption about the distribution, we have succinctly expressed the variability of the data in two numbers: a *mean* and a *standard deviation*. For each performance function, the variability can be quickly assessed by making intelligent assumptions about the distribution of performance. Clearly, the right distribution and accurate parameter values must be carefully chosen to reflect the behavior of the performance attribute as realistically as possible. Estimates of the parameters may be made from experience, from experiments, or from observations of similar services.

The choice of a proper distribution to represent variability depends on the nature of the performance attribute being modeled. The first choice is to select between *discrete* and *continuous* distributions. Discrete distributions are used for phenomena that can only take discrete values, such as the number of customers arriving at a service facility in a given time interval. A *Poisson* distribution is popular for modeling this process. This distribution can be used to calculate the probability of a specific number of arrivals (0, 1, 2, 3, etc.) arrivals in a specified time interval, given an average arrival rate. Table 6.13 gives the Poisson probabilities of 0 through 4 arrivals at a service facility in one minute when the average arrival rate is 45/hour (0.75 per minute).

Variables such as time that can adopt continuous values are modeled using continuous probability distributions. In addition to the normal distribution described above, the *uniform, exponential, gamma, beta,* and *Weibull* distributions are commonly used for simulation. We will not describe these distributions in detail here; the reader is referred to a statistics textbook such as the one by Larsen and Marx (1986). The exponential distribution is used to represent the time between arrivals when the arrivals themselves follow a Poisson probability distribution. The gamma, beta, and Weibull distributions take on a wide variety of shapes and are therefore flexible enough to represent many practical situations. The gamma distribution is often used to model the time taken to complete process activities, especially when the mean completion time is relatively small but the tails are long. This means that

Table 6.13   Probability of arrivals from Poisson distribution with mean = 0.75/minute

Arrivals/min	Probability
0	0.47
1	0.35
2	0.13
3	0.03
4	0.01

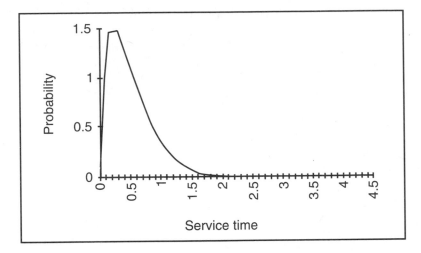

Figure 6.9: Gamma distribution for service completion times

most service requests are processed quickly, but a few may take a very long time. Figure 6.9 shows an example of this distribution. Beta distributions are used to model the variability in phenomena that are expressed as proportions, such as the percentage of resources consumed. Weibull distributions are often used in reliability studies to model the mean time between failures of equipment or hardware.

6.6   PROPERTIES OF A GOOD DESIGN

In the previous sections, we completed the first three of the seven detailed design activities described earlier in this chapter. They are:

Activity 1: Partition concept into design components.

Activity 2: Generate design alternatives for each component.

Activity 3: Predict performance of each design alternative.

The next step is to evaluate the performance of each alternative, and to select those that are the most suitable for further analysis, testing, and implementation. Before we do that, however, we need to clearly understand the criteria that we will use to evaluate a design. Clearly, to be considered acceptable for implementation, the performance of a design should meet or exceed the design performance standards. But suppose there are two designs that meet the standards. We then need some way of comparing these designs. Since the performance of a design is characterized by an average level and variability, any assessment of the quality of a design has to include both these components.

In this section, we will describe two related concepts that can help us with the assessment of a design's quality. The first, *design capability*, refers to the ability of a design to consistently and reliably perform at a level that meets the standards. The second, *design robustness,* was mentioned earlier and refers to the sensitivity of the design to uncontrollable sources of variability. Together, these concepts provide a benchmark for evaluating the worth of a design. Of all possible design alternatives that meet the performance standards, the design with the best performance is the one that is the most capable and the most robust. Let us examine what this means in more detail.

Design capability

We will demonstrate the concept of design capability through a series of examples. Consider the design of a process that is required to deliver a service in between 8 and 12 minutes. Suppose that the operating characteristics are specified and invariant, so that the average performance level remains constant. Suppose also that customers are equally satisfied with any level of performance within the required interval.

How should we design this process? Suppose, for a moment, that there is no random variability in the performance of the process. In other words, the process output is always delivered at precisely the same performance level. In this case, since the customers are indifferent to the exact delivery interval as long as it is between 8 and 12 minutes, all we need to do is to ensure that any process that we design performs to these standards. It does not matter if the delivery interval is 9 minutes or 9.5 minutes or 10.32 minutes or 11.87 minutes. If there is no variability, each of these designs is identical in its ability to satisfy customers.

In practice, however, every process has random variability. What should we do in this case? Clearly, we must make sure that performance of design will meet the standards even under conditions of maximum variability. In other words, even at the extreme points of the distribution (called the *tails*), the performance should still be acceptable to the customer. Now the *average* performance of the design becomes important. Can we accept a design that has an average performance of 11.87 minutes? Clearly not, because unless the process has very, very small variability, it is likely that there will be many occasions when the service delivery interval is more than 12 minutes. We therefore need a design whose average performance is approximately at the center of the range and whose variability is small enough so that the delivery interval remains within the acceptable bounds. We call such a design *capable* of meeting the performance requirements.

The performance of one such design is shown in Figure 6.10 (a). The points on the graph show the service delivery time for ten service encounters. The average service delivery interval for this design is 10 minutes, and the performance is normally distributed with a standard deviation of 1 minute. Even though the performance in these ten encounters seems to be biased toward delivery intervals between 8 and 10 minutes (i.e., there are more intervals in that range), the performance is always within the standards. This indicates that the process is capable.

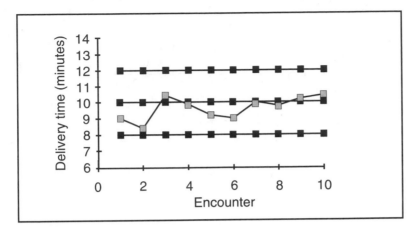

Figure 6.10 (a)   Performance of design (std. dev. = 1)

Now consider the design shown in Figure 6.10 (b), which also has an average service delivery interval of 10 minutes, but this interval is normally distributed with a standard deviation of 2 minutes. At this level of variability, there are several encounters when the process performance breaches the lower and upper performance standards. This process is *not capable*.

Now consider the design shown in Figure 6.10 (c). The performance of this design also has a standard deviation of 1 minute, which is the same as that of Figure 6.10 (a). However, in this figure, the average delivery time has dropped from 10 to 9 minutes. It can be seen once again that the process performance does not meet the standards for several encounters. Once again, this design is not capable.

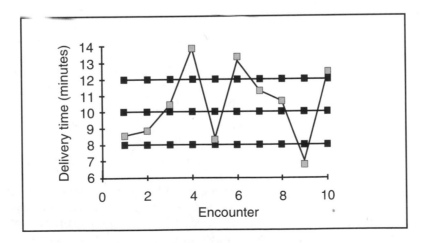

Figure 6.10 (b)   Performance of design (std. dev. = 2)

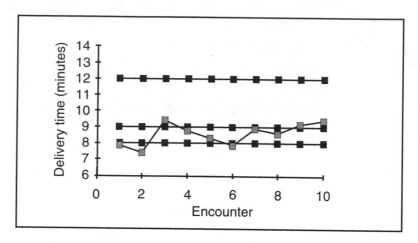

Figure 6.10 (c)   Performance of design (mean = 9)

We can see there are two reasons why a design may not be capable. First, the performance variability may be too high. Second, the average performance may not be adequately centered (or may not be low enough, if the only standard is an upper bound, such as: "delivery interval should be less than 12 minutes").

We have defined the circumstances under which the capability of a design is reduced. But can we *increase* the capability? For example, is there a design that is more capable than that shown in Figure 6.10 (a)? Intuition would suggest that capability can be increased by further reducing the random performance variability. This is indeed the case. A design with a lower variability is said to be more *robust*. The more robust a design, the higher its capability.

Design robustness

The notion of capability above was introduced in the context of a single value of service performance. Robustness refers to the performance of the design over the entire range of possible operating characteristics. We can improve the robustness of a design by reducing its sensitivity to all forms of uncontrollable variability over its performance range. As discussed in Section 6.3, this includes:

- Variability in average performance due to variability in operating characteristics
- Random variability that results in a spread around the average performance

As far as possible, we should develop designs whose average performance is relatively invariant to changes within the normal range of operating characteristics or environmental conditions. We should also develop designs with little scatter or spread around a particular average performance value. Let us discuss each of these in more detail.

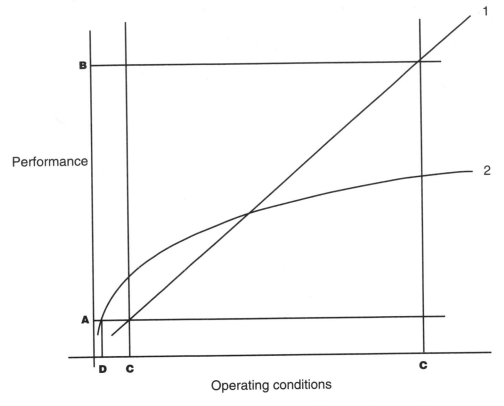

Figure 6.11 Evaluating stability of performance with operating conditions

Variability in average performance: Variability in average design performance occurs as a result of changes in the operating characteristics or environmental conditions. The greater the *slope* of the performance function, the greater the sensitivity of the performance of the design to changes in operating conditions. Consider the two designs shown in Figure 6.11 with performance functions labeled 1 and 2. Function 1 has a steeper slope than function 2. Suppose the performance standards that the design is required to meet are between the values labeled A and B. It can be seen that design 1 will meet these standards as long as the operating conditions lie between the two lines labeled C. Design 2, on the other hand, is less sensitive to operating conditions and will meet the design standards for all values of operating conditions to the right of the line labeled D. The average performance of design 2 is therefore more stable to changes in the operating characteristics.

Spread in performance: Consider once again the process design shown in Figure 6.10 (a). Recall that this process is capable of meeting the requirement that the service should be delivered between 8 and 12 minutes. Over time, suppose customer expectations change, or competitors improve their level of service, and as a result,

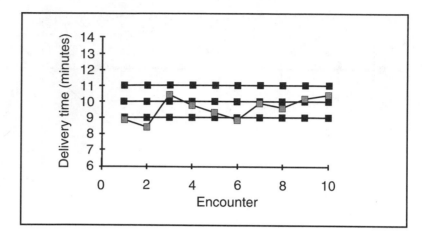

Figure 6.12   Design performance with tighter performance
standards

the performance requirements for the design become more stringent. Suppose customers now want their service to be delivered between 9 and 11 minutes. Is the process capable of meeting these new standards? Figure 6.12 shows that it is not. It can be seen from this figure that the design does not meet the service requirements in at least one encounter.

How can we solve the problem of variability in design performance? Two solutions are possible. The first solution is to change the design in response to changes in operating characteristics or performance standards. The second solution is to initially *design* the service so that it is more *robust*, by attempting to remove sources of variability from the design so that the standard deviation of the service delivery cycle time is smaller than that shown in Figure 6.12. This is a much better solution. Modifications during the design stage are much easier to implement than changes to operational services. The design team should therefore make all possible attempts to reduce performance variability while designing the service.

Let us return to the question we posed at the beginning of this section: How can we select the best performing design from among several that meet the performance standards? Of a set of candidate designs, an optimal design is one that has the following properties:

1. Its average performance is at or *closest to the desired performance.*

2. *Its performance function has the smallest slope* over the range of operating characteristics.

3. It has the *smallest spread of performance* around the average value.

In order to identify the best design, we predict the performance of each candidate design under a variety of operating and environmental conditions. *Process simulation*, described in Chapter 7, is often used to do this. The results from the simulation are used to compare the candidate designs. Based on the simulation results, some designs may need to be modified to further reduce variability. This cycle of evaluation and modification is iteratively carried out until satisfactory reduction in the variability of one or more designs is achieved. The best design is then chosen for implementation.

Design principles for reducing performance variability

The following are some general design principles that assist in reducing variability in design performance:

- Selection of technologies with large capacities so that resources are not stressed

- Use of modular designs where it is easy to add incremental capacity units

- Multiple/backup service centers that provide better ability to manage volumes

- Accurate distribution of input volumes by using automated telephone systems

- Transferring some functional responsibilities to the customers through better partnerships

- Designing processes to address special events or natural disasters

- Automation of routine and repetitive steps

- Process simplification and reduction of steps

- Reduction of paper flow using information technology

- Convenient electronic access to documentation

- Procedures for efficient cross-organizational/cross-process hand-offs

Design solutions vs. operational solutions

Our primary focus on this chapter has been on *design* solutions to improve service capability and reduce variability. However, in some cases, an *operational* solution for improving service performance may sometimes be available. For example, suppose the average cycle time for the delivery of a service depends on how busy the service provider is. Suppose there is a high degree of variability in the number of delivery requests (which influences the utilization of the installers) from week to week. This results in a high degree of variability in the service delivery cycle time.

To reduce this variability, the service performance can be improved in two ways: (1) by altering the service design so that process performance is less sensitive to changes in the volume of requests, or (2) by adding additional resources when volumes are high so that the service providers are not overextended. The first is the design solution, and the second the operational solution.

The operational solution is a *reactive* approach, while the design solution is a *proactive* attempt to design stable performance into the service. In most cases, the design solution is a better long-term strategy. It is usually not efficient to try and maintain a balanced, stable performance over time by constantly adjusting the operations of the service in reaction to variability in the operational characteristics. An operational solution may be appropriate to handle special circumstances that do not occur very often. For example, a sudden unusually high volume of delivery requests may justify a temporary addition of staff. However, if this high volume persists, it may be better to seek more permanent improvements to the service design.

6.7 CONCLUSION

Summary

The following is a summary of the topics described in this chapter. The section in the chapter where a particular topic is covered is indicated in parentheses.

Definition of detailed design (Introduction)

- A blueprint that details the elements needed to deliver and maintain service.
- Specifies functions that need to be performed for each process.
- Identifies people who perform these functions.
- Determines how these functions are performed.
- Specifies the average expected performance and performance variability.

Detailed design activities (Introduction)

- Activity 1—partition concept into process-level design components.
- Activity 2—generate design alternatives for each component.
- Activity 3—predict performance of each design alternative.
- Activity 4—evaluate and select alternative for each component.
- Activity 5—test performance of overall design assembled from selected alternatives.
- Activity 6—make any necessary modifications to the design.
- Activity 7—specify detailed functional performance requirements.

Partitioning service-level specifications to process specifications (6.1)

- Use the second matrix in the QFD hierarchy (service/process matrix).
- Use service specifications as matrix rows.
- Use process specifications as matrix columns.
- Partition service performance requirements into process requirements.

Documenting detailed process functions (6.1)

- Expand FAST diagrams to identify process functions.
- Identify a few important process types.
- Eliminate unnecessarily complex and non–value-added activities.
- Emphasize error avoidance over error correction.
- Draw flow charts of process activities.
- Integrate various levels of flow charts using consistent numbering scheme.
- Check process flow diagrams for continuity and completeness.

Identifying common design elements (6.1)

- Identify processes that share common resources.
- Identify processes with common databases.
- Identify processes with similar functions.
- Identify processes with common attributes.
- Identify processes with common "look and feel."
- Specify the commonality level between design components.
- Specify sequence in which components need to be designed.

Generating design alternatives (6.2)

- Identify the appropriate design units.
- Specify performance requirements for each design unit.
- Identify constraints placed on the design by previously designed subsystems.
- Identify the key dimensions that influence the performance of each design unit.
- Create design alternatives for each dimension.

Identifying factors affecting design performance (6.3)

- Identify environmental conditions affecting performance.
- Identify the operating characteristics affecting performance.
- Identify the design factors affecting performance.
- Specify the relationships between these factors.

Predicting average performance and variability in performance (6.4, 6.5)

- Specify performance functions to predict the average performance.
- Select only those factors that are relevant to the design alternatives.
- Understand causal links between factors.
- Select only unusual or complex relationships.
- Simplify the specification of the performance function.
- Specify distributions to predict random variability.

Properties of a good design (6.6)

- Capability and robustness are characteristics of a good design.
- Capability refers to the ability of a design to consistently and reliably meet standards.
- Robustness refers to the sensitivity of the design to uncontrollable sources of variability.

Suggested Reading

The following texts are recommended for further reading on concurrent engineering. This is not an exhaustive list, but a collection that provides a good overview of different aspects of these topics. Some of these texts have already been referenced in this chapter.

Turtle (1994) provides a very detailed explanation of the concepts of concurrent project management functions such as scheduling, planning, and control. Hartley (1992) is an overview of examples, tools, and techniques and implementation of concurrent engineering. It is a good general text.

Shina (1994) includes case studies of implementation of concurrent engineering in various industries. Carter and Baker (1992) is another text on this topic.

Chapter
7

Performing Detailed Process Design—Part 2: Evaluating and Testing Alternatives

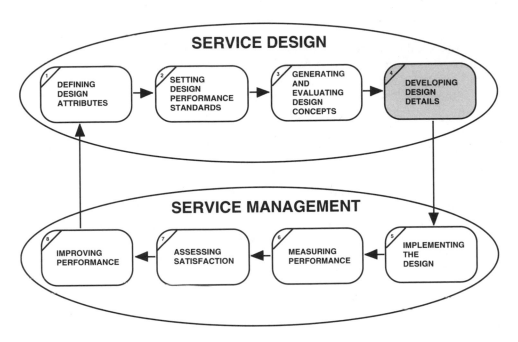

- *Evaluating design alternatives*
- *Introduction to simulation models*
- *Service Edge simulation model inputs*
- *Service Edge simulation model structure*
- *Service Edge simulation model results*
- *Analyzing and modifying designs*
- *Functional design*
- *Conclusion*

In Chapter 6, we listed the following activities required to develop a detailed design:

Activity 1: Partition concept into design components.

Activity 2: Generate design alternatives for each component.

Activity 3: Predict performance of each design alternative.

Activity 4: Evaluate and select alternative for each component.

Activity 5: Test performance of overall service design assembled from selected alternatives.

Activity 6: Make any necessary modifications to the design.

Activity 7: Specify detailed functional performance requirements.

We discussed the first three activities in Chapter 6. At the end of activity 1, the service was partitioned into processes and subprocesses, and the performance requirements for each process were determined. For each process, activity 2 involved the identification of design units and the creation of design alternatives for each unit. During activity 3, performance functions were specified to predict the change in average performance of each design alternative with the operating characteristics. The use of distributions to measure the random variability in performance of each alternative was also described.

The focus of this chapter is on activities 4, 5, 6, and 7. We begin this chapter with activity 4, covered in Section 7.1. In this section, we describe how the design alternatives can be evaluated to identify the alternatives that are potential candidates for implementation. This evaluation compares the *average* predicted performance of each alternative with the design standards. The effects of random performance variability of each alternative are not considered at this stage. This is because we first want to separate potentially acceptable designs from unacceptable ones. A design whose average performance meets the standards needs to be tested further for robustness and capability; one that does not even meet the standards on the average is clearly unacceptable. During the course of this activity, we also evaluate the cost and implementability of each design that meets the performance standards to determine whether the design can be implemented at a cost that keeps the company profitable at the projected level of demand for the service.

The output of activity 4 is a set of designs for each process with acceptable average performance and acceptable costs. In activity 5, these process designs are assembled into an end-to-end model of the service. The performance of the service is simulated under a variety of operating and environmental conditions, and design components with excessive performance variability are identified. Section 7.2 is a general introduction to simulation, and Sections 7.3, 7.4, and 7.5 demonstrate how simulation can be applied to the Service Edge restaurant service. The simulation will help us to identify the parts of the overall design that need to be modified.

These modifications are undertaken in activity 6 and are described in Section 7.6. At the end of this activity, we should have produced a robust design that is capable of meeting the performance standards with little variability across the desired range of operating and environmental conditions. We can then develop detailed specifications for each process at the functional level, which is undertaken in Activity 7. The development of functional level specifications is described in Section 7.7. Section 7.8 is a chapter summary.

7.1 EVALUATING DESIGN ALTERNATIVES—DETAILED DESIGN ACTIVITY 4

As mentioned above, the objective of this activity is to compare the design alternatives generated in Activity 2 (Chapter 6, Section 6.2) on the basis of their *average* performance. This evaluation is carried out through the following steps:

Step 1: Specify the range of operating characteristics under which the design is required to function reliably.

Step 2: Specify design factors for each alternative and set reasonable initial values for them.

Step 3: Combine subprocess-level design alternatives to create feasible process designs.

Step 4: Predict the average performance of each design using the performance functions.

Step 5: Compare the predicted performance of each design with the standards and make any necessary modifications.

Step 6: Evaluate the cost, implementability, and compatibility with other designs that meet or exceed the standards.

Step 7: Select a set of candidate designs for further analysis.

We will demonstrate these steps using a concrete example. We will continue the design of the order-taking process for the Service Edge restaurant. The reader will recall from Section 6.2 (see Table 6.9) that nine design alternatives were created for this process. These alternatives were based on the following four design dimensions:

- Screen display (three alternatives)
- Menu display interval (two alternatives)
- Availability verification (two alternatives)
- Validation procedure (two alternatives)

The description of each alternative from Table 6.9 is repeated in Table 7.1. We will follow the eight steps described above for designs created from these alternatives.

Table 7.1   Description of design alternatives for order-taking process (repeat of Table 6.9)

Design Dimension	No.	Description of alternative
Screen display	SD1	One menu item displayed per page, with a detailed description of item on the page
	SD2	All items displayed on one page with item descriptions on a separate help screen
	SD3	Appetizers, entrees, desserts, and beverages on separate pages, with a brief description of items following each entry
Menu display interval	DD1	Two-minute wait before prompting for input
	DD2	Four-minute wait before prompting for input
Availability verification	AV1	Verification of availability of each item is done immediately after ordering the item
	AV2	Verification of availability is done once for all items after the order is completed
Validation procedure	VP1	Waiter sends order to kitchen immediately on receipt of order; any corrections are sent subsequently after validation with customer
	VP2	Waiter holds order until validation is complete; all corrections are made before the order is sent to the kitchen

Step 1: Specifying the operating range

Recall from Section 6.3 that three factors affect the performance of a design: the operating characteristics, the environmental conditions, and the design factors. In Figure 6.5, we showed how the environmental conditions and the design factors influence the operating characteristics, which in turn affects the design performance. During normal operations, the service may be subjected to many different operating characteristics. In addition, random variability in the operating characteristics may result in unpredictable variability in performance. Our objective should be to develop a design that will deliver the required performance (specified by the performance standards) through a realistic range of operating conditions and despite the uncertainty introduced by the random variability.

How can we do that? We can define an *operating range* within which the design should deliver the required level of performance. For example, suppose a courier service wishes to guarantee overnight delivery of packages in a variety of weather conditions. The range of temperature, the maximum amount of precipitation, and the minimum visibility are examples of parameters that will help set the operating range for the service. In another example, a supermarket checkout counter may wish to deliver a guaranteed waiting time to express customers at all times of the day. The expected number of customers and the anticipated variability in customer arrivals at different times of the day are data that will help specify the operating ranges.

How do we specify an operating range for a design? The range should realistically reflect the normal conditions of operation of a service, with some buffer for unexpected variability or growth. However, extreme conditions that occur only as exception should not be part of the operating range, because this may result in a wasteful over-design of the service to meet situations that are rarely experienced. The only exception should be in situations where rare and exceptional situations affect safety, or cause severe or irrevocable customer dissatisfaction.

If service operations are seasonal or cyclic, the operating range should be defined for each season or cycle. It is preferable to have a single design that is robust across seasons, but if this not feasible, it is better to have two separate designs than one that is forcibly applied to all situations. For example, different check-in and boarding processes may be designed for an airline gate at peak and off-peak hours.

Operating range for the order-taking process of Service Edge restaurant

Table 7.2 shows some operating characteristics and their anticipated range for the order-taking process of the Service Edge restaurant. This process was introduced in Chapter 6 (Section 6.2). For a review of this process and its subprocess, see Figure 6.2 and Tables 6.7 and 6.8.

Table 7.2 shows three values for each operating characteristic: a minimum value, a maximum value, and an average value. The average may sometimes be replaced

Table 7.2   Operating range for characteristics of the order-taking process

Operating characteristic	Min. value	Ave. value	Max. value	Order-taking subprocess design attributes affected
Arrival rate of customers (tables/hour)	10	45	60	Validation wait time
Number of customers per table	1	2.5	4	Validation wait time Ordering time Verification time
Number of items ordered per customer	1	3	5	Ordering time Verification time
Time taken to read menu page (seconds)	5	10	15	Ordering time

by the most likely value. For a new design, these values can be generated in two ways. In some cases, described in Chapter 6, they can be influenced by the design alternative. For example, the capacity of a service facility may be constrained so as not to allow more than a pre-specified arrival rate. In other cases, the values may be obtained by observing the operations of similar services.

Step 2: Specify reasonable initial values for design factors of each alternative

As mentioned before, the design factors are the parameters that are within the control of the design team. Staffing requirements, technology decisions, experience and skill levels, training needs, documentation design, etc., are all design factors. The values of these factors can be set by the design team. The values of the design factors should be set at levels that can produce the required performance over the operating range, within the limits of the capability of the technology, specified by the design alternative.

Typically, once the operating range is specified, the design team sets *reasonable initial values* for the design factors of each design alternative based on an initial assessment of the required performance levels and an understanding of the technological capability of each design alternative. As the designs are evaluated, and the performance of each design alternative can be assessed more precisely, these values may be modified. Let us consider an example of how this is done.

Design factors for the order-taking process of the Service Edge restaurant

Let us now see how we can identify the design factors and specify reasonable initial values for these factors for the order-taking process of the Service Edge restaurant. We begin by referring back to Table 7.2 where we indicate the subprocess design attribute that is affected by the operating characteristic. For example, the arrival rate of customers affects the waiter workload. As a result, customers have to wait longer for their orders to be validated.

How do we identify design factors for a design alternative? A design factor is a dimension of the design alternative that affects the performance of one or more design attributes. For the order-taking process of the Service Edge restaurant, we ask the question: *What technological characteristics of each design alternative shown in Table 7.1 influence the performance of the subprocess design attributes shown in Table 7.2?* We use the word "technology" loosely in this context to refer to the key dimensions by which the design alternatives vary. Consider the four sets of design alternatives for the Service Edge restaurant order-taking process in Table 7.1. Let us start with the screen display format alternatives (SD1, SD2, and SD3 in Table 7.1). Clearly, these designs differentiate themselves by the *number of menu pages*. The number of menu pages affects the total time taken to read the menu, and therefore the ordering time in Table 7.2. The number of menu pages is therefore a design factor for the order-taking process. Similarly, designs DD1 and DD2 vary by the *menu display time*. This factor affects the amount of time available for browsing the menu, and consequently the ordering time. Designs AV1 and AV2 vary by the number of times the availability verification process is invoked. Since each call for verification takes some time, the *time taken by the system to process each availability verification inquiry* is a design factor that affects the attribute "verification time" in Table 7.2. For these design alternatives, *the percentage of unavailable items in the menu* is another design factor that affects the verification time attribute. Finally, for the design alternatives VP1 and VP2, the *time taken to validate an order* is a design factor that affects the performance of the process. The design factors just described are shown in Table 7.3.

In addition to these factors, the last row of Table 7.3 shows a design factor common to all design alternatives. This is the *maximum fraction of a waiter's time that should be spent in planned meal service functions,* which affects the time that guests have to wait for their orders to be validated. This factor is referred to as *waiter utilization* in Table 7.3.

Setting initial values for the order-taking process design factors

The initial values for the design factors are also shown in Table 7.3. How are these specified? For each design factor, we look for the range of the appropriate operat-

Table 7.3   Design factors for the order-taking process

Design factor	Value	Affected performance measure
Number of menu pages	SD1=15 SD2=6 SD3=1	Ordering time
Maximum menu display time	DD1=2 mins. DD2=4 mins.	Ordering time Browsing time
Availability verification time for alternatives AV1 and AV2	Access time=10 sec. Inquiry time=5 sec/item	Verification time
Percentage of unavailable items	15%	Verification time
Time taken to validate order for design alternatives VP1 and VP2	30 sec.	Validation time
Waiter utilization for all design alternatives	Maximum=0.8	Validation wait time

ing characteristics within which the design is to operate. The value of the design factor is then set to accommodate this operating range, using judgment and experience. It is enough for the initial values to be good realistic guesses that are starting points for the evaluation of the alternatives. These values can always be adjusted as the design is analyzed in greater detail.

For an example of the approach used to specify the values for these factors, consider the item *number of menu pages* in Table 7.3. This factor affects the ordering time, since an increase in the number of pages increases the time taken to read the menu. The value of this factor should clearly depend on *the time taken to read a menu page*. Table 7.2 shows that this time can vary from 5 seconds to 15 seconds per page. Let us estimate the time taken to read the menu assuming the maximum interval of 15 seconds per page. The average number of items on a typical menu is about 15. Under the first screen display format (SD1, with one item on each page, see Table 7.1), this would mean that the menu would consist of fifteen pages. The maximum reading time for this menu would be $15 \times 15 = 225$ seconds, or approximately 4 minutes, which is not an unreasonable interval to read a menu. The value of this design factor for the SD1 alternative is therefore set to 15.

For another example, consider the factor *waiter utilization*. This factor is set as a trade-off between cost and performance requirements. Cost or efficiency considerations dictate that a waiter should spend as much time as possible serving customers. On the other hand, waiters have greater flexibility to pay individual attention to customers and to be more responsive when they serve fewer customers. Serving customers no more than 80% of the time seems like a reasonable compromise between these two requirements. This is the figure seen in Table 7.3.

The initial values for the other design factors in Table 7.3 are similarly specified. These examples show that there are no rigid rules to follow for setting the values of the design factors. Rather, it is a flexible process for making an *educated first guess* about the design values that will provide the required performance level over the operating range. This first guess continues to be fine-tuned as more precise information about the design performance is obtained.

Step 3: Combine subprocess-level design alternatives to create feasible process designs

Let us continue with the example of the order-taking process. As mentioned previously, twenty-four designs can be created from the alternatives of Table 7.1. All combinations of the alternatives may not be feasible, and so only a subset of the total number of designs may be relevant. Even if this is not the case, the design team may choose to concentrate on only a few key designs. If some attributes are more important than others, then designs which emphasize these attributes may be selected. Some designs may be inferior to others on all dimensions; clearly, there is no point in evaluating these designs. In any case, the team should narrow the choices to five or six strong alternatives. Four designs for the order-taking process

Table 7.4   Selected designs for the order-taking process

Design Number	Screen	Display	Availability	Validation
1	SD2	DD1	AV2	VP2
2	SD2	DD2	AV2	VP2
3	SD3	DD1	AV2	VP2
4	SD3	DD2	AV2	VP2

of the Service Edge restaurant are shown in Table 7.4. Let us examine the characteristics of these designs.

1. Screen design and menu display alternative selection (SD and DD): The four designs in Table 7.4 represent various combinations of the alternatives SD2, SD3, and DD1, DD2. Alternative SD1 was not selected because it was thought that a single menu item on each page would make the menu too tedious to read. A SD2/DD1 combination as in design 1 in Table 7.4 emphasizes the quickness of ordering time since it combines the smallest number of pages with the shortest menu display interval. Design 4, which combines alternatives SD3 and DD2 will result in a longer time to place an order, but reflects an emphasis on the knowledge and patience attributes because it combines more detail on the menu pages with more time to browse the menu. The two other designs fall in between.

2. Availability verification procedure selection (AV): All four designs use the same alternative AV2 (which is the time taken to access the system). As shown in Table 7.3, each item availability inquiry requires an *access time* and an *inquiry time* (which is the time taken to make the inquiry). Alternative AV1 queries availability one item at a time; therefore it requires multiple accesses to query the availability of the same number of items that alternative AV2 queries in a single pull. Thus, it takes more time to verify availability for alternatives AV1 than AV2. Moreover, it may be more annoying for the customer to interact with AV1 because it requires the customer to wait for verification after each input. AV2 is therefore clearly the superior alternative and is selected for all designs.

3. Order validation method (VP): The four designs also use the same method VP2 for validating the order. The design VP1 (see Table 7.1) requires the order to be shipped to the kitchen before validation is complete, while design VP2 holds the order until the validation is completed and then sends it to the kitchen. From the order-taking process perspective, there is no difference in the total order validation time between the two designs. However, the difference between the two alternatives will affect the *meal delivery time* of the meal delivery process. If there are no ordering errors, VP1 is faster because the kitchen can begin to prepare the meal before the validation is complete. However, under this design, mistakes will take longer to correct because the orders have been sent to the kitchen. The decision to adopt alternative VP2 should be based on the risk associated with dissatisfying a customer by preparing the wrong meal compared to the gain in efficiency and meal delivery speed due to quicker processing of the order. The order validation methodology therefore is a *common design element* between the order-taking and meal-delivery processes. The selection of the design alternative must jointly be made by the design subteams for both processes.

Step 4: Predict the average performance of each design using the performance functions

We will first present the important performance functions for the restaurant order-taking process. Two considerations mentioned in Chapter 6 (Section 6.4) will help to reduce the number of performance functions that need to be specified. First, we specify performance functions for only those service parameters that *directly* affect performance. Second, we only specify performance functions if the relationship between a factor is nonlinear, discontinuous, or unusual in some other way.

An example of the first consideration is shown in Figure 7.1. In Table 7.2 we saw that the arrival rate of customers and the number of customers in a group affect the validation wait time. However, these variables do not affect the performance measure directly. The number of arriving customers and the number of available waiters jointly determine the *waiter utilization level*, as shown in Figure 7.1.

This factor *directly* determines the amount of time customers need to wait before their order is validated. Only this relationship needs to be specified by the performance function, as shown in Figure 7.2 (a).

Figures 7.2 (a) and 7.2 (b) are also examples of the second consideration. Notice that the relationship between waiter utilization and the order validation wait time in Figure 7.2 (a) is nonlinear, with the wait time sharply increasing when the utilization is higher than 0.8. Similarly Figure 7.2 (b) shows the performance function for

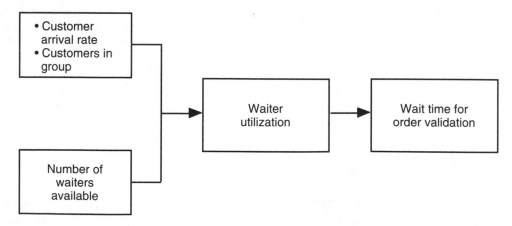

Figure 7.1   Relationship between the factors affecting order validation wait time

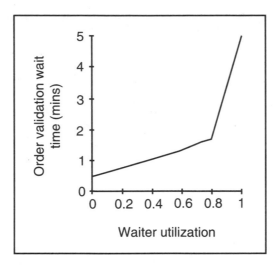

Figure 7.2 (a)   Performance function for
order validation wait time

order-taking patience as a function of the time allowed to browse the menu. This is a discontinuous function, since patience is measured on a discrete scale (1= poor, 6 = exceptional). Each value of the rating is applicable for a range of browsing times.

For the design of the order-taking process, the design team decided that only these two functions were necessary.

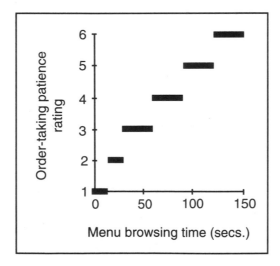

Figure 7.2 (b)   Performance function for
order-taking patience

The next step is to use the performance functions to calculate the average performance of each design shown in Table 7.4. Before we do this, we need to select a *set of values for the operating characteristics* at which the performance is to be calculated. These operating characteristics must be chosen carefully, because if the design meets the performance standards at these values, then we can assume that the design will perform acceptably at less stringent values of these characteristics. The values must therefore be chosen so that they reflect a realistic end point of the operating range. For example, Table 7.2 shows that the customer arrival rate can vary from ten to sixty per hour. Clearly, the operating characteristics chosen to evaluate the performance of the design should be closer to sixty than to ten. If the design operates satisfactorily at the highest possible arrival rate, it will function acceptably at lower values as well.

We now show how the average performance is calculated for each design of the order-taking process in Table 7.4. We will demonstrate the methodology in detail for *design 1*. The performance of the other designs can be similarly determined. We will predict the performance of the design for the three order-taking process attributes specified in Chapter 6 (see the service/process matrix in Table 6.1). They are:

1) time interval between menu delivery and order-taking (promptness)

2) amount of time available to browse the menu and study options (patience)

3) amount of information available about menu items (knowledge)

Example: Calculating the average performance for the order-taking process designs

Recall that design 1 has the following features (notation from Table 7.4 is in parentheses):

- All menu items are displayed on a single page (SD2)
- The menu is displayed for two minutes (DD1)
- Availability is verified for all items after the order is complete (AV2)
- The order is not sent to the kitchen until manual validation is complete (VP2)

Let us predict the performance for each attribute in turn for design 1.

1. PROMPTNESS ATTRIBUTE—TIME BETWEEN MENU DELIVERY AND ORDER-TAKING

This interval can be segmented into the following parts:

A. the time taken to read the menu
B. the time taken to place an order
C. the time taken to reorder

   D. the time taken to verify the availability of an item

   E. the waiting time to for order validation

   F. the actual time taken to validate the order

We will calculate the time for each subprocess interval separately, and total them to determine

   G. the total time between menu delivery and order-taking

A. *Menu reading time:*

   No. of menu pages in design: 1 (alternative SD2, see Table 7.3)

   Time taken to read each menu page : 15 seconds (maximum value of operating characteristic chosen from Table 7.2).

Therefore, the *total time to read the menu under the SD2 option is 15 × 1 = 15 seconds*

B. *Time taken to order:*

   Menu display interval: 120 seconds (alternative DD1, see Table 7.3)

   Time taken to read menu: 15 seconds (maximum value of operating characteristic)

   Maximum time taken to order: 120 − 15 = 105 seconds

The menu display remains on the screen for 2 minutes. If 15 seconds are taken to read the menu, 105 seconds remain to place the order before the menu display vanishes. This is the worst case. If the design meets the standards for this case, it will meet the standards under less stringent conditions.

C. *Time taken to reorder:*

   Most likely value of items ordered per customer: 3 (value of operating characteristic chosen from Table 7.2. Note that in this case, the maximum value was *not* chosen).

   Percent of unavailable items: 15% (design factor value from Table 7.3).

   Percentage of items unavailable per customer: 0.15 × 3 = 0.5 items per customer, approximately. Each customer orders 3 items and 15% of these are not available. So on an average, each customer has to reorder 0.5 items, or more realistically, every second customer has to reorder an item.

   Time taken to read the menu again = 15 seconds (as before)

   Maximum time taken to reorder per customer = 15 seconds × 0.5 (average number of reorders per customer) = 7.5 seconds

D. *Availability verification time:*

Computer access time for availability verification: 10 seconds (design factor value from Table 7.3)

Inquiry time: 5 seconds per item (design factor value from Table 7.3)

Most likely number of items ordered by a customer: 3 (operating characteristic value from Table 7.2)

Total availability verification time for the first order: 10 seconds (access time) + 5 seconds (inquiry time/item) × 3 (items) = 25 seconds.

We now need to calculate the average verification time for a reorder.

Average number of items reordered per customer: 0.5 (from Part C above)

The expected verification time for a reorder: 0.5 × 10 (access time) + 0.5 × 5 (inquiry time) = 7.5 seconds.

The total availability verification time: 25 + 7.5 = 32.5 seconds

E. *Order validation waiting time:*

Maximum utilization level permitted by the design: 0.8 (design factor value from Table 7.3)

Wait time corresponding to this utilization: 120 seconds [performance function Figure 7.2 (a)]

This is the worst case. If the performance meets the standards for this case, it will meet the standards for less stringent conditions.

F. *Actual order validation time:*

Actual order validation time: 30 seconds (design factor value from Table 7.3).

G. *Total time between menu delivery and order taking:*

The total interval between menu delivery and order taking for *design 1* is the sum of the quantities A, B, C, D, E, and F and is equal to 15 + 105 + 7.5 + 32.5 + 120 + 30 = *310 seconds.*

The interval can be similarly calculated for other designs. Table 7.5 shows this interval and its constituents for each of the four designs in Table 7.4.

2. PATIENCE ATTRIBUTE—ORDER-TAKING PATIENCE RATING:

The order-taking patience rating refers to the customers' perceptions of their ability to ask questions about the menu without feeling rushed to order. For this particular concept, where the ordering is done on a terminal, the patience attribute translates into the amount of time available to the customer to read the menu before being prompted to order. The predicted rating is calculated as follows for design 1:

> Menu display (browsing) time: 120 seconds (alternative DD1, see Table 7.3)

> Patience rating: *Exceptional* [from the performance function Figure 7.2 (b)].

3. KNOWLEDGE ATTRIBUTE—KNOWLEDGE OF MENU ITEMS

This refers to the amount of knowledge that the waiters have about the history, contents, and method of preparation of the menu items. For this concept, this translates into the amount of information about the menu items in the ordering system.

Design 1 includes alternative SD2, which provides information about the menu on a separate help screen. Customers perceive this alternative as providing less information than it actually does, because the information is not as easily accessible as it would be if it were provided on the screen. The alternative therefore receives an *excellent* knowledge rating, which is one step below the best possible *exceptional* rating.

Performance summary for all design alternatives

The average performance for all the designs can be calculated in a similar manner. Table 7.5 summarizes the predicted performance of the promptness attribute for all four design alternatives shown in Table 7.4.

Table 7.6 summarizes the performance of the patience and knowledge attributes for the four designs.

Step 5: Compare the predicted performance of each design with the standards and make any necessary modifications

We now compare the designs against the performance standards. If none of the designs meet all standards, then it is necessary to modify them. If no modifications are possible, the team should re-evaluate the constraints placed on the design by any common subsystems that may have been designed earlier. If it appears that the con-

Table 7.5   Interval from menu delivery to order-taking for the four designs

Design	Menu reading and ordering	Availability verification	Order validation	Total interval
Design 1	127.5 sec.	32.5 sec.	150 sec.	310 sec.
Design 2	247.5 sec.	32.5 sec.	150 sec.	430 sec.
Design 3	127.5 sec.	32.5 sec.	150 sec.	310 sec.
Design 4	247.5 sec.	32.5 sec.	150 sec.	430 sec.

Table 7.6   Summary of knowledge and patience ratings for the four designs

Design	Knowledge rating	Patience rating
1	Excellent	Exceptional
2	Exceptional	Exceptional
3	Excellent	Exceptional
4	Exceptional	Exceptional

straints do not allow the opportunity to consider many flexible design options, the team may have to modify or drop some elements of the common design. Several iterations between the individual and common designs may be necessary before an acceptable design is obtained. If it is not possible to modify any common elements, or if the designs do not meet the standards even after modifications, then the team may be forced to relax the performance standards and experience the resultant decrease in satisfaction. The team must return to the performance/satisfaction functions and identify the attributes whose relaxation will cause the least degradation in satisfaction. As far as possible, the standards for only these attributes must be relaxed until they match the predicted performance of the design. This should be a last resort option, and the firm should reassess the feasibility of competing in the market in the long run before it designs and implements a service that does not meet the performance standards.

Comparing the predicted performance of the order-taking process designs

Table 7.7 compares the predicted performance of each attribute of the four order-taking process designs to the standards.

From Table 7.7, it is clear that none of the designs meet all the standards. In fact, none of the designs meets the promptness standard. Designs 3 and 4 are the best candidates because they meet the standards for two out of the three attributes. Between these two designs, design 3 has the smaller performance gap relative to the standard for the promptness attribute. This can be seen from Table 7.5, which

Table 7.7   Comparison of order-taking process designs against standards

Design	Promptness	Knowledge	Patience
Standard	300 sec.	Exceptional	Exceptional
1	No	No	Yes
2	No	No	Yes
3	No	Yes	Yes
4	No	Yes	Yes

shows that the total order-taking interval is 310 seconds for design 3 compared to 430 seconds for design 4. The performance gap relative to the standard is therefore 10 seconds.

Ten seconds is a small amount and can generally be ignored. However, even if we manage to reduce the order-taking interval by 10 seconds to make the average performance exactly 300 seconds, it is not good enough. Because of random variability (see Section 6.3), the average predicted order-taking interval needs to be much shorter (about 250 seconds) for the process performance to consistently meet the standards under all the conditions of random variability. The required improvement in the order-taking interval should therefore be of the order of about 60 seconds.

Modifying the design to meet the performance standards

How should this improvement be made? The design team should investigate the different methods by which the order-taking interval can be reduced. Each method will involve some trade-offs and costs. For example, one possibility for reducing the order-taking interval by 1 minute is to reduce the menu display interval to 1 minute instead of 2. From Figure 7.2 (b), it can be seen that this will cause a significant drop in the patience rating. Since patience is a more important attribute (see Table 3.9) than the order-taking interval, this may not be the best solution.

Another solution is to reduce the maximum waiter utilization from 0.8 to 0.5. It can be seen from Figure 7.2 (a) that this results in a reduction in the validation wait time of 1 minute. However, this requires the number of waiters to be doubled, which is clearly very expensive. The team must balance the benefits of reducing the order-taking time against the costs of doing so, and make the appropriate decision.

Once again, it must be emphasized that the design team's philosophy should not be "quality at any price." Rather, the team must carefully evaluate the costs and benefits of various design modifications and implement the ones that are profitable.

Step 6: Evaluate the costs, the implementability, and the compatibility with other subsystems for each design that meets or exceeds the standards

When there are several attractive design options that meet the performance standards, they must be compared on the cost associated with their implementation and operation. Some alternatives may involve high setup costs, if hardware or software have to be purchased, new employees recruited, or training provided. Other alternatives may have low initial costs, but may be expensive to maintain and operate. Nonfinancial considerations may also play a part in the evaluation of designs. For example, the time needed to implement the design, ease of managing the service, the ability of the design to accommodate future changes in performance standards, and the potential of the design to assist in strategic growth of the business are all factors that should be considered before the final selection of candidate designs is made.

Other considerations are the compatibility of the designs with those of other processes, especially where resources or technology are shared. For example, some process designs that meet the performance and cost requirements may not have the same "look and feel" as other, similar, processes. Other designs may not share resources effectively between processes, or may not interface smoothly with other processes. In other cases, a design may meet operational effectiveness and efficiency criteria but may result in poor quality of face-to-face interactions between the customers and service providers. As mentioned in Chapter 5 (Section 5.2), the operational activities should never be designed alone without considering their impact on the intangible customer service activities for any process. The performance of the customer service activities must seamlessly integrate with those of operations.

Even in cases where only a single design solution meets the performance standards, or no design meets the standards, the financial and nonfinancial analyses described above must be performed. The bottom line is to ensure that the design contributes to the firm's profitability. In conclusion, a suitable candidate for implementation, therefore, not only performs well, but also can be easily deployed and managed, is cost-effective to operate, and maintains a good "fit" with the rest of the service.

Step 7: Select a set of candidate designs for further analysis

For the order-taking process, let us assume that the design subteam selects *design 3* as a candidate based on the predictions of its average performance and on the other considerations mentioned above. The design subteams for other processes choose their candidates on similar criteria. A design that meets these criteria has been shown, on the average, to meet the performance standard for the required range of operating conditions. Up to now, no systematic analysis of the effect of *variability* on performance has been carried out to identify the robustness of each design. Moreover, the performance of the designs when they all operate together to deliver an end-to-end service has not yet been determined.

In order to perform these analyses, it is necessary to *simulate* the entire restaurant service and evaluate the *robustness* of performance under different operating and environmental conditions. This is described in the following sections. We will first begin with a general description of a simulation model, and then apply the techniques to simulate the service of the Service Edge restaurant.

7.2   INTRODUCTION TO SIMULATION MODELS

The model described in this chapter is called a *discrete event simulation model*. This means that the model simulates activities in discrete increments of time. The total duration of the simulation is a specified time interval. This interval is segmented into discrete increments. The size of these increments depends on the length of the simulation. If the model simulates intervals that occur during a 5-minute period, then 5-second increments may be appropriate. If the duration is several hours, then the clock may be advanced at intervals of a minute.

From the start of the simulation, the model steps successively through each time increment until the end of the interval is reached. There are two possibilities for each time increment: *something happens* or *nothing happens*. The "something," referred to as an *event*, is a change in the state of the system, usually triggered by the start or the completion of an activity during the delivery of a service. One or more events can take place in each time increment. In the case of a restaurant service, for example, the arrival of a new customer, the departure of an old one, the completion of an order, and the collection of payment for a meal are all examples of events. At each event, the applicable model parameters are updated and relevant performance statistics collected. In the following section, we will make this description more concrete through an example of a generic process for handling a service request.

It must be noted here that discrete event simulation is only one of several available simulation techniques. Other approaches may be appropriate, depending on the nature of the application and the objective of the simulation. The reader is referred to a simulation text such as the one by Law and Kelton (1991), or to one of the other texts on simulation suggested at the end of the chapter, for a description of other simulation techniques.

Simulating service request fulfillment process—no variability

The logic of the discrete event simulation approach followed in this chapter can be illustrated by the simple example presented in Figure 7.3. This figure shows a flow diagram for a customer service agent processing service requests. If the agent is free, the request is immediately processed. If the agent is busy, the request is queued. After the completion of the current request, the agent sequentially processes queued requests. If no items are queued, the system is empty and the agent waits for the next request.

Let us start at some arbitrary time $t = 0$, and simulate the process at intervals of one minute. At the start of the simulation, the agent is available, and no requests are in queue. Let us first consider a situation with *no random variability*. Suppose service requests enter the process *alternately at intervals of 3 and 6 minutes*. Since there is no variability, these intervals are exact. This means that if the first request enters at time $t = 3$, the second enters at $t = 9$, the third at $t = 12$, and so on. Suppose also that the time taken to process a service request is exactly 4 minutes.

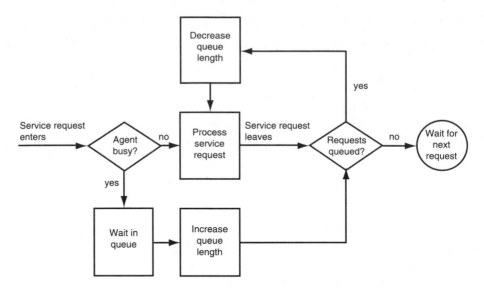

Figure 7.3　Flow chart for service request fulfillment example

To understand how this process can be simulated, let us walk through the first few minutes of the operation of the process. Since the first service request occurs 3 minutes after the start, nothing happens at times $t = 1$ and $t = 2$. At time $t = 3$, the first service request enters the process. Since there is no queue, this request immediately begins to be processed. The agent becomes busy, and remains so for the next four minutes until the time $t = 7$. Nothing happens at times $t = 4, 5$, and 6. At $t = 7$, the agent completes the processing of the request, becomes free, and awaits the next arrival. This takes place at time $t = 9$ (6 minutes after the previous arrival), and once again, since there is no queue, the processing begins immediately. In this cycle, however, the next arrival takes place at $t = 12$, since arrivals alternate every 3 and 6 minutes. However, the customer who arrived at $t = 9$ remains in the process until $t = 13$. The service request arriving at $t = 12$ is therefore put in queue. At $t = 13$, when the agent is available again, this request is removed from queue and processing begins. Table 7.8 shows the events that occur for the first 20 minutes of this simulation.

At every time interval in which an event occurs, statistics on the process are continuously updated as shown in the third and fourth columns of Table 7.8. The model keeps track of two kinds of measures: *status metrics* and *performance metrics*. Status metrics provide instantaneous information on the immediate state of various process performance parameters, and are reset as often as necessary during the simulation. An example of such a metric in Table 7.8 is the *queue length,* which measures the current length of the queue. Note that this metric is reset at times $t = 12$ and $t = 13$ as the request enters and leaves the queue. Other examples of status metrics (not shown in Table 7.8) are a binary variable tracking the availability of the server in each time period (1 = busy, 0 = free) or a variable on a three-point scale indicating the state of each service request (1 = in queue, 2 = in process, 3 = completed).

Table 7.8   List of events in the first 20 minutes of the simulation

Time	Event	Performance metrics	Status metrics
1	No event		
2	No event		
3	Service request 1 arrives Processing of service request 1 begins	Requests received=1	
4	No event		
5	No event		
6	No event		
7	Service request 1 completed	Requests processed=1	
8	No event		
9	Service request 2 arrives Processing of service request 2 begins	Requests received=2	
10	No event		
11	No event		
12	Service request 3 arrives Service request enters queue	Requests received=2 Total # items queued=1	Queue length=1
13	Service request 2 completed Service request 3 removed from queue Processing of service request 3 begins	Requests processed=2 Total queue time=1 min.	Queue length=0
14	No event		
15	No event		
16	No event		
17	Service request 3 completed	Requests completed=3	
18	Service request 4 arrives Processing of service request 4 begins	Requests received=1	
19	No event		
20	No event		

Performance metrics are collected each time an activity begins or ends and are indicators of the overall efficiency and effectiveness of the simulated service. These measures are usually aggregated or averaged over the entire simulation interval. Examples include the following:

- *Number of requests received* or *requests completed* in a fixed time interval measure the throughput of the process

- *Total queue time* accumulated over the simulation interval measures the aggregate amount of delay encountered by customers

- *Average delay per service request* is calculated by dividing the total queue time by the number of service requests queued during the duration of the simulation

Simulating service request fulfillment process—variability included

So far, we have not introduced variability into the simulation. In the results shown in Table 7.8, service requests arrive at exactly the prespecified intervals, and it takes precisely the same time to process each request. Variability in either or both of these times will cause random variability in the overall service performance. As mentioned in the previous chapter (Section 6.5), random variability is represented by assuming a probability distribution for each variable. The value of this variable is no longer a fixed quantity; it is generated by randomly selecting a point from this distribution. Let us introduce variability into our service request fulfillment process by assuming distributions for the following variables:

(a) time taken to process each order (service time)

(b) time between arrivals of service requests

(a) Variability in service time: Instead of the previously assumed constant value of 4 minutes, suppose the time taken to process a service request is now *normally distributed* with a *mean of 4 minutes* and a *standard deviation of 1 minute*. The first column of Table 7.9 shows ten random values of service time from this distribution, ranging in value from 2.41 to 4.36, obtained using a random-number generator available in a popular software spreadsheet package.

(b) Variability in inter-arrival time: Now suppose that instead of constant values of 3 and 6 minutes, the time between arrivals of service requests into the process alternates between two *exponential distributions* with *mean values of 3 and 6 minutes*. Ten random observations from these distributions are also shown in Table 7.9. The inter-arrival times range from 1.3 to 8.6 and from 0.07 to 21.3 minutes, respectively.

Table 7.10 shows the results for the first 20 minutes of a simulation that uses the service time and inter-arrival time values from Table 7.9. It can be seen from this table that the first arrival doesn't take place for 8.63 minutes (from the second column of Table 7.9) and the second until (8.63 + 7.94) = 16.57 minutes (from the third column of Table 7.9). However, the succeeding arrival times from Table 7.9 (second row) are 1.38 and 0.06 minutes, resulting in two arrivals in the 18th minute and the

Table 7.9   Distributions for service request processing and inter-arrival times

Service request processing time (minutes)	Inter-arrival time 3 minute mean	Inter-arrival time 6 minute mean
2.90	8.63	7.94
2.41	1.38	0.06
4.33	2.37	1.47
3.88	4.57	1.17
3.25	5.97	21.32
2.96	2.17	8.97
3.98	2.86	6.86
3.70	1.65	13.42
4.19	1.33	2.26
4.36	5.99	9.64

build-up of a queue. The reader should contrast the results of Table 7.10 with the perfectly predictable results of Table 7.8. Clearly, they are very different.

Every run of the fixed model of Table 7.8 will produce the same result, since all the performance parameters are fixed and perfectly known. On the other hand, each run of the probabilistic model of Table 7.10 will produce a different result, since the parameters are random values from a distribution. Each run of the model is therefore a single manifestation of service operations—for example, a snapshot of a single day of processed service requests. The overall behavior of the process cannot be generalized from the results of a single run. The model needs to be run many times, each with different random values of the performance parameters. The average results from these runs indicate the process performance trends.

Inputs needed to develop simulation model

What inputs were needed to run the service request simulation model? We needed to know the *activities of the process,* shown in Figure 7.3. We had to specify the *units* that flowed through the process, i.e., service requests. We needed to define the *performance metrics* for measuring the output of the simulation. We specified the *design factors* (4 minutes/service request) and the *operating characteristics* (arrival rate). We defined the *form* and the *parameters* of the distributions.

These can be generalized into the following list of inputs that are needed to develop and run a simulation model for evaluating a service design:

1. The list of processes and their interactions

2. The flow units (e.g., customers, orders, projects) for each process

3. The key design performance attributes for each process/subprocess

Table 7.10 Results of first 20 minutes of simulation with variability

Time	Event	Performance metrics	Status metrics
1	No event		
2	No event		
3	No event		
4	No event		
5	No event		
6	No event		
7	No event		
8	No event		
9	Service request 1 arrives Processing of service request 1 begins	Requests received=1	
10	No event		
11	No event		
12	Service request 1 completed	Requests processed=1	
13	No event		
14	No event		
15	No event		
16	No event		
17	Service request 2 arrives Processing of service request 2 begins	Requests received=2	
18	Service request 3 arrives Service request 3 in queue Service request 4 arrives Service request 4 in queue	Requests received=4	Queue length=2
19	No event		
20	Service request 2 completed Service request 3 removed from queue Processing of service request 3 begins	Requests processed=2 Total # items queued=1 Total time in queue= 2 min.	Queue length=1

4. The performance standard for each attribute of each process

5. The operating characteristics for each process/subprocess

6. The design factors for each process/subprocess

7. The performance function for each applicable operating characteristic

8. The form and parameters of distributions representing random variability in each process/subprocess performance attribute

These inputs are usually determined during the concept generation stage and during the first four detailed design activities described in Chapter 6 and in the first part of this chapter. Notice that the items described above are all specified at the process/subprocess level. This is usually an appropriate level of detail for a simulation. The team should not spend time trying to accurately model every nuance of each service function. The additional insights gained by this much detail do not usually justify the effort expended. At this stage, it is enough to identify potential design problems at the process or subprocess level. After several iterations of design improvements, when a process is ready for implementation, the team may wish to study the performance of a few processes in greater detail to identify bottlenecks or inefficiencies at the function level. A more detailed simulation is appropriate at this stage.

We will now evaluate the Service Edge restaurant service design using simulation. This corresponds to Activity 5 of the seven detailed design activities. In Section 7.3, we describe the model inputs. In Section 7.4, we discuss the model structure. Finally, in Section 7.5, we present the results from the simulation.

7.3 SERVICE EDGE RESTAURANT SIMULATION INPUTS— DETAILED DESIGN ACTIVITY 5

As we begin this example, we assume that the first four detailed design activities are complete. The team has decomposed the service into its constituent processes and subprocesses. Design alternatives have been generated for each process or subprocess, and the applicable performance functions and distributions needed to predict their performance have been defined. The design alternatives for each process have been evaluated, and the one or two whose average performance meets the standards and which meet the implementability and cost constraints have been selected for further analysis. This section describes this analysis.

In the previous section, we listed the seven inputs needed to develop a simulation model. In this section, we will describe these inputs for simulating the operations of the Service Edge restaurant under a particular design. Most of the inputs have already been defined in Chapters 5 and 6, and we repeat and consolidate them in this section.

List of processes and their interactions

The processes that make up restaurant service and a flow diagram of their interactions were listed in Chapter 5 (Table 5.1 and Figure 5.4). These are repeated in Table 7.11 and Figure 7.4.

Flow units

Clearly, the flow units of the process are the guests who dine at the restaurant. However, we need to keep track of these customers at two levels during our simulation:

- Number of customer *groups* (i.e., tables)
- Number of *guests* (i.e., size of each arriving party)

Some aspects of the design performance, such as the number of guests forced to wait for a table, depend on the *number of tables* occupied, irrespective of the number of occupants at each table. Other performance attributes, such as the amount of time taken to prepare an order, depend on the number of orders in queue, which in turn depends on the *number of guests* who have ordered a meal, irrespective of the number of tables occupied. Flow through the processes should be measured in both these terms.

Key design attributes for each process/subprocess

In Chapter 6 (Section 6.1), when we described activity 1 of the seven detailed design activities, we showed how the service design attributes could be partitioned into the process level using the *service/process matrix*. This matrix, presented in Table 6.1, is summarized in Table 7.12.

Table 7.11   Process definitions for restaurant service (Table 5.1 repeated)

Process name	*Begins*	*Ends*
Greeting and seating	Customer arrives	Customer is seated
Menu delivery	Customer is seated	Customer receives menu
Order-taking	Customer receives menu	Customer orders meal
Meal delivery	Customer orders meal	Customer receives meal
Meal service	Customer is seated	Customer leaves table
Billing	Customer requests bill	Customer receives bill
Payment collection	Customer receives bill	Customer pays
Bill settlement	Customer pays	Bill is settled
Leavetaking	Customer leaves table	Customer departs
Problem resolution	Customer has problem	Problem is resolved

Problem Resolution Process

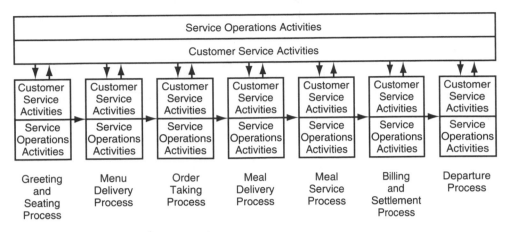

Figure 7.4 Flow chart of processes for restaurant service (repeat of Figure 5.4)

Design standard for each process attribute

In Section 6.1, we also showed how the service-level design standards from the House of Quality matrix can be partitioned into process-level performance standards. These standards were shown in Table 6.3. They are also summarized in Table 7.12.

Operating characteristics for each process/subprocess

The following are the assumptions made about the main operating characteristics for the model. For simplicity, only a few key characteristics have been assumed. We assume that the values of the operating characteristics represent realistic conditions under which the design is expected to operate.

However, the reader should note that for the purposes of the simulation, *some of the assumptions about operating characteristics and design factors are not totally realistic depictions of operating procedures at restaurants, but have been made because they simplify the model.*

Three operating characteristics are considered:

(*a*) *Arrival rate of customers:* Groups of guests (i.e., occupants at a table) are assumed to arrive at the restaurant at an average rate of 0.75 per minute (45 per hour). The arrival rate is assumed to be constant throughout the duration of the simulation.

(*b*) *Number of guests in party:* An average of three guests per party is assumed.

(*c*) *Number of menu items ordered per customer:* Each customer is assumed to order a single item that needs preparation.

Table 7.12   Performance attributes and design standards for restaurant processes (from Tables 6.2 and 6.3)

Process	Performance attribute	Design standard
Greeting	Degree of friendliness of greeting	Exceptional
Meal service	Degree of friendliness of meal service	Exceptional
Meal service	Degree of responsiveness of meal service	Exceptional
Leave taking	Degree of friendliness of leave taking	Exceptional
Menu delivery	Time between seating and meal delivery	< 5 minutes
Order taking	Time between menu delivery and order taking	< 5 minutes
Order taking	Degree of knowledge about menu	Exceptional
Order taking	Degree of order taking patience	Exceptional
Meal delivery	Time between ordering and meal delivery	> 10 and < 15 minutes
Billing	Percent of bills produced without error	> 92%
Payment collection	Percent of bills settled without error	> 92%
Problem resolution	Degree of effectiveness in problem resolution	Excellent

Design factors for each process/subprocess

We assume that the initial values of the design factors are set using the approach outlined in Section 7.1 and have been modified through several iterations of performance evaluations of the design.

Four design factors are considered:

(*a*) *Length of simulation run:* Each run lasts for 5 hours, which is the length of an average evening of dinner service. Time is incremented in units of 1 minute in this interval.

(*b*) *Restaurant capacity:* The restaurant is assumed to have sixty tables, arranged in sets of four. Each set of four tables is assumed to be exactly identical to the others. We will refer to this set as a *waiter station*. The arriving guests are assumed to be distributed sequentially to the fifteen waiter stations (i.e., if the last guest was assigned to station 5, the next guest is assigned to station 6 even if all the tables at this station are occupied). This implies an arrival rate of three customers per hour at each waiter station. If all four tables at the waiter station are occupied, the guest is assumed to wait in queue until a table becomes free at that station. The guest is not permitted to leave the queue to occupy a free table at another station.

(c) Kitchen capacity: For each waiter station, it is assumed that up to three dishes can be prepared simultaneously. If more than three items are currently on order, the remaining items are queued. The queue is cleared on a first-come-first-served basis. No transfer of orders is possible between waiter stations.

(d) Waiter assignment: One waiter is assumed to be assigned to each waiter station. This is intended to result in an average waiter utilization of 0.75 or less over the course of an evening. However, since queues can build up in this model, there is a possibility for a waiter to be more heavily utilized at some points during the course of an evening.

Performance function for each process/subprocess

The performance function measures the relationship between performance attributes and various design factors and operating characteristics. We do not show each performance function here, but indicate the factors affecting the performance of some key process attributes in Table 7.13. For some processes, such as order-taking or meal delivery, each subprocess performance attribute is affected by a different factor. In these cases, the attributes are decomposed to the subprocess level. For example, the meal delivery interval is partitioned into the following subintervals:

- The time taken to deliver the order to the kitchen (order delivery time in Table 7.13)

- The time for which the order waits before it is prepared (order wait time)

- The time taken to prepare the meal (meal preparation time)

- The time taken to deliver the meal to the customer (meal delivery time)

Following the approach suggested in Section 7.1, only those relationships that are nonlinear or discontinuous, or that involve the most important processes, are included in this table.

The reader should note two points from Table 7.13. First, some factors affecting performance depend on the number of guests in the restaurant, while others depend on the number of tables occupied. For example, the effectiveness of problem resolution depends on the number of problems generated, which in turn depends on both the arrival rate of guests and on the number of guests in each party.

On the other hand, attributes that measure the quality of service provided by the waiter, such as the order-taking and meal-delivery intervals, or the level of waiter friendliness and responsiveness, are functions of waiter utilization, which we assume depends on the *number of tables occupied*. The reason for this is that a certain set of activities has to be performed by the waiter for any occupied table (e.g., take the order, deliver the meal, provide service during meal), which takes a fixed quantity of time. A table that has several guests will require some additional time because of the larger number of interactions, but this additional time is assumed to be small compared to the fixed time taken to service a table.

Table 7.13   Factors affecting performance of restaurant processes

Process	Process performance attribute	Subprocess performance attribute	Factor affecting performance
Meal service	Degree of friendliness		Waiter utilization
	Degree of responsiveness		Waiter utilization
Menu delivery	Menu delivery promptness		
Order-taking	Order-taking promptness	Menu reading time	Ave. time to read page
		Availability verification time	No. of items ordered
		Wait time for order validation	Waiter utilization
	Order-taking patience		Menu browse time
	Order-taking knowledge		
Meal delivery	Meal delivery promptness	Order delivery time	
		Order wait time	Guest arrival rate Party size
		Meal preparation time	
		Meal delivery time	Waiter utilization
Billing	Bills produced accurately		Guest departure rate
Payment collection	Bills settled accurately		Waiter utilization
Problem resolution	Problem resolution effectiveness		Guest arrival rate Party size

The second point to be noted from Table 7.13 is that the performances of some at-tributes, such as the degree of knowledge or the menu delivery interval, are not af-fected by any factor. This is because these attributes are not sensitive to changes in operating characteristics for this design. Recall that the design concept involves a permanently available menu screen at each table. The menu delivery interval is therefore constant under this design. Also, the menu information screens provide a complete description of the menu items. The degree of knowledge about the menu items is therefore always perceived to be exceptional. For this design, the performance of these attributes is invariant across the entire operating range of the design.

Distributions

Distributions are used to model variability in three sets of variables:

(a) Arrival rate (of groups)

(b) Party size (i.e., number of guests per group)

(c) Process performance

(*a*) *Arrivals (of groups):* We noted above that guests arrived at the restaurant at the average rate of 0.75 groups/minute (45 per hour). The variability in arrivals is modeled by a Poisson distribution. Recall that the probability of 0,1, 2, . . . , etc., guests arriving within 1 minute at this arrival rate was presented in Table 6.13.

(*b*) *Party size (number of diners per group):* We also noted above that each arriving party had an average of three members. The distribution of party size is represented by the discrete distribution shown in Table 7.14. Of the groups, 10% have a party size of 1, 30% a party size of 2, and so on. The average value of a discrete distribution can be calculated by multiplying each value of the distribution with its associated probability, and summing the results. The average of the party size distribution is $(1 \times 0.1 + 2 \times 0.3 + 3 \times 0.2 + 4 \times 0.3 + 5 \times 0.1) = 3$.

(*c*) *Process performance:* Variability in the *cycle times* of order-taking and meal delivery are modeled by gamma distributions. For billing accuracy, a normal distribution is used. The average values for these distributions is obtained from the performance functions that link performance to the factors presented in Table 7.13. Unlike the arrival rate and party size variables, the cycle times do not have a fixed average, since the average performance in any given minute depends upon the operating characteristics during that particular minute. The performance function therefore has to be evaluated at each time increment.

Reasonable parameter values (from judgment) are used for each distribution. For some attributes, the standard deviations are assumed to be constant over the entire

Table 7.14   Distribution of party size

Party size	Probability
1	0.1
2	0.3
3	0.2
4	0.3
5	0.1

operating range. For others, different values of standard deviations are selected that depend on the average level of performance of the attribute. For example, consider the meal delivery interval. As the waiter utilization increases, the meal delivery interval not only may take longer, but may be more variable as well, because of the decrease in the ability of the waiter to respond flexibly to unexpected situations (such as spills, wrong orders, or irate customers). In such a case, both the mean and the standard deviation of the meal delivery cycle time distribution will be higher at higher utilizations.

This is illustrated by the two gamma distributions shown in Figure 7.5. In this figure, the narrower curve to the left shows the cycle time distribution when the waiter utilization is 0.25. As the utilization increases to 0.5, the curve moves to the right and widens, indicating that both the mean and the spread of the distribution has increased. Where appropriate, these considerations have been included in the model.

We have described the inputs that are needed for a model simulating the processes of the Service Edge restaurant. We now describe the structure of the model.

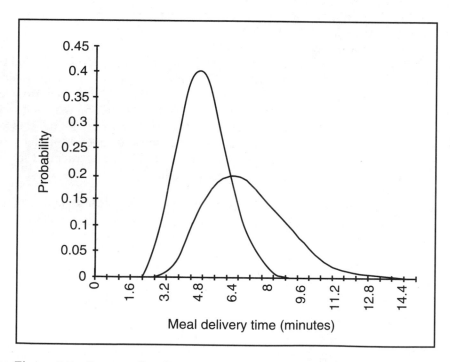

Figure 7.5 Gamma distribution function of meal delivery time at two waiter utilization levels

7.4 SERVICE EDGE SIMULATION MODEL STRUCTURE— DETAILED DESIGN ACTIVITY 5

The model simulates the flow of customers through the restaurant, from the time they enter, through their meal, until the time they depart. We will not describe the model in much detail, but will focus on three important topics:

- Representation of customer service activities of each process

- Generating events from distributions using random numbers

- Overview of model logic

We will describe each of these in sequence.

Representation of customer service activities of each process

Recall from Figure 7.4 that each Service Edge restaurant process has two sets of activities: *service operations* and *customer service*. As mentioned in Chapter 5, the service operations activities represent the steps that need to be performed to deliver the service, while the customer service activities refer to the interactions between the service provider and the customer during the delivery of the service.

Since the simulation is activity- or event-driven, only the service operations activities are explicitly modeled. Customers enter the restaurant, receive their menus, order their meals, eat their meals, pay their bills, and leave. But in the act of performing these activities, they affect those factors that influence the level of service of the customer service activities. For example, in any time increment, outputs of the operations activities such as the number of items ordered, the length of time taken to prepare a meal, or the number of bills paid affect the utilization of waiters and other service providers. This, in turn, affects the quality of the interactions between the customer and the service provider, and therefore the customer service activities.

Let us illustrate this further by a hypothetical quantitative example. Suppose we are simulating the responsiveness of waiters at a restaurant with four tables. Suppose the responsiveness is a function of the waiter utilization, which is simply defined as the proportion of tables occupied (for example, if three tables are occupied, the utilization is 0.75). Table 7.15 shows ten time periods of this simulation. Even though our interest is in waiter responsiveness, note that this is not what we are simulating. We are simulating the *arrival and departure of customers*. In each time period, the number of arriving and departing customers affects the number of occupied tables, and consequently the waiter utilization.

Notice from Table 7.15 that, because of the arrival and departure of customers, the utilization changes from time period to time period. From the waiter utilization value for each time period of the simulation we can indirectly estimate the perfor-

234 *Design and Management of Service Processes*

Table 7.15 Variation of average meal delivery interval in ten simulation time periods

Time period	Arriving guests	Departing guests	Occupied tables	Waiter utilization	Responsive-ness
1	1	0	1	0.25	6
2	2	0	3	0.75	5
3	0	0	3	0.75	5
4	0	1	2	0.50	6
5	1	2	1	0.25	6
6	0	1	0	0.00	6
7	3	0	3	0.75	5
8	0	0	3	0.75	5
9	0	0	3	0.75	5
10	1	0	4	1.00	4

mance of the responsiveness attribute by using a performance function that represents the relationship between waiter utilization and responsiveness. For our example, suppose this relationship is a discrete function that assumes the following values:

- responsiveness rating of "6" if utilization is less than or equal to 0.5
- responsiveness rating of "5" if utilization is between 0.51 and 0.75
- responsiveness rating of "4" if utilization is between 0.76 and 1.0

Using this function, we can translate the utilization levels for each time period to a responsiveness rating. This is shown in the last column of Table 7.15. The performance of all customer service activities for the Service Edge restaurant is modeled in a similar manner.

Generating events from distributions using random numbers

How are events in a simulation generated from distributions? We will illustrate this using a discrete distribution. The logic is similar for continuous distributions.

We will demonstrate how a Poisson distribution can be used to generate arrivals to the restaurant. Table 7.16 shows the probabilities of 0, 1, 2, 3, and 4 arrivals/minute from a Poisson distribution with a mean arrival rate of 0.75/minute. To generate the number of arrivals in a given time interval, a random number generator is used to produce a uniformly distributed random number between 0 and 1. Since the number is uniformly distributed, it will fall between 0 and 0.47 with a probability of 0.47, between 0.47 and 0.82 with a probability of 0.35, between 0.82 and 0.95 with a probability of 0.13, and so on. We can therefore *assign* 0 arrivals to the interval from 0–0.47, 1 arrival to the interval 0.47–0.82, and so on. This is also shown in Table 7.16.

Table 7.16   Probabilities of arrivals from a Poisson distribution (repeat of Table 6.13)

Arrivals/min.	Probability	0–1 Range
0	0.47	0.00–0.47
1	0.35	0.47–0.82
2	0.13	0.82–0.95
3	0.03	0.95–0.98
4	0.01	0.98–0.99

For any given random number, therefore, the range from Table 7.16 in which the value of the random number falls determines the number of arrivals. For example, suppose a random number with a value of 0.35 is generated in a time period. This corresponds to no arrivals in the time period, because it falls between 0 and 0.47. Similarly, a value of 0.8 corresponds to one arrival, and a value of 0.9 corresponds to two arrivals. Over a number of generations, the distribution of simulated arrivals will be close to the probabilities of Table 7.16.

Overview of model logic

An overview of the structure of the Service Edge restaurant simulation model is shown in Figure 7.6. This figure shows the sequence of steps followed by the simulation *in each time increment*. It is important to emphasize this: *all the steps in Figure 7.6 are repeated at every time interval*. For clarity, however, we will follow a single guest through the steps of the simulation.

The arrival of the customer is generated in the *arrival and seating* step. Suppose we are currently at some arbitrary time interval $t = 100$, when our guest arrives. The party size distribution from Table 7.14 is used to generate the number of guests in the party. Suppose our guest is a solitary diner. She is sequentially allocated to a waiter station, and the model assigns her a table if one is available. If no table is available, she is placed in a queue. Let us assume that she has the good luck to immediately find a table. She is then transferred to the *ordering* step. In this step, the time required for ordering the meal is generated for all new arrivals, from the order cycle time distribution. Suppose the interval generated for our guest is 5.2 minutes. This means that it takes her 5 minutes to place an order, and that this activity should be complete by the time t = 105. At this time she is ready to receive her meal. Therefore, she will move to the *meal delivery* step, and the time taken for the delivery of the meal is generated from the appropriate cycle time distribution. When this time comes, our guest is ready to begin her meal and enters the *meal completion and billing* step. In this step, the meal completion time for customers who have received a meal is calculated. Suppose it is now $t = 110$, and our guest is expected to finish her meal in 42 minutes. When the guest's departure time (t = 152) is reached, she enters the *departure* step, and statistics are collected on the performance of the design attributes shown in Table 7.13 for this guest. In the *update*

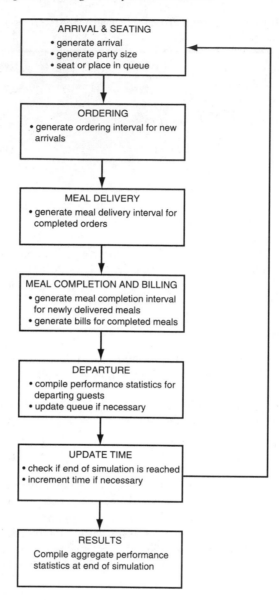

Figure 7.6   Structure of restaurant service simulation model

time step, the model checks if the end of the simulation interval is reached. If this is the case, the simulation is stopped, and aggregate statistics are compiled for the entire simulation in the *results* step; otherwise, time is incremented by another minute and the steps of Figure 7.6 are repeated once more.

In the following section, we will describe how the results from the Service Edge restaurant simulation can be used to test the performance of the designs.

7.5 SERVICE EDGE SIMULATION MODEL OUTPUTS— DETAILED DESIGN ACTIVITY 5

In this section, we describe the results obtained from the simulation model and discuss their implications for modifying and improving the designs. We first describe the metrics used to measure the model outputs, and then the performance predicted by the model on these metrics.

Performance metrics for measuring model output

The metrics used for measuring the performance of each design attribute from Table 7.12 are presented in Table 7.17. The associated design standards are also presented in this table. The metrics compare the performance of the simulated

Table 7.17   Design attributes, standards, and metrics for restaurant service processes

Process design attribute	Standard	Metric
Degree of friendliness of greeting	Exceptional	% time periods meeting standards
Degree of friendliness of meal service	Exceptional	% time periods meeting standards
Degree of friendliness of leavetaking	Exceptional	% time periods meeting standards
Degree of responsiveness of meal service	Exceptional	% time periods meeting standards
Time between ordering and meal delivery	> 10 & < 11.5 mins.	% customers with interval > 10 & < 11.5 mins.
Degree of order-taking patience	Exceptional	% time periods meeting standards
Time between seating and menu delivery	< 5 minutes	% customers with interval < 5 mins
Time between menu delivery and order-taking	< 5 minutes	% customers with interval < 5 mins
Degree of knowledge about menu	Exceptional	% time periods meeting standards
Percent of bills produced without error	> 92%	% bills produced without error
Percent of bills settled without error	> 92%	% bills settled without error
Degree of effectiveness in problem resolution	Excellent	% time periods meeting standards

processes against the performance standards. They are therefore expressed in the general units of *percent meeting standards.*

The specific units of each metric in Table 7.17 depend on the attribute. Three types of attributes are shown in Table 7.17:

1. Attributes whose performance is measured at the customer or customer-group level

2. Attributes whose performance is measured at a work unit level (such as orders or bills)

3. Attributes whose performance is measured at a time period level

We will illustrate each with some examples.

1. Attributes measured at the customer or customer-group level: Examples of these are *cycle time attributes,* such as the ordering or meal delivery intervals. Each customer experiences a single value of these attributes during a meal. The percentage of customers who experience cycle times that meet or exceed the design performance standards is therefore used as a measure of the quality of the design. If the process functions perfectly, the value of the metric will be 100%.

2. Attributes measured at the work-unit level: An example of this type of attribute is *billing accuracy.* The performance of this attribute cannot be measured at the customer level, since each customer in a group may not receive a bill. However, the performance cannot be measured at the customer-group level either, since there may be instances where several customers in a group receive bills. This attribute is therefore most appropriately measured at the level of the *individual bill.* In each time period of the simulation, the percentage of accurate bills produced is calculated based on the number of departing customers in that period. These percentages are aggregated across all time periods to produce an overall measure of billing accuracy. For a perfect process, all the bills produced in every time interval will be accurate. The value of this metric will therefore be 100%.

3. Attributes measured at the time period level: The metrics for the customer service attributes such as friendliness and responsiveness are not defined at the individual customer level. Let us see why this is so.

As Table 7.13 shows, the quality of the customer service attributes depends on the utilization level of the waiter. In any time interval, if the waiter is overutilized and cannot operate at the desired level of friendliness or responsiveness, the service quality of *every* customer who happens to be dining at that waiter station will be affected. Therefore, it does not make sense to think of customer service in terms of an individual customer. Instead, in each time period, the quality of customer service is determined by evaluating whether the service level meets or exceeds the standards (for all customers). The overall quality is then given by the percentage of time periods during which the performance standards were met. If the processes perform perfectly, the desired service level will be met or exceeded at every instant throughout the duration of the simulation. The value of the metric will be 100%.

Results from restaurant simulation model

The model was executed twenty times with different random numbers. These may be interpreted as twenty weekday evenings at the restaurant for the duration of a month. These runs produced twenty values for each metric in Table 7.11. For each metric, the minimum, maximum, average, and standard deviation of these twenty values were computed. These values, presented in Table 7.18, are presented in decreasing order of attribute importance (see Table 3.9).

Table 7.18   Performance statistics from twenty simulated evenings at the restaurant

Attribute	*Metric*	*Min*	*Max*	*Ave*	*Std*	*Ok?*
Greeting friendliness	% time periods meeting standards	100	100	100	0	Y
Meal service friendliness	% time periods meeting standards	93	100	99	2	N
Leavetaking friendliness	% time periods meeting standards	99	100	100	0	Y
Meal service responsiveness	% time periods meeting standards	93	100	99	2	N
Meal delivery interval	% customers with interval > 10 and < 11.5 mins.	0	35	16	10	N
Order-taking patience	% time periods meeting standards	100	100	100	0	Y
Menu delivery interval	% customers with interval < 5 mins	100	100	0	0	Y
Order-taking interval	% customers with interval < 5 mins	75	100	92	8	N
Knowledge of menu	% time periods meeting standards	100	100	100	0	Y
Bill production accuracy	% bills produced without error	99	100	99	0	Y
Bill settlement accuracy	% bills settled without error	99	100	100	0	Y
Problem resolution effectiveness	% time periods meeting standards	93	100	99	2	N

In Table 7.18, attributes that meet the standards close to 100% with small performance variability are marked with a "Y" in the last column. The design of these attributes is assumed to be acceptable, and no further modification is immediately necessary, though improvements may be considered in the future. On the other hand, the rows listed in bold in Table 7.18 are the attributes that do not meet the performance standards, as indicated by the "N" in the last column.

The attributes that do not meet the standards can be divided into three categories, listed below in order from most serious to least serious.

1. Attributes that perform so poorly that a complete redesign of the associated process is required

2. Attributes that do not perform satisfactorily and that may require some modifications to the associated process design

3. Attributes whose average performance is close to the standards, but that demonstrate a degree of performance variability that may be cause for concern

In the next detailed design activity (Activity 6), each attribute whose performance is unsatisfactory must be analyzed in detail, the causes for unsatisfactory performance should be determined, and design modifications and redesign solutions should be identified. In the next section, we will show how this is done.

7.6 ANALYZING AND MODIFYING DESIGNS—DETAILED DESIGN ACTIVITY 6

In the previous section, we defined three categories of attributes that did not meet the design performance standards. From Table 7.18, we can easily identify the attributes of the Service Edge restaurant that correspond to each category. An example of the first category in Table 7.18 is the *meal delivery interval*, with an average of only 16% of customers experiencing the desired interval. An attribute belonging to the second category is the *order-taking interval*. An average of 92% of the customers experience service that meets the design standard, but the percentage is as low as 75% on some evenings. Attributes of the third type are the *friendliness and responsiveness of meal service*. For these attributes, satisfactory service levels are experienced for 99% of the time periods on the average, but the performance varies between 93 and 100%. We will now describe the analysis of each of these attributes.

1. Processes needing total redesign—the meal delivery interval

As mentioned above, the meal delivery interval demonstrates the worst performance in Table 7.18, meeting the standards for only 16% of the customers on the average over twenty evenings and for only 35% of the customers on the best evening. Figure 7.7 shows the percentage of meals that are delivered in less than 10 minutes and more than 11.5 minutes for each of the 20 evenings. It can be seen that as many as 80% of the meals are delivered in under 10 minutes for some evenings, and on other evenings, 60% of the meals may take over 11.5 minutes to deliver.

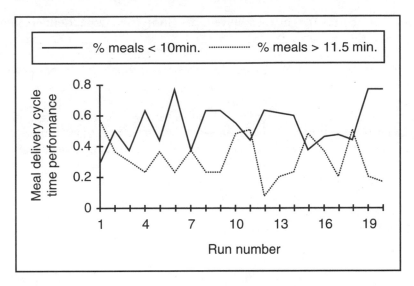

Figure 7.7   Meal delivery cycle time performance from simulation

Figure 7.8 shows the average meal delivery interval for each run of the simulation, where the average is taken across all the customers who are simulated during the run. The horizontal line shows the performance standard of 11.5 minutes. It can be seen from the figure that only two out of the twenty evenings result in an average delivery interval that is between 10 and 11.5 minutes.

These results show that this design of the meal delivery process needs to be significantly modified. From Figure 7.8, it appears that the average performance of the design on the attribute is highly unpredictable, varying from as little as 9 minutes to as much as 16 minutes. And since this is the variability in the *average* in-

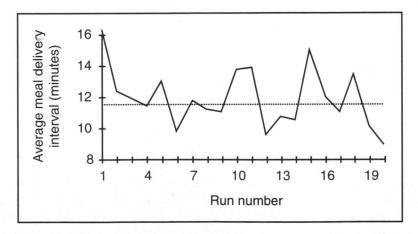

Figure 7.8   Average meal delivery interval from simulation

terval, this suggests a larger variability in the individual meal delivery times experienced by the customers.

The variability in performance could come from various causes, such as the following:

1. Design instability: The design is unable to quickly adjust to changes in operating characteristics, so that small changes in the arrival rate of customers or in the ordering rate cause large shifts in performance. Even if the performance function indicates that the process can deliver the required performance across the operating range on the average, sudden *changes* in the operating conditions may cause rapid fluctuations in process performance.

2. High unit-to-unit performance variability: There is a high degree of variability in the meal preparation process, either from cook to cook or from item to item.

3. Unbalanced use of resources: An inefficient order distribution system in the kitchen causes uneven utilization of kitchen staff. This may cause some staff members to be over-utilized and others to be underutilized, so that some orders are completed earlier than required while others are completed later than required.

Whatever the reason, the meal delivery process needs to be evaluated and redesigned. The team must return to the design alternatives generation step described in Chapter 6 (Section 6.2), and generate new design alternatives that can be re-evaluated and tested. If it is not possible to redesign the process, the design team should revisit the concept and investigate the possibility of a whole different approach to meal delivery.

2. Processes needing modification but not redesign— the order-taking interval

From Table 7.18, we can see that averaged over the twenty evenings, 8% of the customers experience intervals that are greater than 5 minutes in duration. Figure 7.9 shows this percentage for each of the twenty simulation runs. It can be seen from this figure that as many as 25% of the customers are affected on some evenings. Some modifications to the design are therefore needed.

Figure 7.10 shows the average value of the order-taking interval for all the customers on a given evening. It can be seen from this figure that the average interval is fairly stable at 4.5 minutes or less, except for two instances where it is higher than the 5-minute design standard. This relatively stable average, which occurs despite the wide variability in the percentage of customers who experience unacceptable service from one evening to the next (Figure 7.9), indicates a high degree of customer-to-customer variability in the order-taking interval. On most evenings, it appears that many short intervals compensate for a few very long ones, leading to an acceptable average performance. On some evenings, indicated by the spikes

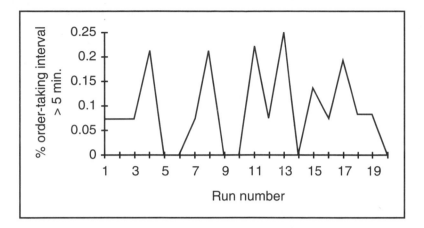

Figure 7.9 Order-taking interval performance from simulation

in Figure 7.10, this fails to happen, and the average order-taking interval fails to meet the standards. Some improvements to increase the robustness of the design and lower the variability of the order-taking interval are therefore necessary.

The customer-to-customer variability in the order-taking interval can be seen in Figure 7.11, where we plot the value of this interval for fifteen random customers. While most of these customers experience an order-taking interval that is shorter than 5 minutes, the jagged nature of the graph shows how the performance varies.

What could be the reason for this variability? Recall the design of the order-taking process for the Service Edge restaurant. Customers read their menu from a screen that displays the menu for 2 minutes. Once customers have ordered, their order is

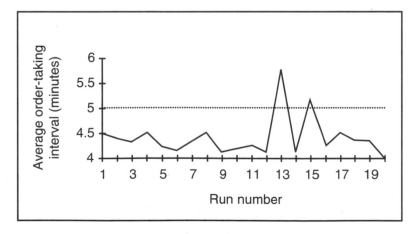

Figure 7.10 Average order-taking interval for each evening

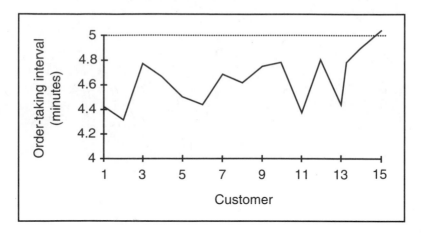

Figure 7.11   Order-taking interval for fifteen random customers

sent to the waiter station, where it waits until a waiter is available to validate the order with the customers. Once the validation is complete, the order is sent to the kitchen for preparation.

Given the design of this process, the variability in performance can come from either the *ordering* part of the process or from the *validation* part. If the variability is in the ordering part, then the source of the variability is the *customer*. It may be that some customers just take longer to read the menu and place their order. Clearly, this is not a design problem; at most some customer education might be required to ensure that customers who take a long time to order do not expect their entire order-taking interval to be shorter than five minutes. One way of achieving this could be by setting an expectation that a customer's order will be validated and sent to the kitchen within three minutes of ordering. This will ensure that the overall interval is five minutes or less for customers who complete their orders within two minutes. For customers who take more than two minutes to order, the overall interval will be longer. If customers are unwilling to accept this scenario, then it may be necessary to redesign the process to provide the restaurant with more control over process performance.

Let us assume for the purposes of this example that there is no variability in the ordering part. The variability in performance is therefore in the validation part. In this case, we need to identify the operating characteristics that affect the time taken to validate the order. What operating characteristic is likely to have the greatest influence on the validation interval? Recall that the only manual part of this process is the validation of the order performed by the waiter. As shown by the performance function in Figure 7.2 (a), the time taken for this activity is a function of waiter utilization. It is therefore conceivable that the variability in performance could be due to variability in the waiter utilization level over the course of the evening.

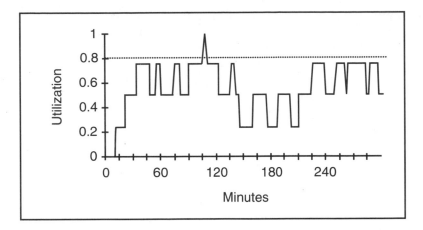

Figure 7.12   Waiter utilization levels on a random evening

To test this, we plot the waiter utilization for a random evening, and for evening 13, which corresponds to the run with the exceptionally high order-taking cycle time in Figure 7.10. The results are shown in Figures 7.12 and 7.13.

It can be seen from these figures that there is indeed a high degree of variability in the utilization from minute to minute during the course of both evenings. In Figure 7.12, the utilization varies between 0.25 and 0.75. In Figure 7.13, the same kind of variability is evident, except that there are several instances where the utilization is close to 1. Since the relationship between the order validation wait time and the waiter utilization is nonlinear [see Figure 7.2 (a)], high utilizations result in a disproportionate increase in the validation wait time, and consequently in the overall interval.

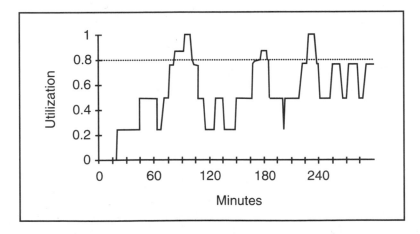

Figure 7.13   Waiter utilization levels for simulation run 13

In this example, therefore, the variability in the order-taking interval can be attributed to the variability in waiter utilization. The same variability is evident in both Figures 7.12 and 7.13, except that the overall utilization in Figure 7.13 is higher, leading to poorer performance than usual on that particular day. Clearly, therefore, the fact that the average performance of the order-taking interval is generally acceptable in Figure 7.10 is not because of an intrinsically robust design, but because the variability in the operating characteristics on an average evening is not enough to stress the design. Should the arrival rate of customers change so that the waiter utilization on a typical evening looks more like Figure 7.13, then the design performance is in danger of rapidly deteriorating. It is therefore important to consider modifications to the design that will make its performance less sensitive to the variations in waiter utilization.

Solutions for reducing the variability of the order-taking process performance

What options are available for improving the performance of the order-taking process? We can consider the following four alternatives:

1. Reduce the variability in utilization by carefully controlling resources (operational solution)

2. Reduce the average order-taking interval through process improvements

3. Reduce the sensitivity of the order validation wait time to utilization (flatten slope of performance equation)

4. Reduce random variability in waiter performance

Let us discuss each of these.

Solution 1—better control of resources: This solution does not address the design, but attempts to improve the performance by controlling the operations. The change in utilization from minute to minute occurs because of variability in the arrival rate of customers and random variability in waiter performance. If historical data is available to accurately predict the arrival rate into the restaurant in 15-minute segments, then it is possible to control the supply of waiters so that the utilization remains approximately constant. This would involve staggering the reporting time of waiters so that more waiters are available when the arrival rate is high, and fewer are available when the arrival rate is low. Many service industries (such as airlines) have developed sophisticated scheduling algorithms to determine optimal staffing requirements during every hour of the day.

This kind of solution is appropriate for fine-tuning the performance of a design *after* implementation, when enough historical data is available to identify systematic demand patterns. However, in the design stage, it is better to seek solutions that are *intrinsically* robust to changes in operating characteristics. This provides a more solid foundation on which future operational solutions can be imposed.

Solution 2—reduce average interval: This solution does not directly address the variability issue. Instead, it attempts to ensure that the standards are met even if the performance is unpredictable by improving the average performance. For example, if improvements could be made to reduce the average order-taking interval from the 4.5 minutes in Figure 7.10 to 3.5 minutes, then the process may meet the standards even under conditions of extreme variability.

This approach is superior to the previous one because its emphasis is on improving the process design. However, while improving the average performance level is not undesirable in itself, it should not be used as a substitute for reducing performance variability. The design that is created as a result of the evaluation steps in Section 7.1 should be an optimal design from the perspective of average performance. If a design solution is available that reduces the order-taking interval by a minute, it should be implemented for its own sake and the variability around this interval should then be further reduced. But this solution should not be pursued to make up for unreliability in design performance.

Solution 3—reducing the sensitivity of wait time to utilization: This solution is focused on reducing the sensitivity of the average order validation wait time to changes in utilization. This requires changes to the design that reduce the slope of the performance function, especially in the nonlinear parts of the curve. Why does the order validation interval depend on the utilization? The reason is that the validation needs to be performed by the waiter. If all tables are occupied, it may take some time for the waiter to arrive at the table and validate the order.

An obvious solution is to remove the order validation step. The process design can be modified so that the customer order is directly transmitted to the kitchen without passing through the waiter station for validation. This solution has the additional benefit of reducing the overall waiter utilization, since it does away with some of the activities that the waiter needs to perform.

However, this is not a viable solution, since it violates the design concept. The reader will recall that when the concepts were evaluated in Chapter 5 (Section 5.4), the validation step was explicitly introduced to provide a human face to an automated process. Removing this step will affect the customers' perception of the friendliness of the service. This trade-off indicates a general principle to be kept in mind when the design team considers opportunities for design modification. Because processes are interrelated, changes to a process to improve one attribute may negatively affect the performance of other processes and other attributes. Each potential modification to a process should therefore be carefully evaluated to assess its impact on the entire service design.

Since it is not feasible to remove the validation step, the design team needs to look for solutions that improve the efficiency of the validation task. This can be done in several ways. For example, the process can be designed so that the order validation for all guests at the restaurant is the responsibility of a single "guest service representative." This could be the only function performed by this person, and therefore order validation would not compete with the other tasks that need to be performed by the waiter. Another option is to utilize a waiter's time more efficiently by combining the validation activity with other tasks. For example, instead of the waiter having to return to the station to check whether an order is ready for validation, a call light could be turned on at the table when the order is complete (similar to the light summoning a flight attendant to a particular seat when the call button is pressed). The waiter could then validate the order in conjunction with some other tasks such as delivering a meal to a nearby table. This would have the double benefit of reducing both the ordering interval and some waiter stress. This solution could be combined with a facility design that placed the waiter station close to the tables—the waiter can then see customers completing their orders and may be able to walk over immediately for validation.

Solution 4—reducing random variability in waiter performance:

At any level of utilization, random variation in the order validation time can result from a variety of causes. Clearly, there is some dependence between the number of customers at a table and the validation time. Shorter validation times may be the effect of tables with one or two guests. Other factors may also contribute. Some customers may wish to converse with the waiter; similarly, some waiters may be more talkative than others. Shorter intervals may be seen when a waiter is in a hurry and rushes through the validation task. Other random causes will also affect the validation interval.

In general, random variability can be reduced by standardizing or systematizing a process, by increased levels of automation, or by enhanced training. The design solution should try to eliminate both very long and very short ordering intervals. Very short ordering intervals may leave the customer feeling rushed. Also, customers who randomly experience short or long intervals during several visits to a restaurant may feel that the service is sloppy and uncoordinated. Solutions should therefore seek to consistently drive the order-taking interval as close to the average of 4.5 minutes as possible.

One method of achieving this is to require all waiters to follow a script to interact with the customers. This script may be a series of questions that need to be asked in sequence. Another solution may be to design the display of the customers' order on the waiter's terminal or printout in such a way that validation can be easily accomplished by systematically checking off a series of fields.

Clearly, a balance must be maintained between the efficiency gains from standardization and the potential loss of spontaneity and responsiveness. The design improvements must seek to reduce variability that occurs because of improper or inefficient implementation of the process, but must strive to keep some flexibility in the process to allow the waiter to provide a personal touch to each encounter. Customers are not likely to appreciate a waiter who follows the script like a robot without any accommodation of personal styles and interaction needs.

Selecting the best solution

We have discussed four ways to modify the design or operations of a process so that the effect of variability in the process cycle time can be mitigated. Which of these is the best approach? The answer is that a different combination of solutions may be appropriate for each specific situation. In general, the first two approaches should not be the only design solutions considered. The third and fourth types of solution (reducing impact of operating characteristics on performance, and reducing random variability) are the most promising at this stage, and should be pursued most diligently. Several options may be available for each solution. The team has to evaluate the options in terms of their effectiveness, the resources required for their implementation, and their influence on the other design attributes. It may be necessary to simulate some of the options to test their impact on the performance of the overall service design. The best solution package that meets all the performance needs and is feasible to implement should be selected.

3. Processes needing monitoring but no immediate change— friendliness and responsiveness of service

Figure 7.14 presents results for the performance of the friendliness and responsiveness attributes for twenty runs (evenings) of the simulation. For the purposes of this example, we treat the two attributes identically. As shown in Table 7.17, the performance metric is the percentage of time increments (out of 300) in each run that the performance standards are met. Figure 7.14 shows that most evenings, the standards are met for over 98% of the time periods. The exception is evening number 13, which, as described above, saw periods of very high waiter utilization. As

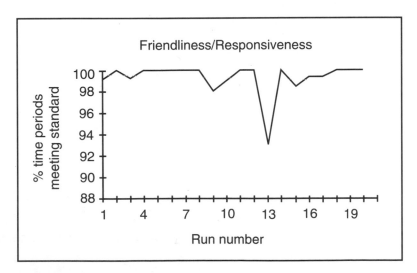

Figure 7.14:   Degree of friendliness and responsiveness from simulation

a result, the waiters were busier than usual, and did not have the time to attend to the customers in the most personal and responsive manner. This would result in a deterioration in performance for that evening. Apart from this exception, the service performance on these attributes appears to be acceptable under the current operating conditions.

The major issue with these attributes therefore is not their *current* performance, but their sensitivity to changes in the operating characteristics. The reason for this is that friendliness and responsiveness are the first and second most important attributes of the quality of restaurant service (see Table 3.9). Even though the current performance is satisfactory, it would be important to know the conditions under which the performance would begin to be unacceptable. These points are known as *failure points* of the design. Identifying the failure points serves two purposes. First, it allows the design team to decide whether modifications or improvements to the design are immediately necessary. Second, it allows the service manager to anticipate deteriorating performance after the service is implemented, and to take corrective action if the service is operating near a failure point.

Figure 7.15 shows the simulated performance of the design on the friendliness and responsiveness attributes as the arrival rate of customers to the restaurant increases. The processes are designed to perform effectively up to an arrival rate of 45 customers per hour, and Figure 7.15 shows the performance up to an arrival rate that is approximately double that amount.

The graph in Figure 7.15 shows that the performance of friendliness and responsiveness attributes is robust up to an arrival rate of about 70 arrivals/hour. Beyond this point, however, the performance deteriorates rapidly. A point between 65 and 70 arrivals per hour, say 66, can be chosen as the *failure point* for these attributes.

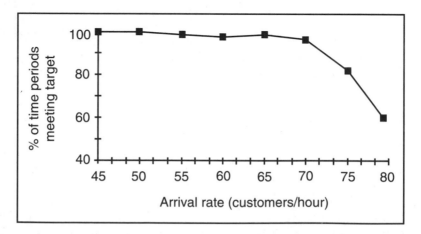

Figure 7.15   Change in friendliness and responsiveness with arrival rate

From these data, the design team should determine whether modifications to improve the robustness of the design are immediately necessary, or whether the design can be implemented at the current performance and monitored over time. The answer to this question depends on the design team's prognosis for the growth of the restaurant. If it is expected that business will grow quickly, so that arrival rates at or close to the failure point are realistic possibilities in the not-too-distant future, then design modifications must be improved at this stage. On the other hand, if the forecast is that business will remain steady, it may not be too critical to make immediate design changes. In this case, the service management team (see Chapter 9) that is responsible for the service after implementation should continuously monitor the performance of these attributes, and the arrival rate. Plans for improving the design must be developed and implemented *before* the failure point is reached.

7.7 FUNCTIONAL DESIGN—DETAILED DESIGN ACTIVITY 7

At the end of several iterative cycles of evaluation, simulation, and modification of the design, we should have a service that is both robust and capable of meeting the design performance standards. It is now time to perform activity 7 of the seven detailed design activities. This activity is the final and most detailed step in the design of the service. In this step, the design of the individual functions of each process must be specified. This includes the development of software with the performance specifications that will allow the process to meet its design standards, the detailed description of how each activity should be performed, the definition of materials for on-the-job employee training and reference, and other details that are necessary for the practical implementation of the service. At its later stages, this activity begins to overlap with *service construction*, described in Chapter 8 (Section 8.2), where the service is actually built for deployment. At this stage, other personnel may join the design team as it begins to share the functional details of the design with those responsible for its implementation and management. If properly managed, functional design can serve as the transition from the design stage to the management and improvement stage of the service process design and management model.

The fourth matrix of the QFD hierarchy, called the *subprocess/function matrix*, can be used to guide the functional design. This matrix translates the performance requirements of the subprocesses into the specifications for the process functions. The rows are the subprocess attributes from the columns of the *process/subprocess matrix* (see Table 6.7 for the process/subprocess matrix of the order-taking process); the columns are the engineering requirements for the functions. At this level, these requirements are expressed in terms of the engineering elements that are used to create the process. For example, the functional requirements may specify response requirements of hardware, the look of a menu or screen, the contents of a script to be followed by an employee, or the dimensions and weights of parts. This information is used by the implementation team members who are responsible for constructing the service. Table 7.19 shows the subprocess/function matrix for the order-taking process.

Table 7.19   Sub-process/function matrix for the order-taking process

WHATs vs. HOWs Legend		
Strong	●	9
Moderate	○	3
Weak	△	1

	Number of menu pages	Number of menu items per page	Menu display interval	Page refreshment interval	Design of help screens	Help screen retrieval interval	Number of items on order entry screen	Order acknowledgment response time	Accessing time for availability verification	Inquiry time for availability verification	Order transmission rate	Maximum time for order validation
MENU READING AND ORDERING												
Time taken to read menu	●	●	●	●								
Time taken to enter order			●	●			●					
Time available to browse menu			●		●	●						
Amount of explanation of menu items	●	●			●	●	●	●				
AVAILABILITY VERIFICATION												
Time taken to verify order availability									●	●		
ORDER VALIDATION												
Time to validate customer order								●			●	●

7.8   CONCLUSION

Summary

The following is a summary of the topics described in this chapter. The section in the chapter where a particular topic is covered is indicated in parentheses.

Evaluating design alternatives—detailed design activity 4 (7.1)

- Specify the range of operating conditions under which the design should function reliably.

- Specify design factors for each alternative and set reasonable initial values.
- Combine subprocess-level design alternatives to create feasible process designs.
- Predict the average performance of each design using the performance functions.
- Compare the predicted performance of each design with the standards.
- Evaluate the cost, implementability, and compatibility of each design with the standards.
- Select a set of candidate designs for further analysis.

Simulating service performance—detailed design activity 5 (7.2, 7.3 & 7.4)

- Specify the list of processes and their interactions.
- Specify the flow units for each process.
- Specify the key design attributes for each process/subprocess.
- Specify the performance standard for each process attribute.
- Define the operating range and initial design factor values.
- Define the performance function for each applicable design factor or operating condition.
- Define the form and parameters of the distributions for each performance attribute.

Analyzing simulation results—detailed design activity 6 (7.5 & 7.6)

- Define the appropriate metrics for measuring service performance.
- Identify the processes that need to be completely redesigned.
- Identify the processes whose designs need to be modified.
- Identify the processes whose robustness needs to be improved.
- Perform the necessary design modifications.

Perform design of process functions (7.7)

- Use the fourth matrix of the QFD hierarchy (subprocess/function matrix).
- Use subprocess specifications as matrix rows.
- Use function specifications as matrix columns.
- Specify detailed functional requirements for the design.

- Identify service construction team members.
- Transition design to service construction team.

Suggested Reading

The following texts are recommended for further reading on the topics covered in this chapter. This is not an exhaustive list, but a collection that provides a good overview of different aspects of these topics. Some of these texts have already been referenced in this chapter.

For a discussion of simulation, Law, and Kelton (1991) is a detailed but difficult-to-read text on how to use simulation for practical modeling applications. Pidd (1992) is a readable introduction to the concepts of discrete simulation, and the simulation of events, activities and processes. It provides Pascal programs that can be used as modules for a variety of applications.

For an overview of statistics and distributions, Masson (1986) includes more than ten chapters of information on distributions and how they are used. The text is very comprehensive. Hildebrand and Ott (1987) is a basic statistics text covering most important topics. Larsen and Marx (1986) is another basic text, at a slightly higher mathematical level. It includes good examples.

Part

3

Management and Improvement

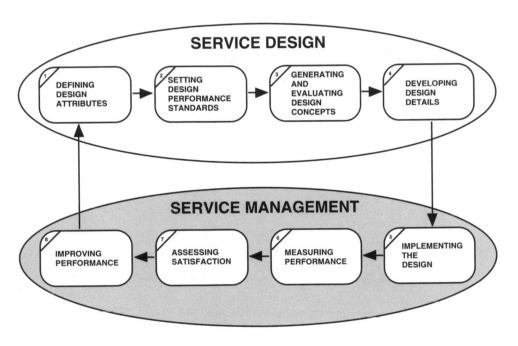

Chapter
8
Implementing the Design

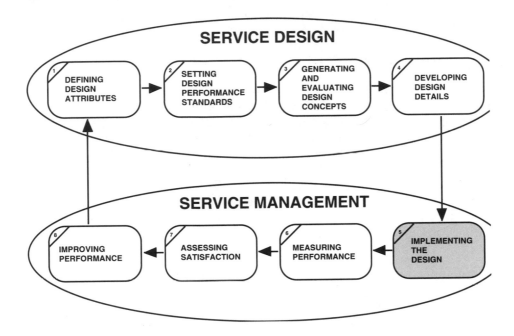

- *Design implementation plan*
- *Service construction plan*
- *Testing plan*
- *Communications plan*
- *Rollout and transition plan*
- *Service management plan*
- *Conclusion*

In this chapter, we describe Stage 5 of the service design and management model. This stage is a transition between the design stages (1, 2, 3, 4) and the management and improvement stages (5, 6, 7). In the preceding chapters (3 through 7), we described methods for developing processes that consistently deliver the level of performance desired by the customers of the service. In the following three chapters (9, 10, and 11), we will discuss how the operations of these processes must be managed so that they are able to sustain their expected performance, and how they can be modified and improved to anticipate or respond to changing customer expectations.

Between design and management lies *implementation*, which is the topic of this chapter. We describe the steps that are needed to transform the design—which, so far, is a set of decisions on paper—into a working service. Specifically, we emphasize the activities required to *plan* for the implementation, so that the new service is rolled out in a smooth and coordinated manner and can function efficiently from the first day of operations.

The success in the market of even the best-designed service is determined by how effectively it is implemented. The implementation critically affects the quality of the service provided to its customers. Recall from Chapter 1 (see Figure 1.1) that the quality of a service is determined by the balance between the *stable, reproducible elements* and the *customized, personal elements* of service provision. The design implementation process affects both of these elements. If the implementation is incomplete, disorganized, or untested, the deployed service cannot reliably meet the performance standards expected by the design. Moreover, the service can rarely delight customers with extraordinary individualized service, since much of the employees' resources will be used to compensate for these deficiencies in performance. Therefore, customers experience neither stable service nor personal attention.

Another factor that determines the ability of a new design to provide sustained high-quality service is the extent to which the employees of the organization actively support the design. This is also determined by how the design is implemented. The implementation stage is a time of great uncertainty for the company. Up to this stage, most activities have been performed by the design team, with little direct participation from other employees. Many employees may have heard of impending changes only through rumors, and uncertainty and fear may foster a negative predisposition to the new design. The implementation is usually the first time that the details of the design are presented to the general population of employees. An implementation process that is not perceived as being open and honest, or one that does not actively encourage the participation of all employees, will only reinforce the feelings of alienation or suspicion. Under these circumstances, it is very difficult to create an environment within which exceptional, customer-delighting service quality can be delivered.

In summary, therefore, the implementation process should involve and engage all employees. The key components of the implementation should be decentralized to encourage the participation of employees from all parts of the organization. Moreover, the implementation should be customized to the particular organizational culture and environment within which the service is to perform. These requirements should be carefully planned into the implementation process.

Table 8.1 Design implementation steps

Step	Planning	Execution	Execution level
1	Plan implementation strategy	Coordinate implementation tasks	Organization
2	Coordinate service construction	Construct service	Organization
3	Develop testing plan	Pilot and test service	Selected work location
4	Plan regular communications	Communicate with employees and customers as planned	Work location
5	Develop rollout and transition plan	Manage change during transition	Organization/ work location
6	Plan ongoing management of service	Continue to monitor service performance	Work group

What steps are needed to translate the design into a working service and to manage this service through its life? Six steps are shown in Table 8.1:

- Implementation strategy
- Service construction
- Piloting and testing
- Communications
- Rollout and transition
- Service management

The *implementation strategy* is the blueprint that determines how the different parts of the implementation are completed and coordinated. *Service construction* refers to the development of the systems, the documentation of process functions and procedures, and the training of employees needed to realize the design. *Testing* involves the development of a pilot or prototype of the design. *Communications* are the means by which customers, employees and management are informed about the features of the new service, especially if it is significantly different from current operations. *Rollout* refers to the logistics of preparing the organization for the changes resulting from the new design. Finally, *service management*, which is the primary focus of Chapters 9, 10, and 11, comprises the activities that need to be performed to monitor and improve the performance of the service over time.

Notice that each step in Table 8.1 has two functions. The first is a *planning* function, in which the activities that need to be performed, their sequence, the time frame, and the persons responsible for their execution are identified. The second is an *execution* function, where the planned activities are accomplished. We have distinguished between the two functions to emphasize the point that planning is a separate and indispensable part of the implementation process. We cannot overstate its importance. It is a matter of common sense that something cannot be implemented without a knowledge of what needs to be done, when, and by whom. Yet, in many cases, implementation teams view planning as a waste of time and are anxious to "get down to the real thing." This results in a chaotic descent into detailed execution, resulting in poor coordination and a disorganized implementation that takes time and effort in the future to stabilize and correct. Some initial time spent in planning can often avoid a lot of rework later.

For this reason, our approach in this chapter emphasizes the *planning* aspects of design implementation, i.e., we describe what should be done. We concentrate less on the execution and control of the plan. For example, we do not describe what to do when the plans are not being followed or the schedules are not met, or how employees should be motivated to adopt the new service, or the role of senior management in overcoming resistance to change. These are important topics, but many texts on project management, team empowerment, and change management discuss them in the detail they deserve. The suggested reading at the end of this chapter refers the reader to some of these texts.

Table 8.1 also presents the organizational level at which each implementation step is carried out. An increasing amount of decentralization takes place as we move from planning the implementation strategy to managing the service. This is consistent with the general objective of providing employees with the ownership of their operations. The testing, training, communications, and management functions are performed locally under the coordination of the overall project plan which is constructed for the entire organization. This encourages local participation while ensuring a common implementation across the organization.

Each section of this chapter describes the planning of one of the six steps in Table 8.1. Each step is generically referred to as a *plan*. Step 1 (implementation strategy) is defined in the *design implementation plan,* and the other steps form the *component plans.* Each plan is presented in the following format:

- The activities that need to be planned

- The structure of the team implementing the plan

- The scheduling and coordination requirements to ensure the smooth execution of the plan

The design implementation plan is described in Section 8.1. Planning the construction of the service is described in Section 8.2. Designing a pilot implementation is the topic of Section 8.3, and communications planning that of Section 8.4. Planning for rollout and transition from existing operations to the new design is discussed in Section 8.5. Section 8.6 describes the plan for managing the performance of the service after the implementation is completed. Section 8.7 is a chapter summary.

8.1   DESIGN IMPLEMENTATION PLAN

The design implementation plan is a "plan of plans" that oversees the implementation and integration of each component plan. It serves as the framework for managing the entire implementation, and at any time provides a high-level overview of the status of the project. The plan is executed by the *design implementation team*. This team is the "steering committee" for the entire implementation and is responsible for coordinating all implementation activities and for communicating the progress of the design deployment to senior management. The team is also the primary link to the design team for initiating any major design modifications, though individual design team members will be associated with component teams to make small, localized changes to the design as necessary.

Activities included in the design implementation plan

The following overall project level activities should be incorporated in the design implementation plan:

1. Specification of the objectives of each component plan

2. Identification of the leaders of each component team

3. Coordinating the timelines of the component plans

4. Communicating progress of implementation to senior management and customers

5. Resolving unexpected timing and implementation conflicts

Design implementation team structure

The overall project plan is created and managed by the *design implementation team*. Figure 8.1 shows the composition of this team. As is evident from the figure, the design implementation team has representatives from each component team and from the design team. The design implementation team representatives from the component teams should have the ability to influence changes in their respective teams to reflect decisions made at the overall project level. For example, if the pilot test is delayed, it may be necessary to adjust the communication and rollout schedules. It is therefore preferable for the team leaders of each component team to be the members of the design implementation team.

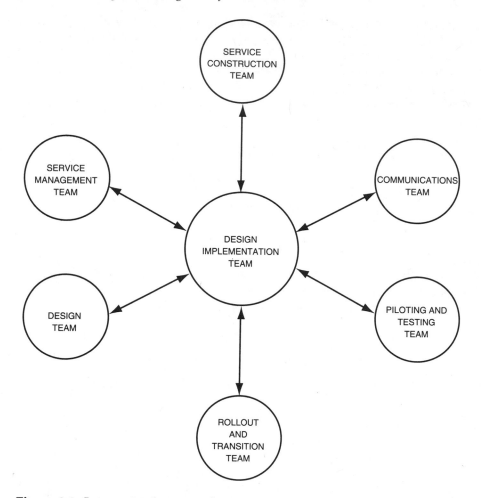

Figure 8.1 Interaction between design implementation team and component teams

The design implementation team should be supported by a *project mentor* or *champion*. This is usually a senior manager who acts as the sponsor for the project. The role of the champion should be to encourage, coach, and motivate the team members and to facilitate communication between the project team and other members of senior management. The team should also contain *subject matter experts* as extended or part-time members. For example, it is useful for a professional trained in the principles of quality management to be part of the team as a facilitator and guide. Personnel skilled in project and change management may also be to involved to advise and direct the team.

The design implementation team is best managed as a self-directed team of equals. This does not mean that all members of the team should be at the same hierarchical level in the organization. Organizational level should not be a criterion for membership to the team. Instead, the team members should be chosen for their understanding of the vision of the design and for their ability to effectively lead their individual teams to implement the details of the design. Each member of the team should have an equal voice, and all team members should share the responsibility for directing the course of the project. Facilitation, logistics, and meeting management functions usually performed by a team leader should be rotated among all members of the team.

Scheduling and coordination requirements

Since the design implementation plan is the road map for managing the entire project, procedures should be developed to ensure that the plan is systematically executed and that its activities are effectively coordinated. Some elements that should be included in these procedures are the following:

- Frequency of face-to-face meetings

- Frequency of telephone meetings

- Medium of communication among team members (paper, fax, electronic mail)

- Project milestones and critical dates

- Frequency of communication to senior management

- Process for issuing timely warning about delays or impediments

These procedures should be finalized and documented during the first few meetings of the implementation team. They should then be diligently followed, and should be the framework for establishing schedules and coordination requirements for the component plans.

8.2   SERVICE CONSTRUCTION PLAN

Service construction is the largest and most important segment of design implementation. The service is "built" during service construction. The service construction activities include the documentation of the procedures needed to operate the service, the development of the systems supporting the delivery of the service, and the training of personnel. The service construction plan systematically documents the details of these activities and the scheduling and coordination requirements for their effective completion.

Activities included in the service construction plan

The following are the most important activities that should be incorporated into the service construction plan:

Overall planning:

1. Identify service construction team members.

2. Identify subteam leaders and subteam members.

A. Operating procedures:

1. Specify functions or processes for which operating procedures should be written.

2. Define medium for storing operating procedures (e.g., paper, electronic storage).

3. Define format for operating procedures (e.g., index cards, book with index, electronic storage with index, electronic storage with on-line keyword search capabilities).

4. Specify distribution of operating procedures (e.g., paper copy at each desk, centralized paper copy at each work site, electronic access at each desk, centralized electronic access, distributed to supervisors).

5. Develop links between procedures and other necessary process documentation (such as flow charts, instruction sheets, and performance reports).

6. Write the procedures for each appropriate function.

B. Systems development and integration:

1. Evaluate and select hardware/software options that meet the functional design specifications (e.g., mainframe or networked desktop systems, internal development or off-the-shelf software).

2. Define system integration requirements (e.g., common hardware and software to be used by all processes, customer information databases shared by all systems, common format for all input screens).

3. Define user-interface requirements for each system (e.g., screen display format, menu appearance, keyboard or mouse interface).

4. Define reporting requirements for each system (e.g., prespecified reports distributed at regular intervals, prespecified reports available on demand, real-time user-generated reports).

5. Develop and integrate the various system elements as required.

C. Organizational design:

1. Specify the skills required for performing each subprocess or function.

2. Define job categories that meet these skills.

3. Specify organizational structure to manage and support the operation of the service.

D. Training requirements and delivery plans:

1. Define training requirements for each job function (e.g., operating procedures, use of systems, interaction with customers).

2. Identify any training required for customers (e.g., on new service features).

3. Specify how the training for each job function and customers will be delivered (e.g., classroom training with instructor, classroom training with video, documentation, job aids).

4. Develop appropriate materials for each job function and customers (e.g., manuals, computer programs, videotapes).

Service construction team structure

The service construction plan is executed by a *service construction team.* Apart from the design team, the service construction team is the most critical for the successful implementation of the design. It is therefore very important to select the members of this team carefully. The choice of team leader is especially important. This person should have the breadth to understand the design team's vision, but at the same time should have a good knowledge of the implementation details. The team leader should be able to manage the details of the implementation without losing sight of the intent of the overall design concept. Moreover, the leader should be able to impart this intent to the other team members.

For small projects, the same team that is responsible for the detailed design may also construct the service, but this is difficult for large projects. There are several reasons for this. First, a large project requires more resources than the design team can provide. Second, a good design team should consist of members who are familiar with, but are not immersed in, the day-to-day details of existing service operations. This gives the team the objectivity and the distance needed to generate innovative design ideas, but does not give them the intimate familiarity with the details required to deploy the design in an operational environment. Third, involving other members of the organization in the implementation process broadens the base of support for the design within the organization.

For these reasons, it is preferable for the service construction team to have different members than the design team. However, the two teams should remain closely connected, and some design team personnel should be full-time members of the service construction team. This will help to ensure that the design team's intent is accurately interpreted throughout the implementation process.

The service construction team members should clearly understand the impacts of the implemented design on the day-to-day operations and on the users (customers) of the service. The members of this team should therefore be chosen from personnel who will be responsible for the operation of the new design, and the team leader should be a future manager of the new service. In addition, this team should contain members who will provide the links to the sales, advertising, and customer-education organizations. It is important to select team members who are able to overcome their resistance to change, and who are willing and open to adopt new concepts and ways of doing work. All processes and functions affected by the design should be represented in the service construction team.

The actual work of constructing the various parts of the service may be performed by one or more *subteams*. For example, there may be a systems development subteam, consisting of members who are systems requirement writers and programmers, led by a manager who will be responsible for ongoing system maintenance during regular operations. The responsibility of this subteam would be to complete the development of the system or systems that are needed to support the processes. Another subteam may use educational technologists and trainers to assist with the development of training materials. The service construction team leader should coordinate the activities of the various subteams. Team facilitators may assist the leader in this task.

Scheduling and coordination requirements

The service construction team must function as a single cohesive entity with all team members available and involved through the duration of the service construction project. It is often more difficult to find dedicated resources to staff implementation teams than it is for design teams. The reason is the difference in the organization's perception of the role of each team. The design team is viewed as being removed from everyday business; management is therefore usually more willing to let the team members dedicate themselves to the design task. Implementation, on the other hand, is assumed to be a transition that can be carried out as a natural extension of one's work; dedicating resources to this task is not perceived to be a need. Very often, team members are selected only because they are immediately available, with no thought about their long-term ability to remain involved. This practice ultimately affects the quality of the implementation.

In order to maximize the availability and involvement of all team members, the enumeration and scheduling of the service construction activities should be one of the first priorities of the team, and should be completed in the first few team meetings. The schedules should be based on the following considerations:

- The estimated time taken for each activity

- The sequence in which the activities need to be performed (e.g., training documents cannot be written for a job function until procedures are complete)

- Activities that need to be performed simultaneously

- Activities with the greatest uncertainty and possibility of delay (e.g., systems development may be more uncertain than procedures documentation)

- Activities that need to be completed to meet the testing schedule

- Activities that need to be completed before communication to customers or advertising can begin

Once the schedule is complete, team members should be asked to commit to being available and involved during this period. Alternates must be found for members who cannot guarantee their availability. As far as possible, all changes in team membership must be completed at this early stage of the project. Replacements made later in the project severely disrupt the cohesiveness of the team.

In addition to the schedule, the following are some other items whose specification in the early stages of the project facilitates the coordination of the service construction activities:

- The day or days of the week when team meetings are scheduled (the same day should be chosen every week to facilitate planning)

- A procedure for setting team meeting agendas

- The format of team meetings

- The medium of communication among team members (e.g., paper, fax, or shared files on network)

- A procedure for replacing team members

- A procedure for informing part-time team members about when they should participate

- A procedure for documenting progress at the team and subteam levels

- A procedure for indexing, storing, and accessing team documents

When all the activities detailed in the service construction plan are completed, the service should be ready for operation. The operations of all aspects of the service should be completely tested before the service is generally available. Some components of the service may need to be tested even as they are being developed. Testing therefore needs to be coordinated with the service construction activities. In order for the tests to be accurate and credible, and for their results to a meaningful predictor of service operations, they must be carefully planned and systematically executed. A *testing plan* needs to be developed for coordinating the testing activities. The contents of such a plan are described in the following section.

8.3 TESTING PLAN

Before the design is globally deployed, it is useful to test its performance through a *pilot implementation*. This is a limited operation of the design under controlled conditions. The pilot serves two purposes. First, it helps to test whether the major components of the design perform as expected when the service is operational. Second, it allows the team to demonstrate to customers, senior management, and other employees that the design is feasible, and so helps to build a broader base of support within the organization. The pilot could be an implementation that is restricted to a small set of customers, a few employees, or only the most important processes. This restricted scope and the controlled conditions reduce the influence of random variability from the operating environment on the results of the test. Any problems in performance observed during the pilot can then be more readily attributed to deficiencies in the design. However, care must be taken to ensure that even under the restricted scope, the operating conditions are still realistic. Results obtained from a pilot tested under excessively relaxed conditions may not apply to the normal operations of the service.

Activities included in the testing plan

The most important activities that should be incorporated into the testing plan are listed below:

1. Select the members of the testing team.

2. Select the customers to be involved in the test.

3. Select the locations for the test.

4. Specify the design characteristics to be tested.

5. Define the measures for evaluating the performance of the design during the test.

6. Conduct test, collect data, and analyze performance.

7. Determine causes of performance problems.

8. Correct deficiencies in design, implementation, and testing.

It is important to select the right customers and sites for the pilot. Some companies have a core of key customers who act as advisors to the service; some of these customers may be asked to volunteer for the pilot. Another option is to select the customers who provided the needs and benchmarks for service performance during the QFD study, though it is sometimes better to use a fresh set of customers to test the appeal of the service to a wider customer base. A third possibility is to ask customers who would be affected most by the new design to volunteer for the pilot; these would be the highest-volume customers, or those who use the most complex features of the service. For example, the Service Edge restaurant testing team may wish to select customers who dine out most frequently, or those who often visit restaurants in large groups. In some cases, especially where "back-room" process designs are being tested (i.e., those not seen by the customer), the choice may be made to use all the customers associated with a particular service location. If it is difficult to find volunteers for the pilot, the organization can provide incentives such as discount coupons or free service to customers willing to participate. In this case, the team must ensure that a broad range of customers is represented in the sample and that no selection bias (e.g., only customers who are interested in discount coupons) is present in the data.

It is preferable to test new designs at work sites where they will ultimately be deployed. Companies with multiple locations can select one or more existing sites for the trial. Such locations will provide customers and employees with a more authentic test setting than a laboratory or a prototype facility, and will facilitate a more realistic test of the design. However, in some cases it may not be possible to use an existing site without disrupting current operations, and it may be difficult to separate the test customers from the regular ones. If this is the case, or if the new design requires the construction of a new service facility, a prototype facility set up in a test lab may be used for the trial. Clearly, the test conditions at prototype facilities must simulate regular operations as closely as possible.

The design characteristics that are typically tested during a trial include the following:

- *Design completeness:* Does the design contain all the required features?

- *Design performance:* Do all processes perform to the standards in the range of operating conditions tested by the pilot? Is the random performance variability within acceptable limits? Are the resources used and their utilization within acceptable limits? Are there any aspects of the performance that fail to satisfy the test customers? Does the facility design adequately support the performance of the processes?

- *Design cost:* What are the costs of developing and implementing the design? What are the projected fixed operating costs? What are the projected variable operating costs at various levels of demand? What should be the optimal volume or revenue rate for maximum profitability?

- *Process continuity:* Do materials and information flow smoothly through the processes of the service? Are there any gaps in the design?

- *Process interface integrity:* Are the hand-offs at the process interfaces completely defined? Is there a common format for information transfer across process interfaces? Do delays and reworks occur at the interfaces because of system incompatibilities? (For example, does data entered into one system have to be manually re-entered into another to perform a different service function?)

- *Technology performance:* Do the technologies supporting the processes perform as required by the specifications? Do the systems contain the complete range of required functionality? Are the system response times acceptable? Do the screens and menus have the required fields in convenient formats? Are system-generated reports complete and accurate? Are the help menus readable and useful?

- *Documentation completeness:* Are descriptions of all process functions documented? Have procedures for performing process activities been written where required? Are these procedures easy to follow and readily accessible?

- *Training effectiveness:* Are all documents, tools, and job aids for training customers and employees complete? Is the training provided by these materials complete and accurate? Are there any ambiguities or gaps in the training and instructions? Does the training produce the required performance results?

As far as possible, the performance of the service on the characteristics just listed should be carefully documented. Quantitative metrics of performance should be used where applicable. Where these are not appropriate, a systematic results documentation format should be employed for all customers and all locations where the trials are conducted. This increases the credibility of the test results. Some examples of data that can be used to measure the performance of the design characteristics described above are shown in Table 8.2.

Systematic procedures for collecting and analyzing this information should be specified in the testing plan. Performance problems that are discovered during the pilot could be due to a variety of causes: (1) the design itself could be faulty, necessitating a modification of the design; (2) the implementation could be faulty, which requires a change in the implementation details; or (3) the pilot data could be faulty, which may require a change to the performance measure or the manner in which the data is collected. Each of these situations may require a different solution approach, and possibly a different team to correct the problem. The testing plan should also explicitly document the procedures by which the performance discrepancies identified during the test will be corrected.

The testing plan should also be the starting point for identifying the potential profitability of the service. Up to this stage, the costs associated with the design have been defined very broadly. The pilot implementation is a good place to obtain estimates of the costs of implementing the design and of operating the service over time. "Break-even" analysis of the volume or revenue required to match the implementation and operating costs should be performed at this stage. It is still possible to make modifications to the design if there are any doubts about its potential profitability. Many design teams are so focused on ensuring that the implemented design meets the performance requirements that they pay no attention to cost. As a result, the service is introduced without a clear understanding of the costs of the design, and fails to make a profit. The pursuit of quality without regard to its cost is not a good formula for profitability.

Structure of the testing team

The composition of the testing team depends on how the trials are conducted. If an existing service operations center is used for the tests, the team should be a blend of service construction team members, design team members, and employees and managers from the test site. The pilot team leader may be a manager from the test

Table 8.2   Measures to test pilot design performance

Design element tested	Performance measures
Design completeness	Checklist of features not adequately provided by the design
Design performance	Process/subprocess/function performance against standards
Design costs	Fixed and variable cost data
Process continuity	Documentation of process gaps with supporting examples
Process interface integrity	1. Percent of transmission errors at each interface
	2. List of interfaces where data transformation is required
Technology performance	Performance against system functional specifications
Documentation completion	List of incomplete documents with supporting examples
Training effectiveness	Rating of training effectiveness by pilot team members

facility. If the pilot is carried out under laboratory conditions, the test may be conducted by selected members of the service construction team and the design team. In addition, the team should be supported by personnel skilled in data collection and in statistical and qualitative data analysis.

Scheduling and coordination requirements

The important coordination issues surrounding the testing plan relate to the manner in which the study should be conducted so that the results reflect the performance of the design without bias. Several factors may affect the validity of the trial results. A common error during pilot studies is to generalize results obtained from a very small and unrealistic experiment. This is because teams assume that a trial can be controlled only if every service encounter can be individually monitored. This is not true. Extreme operating conditions should not be experienced during the trial, but the testing should still be conducted within the range of anticipated normal operations. For example, consider the design of a customer service process that is expected to handle a normal volume range of 40 to 60 calls per hour. During the pilot, it is appropriate to restrict the number of calls to 45 or 50 an hour to ensure that the process is not operating at the limits of its capacity. However, it is not enough to test the design at a volume rate of 5 or 10 calls an hour when it is possible to influence the quality of each call.

Another common error is to give specialized treatment to the most important customers participating in the trial. This is especially true where customers who are likely to be most severely affected by the new design are chosen as trial customers. In an effort to keep these customers happy, pilot teams often deliver a level of service that cannot be matched in regular operations. A biased view of the design performance is therefore obtained.

A third source of bias can occur in the selection of the test site and the test team. If the teams are employees from existing sites, the managers at these sites may place their best employees on the team to demonstrate the quality of their staff. The team working on the pilot may therefore be more skilled and experienced than an average team during normal operations. This factor, especially when combined with lower-than-normal utilization levels, may produce performance levels that are significantly better than what can be achieved in regular day-to-day operations.

The duration of the trials can also affect the validity of the results. The pilot should be long enough that all the data that are needed to test the performance of the design thoroughly and completely can be collected. Characteristics of the design that need unusually long testing intervals may continue to be piloted after the rest of the service is in operation by making prior arrangements with some customers. In any case, the important point to note here is that the pilot should not be terminated *before* all design characteristics have been tested. If the initial results are positive, pilot teams often come under pressure to terminate their testing and move quickly to the final implementation stage. However, initial results are often erroneous because they may reflect the effects of unrealistic operating conditions during the initiation of the pilot or the efforts of employees trying unusually hard to achieve high performance in the first few days of the trial. The trial must be given time to reach steady state before accurate performance data can be collected.

The following considerations determine the duration for which the pilot should be implemented:

- The design characteristics that need to be tested (longer duration if many characteristics need to be tested)

- The amount of quantitative data that needs to be collected (longer duration if a large amount of data needs to be collected)

- The method used to collect this data (longer duration if data is collected manually, to incorporate learning period)

- The method by which the final version of the design will be deployed (a shorter pilot is adequate if the design is deployed in a phased manner across the organization; a longer pilot is needed if the entire organization simultaneously switches to the new design)

- The amount of disruption to current operations caused by the pilot (a short but intense pilot may be the best possible if the disruption caused is substantial)

- Other market and organizational factors (e.g., the speed with which the service needs to be introduced into the market, service construction schedules)

8.4 COMMUNICATIONS PLAN

The communications plan lists, schedules and coordinates the activities required to disseminate information about the new service and the progress of the implementation. The plan specifies who should be kept informed, how often, and by what means.

Communications activities should be planned with two target populations in mind:

- Customers of the service
- Employees of the organization who are not directly involved with the design or the implementation

Two kinds of information need to be provided to customers. The first is advertising information describing the key features and performance characteristics of the new service. This information is directed towards both current and future customers of the service. The second is a more detailed description of how the service features operate, instructions on how to use the service, or information on how to resolve service problems. This information may be provided to current customers of the service, to new customers at the time of subscription (for services such as a telephone service or a bank), or during a service encounter (e.g., instructions on using an automated ticket purchase facility). Timely and accurate communication results in more sophisticated usage of the service by the customers, and may increase the revenue produced by the service.

For example, recall the design of the ordering process for the Service Edge restaurant described in Chapters 6 and 7. Customers are required to enter their order into a terminal placed at each table. If detailed information about each menu item is provided on help screens that can be accessed from the order input screen, and easy-to-follow directions are available on how to use the help facility, guests will be motivated to select a larger and more varied range of items from the menu, since they are able to obtain information about unfamiliar dishes they would otherwise avoid. This may result in a higher average revenue per customer and may also encourage diners to return to the restaurant more often.

The second purpose of communications activities is to keep employees who do not participate in the design implementation regularly informed about its status. It is common for design teams to remain somewhat isolated from the rest of the organization when the concept and design details are taking shape. The greatest opportunity for gaining the support of the entire organization for the design is during the implementation, and this is best achieved through frequent and open communication. However, employee communication should not be confused with training. Training is obviously important, but cannot be used as a substitute for communication. Before employees are trained, they need to receive satisfactory answers to the questions "What am I getting trained on?" and "Why should I be trained?" The communication plan should be a process to provide employees with timely answers to these questions.

Activities included in the communications plan

Some of the important activities to be included in the communications plan are the following:

1. Identify the communications needs of various customer groups.

2. Determine the information to be passed on to various levels of employees.

3. Select one or more communication vehicles.

4. Specify the format and content of the information.

5. Disseminate timely and accurate information to customers and employees.

6. Collect customer and employee feedback about the quality of the communication.

7. Enhance material and delivery based on this feedback.

Structure of the communications team

For large projects affecting a number of customers, the communications plan may be executed as part of an advertising campaign or a customer education program, conducted by organizations specializing in these functions. Similarly, if a large number of employees needs to be kept informed, this task may be turned over to training managers at each work location. In both cases, members of these organizations should remain closely linked to the appropriate members of the service construction teams. For projects involving a smaller number of customers and employees, the communications activities may be carried out by the members of the service construction team or by the design implementation team, and no separate communications team may exist. However, it is still important to prepare a communications plan that is distinct from the design implementation and service construction plans. Communications activities that are buried in other plans often take low priority as the primary activities of these plans take precedence. In times of stress or schedule delays, the communications activities in these plans tend to get ignored, even though it is usually at these times that effective communications are most required. It is therefore preferable to document and manage the communications separately from the other implementation activities.

Scheduling and coordination requirements

The communications plan should schedule the sharing of information at various points throughout the implementation process. Some points where communication is especially important are the following:

- At the start of the implementation (overview of design, project goals, kickoff for sales promotions and advertising campaigns)

- At each major milestone (e.g., completion of service construction, completion of testing, beginning of rollout, before service goes into operation)

- When the new design has required major changes to existing operations (new technology to be used by customers and employees, organizational changes, customer-affecting process changes)

- At points of variance with the implementation plan (e.g., during delays, testing failures, unexpected problems)

The overall effectiveness of communication depends on two factors: its *timeliness* and its *accuracy*. The communications plan should be coordinated with the other implementation activities to ensure that these criteria are met. The timing of the promotion of new services is especially important. Poor timing may lead to disappointed or dissatisfied customers. For example, suppose customers are informed about or sold new service features before the technology or process infrastructure needed to provide these features are in place. Customers who request these features have to be told that they are not currently available. Another example of poor communication timing occurs when customers are sold new services, but information about these services has not been passed to the service representatives who receive calls from the customers with questions about the service. The representatives are therefore unaware of the existence of the service. To avoid these timing errors, internal communications within the organization must be coordinated with the project milestones so that employees are aware of new services, or of operational or organizational changes, before they are generally announced.

Procedures must also be developed as part of the communications plan to ensure the accuracy of information. It is difficult, and sometimes impossible, to correct errors in perception caused by the dissemination of inaccurate or unsupported information. As far as possible, communications to employees and customers must be supported through documentation such as brochures, photographs, slides, or videotape. The recipients of communications must also be provided with numbers and names of people to contact for additional information or clarification. All communications must clearly identify the sources of "official" information and ensure that these sources are updated regularly so that they provide current and accurate information.

8.5 ROLLOUT AND TRANSITION PLANS

As is evident from the title, this plan consists of two parts. The *rollout plan* addresses the logistics of the deployment of the new service in the organization. The sequencing and scheduling of the deployment across various locations, the preparations needed at each location, the completion of systems implementation and training for all employees, and making the required organizational changes are some of the activities included in this plan. The *transition plan* spells out how a smooth transformation from the old to the new service can be effected when existing operations are being replaced. For example, service operations involving processes that take several days to complete (for example, a telephone service installation process that requires wiring) may have to follow the old and new process methodologies simultaneously during the transition period. If the new design involves a change in systems, data may have to be transferred from the old systems to the new ones, often in a very short time. Organizational changes may require relocation for some personnel, which may have to take place without current operations being halted. The details of how these changes can be accomplished should be the focus of the transition plan. In addition, the transition plan should also include a *contingency plan* that specifies the steps that need to be taken if the new service fails after implementation. We will discuss contingency plans in more detail later in this section.

The rollout and transition plans are the blueprints that specify how the new service should be deployed. However, a satisfactory deployment cannot be achieved merely by mechanically following the steps of the plan. The success of the plan depends as much upon the sensitive management of the *human* issues associated with change as upon the systematic completion of the activities identified in the plan. A rollout of a new service may be a significant imposition on a large number of employees who are suddenly affected by the change. Systematic planning alone is not enough to address the stress, anxiety, and fear that change could cause for the organization. Therefore, in addition to the rollout and transition plan, there is a need for a broad *change management* strategy, where senior management, operational managers, design and service construction team members and other "change agents" are personally involved in minimizing the impact of change. A detailed description of the concepts and techniques for managing change in organizations is beyond the scope of this book, and the reader is referred to the text by Jick (1993) for further reading. Some other books on this topic are also suggested at the end of this chapter.

Activities included in the rollout and transition plan

The rollout plan should be a *local* document that describes the activities needed to implement the service at a particular location. If the service needs to be deployed at multiple locations, a separate plan must be prepared for each location, though the plans may look identical to each other in structure and format.

The following are some of the important activities that need to be incorporated in the rollout and transition plan:

1. Specify deployment date.

2. Define and sequence the activities that need to be completed before the deployment date, such as the following:

   - Facility planning

   - Relocation of employees to new functions

   - Hardware and software acquisition

   - Training of all employees

   - Documentation acquisition and distribution

   - Software implementation and testing

3. Identify and sequence the activities that need to be completed on the deployment date, such as the following:

   - On-the-job training

   - Real-time resolution of problems with processes or systems

   - Real-time customer feedback data collection

   - Employee debriefing sessions (to collect employee feedback, observations, and opportunities for improvement)

   - Other real-time assistance and support to employees

4. Identify and sequence the transition activities (a few days to a few weeks after deployment) such as the following:

   - Continuation of real-time problem resolution

   - Continuation of employee debriefing sessions (these should be held every day if possible until transition is complete)

   - Termination of old processes and systems

   - Removal of old equipment and documentation, if necessary

   - Completion of employee relocation, if necessary

   - Conversion of data from old to new system

5. Develop contingency plans.

Contingency plans

There are many reasons why even the most carefully tested design may fail. A technology that functioned well as a prototype may have some problems when implemented on a large scale. For unexpected reasons, the anticipated operating conditions under which the service was tested may be different from the actual conditions immediately after the new service is implemented. For example, advance publicity about a new service may cause a surge of demand in the first few weeks after its introduction. A new service, and the processes to deliver the service, may therefore be unusually stressed in the first few days of operation. If not properly managed, this stress, combined with the natural uncertainties in performance resulting from employees who are just getting used to new processes and systems, can cause a breakdown in operations.

A contingency plan specifies the alternative strategies to be employed in the event of a failure in a newly implemented service. Such a plan could make the difference between a breakdown in service operations being an inconvenience and it being a major disaster. The plan may specify several options to deal with the contingency of a service failure. One solution is for the old processes and systems to remain operational for a few weeks, so that employees can switch back to these if necessary. Another plan may be to employ a phased implementation, in which locations switch sequentially to the new service. A location that has already completed the transition successfully may be used as a backup to service the overflow demand. Another option may be to streamline volumes by providing an incentive (such as a discount coupon, or a credit towards the next purchase) for overflow customers to return for service at a future, predetermined date.

The applicability of a contingency plan is not necessarily limited to the first implementation of a new service. Service performance failures can occur at any time in the course of normal operations, for a variety of reasons. For example, a cut cable outside the building can cause all the software supporting the processes to shut down. A new sales promotion campaign may result in a large influx of new customers. A contingency plan should be part of the service management strategy to deal with any emergency situation that may result in a restriction or termination of operations.

Structure of the rollout team

Since rollout is a local operation, a rollout team must be assembled at each location, and it must consist mainly of the employees at that location. The rollout team needs to perform two functions. First, members of the team must manage the practical details associated with the introduction and operation of the new service design at the location. Second, team members should be local agents of change to facilitate the adoption of the new service.

The rollout team therefore should consist of a variety of personnel, chosen for different reasons. Some team members are chosen because their job functions provide them with the expertise needed to ensure that the location is adequately prepared before the deployment date. For example, local training personnel should be involved in setting up information overviews and detailed training sessions. Local systems support staff should be involved in procuring the hardware, setting up networks, loading software, and testing. Quality managers should be holding "town meetings" and focus groups with employees to prepare them for the deployment and to answer any questions and concerns.

For the change management function, both local management and nonmanagement employees should be selected as team members. These members should be chosen for their understanding of the new design, their ability to communicate this understanding to other employees, their sensitivity to employees' concerns, and their standing in the organization as well-accepted mentors or champions. During the deployment and transition, these members should "walk the floors" and make themselves available to answer questions about the concepts and details of the design and to solve problems and address issues on the spot.

Scheduling and coordination requirements

A successful implementation of the design at each work location depends upon the ability of the organization to pull together the myriad details that are involved. As mentioned in the previous section, it is most efficient for the rollout to be managed by the local employees, who best understand the culture, skill sets, and facilities of their location. However, despite local differences, the same service should be duplicated at all locations. There is therefore the need for systematic coordination between the service construction team and the local rollout team. The service construction team should identify one or more contacts at each work location who are members of the rollout team and will be responsible for ensuring that the directions of the service construction team are adequately represented. The rollout plan should explicitly document the procedures for the interface between the local contacts and the members of the service construction team. Some items that should be included in these procedures are the following:

- Name and function of each contact at each work location

- List of materials, documentation, and software to be sent to each contact

- Process by which these are sent to the contacts to ensure receipt on schedule

- Process for communicating between the service construction team members and the work location contacts during deployment

- Structure, format, and content of employee briefing meetings

- Process for compiling and delivering feedback on design problems to the service construction team

In addition to specifying procedures for the interfaces, the rollout plan must ensure that all preparations are scheduled to be concluded by the deployment date at each work location. This requires all the materials, documentation, and software to be available at each location in a timely manner. The assembly and testing activities must be scheduled to take place before the deployment date. For each work location, some of the important activities that need to be scheduled in the rollout plan are the following:

- Kickoff date for deployment preparation at work location

- Date by which training materials should be received at work location

- Start and end dates for training at work location

- Date by which software should be available at work location

- End date for hardware and software installation at work location

- Start and end date for hardware and software test at work location

- Date by which process and system documentation must be available and distributed at work location

- Dates for predeployment focus groups and information sharing sessions at work location

- Deployment date at work location

- Date for completion of all employee relocation at work location

- Date by which old processes should be terminated at work location

- Date by which old systems are turned off at work location

The schedule for the delivery of software, process documents, and training manuals at the work location should be jointly negotiated and managed by the local contact and the appropriate member of the service construction team. The local activities should be planned to meet these schedules.

A separate rollout plan must be prepared for each location. The plan must be thoroughly studied and understood by those responsible for its implementation. As the rollout begins, the team must begin to carry out the activities specified in the plan. If the plan is well-thought-out and carefully coordinated, it should be possible to receive early warning of any problems, delays, or impediments that may prevent the execution of the plan. By attending to these problems promptly, the new design can be rolled out smoothly and efficiently, with minimal impact on the customers and on the employees.

8.6   SERVICE MANAGEMENT PLAN

Service management refers to the management of the service after the implementation is complete and the new design is in stable operation. Service management activities involve the systematic and regular monitoring of service performance to confirm that the design is continuing to meet the performance standards, and to identify areas where improvement may be necessary. These activities are performed by a *service management team.*

The concept of service management must be distinguished from that of the day-to-day *operations management* of the service, carried out by a *service operations* team. Consider the example of a restaurant. The operational management is carried out by the restaurant managers and their staff, whose job is to make sure that the restaurant functions smoothly from day to day. The responsibilities of the team include the hiring and management of employees, management of inventory, settlement of accounts, and opening and closing the restaurant, as well as taking care of problems that customers experience during the meal. The service operations team is therefore the first line of contact with the customers. The performance of this team has an *immediate, real-time* impact on service quality and satisfaction.

By contrast, service management activities focus more on managing the performance of the design of the service. The service management team, which must include some members from operations, serves two primary purposes. First, the team functions as a *postimplementation monitoring team* and checks for deviations in performance from the design standards, and for large deviations in cost from projected values. A service that has been properly designed and tested should meet the performance standards after implementation. Over the course of time, changes in operating conditions, obsolescence of process documentation, and replacement of experienced employees with new ones may cause the performance of the service to deteriorate. The task of the service management team is to identify areas where improvement is necessary and to plan and implement these improvements. As far as possible, this should be done *proactively,* so that problems can be anticipated and corrected before a crisis situation is reached.

The second purpose of the service management team is to function as a *postimplementation design team* and to maintain continuity between the design and the service management stages in the service design and management model. In this role, the team is responsible for *strategic service improvement*. This involves identifying the areas where improvement has the greatest impact on customer satisfaction or on customers' willingness to purchase more of the service. The team then designs improvements in these areas.

In summary, the service management functions should be different from those of everyday operations in two ways. First, they should be *strategic* in nature. Second, they should be *broader* than operations, encompassing all the functions that are needed to sell, provide, and maintain the service over time in the market. This does not mean that the service operations team should not improve their processes, and should leave all improvement efforts to the service management team. On the contrary, performance improvement at the operational level goes a long way towards maintaining the quality of the service. Moreover, the ability to influence quality through service delivery (making each service encounter special) is almost entirely within the control of operations. The day-to-day management of the service therefore has a fundamental impact on its quality.

However, a planned and sustained range of improvements that carefully targets strategic business growth areas is indispensable to the continued success of the service in the market over time. Most service operations teams have neither the span of control nor the time to develop or execute such improvement plans. There is therefore the need for a team whose primary responsibility is to coordinate and direct improvement efforts so that resources can be spent where the greatest benefits can potentially be achieved, and the profitability of the service can continue to be enhanced. The service management team fulfills this role.

Ideally, the service management team should be assembled and ready to function as soon as the service enters regular operations. Often, however, this is not the case. Process improvement is usually left to the independent, unstructured, and uncontrolled efforts of service operations teams, which do the best they can. The service management team, if one exists at all, is often not formed until months after the service is in operation. Sometimes, the team is not created until there is a crisis caused by a severe deterioration in the quality of the service and a large number of customer complaints have been received. By this time, the team is forced to reactively respond to accumulated performance problems and use all its resources to repair damage that could have been avoided by regular monitoring of the service. This leaves no time for the service management team to proactively make design improvements to the service.

To avoid this situation, the activities, schedules, resources, and coordination requirements of service management should be defined, at least in outline form, in a *service management plan*. This plan should be developed as part of the design implementation planning process, and should be in place before the deployment is complete. The key elements of such a plan are described below.

Activities included in the service management plan

Service management activities should be defined at the level of a process or other service elements (such as a service feature or the facility through which service is delivered) that can influence customer satisfaction. The following activities, addressing both short and long term objectives of the service management team, should be included in the plan:

A. Performance monitoring and stabilization:

- Measure performance of the service
- Measure cost of service and utilization of resources
- Analyze areas of unsatisfactory performance or excessive cost
- Resolve service performance problems

B. Strategic service improvements:

- Determine the satisfaction of customers with the service
- Evaluate the financial or market impact of improved customer satisfaction
- Identify attributes where satisfaction improvement has the greatest impact
- Develop service improvement alternatives for these attributes
- Determine the amount of effort to be expended on these alternatives
- Select and implement feasible and cost-effective alternatives

Structure of the service management team

Similar to many other teams that are described in this book, the service management team is a "team of teams," and it exists at many levels. At the highest level, the members of this team should be responsible for managing the performance of the *entire service*, i.e., all the features, facilities and processes. This team should therefore have members from all organizations involved in planning, selling, delivering, maintaining, and billing for the service. Some key functions that need to be represented (either as members or through delegates) on the team are the following:

- Market strategy
- Market research
- Service marketing
- Sales
- Service provisioning
- Service maintenance
- Customer service and problem resolution
- Order processing
- Billing and claims processing
- R & D
- Technology planning
- Systems development

Depending on the service, a single person may represent more than one function, or several persons can represent a single function. For example, at the level of operations of a single restaurant such as the Service Edge, all the functions can be represented by a small team consisting of managers and supervisors, waiters, hosts, cashiers, kitchen staff, and cleaning staff. The market strategy, market research, service marketing, and sales functions together correspond to the activities of advertising, sales promotions, collecting competitive intelligence, and preparing, administering, and analyzing customer surveys. Service provisioning activities include the preparation and the delivery of the meal, and the back-room functions associated with ordering, storage, and control of supplies. Service maintenance refers to the activities that are needed for the upkeep of the restaurant, such as cleaning the facility, preparing the tables, and designing the menu. Customer service and problem resolution incorporate the greeting and seating functions, service during the meal, and the real-time handling of complaints. Order processing corresponds to the activities required to take a customer order. Billing and claims processing correspond to the cashier functions. R & D, technology planning, and systems development may be the responsibility of a MIS person, or may be contracted to an external vendor.

For larger organizations with multiple locations and complicated processes, several levels of sub-teams may be needed. An example of a possible configuration is shown in Figure 8.2. In this figure, the service management team is supported by *functional subteams* that are responsible for the details of each function represented on the main team. Each subteam is led by an appropriate member of the main team. Some subteams, such as the one for market research, or one for systems development, may not be specific to any location. Others, particularly those that relate to service operations, consist of members selected from various locations. These members in turn are leaders of *location subteams* whose responsibility is to manage the service at their respective sites. Strategic decisions made about the service by the main team are converted into work activities by the functional subteams and implemented at each work site by the location subteams.

An organization of subteams such as the one shown in Figure 8.2 may look complicated, but it forms the foundation that is needed for successful management of the service. It should be remembered that—unlike the design implementation process, which is executed once for each design—the service management process needs to operate throughout the life of the design. In this period, various *organizational* initiatives have to be *locally* implemented and managed. This requires the local management at each work location to have ownership for their own operations, but at the same time remain linked to the strategic growth of the service. The multilevel, linked team structure is an effective way of accomplishing this.

Scheduling and coordination requirements

As mentioned before, the service management activities are ongoing through the period of operation of the service. The coordination issues for managing these activities are similar to those identified for rollout, and have to do with the identification of contacts, the establishment of communication links, and the development of processes required to replicate service changes across the entire organization. These changes may sometimes require the modification of service components that are common to several locations or functions, such as systems, process documentation, and training manuals. The service management plan must clearly identify the per-

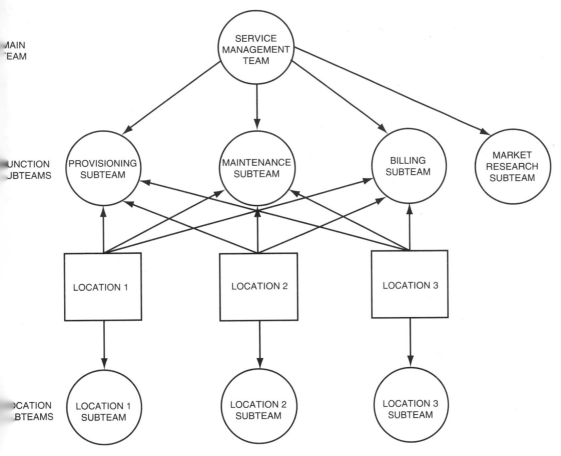

MAIN
TEAM

FUNCTION
SUBTEAMS

LOCATION
SUBTEAMS

Figure 8.2 Example of service management subteam configuration

sonnel responsible for managing these components, the processes that must be used to transmit change requests to the owners, the manner in which the changes will be implemented in all locations, and the procedures for removing old and obsolete material.

The *execution* of the service management plan is the subject of Chapters 9, 10, and 11. In Chapter 9, we address the *service monitoring and stabilization activities* and present the effectiveness, capability, and efficiency measures that can be used to evaluate the performance of the service. We also discuss the analysis needed to isolate the causes for unstable performance, and show how the results of this analysis can be used to make changes to the service. Chapters 10 and 11 present the strategic service improvement activities of the service management team. In Chapter 10, we describe the measurement of customer satisfaction. In Chapter 11, we discuss how these satisfaction measures can be used to identify service improvement alternatives and to select an optimal improvement plan.

8.7 CONCLUSION

Summary

The following is a step-by-step summary of the topics described in this chapter. The section in the chapter where a particular topic is covered is indicated in parentheses.

Design implementation plan (8.1)

DESIGN IMPLEMENTATION ACTIVITIES

* Specify the objectives of each component plan.
* Identify the leaders of each component team.
* Coordinate the timelines of the component plans.
* Communicate progress of implementation to senior management and customers.
* Resolve unexpected timing and implementation conflicts.

DESIGN IMPLEMENTATION TEAM STRUCTURE

* Consists of team leaders from component teams.
* Should be supported by a project mentor or champion.
* Subject matter experts should be included in the team.

DESIGN IMPLEMENTATION PLAN COORDINATION ELEMENTS

* Frequency of face-to-face meetings.
* Frequency of telephone meetings.
* Medium of communication among team members (paper, fax, electronic mail).
* Project milestones and critical dates.
* Frequency of communication to senior management.
* Process for issuing timely warning about delays or impediments.

Service construction plan (8.2)

SERVICE CONSTRUCTION ACTIVITIES

* Identify service construction team members.
* Identify subteam leaders and subteam members.
* Define contents, format, and distribution of operating procedures.

- Write operating procedures.
- Define system integration requirements.
- Define reporting requirements.
- Develop systems to support new design.
- Specify organizational structure to manage and support new service operations.
- Define training requirements for employees and customers.
- Develop required training materials.

SERVICE CONSTRUCTION TEAM STRUCTURE

- Members should be personnel responsible for operation of the new design.
- Construction activities can be performed by designated subteams.

COORDINATION ELEMENTS

- Team members must be available for the duration of the entire project.
- Enumeration and scheduling of activities should be clearly specified.
- Schedules, formats, and contents of team meetings should be clearly documented.

Testing plan (8.3)

TESTING ACTIVITIES

- Select the members of the testing team.
- Select the customers to be involved in the test.
- Select the locations for the test.
- Specify the design characteristics to be tested.
- Define the measures for evaluating the performance of the design during the test.
- Conduct test, collect data, and analyze performance.
- Determine causes of performance problems.
- Correct deficiencies in design, implementation, and testing.

TESTING TEAM STRUCTURE

- Team members should be a blend of design team members, service construction team members, and managers from the test site.

COORDINATION ELEMENTS

- Testing should be carried out under realistic conditions.

- Test should not give specialized treatment to trial customers.

- Test team should not consist only of best employees.

- Test should be carried out for a long enough duration to obtain accurate information.

Communications plan (8.4)

COMMUNICATIONS ACTIVITIES

- Identify the communications needs of various customer groups.

- Determine the information to be passed on to various levels of employees.

- Select one or more communication vehicles.

- Specify the format and content of the information.

- Disseminate timely and accurate information to customers and employees.

- Collect customer and employee feedback about the quality of the communication.

- Enhance material and delivery based on this feedback.

COMMUNICATIONS TEAM STRUCTURE

- For large projects, the communications plan may be part of an advertising campaign.

- Training managers may be used to inform a large number of employees.

- For small projects, service construction or design implementation team members may be used for communications.

- It is better to separate the communications plan from the design implementation and service construction plans.

COORDINATION ELEMENTS

- Effectiveness of communication depends on timeliness and accuracy.

- Communications must be coordinated with project milestones to improve timeliness.

- Procedures must be developed to assure accuracy of information.

- As far as possible, communications must be supported by documentation.

Rollout and transition plan (8.5)

ROLLOUT AND TRANSITION ACTIVITIES

◆ Define, sequence, and carry out the activities that need to be completed before the deployment date at each work location.

◆ Define, sequence, and carry out activities that need to be completed on deployment date.

◆ Define, sequence, and carry out transition activities a few days to few weeks after deployment.

◆ Develop contingency plan in case deployment fails.

ROLLOUT AND TRANSITION TEAM STRUCTURE

◆ Rollout team members must manage the implementation details at each work site.

◆ Rollout team members need to be local agents of change.

◆ Rollout team at each location should encompass a variety of job functions.

◆ Change management function should be performed by both managers and nonmanagers.

COORDINATION ELEMENTS

◆ Systematic coordination is needed between the service construction team and rollout team.

◆ Interface between service construction team and local rollout representatives should be clearly documented.

◆ Rollout plan must ensure that all preparations are complete by the deployment date.

Service management plan (8.6)

PERFORMANCE MONITORING AND STABILIZATION ACTIVITIES

◆ Measure performance of the service.

◆ Measure cost of service and utilization of resources.

◆ Analyze areas of unsatisfactory performance or excessive cost.

◆ Resolve service performance problems.

STRATEGIC SERVICE IMPROVEMENT ACTIVITIES

◆ Determine the satisfaction of customers with the service.

◆ Evaluate the financial or market impact of improved customer satisfaction.

◆ Identify attributes where satisfaction improvement has the greatest impact.

◆ Develop service improvement alternatives for these attributes.

◆ Determine the amount of effort to be expended on these alternatives.

◆ Select and implement feasible and cost-effective alternatives.

SERVICE MANAGEMENT TEAM STRUCTURE

◆ Service management team different from day-to-day service operations team.

◆ Service management team is a postimplementation monitoring team.

◆ Service management team is a postimplementation design team.

◆ Service management team should have members from all organizations involved in planning, selling, delivering, maintaining, and billing for the service.

COORDINATION ELEMENTS

◆ Service management may require changes to the service and the organization over time.

◆ Service management plan must clearly specify how these changes are coordinated and implemented.

Suggested reading

The following texts are recommended for further reading on the topics covered in this chapter. This is not an exhaustive collection, but it provides a good overview of different aspects of these topics.

Project Management: For project management, Oberlender (1993) provides a detailed description of all project management functions, including scheduling, tracking, coordination, and some discussion of people issues. It is a readable text that describes how to manage plans during execution, and it makes a good companion text to this chapter. Lewis (1991) is a more analytical approach to project management than Oberlender with a description of statistical techniques and quantitative tools.

Teamwork and Change Management: On the subject of teamwork and change management, Fisher (1993) covers a broad range of topics on the functioning of teams and the role of team leaders in empowering change. Jick (1993) is an academic text on change management, but with several interesting and enlightening case studies about how change is managed in different industries. Belasco (1990) is a readable, but simple, overview of the factors that affect change in organizations. Quirke (1995) is a general book about how to communicate impending change to customers and employees. LaMarsh (1995) is another text on this topic.

Chapter
9

Measuring Performance

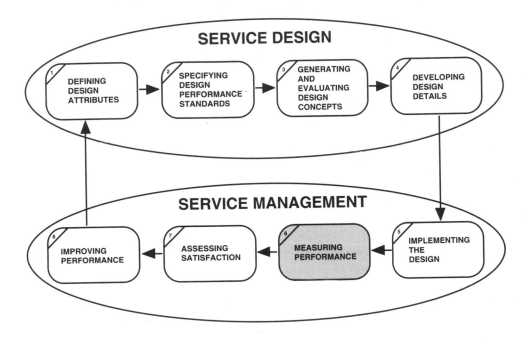

- *Performance monitoring and stabilization procedure*
- *Service performance metrics*
- *Collecting the right data for service management*
- *Data analysis and reporting*
- *Monitoring service performance—Service Edge restaurant example*
- *Conclusion*

In the previous chapter (Section 8.6), we described the structure of the service management team responsible for postimplementation management of the service. We stated in that section that the team has two major objectives. The first is to function as a *postimplementation monitoring* team. In this role, the team ensures that the current service sustains the performance level specified by the design standards, as long as the operating and market conditions remain unchanged. The activities to fulfill this objective correspond to stage 6 of the service design and management model. The second objective is to function as a *postimplementation design/redesign* team. In this role, the team addresses the future evolution of the design in response to changing customer expectations and the behavior of competitors, and looks for opportunities to improve the service so that the strategic competitiveness of the service in the market is maintained or enhanced. The activities for this objective correspond to stages 7 and 8 of the service design and management model. The first objective is the focus of this chapter. The second objective is the topic of Chapters 10 and 11.

To fulfill its first objective, the team asks the question:

- Is the service currently performing as expected by the design specifications?

The second objective requires answers to two further questions:

- How does service performance affect customer satisfaction?
- How does the behavior of satisfied customers influence future company profitability?

The team's ability to effectively control and improve the service depends on the accuracy with which the preceding questions can be answered. The accuracy, in turn, depends on the extent to which the analysis of quantitative data is used as the basis for making service management decisions.

Measures for service monitoring and improvement

To ensure that the right information is accurately collected and available when needed, the service management team's first priority should be to set up processes for regularly collecting *quantitative measures* of the performance of the service. Each question posed above requires a different set of measures, but these measures should be linked together to provide a single coherent view of service performance and its impact on the market. Figure 9.1 shows the complete set of measures that are needed to monitor and manage the service and their relationships. The questions that the measures help to answer are also listed in the figure.

In Figure 9.1, *service performance measures* evaluate the current performance of the service and ensure that it is continuing to reliably meet the design specifications. *Customer measures* indicate the impact of service performance on the customers. *Financial measures* are indicators of the financial health of the organization. The correlation between the financial and customer measures determines the revenue-generating potential of the service. This correlation can indicate the increase in customer satisfaction needed to achieve a specified market share gain or a strategic financial objective, which can then be used to set service improvement targets or new performance standards. The relationship between service performance

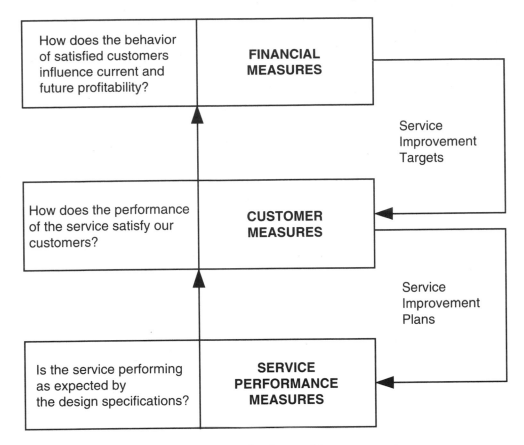

Figure 9.1 Measures for service monitoring and improvement

measures and the customer measures determines the operational improvements that can achieve the required increase in customer satisfaction. This is used to make improvement plans that specify how the current design should be improved.

This focus of this chapter is on the collection and analysis of service performance measures. The other measures are covered in Chapters 10 and 11. We develop some key service performance measures and describe how they should be displayed and reported to provide accurate and meaningful information about the performance of the service. We also show how data on service performance can be analyzed to determine the causes of excessive performance variability or unexpected deviations in performance from the design standards.

Importance of service performance measures

Why is it so important to ensure that the service continues to meet or exceed the performance requirements specified by the design? To understand why, recall the approach used in Chapters 3 and 4 to set the design performance standards for a service. First, customer needs were identified. These needs were translated into design attributes. Technical benchmarks of the competitors' performance were obtained for these attributes. The benchmarks were used to generate service profiles for estimating the satisfaction/performance relationship for each attribute. The required level of customer satisfaction to be achieved by the design was specified. The satisfaction/performance relationships were used to determine the performance levels at which the required satisfaction could be attained. These performance levels were selected as the design standards. The standards are therefore *customer-generated service performance requirements* that must be met by a service that satisfies its customers. In Chapters 6 and 7, we showed how the design team should take great care to ensure that the selected design is capable of meeting these requirements with little variability over a wide range of operating conditions. It is now the service management team's responsibility to continue to sustain this level of performance. At the same time, the service performance team must also monitor the costs of operating the service to ensure that they are being maintained within acceptable limits. These two criteria will ensure the continued profitability of the firm until market or operating conditions change sufficiently to necessitate a new design.

In Section 9.1, we present an eight-step *performance monitoring and stabilization procedure* for measuring service performance and correcting observed deviations. Different kinds of performance measures and their use are described in Section 9.2. Sections 9.3 and 9.4 address data collection, analysis, and reporting issues. In Section 9.5, we apply the eight steps of Section 9.1 to monitor the performance of the order-taking process of the Service Edge restaurant. Section 9.6 is a summary of this chapter.

9.1 PERFORMANCE MONITORING AND STABILIZATION PROCEDURE

At regular intervals (weekly or monthly, and in some cases hourly or daily), the service management team should collect and analyze service performance data. This procedure should follow the steps listed below:

Step 1: Select the design attributes to be analyzed.

Step 2: Measure the performance effectiveness of each selected attribute.

Step 3: Measure the capability of each selected attribute.

Step 4: Measure the efficiency of key processes.

Step 5: Identify attributes whose performance does not conform to standards or shows unusual change.

Step 6: Analyze the attributes identified in Step 5 in detail to determine the cause for poor performance or for unusual change in performance.

Step 7: Decide whether any corrective action is necessary, and if so, what steps need to be taken.

Step 8: Take the corrective action.

Description of steps

In *step 1*, the team selects a few important design attributes to analyze. It is advisable, though not necessary, to select the same attributes every month. Typically, the attributes that are most important to customers or those whose performance/satisfaction relationships have a steep slope should be regularly monitored. Other candidates may be attributes whose performance has been unstable over time. Attributes whose performance has generated customer complaints may also be selected for observation. If the number of attributes is small, all attributes may be chosen.

Three characteristics of performance are analyzed in *steps 2, 3, and 4*. They are *effectiveness, capability,* and *efficiency. Effectiveness* measures whether (or the extent to which) an attribute meets the design standards. We introduced the concept of *capability* in Chapter 6. It is a measure of the ability of the service to meet the standards for the attribute. Finally, *efficiency* measures are used to determine the costs of providing the service and the resources utilized.

In *step 5,* the team identifies attributes whose performance has changed since the last monitoring period, or whose performance fails to meet the standards. If the operating characteristics remain stable, the only change in performance from month to month should because of random variability. A significant change in performance that cannot be attributed to random effects should signal a need for additional analysis. The same is true for large changes in cost. This analysis is performed in *step 6* and usually involves examining the data at the subprocess or activity level to isolate the particular function, system, or feature that is responsible for the performance change. The team then determines whether the performance problem can be attributed to some uncontrollable and unique circumstance that is unlikely to be repeated, or whether there is a problem with service operations. Once the underlying cause of an unexpected performance or cost change has been identified, the team decides what action, if any, should be taken in *step 7*. Obviously, if the cause is a unique event, no further action may be necessary except to test whether the occurrence of a similar event can be predicted in the future. In other cases, some action may be necessary. Any reasonable modifications to service operations that may be needed are implemented by the team in *step 8*. If changes in market conditions or operating strategy require major modifications to the service, the team may package and prioritize these modifications as part of a larger service improvement effort.

Before we move on, it is important to explain the term *changes in performance*. Many teams take this to automatically imply that only changes in a negative direction are worthy of further analysis. Improvement in performance is often treated as good news and ignored. In reality, however, changes in *both* directions represent an instability in performance and should be investigated. Unexpectedly good performance that occurred because of some special circumstances may be systematized and realized on a regular basis. Under a more pessimistic scenario, unexpectedly good performance may be the result of diminishing work volumes arising from decreased demand. Both unexpectedly good and unexpectedly poor performance deserve scrutiny.

Need for accurate data

What is the key determinant of the service management team's ability to successfully execute the eight steps described above? Note that three steps begin with words "measure" and one step contains the word "analysis." It is impossible to underestimate the importance of quantitative analysis using current and accurate data. This requires the following:

- Metrics must be correctly defined to ensure that the *right information* is available.

- Data collection procedures must be implemented and tested so that *accurate information* is available.

- Aggregation, reporting, and distribution processes should be designed so that the information is available to the team in a *timely* manner.

- Team members should be trained in *interpreting* analysis results, charts, and diagrams.

- The data should be stored in a system that allows easy access to *historical performance information.*

Designing a system and/or a process to satisfy these requirements, called a *performance management system,* should be the first activity of the service management team. This activity should be begun while the service is being implemented so that the system is in place when the service goes into operation. In practice, however, many teams responsible for managing a newly designed service do not take the time to develop a complete and integrated performance management system. This is usually because the teams are assembled several months (or years) after the service is in operation, by which time it is difficult to replace the dozens of local reports and data collection techniques that are already in place. Many service management teams believe they base their decisions on quantitative data, but very often the metrics used are inaccurate or incomplete, and present an erroneous picture of the performance of the service. Incorrect data is sometimes more detrimental than no data at all, since misleading or even counterintuitive results obtained may be unquestionably accepted just because they are presented as the output of quantitative analysis.

In the absence of good and complete data, many teams focus only on those aspects of service performance that they can measure, such as completion intervals for a process. As a result, many service improvement efforts are directed only towards achieving shorter and shorter completion intervals, well after this attribute loses its importance to customers. Ultimately, improper measurements and the lack of adequate data leads to poorly planned service improvements that neither satisfy customers nor affect the company's profitability.

9.2   SERVICE PERFORMANCE METRICS

Recall from steps 2, 3, and 4 of the performance monitoring and stabilization procedure that effectiveness, capability, and efficiency are the three characteristics of performance measured by the service management team. The metrics that are used to measure these characteristics are correspondingly called *effectiveness metrics*, *capability metrics*, and *volume and efficiency metrics*.

Effectiveness metrics

Consider the following metrics:

- Percent of orders delivered within 5 hours

- Number of bills produced with no errors

- Number of customers rating service provider "exceptionally reliable"

How are these three metrics similar? Each metric measures the performance of an attribute *relative to a target or a standard*. For the first metric, the target is 5 hours. For the second, the standard is zero errors. For the third, the standard is the "exceptionally reliable" rating. Each metric measures the extent to which the performance of the service meets its standard. These kinds of metrics therefore measure the *effectiveness* of the performance of the attribute.

All effectiveness metrics *must* have an associated standard. For some set of standards X, Y, and Z, these metrics are constructed using wording such as "Percent of customers less than X" or "Number of parts greater than Y" or "Number of ratings equal to Z." The standards used depend on the application. For a newly designed service, the standards may be the design performance targets for the attributes estimated from the satisfaction/performance relationships (see Chapter 4). In some cases, performance standards may be set by the customers. For manufactured goods, the dimensions may have to conform to national or international standards. An organization may adopt published "best-in-class" benchmarks as a standard. The performance level of close competitors may be adopted.

The service management team must ensure that the standards that are used are the most appropriate for providing the required information about the performance of the service. The same standards should also be consistently used every time. Standards that are not based on any criteria, but which "seem reasonable," should be avoided. Often, if design standards are not available, teams make up internal targets and use these to define their effectiveness metrics. Metrics defined in this way are meaningless and can even be counterproductive.

How do we select an appropriate standard? This depends on the application. For example, suppose customers of a telephone service want it installed within 24 hours, while the best-in-class industry benchmark is 48 hours. If the objective is to measure the effectiveness of service performance to the *customer*, the metric should be "the percentage of customers who have service installed in 24 hours or less." If the objective is to compare performance relative to the industry, the metric should be "the percentage of customers who have service installed in 48 hours or less." One metric should not be substituted for the other.

Effectiveness metrics for the Service Edge restaurant

Table 9.1 shows the effectiveness metrics for the process design attributes of the Service Edge restaurant. The performance standard for each attribute is taken from Table 7.12.

The reader should note the following points from Table 9.1:

1. Some metrics are obtained through objective measurements while others are customers' ratings of performance. For example, the metric "% of customers served between 10 and 11.5 minutes" can be measured from data on service operations, while the metric "% of customers rating meal service friendliness 'Exceptional' " is obtained by surveying customers. We should point out a conceptual difference between these two types of measurements. The first type of measurement is an indicator of *objective quality*, while the second measures the *perceived quality* of the process.

As far as possible, we should always measure the performance of the intangible attributes of the service from customers' ratings. This is because customer satisfaction is affected by the gap between perceptions and expectations. This is referred to as the "disconfirmation paradigm" in the service quality literature (Oliver, 1993), which we will describe in greater detail in Chapter 10. Under this paradigm, customers are satisfied if their perception of service performance exceeds their expectations; otherwise, they are dissatisfied. Therefore, we want to be able to regularly monitor customers' perceptions of the quality of each attribute of the service. The obvious problem associated with obtaining perception ratings is that all information needs to be collected from the customers, and this is not always easy. Objective performance measures are always easier to collect. For tangible attributes such as the order-taking interval, an initial study can be conducted where a sample of perceived quality ratings is calibrated against a parallel set of objective measures of the interval. This calibration can then be used regularly to predict the perceived quality from data collected on the objective measures.

This is not so easy for the intangible variables. In theory, it is possible to calibrate ratings of these variables against objectively measurable "bundles of characteris-

Table 9.1 Effectiveness metrics for Service Edge restaurant

Service attribute	Effectiveness metric
Degree of friendliness of greeting	% of customers rating attribute "Exceptional"
Degree of friendliness of meal service	% of customers rating attribute "Exceptional"
Degree of responsiveness of meal service	% of customers rating attribute "Exceptional"
Degree of friendliness of leavetaking	% of customers rating attribute "Exceptional"
Time between seating and menu delivery	% of customers with menu delivery interval less than 5 minutes
Time between menu delivery and ordering	% of orders taken in less than 5 minutes
Degree of knowledge about menu	% of customers rating attribute "Exceptional"
Degree of order-taking patience	% of customers rating attribute "Exceptional"
Time between ordering and meal delivery	% of customers served between 10 and 11.5 minutes
Percent of bills produced without error	% of bills produced without errors
Percent of bills settled without error	% of bills settled without errors
Degree of effectiveness in problem resolution	% of customers rating attribute "Excellent"

tics" (recall that we used these bundles to set scale values for the intangible attributes in Chapter 3). For example, some characteristics relating to meal-service friendliness may be the number of times the waiter stops by the customers' table, the length of each conversation, the topics covered, etc. Even though these characteristics can be measured without the customer's assistance, it is usually cumbersome and time-consuming to observe and collect accurate data on the nature of the transactions between the waiter and the customers. It is still easier to directly measure the customers' perception of the quality of these attributes.

2. Note also from Table 9.1 that the effectiveness metrics are defined for the *end-to-end* processes. This is very important. In Chapter 5 (Section 5.2), we stated that it was necessary to define processes that began and ended with customers, since it would otherwise be difficult to evaluate the impact of process performance on the customers. For exactly the same reason, it is important to design effectiveness metrics that span the entire process. Many teams confronted with inadequate data or with processes that span organizational boundaries define effectiveness metrics that only affect the parts of the process they can control or measure. Without an end-to-end process performance measure, these partial metrics have no value. However, when used in conjunction with these measures, the partial metrics provide useful diagnostic information about the effectiveness of subprocesses.

Capability metrics

How can we measure the capability of the attributes of a service? The reader will recall from Chapter 6 (Section 6.4) that the capability of a process is its intrinsic ability to reliably meet the performance standards. The capability therefore depends on the *shape* and *spread* of the performance distribution of the attribute. The average performance and the variability of performance (measured by the standard deviation) are two obvious metrics of these characteristics. In general, any descriptive statistic of the performance of a service attribute is a potential capability metric. Depending on the application, minimum values, maximum values, ranges, medians, quartiles, etc., can all be used to measure the extent of variability of performance.

Table 9.2 shows the capability metrics for the attributes of the Service Edge restaurant. We have only shown the mean and standard deviation for all attributes, but the maximum, minimum, or median values are also needed for attributes whose performance distribution is skewed. Just as in the case of the effectiveness metrics, the capability metrics should also be measured end-to-end so that the ability of the service to satisfy the customers can be ascertained.

The reader may have come across formulas for capability in texts on statistical process control, especially in the manufacturing context (see, for example, Juran and Gyrna, 1990). In these texts, capability is measured by the *capability ratio* C_p and the *capability index* C_{pk}. Conceptually, these coefficients are a compact way of representing (1) the distance between the performance standard and the mean performance level of the process, and (2) the spread (variability) of process performance. In other words, the ratios are derived from the mean and standard

Table 9.2 Capability metrics for Service Edge restaurant

Service attribute	Capability metric
Degree of friendliness of greeting	Mean, standard deviation of performance rating
Degree of friendliness of meal service	Mean, standard deviation of performance rating
Degree of responsiveness of meal service	Mean, standard deviation of performance rating
Degree of friendliness of leavetaking	Mean, standard deviation of performance rating
Time between seating and menu delivery	Mean, standard deviation of menu delivery interval
Time between menu delivery and ordering	Mean, standard deviation of ordering interval
Degree of knowledge about menu	Mean, standard deviation of performance rating
Degree of order-taking patience	Mean, standard deviation of performance rating
Time between ordering and meal delivery	Mean, standard deviation of meal delivery interval
Percent of bills produced without error	Mean, standard deviation of production error rate
Percent of bills settled without error	Mean, standard deviation of settlement error rate
Degree of effectiveness in problem resolution	Mean, standard deviation of performance rating

deviation of process performance. They are therefore not conceptually different from our definition of capability.

In manufacturing applications, standard values of the indices are used to represent different probabilities that a product meets the design specifications. For example, a defect rate of 100 parts-per-million (i.e., the process does not meet the specifications 100 times out of a million encounters) corresponds to a capability ratio of 1.3. These standard indices and their interpretations are based on the assumption that the performance of the attribute is normally distributed. Many of the attributes in the service context may have skewed distributions. In this case, the individual statistics described above help to present a better picture of the distribution than the standard indices.

Efficiency metrics

The cost of delivering the service and the resources utilized in delivery are measured by the *efficiency metrics*. As described in Chapter 7, the amount of resources needed to deliver the required level of service through the operating range should be specified by the design. If the service operations are stable, we should expect that the utilization of resources and the costs of delivering the service are consistent with the levels predicted during the evaluation of the design. On the other hand, if the actual volume of units processed is larger than the design operating range, or there is a greater amount of rework than expected, then the costs of delivering service will be greater.

The following are some common examples of efficiency metrics:

- Average utilization level of human or machine resources
- Average percentage of reworked items (as a percentage of the total number of items)
- Average time spent in rework for each process (as a percentage of total cycle time)
- Average amount of material wasted
- Average number of overtime hours (by process)
- Average ratio of overhead time to productive time (by process)
- Average absentee rate
- Average system availability rate

When used in conjunction with the effectiveness and capability metrics, the efficiency metrics identify areas where the service might be improved to provide the required performance level at a lower cost, or indicate where additional resources are needed to sustain current levels of performance.

For clarity of presentation, we described the effectiveness, capability, and efficiency metrics separately. In reality, they are interrelated and need to be used together to provide a complete picture of the operations of the service. The data collection process should be designed to reliably deliver *all* the information required by the service management team to monitor and improve the service. In the following sections, we present guidelines for effective data collection, analysis, and reporting.

9.3 COLLECTING THE RIGHT DATA FOR SERVICE MANAGEMENT

As mentioned in Section 9.1, the five requirements that influence the service management team's ability to effectively monitor and control the performance of the service are:

- Metrics must be correctly defined to ensure that the *right information* is available.

- Data collection procedures must be implemented and tested so that *accurate information* is available.

- Aggregation, reporting, and distribution processes should be designed so that the information is available to the team in a *timely* manner.

- Team members should be trained in *interpreting* analysis results, charts, and diagrams.

- The data should be stored in a system that allows easy access to *historical performance information*.

The first requirement (definition of metrics) was covered in Section 9.2. The remaining four requirements deal with the *collection of data*, the *distribution of reports*, the *methods of analysis,* and the *development of systems*. Data collection is discussed in this section. Analysis and reporting are the topics of Section 9.4.

Factors affecting the collection of accurate data

The regular availability of accurate data is the single most critical determinant of the team's ability to effectively manage and improve the service. All too often, however, teams have to deal with insufficient or incorrect information, and in many cases, with no information at all. Some of the factors that impede the collection of accurate data are these:

1. No well-defined process for data collection: Very often, there are no documented plans detailing factors such as:

- What information needs to be collected
- Who is responsible for collecting this information
- Where this information can be found
- At what intervals the information needs to be gathered
- The format to be used for compiling the information
- The method by which the information is transmitted to the service management team

Without planning, data collection becomes an unscheduled and ad hoc activity. Typically, requests (or demands) for data are sent out to all appropriate members of the organization a day or two before the information is needed, usually in response to a crisis or a request from senior management. Personnel in the organization responsible for satisfying this request frantically scramble to produce this information, sacrificing care and accuracy for speed. The data that are finally collected may be in different formats, cover different time periods, span different services, and provide a fragmented and incoherent view of the performance of the service.

2. Manual data collection procedures: Some organizations make data collection a tedious manual procedure that requires a service agent to enter the details of a service transaction on a paper form or into a tracking system every time the transaction takes place, or every time an activity is performed. In organizations that handle large volumes of transactions, it is often very difficult to simultaneously provide service and record its details. As a result, either the required information does not get collected, or it is randomly entered into the system with no thought about its accuracy, rendering much of it unusable.

3. Inadequate training: In many customer service applications, data are collected on the reasons for customer complaints or problems. Since the customer's statement of the problem may not accurately represent what is wrong with the service, agents taking the calls collect information that reflect their best guess about the cause of the problem. In order to collect accurate information, service agents must be trained on the sequence of diagnostic questions they need to ask customers. This training is usually not provided, and as a result, complaint information is often merely an arbitrary interpretation of the person collecting the data.

4. Data collection not integrated with work activities: In many organizations, data collection and performance tracking are perceived to be additional responsibilities that are external to the main functions performed by the organization. As a result, data collection is given low priority, especially if manual procedures are used. Often, personnel enter all tracking information at one time at the end of a day or week, relying on memory, and make up data when their memory fails them. This affects the accuracy of the data.

5. Measurements drive the wrong behavior: In some cases, the reasons for collecting data are not adequately communicated to all members of the organization. In other cases, results are used to punish or reward individuals rather than to identify and correct performance problems. Both situations induce fear and mistrust of the data and encourage manipulation and misrepresentation of the information.

These points indicate that the data collection should be a carefully planned activity that should be undertaken by well-trained personnel who have a good understanding of why the data is important and how the results will be used. Also, the process for collecting data should be streamlined so that it doesn't disrupt the primary service-providing functions of the organization.

Designing effective data collection procedures

The following are guidelines for designing effective data collection procedures:

1. Select a few, critical items for measurement: It is better to collect accurate data on a few key items than to attempt to measure every possible facet of the service. The completion rate will be higher and the data are likely to be more accurate. A few of the most important attributes identified in the QFD matrix (see Chapter 3) or the ones with the steepest performance/satisfaction function (see Chapter 4) provide a good starting set.

2. Sample, if necessary: If the number of service transactions is too large, it is not necessary to collect data on every transaction. A carefully chosen sample is adequate. The sampling plan depends on the nature of the problem. If all service transactions are of the same type, a simple random sample may be adequate. Such a sample may be obtained by a systematic procedure such as measuring every fiftieth transaction. If the transactions are of different types, a *stratified* sample may be appropriate, where a random sample is chosen from each transaction type. In other cases, a double sampling strategy may be adopted, where a small initial sample can be used to design a more detailed sample. More details on different sampling strategies and their use are provided in texts suggested at the end of this chapter.

3. Automate, if possible: As far as possible, the collection of data should be automated, so that it takes place as a natural consequence of the work being performed. Technology should be used where possible to assist in data collection. For example, orders can be bar-coded to track their progress through a service delivery process. The bar codes can be read at various stages of the process to track the flow of the order. Similarly, if an order management system is used to track the steps of a service delivery process, then the system should be designed so that completion times can be captured automatically by the system as each activity is completed. For example, the person delivering the service may merely need to register the completion of each activity in the system, possibly by pointing to an icon on the screen. Technological aids must make it easy to collect accurate data with little human intervention.

4. Avoid paper forms for data collection: As far as possible, databases should be updated directly through electronic inputs. Chances of data entry errors are greater when data are first collected on paper forms and then manually input into data collection systems. Data collected at various field locations should be directly entered into computer forms and electronically transmitted to the database where the information is stored.

5. *Develop easy data access and reporting capabilities:* The data that is collected should be readily available for analysis and reporting. Flexible interfaces should be built into the data collection system so that the information can be sorted and segmented in many ways and different views of the data can be easily accessed. It should be possible for users of the system to define reports or to extract data to meet their specific requirements without sophisticated programming.

6. *Decentralize data analysis:* Resistance to collection or analysis of data often occurs in organizational structures where field or branch managers are required to send information on the performance of their centers to a centralized location for analysis. When this happens, field organizations feel a loss of ownership over their own data, and they are not motivated to seek local answers about how to improve the service. Much time and effort is spent in questioning the results of the analysis.

To avoid this problem, data analysis should be decentralized as far as possible. The organizations responsible for doing the work should also perform their own analysis. Once the data is analyzed, the field organizations may send a summary of the analysis results with recommendations to a central location for further aggregation and reporting. However, the primary analysis should be performed locally.

7. *Make data collection part of job function:* Instead of treating performance measurements as an additional task external to the main job, data collection that is not automated should be integrated into work procedures. For example, the task of collecting satisfaction data from customers can be part of the job responsibility of a customer service representative at a hotel checkout desk. The questions that need to be asked and the required entries in the reservation system should routinely be part of the representatives' training program and should be documented in the work procedures. This will ensure that the data collection function is carried out seriously and competently.

8. *Openly communicate the objective of data collection:* All involved personnel should know and understand what data is collected, how it is analyzed, and what the results will be used for. It must be emphasized to all members of the organization that the collection and analysis of data is part of a collective effort to manage and improve the service and that service performance results will not be blindly used to punish or reward individuals. The more confident the employees feel that their data will not be misused, the more accurate the data will be.

9.4   DATA ANALYSIS AND REPORTING

The availability of accurate data is clearly an important issue for the service management team. How the data is analyzed is no less important. The objective of data analysis should not merely be to produce reports every month; rather, it should be to gain insights about the service performance that will help the team to make intelligent and informed decisions about improving the service. This requires creative *analysis procedures,* the use of the right *analysis tools* and *display methods,* and a well-defined *report distribution process* that ensures that the right information is available to the right people when needed. In this section, we present guidelines that show how these requirements can be achieved.

Routine and ad hoc analysis

Two kinds of analyses are typically needed to gain insights into service performance data. They are *routine analysis* and *ad hoc analysis.* Routine analysis, as its name suggests, refers to the regular, systematic analysis that is performed in every reporting period to evaluate the performance of the service on the effectiveness, capability, and efficiency metrics. Ad hoc analysis is the detailed diagnostic testing that is needed to investigate the reasons for unexpected performance changes. The nature and complexity of ad hoc analysis will differ from situation to situation.

Routine analysis activities should be planned so that they can be performed with the least amount of effort. Many teams are so consumed by the effort needed to produce results every month that little time is left over for interpretation or ad hoc analysis. Yet ad hoc analysis should be the primary focus of the service management team, because it is through the details of this analysis that the most important insights about service performance can be obtained. On the other hand, routine analysis procedures should be *repeatable, documented,* and *decentralized.*

Repeatable means that it should be possible to follow the same analysis steps in every time period. Some teams change their metrics every few months, making it very difficult to obtain a comprehensive picture of the performance of the service over time. As far as possible, analysis procedures must be left unchanged for at least twelve months so that trends can be studied. The procedures for routine analysis should be *documented* so that all individuals performing the analysis will follow the same steps in the same sequence. Proper documentation also assists in the training of new personnel. To the extent possible, the most repetitive tasks of routine analysis should be automated so that they can be regularly reproduced with little intervention. *Decentralization* means that almost all the routine analysis (and as much of the ad hoc analysis as appropriate) should be performed close to where the work is done.

Procedures for sharing analysis results

If the service delivery is distributed across several geographic areas, or if different subprocesses are managed by different organizations, then agreements must be developed that detail how the analysis results will be sent to the service management team, and in what format. Typically, results from the various organizations should be consolidated and aggregated by the service management team. Any ad hoc analysis that is necessary may either be performed by the team, or by the appropriate responsible organization. The service management team may also perform spot checks or audits of the departmental and regional results from time to time.

When all ad hoc analyses are complete, the team should develop a list of interventions that may be required to stabilize the performance of one or more processes, and should then pass these back to the appropriate organizations for implementation. In general, the analysis procedures must be designed to provide the service management team access to all the information that it needs without requiring it to perform large amounts of data analysis on its own. The procedures must also ensure that all regions and departments responsible for managing various service components are equally involved in providing inputs and recommendations to the service management team.

Analysis tools

Results can be displayed either as numbers in tables or in graphical form. With the large number of graphical tools now available for desktop computers, it is easy to produce results in the form of charts or graphs. The advantage of graphical or visual displays is that large amounts of information can be conveniently presented in a manner that can be readily assimilated. The disadvantage of these displays is that they can be manipulated to give the viewer a biased or erroneous first impression of the data. For example, the scale of a graph can be adjusted so that small differences between data points are magnified, leading a viewer to believe that large differences are being presented. Even if the data are not manipulated on purpose, careless or incompetent presentation can result in viewers reaching undesired conclusions. The presenters of graphical data must therefore take care to make sure that the display method chosen is the most appropriate for representing the information, and that visual biases are minimized.

We now briefly describe four versatile methods of graphically displaying data that can be used in a wide variety of applications: *histograms, run charts, scatter plots,* and *control charts*. These methods allow us to visually answer the following common questions asked during any data analysis:

- How are the data distributed?
- How variable is the performance?
- How have the results changed over time?
- What factors affect the observed results?
- How stable is the performance around the standards?
- How close is the performance to the standards?

Space considerations limit us here to no more than a superficial description of these methods, but they are presented in greater detail in some of the texts suggested at the end of this chapter.

Histograms

A histogram is a bar chart that shows the number of times each value of a variable occurs in a sample of observations. The tabulation of the number of occurrences of each value is called a *frequency distribution,* and a histogram is a graphical representation of this distribution. The variables can either be *discrete* (i.e., taking ordinal values such as 1, 2, 3) or *continuous.* We used histograms in Chapter 3 [see Figures 3.4 (a) and (b)] to chart the number of observations of a variable that take rating values 1, 2, 3, 4, 5. Histograms of discrete variables are also referred to as a *bar chart.* Continuous variables such as cycle time are segmented into groups, and the number of observations in each group is charted. The midpoint of each group is usually used as a representative value for the group, though any other value may be used as well. Figure 9.2 shows an example of a histogram for three groups of order processing time. The first bar shows the number of orders between 1 and 4 days, the second the number between 5 and 8 days, and the third the number between 9 and 12 days.

The histogram is a visual picture of the shape of the distribution of the data. Some questions that can be answered from a histogram include the following:

- Is the distribution symmetrical?

- Are there long tails (i.e., large numbers of values at either end of the scale?)

- Are there multiple peaks?

- How wide is the spread in the data (i.e., does the variable take on many values or a few)?

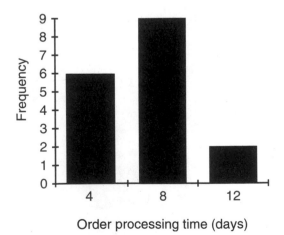

Figure 9.2   Histogram for order processing
time

Special versions of histograms are useful for specific applications. A *Pareto chart* is a histogram where the bars are ordered from the largest frequency to the smallest. This chart can be used to identify the critical few factors that contribute the most to the variability in the data. Pareto charts are useful in analyzing the major causes for defects, in identifying the activities contributing to the greatest costs, or in determining the factors that have the largest impact on customer satisfaction. A special case of a bar chart is a *clustered* or *stacked* bar chart that can be used to compare a variable across multiple discrete dimensions. Figure 9.3 shows a clustered bar chart that compares the volume of orders at three work locations in three months. Each bar in a cluster pertains to one work location.

Run chart

A run chart is a graph that shows the performance of a variable over time. These plots serve the following purposes:

- To identify cyclic performance patterns or seasonal variations
- To determine historical trends in performance
- To evaluate the effect of service improvements on performance
- To identify the time lag between service improvements and changes in performance
- To determine wear or experience effects that cause performance to drift over time
- To assess the gap between the desired and actual performance over time

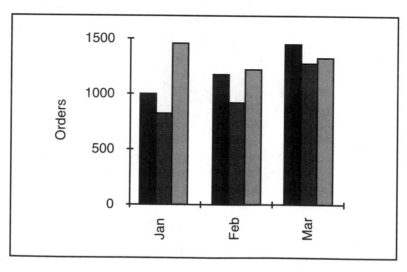

Figure 9.3 Clustered bar chart of order volumes

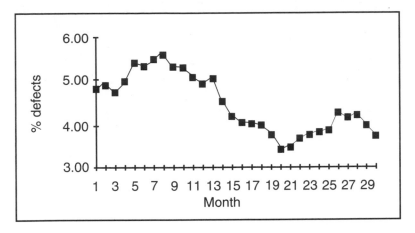

Figure 9.4   Run chart of service defect rate

Figure 9.4 shows a run chart for the defect rate of a service plotted over a period of thirty months. The following is a hypothetical interpretation of the information in this chart:

> It is evident that the defect rate has declined in this period. A service improvement initiative was put in place at month 7 in response to increasing defects. The lag time between the deployment of the initiative and a decrease in the rate of defects is three months, and the effects of the initiative begin to be observed in the tenth month. Overall, the initiative reduced the defect rate by 1.5% over a ten-month period. At the end of this time, because of an influx of new and inexperienced personnel between months 20 and 22, the defect rate began to rise again. The new staff was trained in month 23, resulting once again in an improvement in performance by month 26.

Scatter plot

A scatter plot shows the relationship between two variables such as defect rate and employee experience, or the time taken to complete a service transaction and customer satisfaction. The scatter plot shows the following:

- Whether a relationship exists between two variables

- The shape of the relationship (i.e., linear, curved)

- The amount of random variability in the relationship between two variables

- Whether this variability differs for different values of the two variables

A scatter plot is a graph, with the values of the *dependent variable* (whose value is predicted) on the *y*-axis and those of the *predictor* or *independent variable* (which predicts the value of the dependent variable) on the *x*-axis. Each point on the graph represents a pair of values of the dependent and predictor variables. An

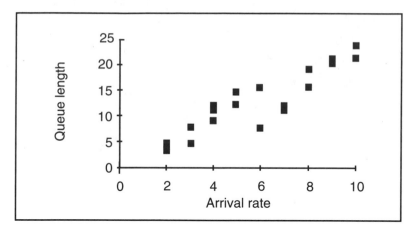

Figure 9.5 Scatter plot of queue length and customer arrival rate at a service
facility

example of a scatter plot is shown in Figure 9.5, which shows the relationship between the arrival rate of customers and the queue length at a service facility. The
queue length is predicted by the arrival rate. The queue length is therefore shown
on the y-axis, and the predictor variable on the x-axis. Each point on the graph represents one combination of arrival rate and queue length.

The slope of a scatter plot shows the extent of the average relationship between
two variables. If the slope is flat, no relationship exists. From Figure 9.5, it can be
seen that the queue length increases with the arrival rate. We can also see that
the relationship is approximately linear. The amount of scatter in the plot (i.e.,
whether the y values are fairly close for each value of x, or whether they form a
"cloud") shows the extent of random variability in the data, and is a measure of
the strength of the relationship between the two variables. In Figure 9.5, the values
of queue length are fairly close together for each value of arrival rate. A strong relationship therefore exists between these variables. A scatter plot is often a useful
first step before estimating a regression equation, because it gives an indication of
the nature, strength, and shape of the relationship between two variables.

The scatter plot can also be used to validate assumptions made during the design
of a service. Suppose a design team is trying to develop a performance function for
a particular service attribute for which the exact functional form is unknown. Suppose the design team approximates the function using a mixture of experience and
judgment. After the service is in operation, a scatter plot can be used to validate
the assumed functional form. The service management team can collect data on
the performance of the attributes at various levels of operating characteristics and
can draw a scatter plot between the performance of the attributes and the operating characteristics. The design may need to be modified if the actual performance
function is significantly different from what was assumed.

Control chart

A control chart is a graphical tool which is part of a methodology known as "statistical process control (SPC)." This methodology is used to measure the variability of manufacturing and service processes with a view to determining whether this variability is attributable to systematic or random causes. SPC is a complex topic with a very large body of literature. In the following paragraphs, we will present a very brief overview of what control charts look like and how they can be used, without any explanation of the SPC methodology itself. References are provided at the end of this chapter for readers wishing to know more about this topic.

A control chart compares the performance of a continuous or discrete variable against statistically computed "control limits." The idea of control limits stems from the fact that the performance of any service attribute is inherently variable because of a variety of random causes that cannot be identified or controlled. This random variability should be the *only* source of variability in a service that has been designed to produce a stable average performance level that is robust to changes within a given operating range. Moreover, this variability should remain within the limits specified by the design. A control chart tests the stability of performance throughout the operation of the service.

Suppose data is collected on the performance of a service attribute during the lifetime of the service. In the absence of large changes in the operating characteristics, we would expect the performance of this attribute to be randomly distributed around a stable mean value with a standard deviation specified by the design. If the performance is normally distributed, then from the properties of the normal distribution, we would also expect that 99.7% of the performance values will lie randomly within three standard deviations of the average value. If these expectations are met by the collected data, the service performance is said to be *in control*. The performance values represented by three standard deviations are referred to as the *control limits*.

The procedure for plotting a control chart consists of two steps: *calibration* and *control*. In the *calibration* step, the mean and variability of the data are calculated from historical process performance data and the control limits are determined. As mentioned above, the control limits are the performance values at three standard deviations on either side of the mean. Various methods exist for estimating the standard deviation of the data. A transformation of the *range* of the observations, which is the difference between the maximum and minimum value, is a commonly used estimate. We will not describe the detailed methods for calculating control limits in this book, but refer the reader to the suggested texts referenced at the end of this chapter.

In the *control* step, current observations of process performance are regularly plotted on the calibrated control chart. If the process is under control, we would expect over 99% of the points on the chart to lie between the upper and lower control limits. We would also expect that the points to be randomly distributed, i.e., no unusual patterns should be seen in the data. Standard tests exist to check for unusual patterns through visual inspection. The reader is referred to a paper by Nelson (1984) or other texts on statistical process control for a description of these tests. If these conditions are not met, then the process performance is *out of control*, and some action may be necessary.

Let us explain these concepts further with an example of a control chart of the temperature of hot coffee at a coffee shop.

Controlling the temperature of hot coffee—an example

Consider a coffee shop that is trying to provide coffee at the temperatures desired by its customers. Suppose market research shows that customers desire coffee at temperatures between 180° and 190°. Therefore, the coffee shop tries to keep the temperature of the brewed coffee as close to 185° as possible. Each batch of coffee that is brewed is placed on a thermostat controlled heater set to 185 degrees Fahrenheit. Because of internal variations in the thermostat timer operations and variability in the number of requests for coffee (that results in variability in the number of times the coffee pot is taken off the heater), the temperature varies around this set value. The coffee shop decides to use a control chart to study whether these temperature variations are under control. Let us examine the calibration and control steps for this example.

1. Calibration step: In the calibration step, the temperature of twenty batches of coffee is measured. To minimize the effect of measurement errors, each new batch of coffee is allowed to sit for 10 minutes until its temperature stabilizes with that of the thermostat. Five temperature observations are collected for each batch in a period of 5 minutes. The average of these five observations is considered to be the temperature of the batch.

After the temperatures of all twenty batches are measured, the average temperature of these batches is calculated (note that this is actually the average of 100 observations, because five observations are collected for each batch). This average represents the *center line* of the control chart. The control limits around this center line are then estimated. Suppose the *lower* and *upper* control limits are calculated to be 182° and 188°, respectively, and that the standard deviation of temperature is 1°. The control limits and the center line are shown in Figure 9.6. The upper and lower control limits are labeled *UCL* and *LCL* respectively, and the center line is labeled *CL*.

2. Control step: After the calibration is complete, observations are collected one batch at a time on the chart to determine whether the performance is under control. As before, five temperature readings are collected for each batch, and these readings are averaged to determine the temperature for the batch. Figure 9.6 shows the temperatures of ten batches plotted on the control chart. If the temperature of these batches is under control, we would expect over 99% of the points on

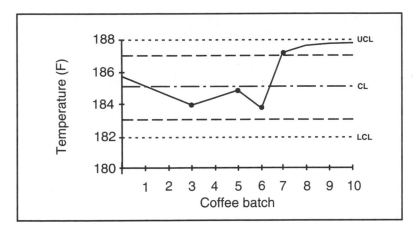

Figure 9.6 Control chart for coffee temperature

the chart to lie between the control limits of 182 and 188. We would also expect these points to be randomly distributed. Let us examine Figure 9.6 to see if this is the case.

3. Analysis of results: From Figure 9.6, it is clear that all ten observations lie between the control limits of 182° and 188°. Let us now examine the pattern of the observations. Two lines at temperature values of 183° and 187° are shown in Figure 9.6. These are the temperatures at two standard deviations on either side of the mean. From the properties of the normal distribution, we would expect no more than three or four observations out of 100 to fall above or below these values, because over 95% of the observations of a normally distributed variable lie between two standard deviations of the average value. However, Figure 9.6 shows that the last four observations (out of ten) show temperatures greater than 187°. This indicates that for some reason, the average temperature of four batches of coffee is systematically higher than the expected average performance of 185°. This indicates that the heating process may not be in control and that further analysis is necessary. We will show the use of control charts once again in our detailed example in Section 9.5.

Control, capability, and robustness—a comparison of concepts

We will close this section with a discussion of the differences between *control* and the two other concepts we have seen earlier that pertain to the variability in performance: *capability* and *robustness* of a process. *Control* is an internal process performance concept that is unrelated to the customers' needs. All that control implies is that the process performance is randomly distributed within three standard deviations of the average value. It merely confirms that process variability is *contained* within certain expected limits, irrespective of the acceptability of these limits to customers or the quality of the design.

Capability, on the other hand, is a measure of the extent to which a service meets the performance standards required by the design. A process in control may not be capable if its variability is too high, or if its average value is not properly centered between the design specifications. On the other hand, a process can be out of control and still be capable of meeting the design standards, if the standards are wide enough. For example, the control chart in Figure 9.6 shows a process whose performance is not randomly distributed between 182° and 188° (and is therefore not in control), but which is still capable of meeting the customers' desired temperature range of 180 to 190 degrees.

Finally, *robustness* is a measure of the sensitivity of the design performance to changes over an entire range of operating characteristics and environmental conditions. A process in control does not necessarily imply a robust design; it could merely be that the operating conditions did not change appreciably during the period when measurements were taken. Similarly, a process out of control does not automatically mean that the design is not robust; the conditions could have changed beyond the operating range for which the process was designed.

In summary, the fact that a process is in or out of control does not by itself provide any information of the quality of the design or its ability to satisfy customers. Control is the *consequence* of a good design, but not its indicator. When properly used, control charts should validate the service management team's expectations of how a well-designed process should perform. In other words, the process should *first* be designed to be capable and robust; it should then be *expected* to be under control. Service management teams sometimes spend a lot of effort in plotting control charts without a good understanding of the design properties (capability and robustness) of the process. In these cases, the control charts do not provide useful diagnostic information about the quality of the design.

Report distribution

After the data analysis is completed, the results and the suggested actions must be shared with those responsible for their implementation. The results may also be sent to senior management. The results need not be presented at the same level of detail for everyone in the organization. For senior management, it is enough to present a short and succinct summary that lists the current and past performance of key indicators, actions to be taken, and their predicted effect on future performance. For managers of individual processes, a summary of the overall performance and details of their process should be provided (for example, effectiveness and capability by work location, region, order, or customer type). For managers of a work location, a summary of overall performance must be supplemented with details of their own work location. The idea should be to provide all the key stakeholders with an overview of the performance of all components of the service, and to provide specific details to those in charge.

In order to ensure that the reporting process is effectively managed, it is important to make the service management team or a group designated by the team the sin-

Table 9.3   Performance information required at each organization level

Organization level	Information required
Senior management	Financial measures summary Customer satisfaction summary Service effectiveness and efficiency summary Performance and market predictions
Service management team level	Financial measures summary Customer satisfaction summary Service performance (effectiveness, efficiency, and capability) summary Root cause analysis of performance discrepancies Service stabilization activities
Process/attribute level	Customer satisfaction summary Service performance summary Attribute specific performance details Subprocess/activity specific performance details Investigation/analysis of performance discrepancies Outlier/exception analysis
Work location level	Customer satisfaction summary Service performance summary Work location specific customer satisfaction details Work location specific service performance details Resolution of customer complaints at work location Benchmarks/comparisons of work location costs and performance Other work location specific details
Work group level	Customer satisfaction summary Service performance summary Work location specific customer satisfaction details Work location specific service performance details Resolution of customer complaints List of defective orders and their resolution List of employees absent, on disability, in training, etc.

gle owner of all summary information. In every reporting period, this owner must ensure that the results distributed from each source cover the same time periods, use similar segmentation or exclusion rules, calculate performance in the same manner, and can be combined, aggregated, and reported with results from other sources. The owner's responsibility should primarily be to manage the reporting of national or aggregate data. Detailed information relevant to a work location or process may be locally managed and distributed as necessary.

The information needed at various levels of the organization is presented in Table 9.3. Note that the data summaries compiled at the level of the overall service are distributed to the entire organization. In addition to these summaries, detailed group specific information is required as we move down the table.

9.5 MONITORING SERVICE PERFORMANCE—SERVICE EDGE RESTAURANT EXAMPLE

In Section 9.1, we listed the following eight steps of the *performance monitoring and stabilization procedure* to measure and analyze the performance of the service:

Step 1: Select the design attributes to be analyzed.

Step 2: Measure the performance effectiveness of each selected attribute.

Step 3: Measure the capability of each selected attribute.

Step 4: Measure the efficiency of key processes.

Step 5: Identify attributes whose performance does not conform to standards or shows unusual change.

Step 6: Analyze the attributes identified in Step 5 in detail to determine the cause for poor performance or for unusual change in performance.

Step 7: Decide whether any corrective action is necessary, and if so, what steps need to be taken.

Step 8: Take the corrective action.

In this section, we demonstrate how these eight steps can be used to analyze the performance of the *order-taking process* of the Service Edge restaurant. The analysis described in this section is far more detailed than what would usually be performed at the level of a single process. Our objective is to use this process to give the reader a detailed view of how analysis should be performed to identify the root causes of performance problems. Depending on the application, these same techniques can be used at whatever level is judged to be the most appropriate.

We will begin with an overview of the order-taking process repeated from previous chapters. We will then describe each step listed above for this process.

Overview of order-taking process

The order-taking process of the Service Edge restaurant begins when the customer receives the menu and ends when an order is placed for the meal (see Chapter 5, Table 5.1). The flow chart of the process, repeated from Figure 6.2, is shown in Figure 9.7.

The *service/process matrix* introduced in Chapter 6 (Table 6.1) partitioned the design attributes of the service into process-level design attributes. Three attributes were identified for the order-taking process:

- Time between menu delivery and order-taking (promptness)

- Degree of order-taking patience (patience)

- Degree of knowledge about menu (knowledge)

In Chapter 6 (Table 6.2), the design performance standards for the three attributes were also specified. These are repeated in Table 9.4.

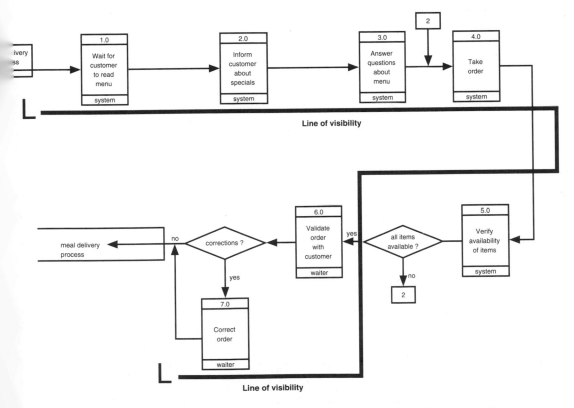

Figure 9.7　Activities of the order-taking process (repeat of Figure 6.2)

Table 9.4   Design performance standards for order-taking process attributes

Order-taking process design attribute	Standard
Time between menu delivery and order-taking	100% orders taken in < 5 minutes
Degree of order-taking patience	100% customers rate attribute "exceptional"
Degree of knowledge about menu	100% customers rate attribute "exceptional"

The design of the order-taking process at the Service Edge restaurant requires customers to enter their orders into a computer terminal placed at their table. The computer checks for the availability of the ordered items and notifies the customer if a particular menu item is not available. When the ordering is complete, the order is manually validated by a waiter who dispatches it to the kitchen for preparation.

Finally, three subprocesses of the order-taking process are identified in Chapter 6 (Table 6.6). The table is repeated as Table 9.5.

Let us now follow the eight steps of the performance monitoring and stabilization procedure for this process.

Step 1: Select the design attributes to be measured

In order to reduce the amount of data needed and the analysis effort required, performance measurements should be restricted to a few key attributes for each process. These attributes should be selected based on their importance specified in

Table 9.5   Subprocesses for the Service Edge order-taking process (repeat of Table 6.6)

Subprocesses	Activity numbers (from Figure 9.7)
Menu reading and ordering	1, 2, 3, 4 Feedback 2
Availability verification	5
Order validation and correction	6, 7

Table 9.6   Effectiveness of order-taking process of Service Edge restaurant

Metric	Target	Performance	No. of observations
% orders taken in less than 5 minutes	100%	88.5%	2110
% customers rating patience "exceptional"	> 95%	95.5%	1876
% customers rating patience "excellent"	> 5%	0.5%	
% customers rating knowledge "exceptional"	> 95%	99.5%	1876
% customers rating knowledge "excellent"	> 5%	4.5%	

the QFD matrix, or based on the slopes of their performance/satisfaction functions. In our example, since only three attributes are defined for the order-taking process, we will select all three attributes (promptness, patience, and knowledge) for analysis.

Step 2: Measure the performance effectiveness of each attribute

The effectiveness of an attribute is its ability to meet the performance standards. As stated in Section 9.2, effectiveness is measured by the *effectiveness metrics*. Table 9.1 shows all effectiveness metrics for the Service Edge restaurant. From this table, the following three metrics measure the effectiveness of the order-taking process attributes:

- % orders taken in less than 5 minutes

- % of customers rating order-taking patience "Exceptional"

- % of customers rating menu knowledge "Exceptional"

We will refer to these as the promptness, patience, and knowledge metrics respectively.

Table 9.6 shows the measured performance level for each effectiveness metric in the previous month. During this month, 2110 guests dined in the restaurant; of these, 1876 rated the restaurant on the patience and knowledge attributes.

Table 9.6 also shows the target performance level that each attribute is required to meet. In theory, these targets should be identical to the design performance standards shown in Table 9.4. In practice, it may be necessary to relax the targets slightly to account for *measurement errors*.

We can see this in Table 9.6 for the two intangible attributes: patience and knowledge. For these attributes, it is impossible to achieve a 100% "exceptional" customer rating even if the process has been designed to deliver a level of service that justifies this rating. The reason for this is that the ratings for these attributes are subject to random variations in customers' evaluation of performance. For example, a customer may never give a service the highest rating on principle, even if its performance is truly spectacular. Another customer's mood may negatively influence the rating. To account for these discrepancies, we need to set a *practical* target against which we can realistically evaluate the performance of the service. This target will be more relaxed than the performance standard, and its value will depend on the attribute. For attributes subject to wide interpretation, the targets should be farther away from the standard. For attributes subject to more consistent interpretations, the targets can be closer to the standard.

In Table 9.6, we set the practical targets for the percentage of customers rating the promptness and knowledge attributes exceptional at 95%. These values may arise from the service management team's experience with these attributes, or be based on a small pilot study where a small sample of customers is asked to explain the reasons for its ratings of the performance of these attributes. In any case, we assume that the performance of the service is satisfactory as long as fewer than 5% of the customers deviate from an "exceptional" rating. If a larger percentage rate the service worse than exceptional, then there may be some systematic deterioration in performance that needs to be investigated.

We can see from Table 9.6 that the promptness attribute does not meet its target, and the other two attributes do. The above discussion indicates the inherent complexity in setting accurate performance targets that meaningfully reflect customers' perception of the service. The reader may wonder why we set the performance standard for the knowledge and patience attributes at 100% in the first place, if we assume that 95% is acceptable. The reason is that the *customers' requirement* is that the service level should be exceptional for these attributes, as shown in Chapter 4. The service management team should always keep in mind that the final objective is to deliver a service level that *every* customer can rate as exceptional. This is the true performance standard and the service should be designed to meet this standard. At the same time, it is also important to realize that customer-to-customer variations in rating do take place, and some practical flexibility must be exercised in interpreting the results. The value of 95% therefore merely serves as an internal benchmark that helps to determine any aggressive intervention to improve the performance level of the attribute is necessary.

The 95.5% rating for the patience attribute in Table 9.6 should be a signal to the team that there is no immediate cause for concern about the performance of this attribute. However, if the ratings persist at this level for several time periods, then approximately 100 customers every month do not feel that their perceived service level is exceptional on this attribute. This should trigger the need for more detailed analysis to investigate why this is happening.

Data collection

How are data collected for the metrics of Table 9.6? As mentioned in Section 9.3, we should streamline data collection procedures so that information can be collected quickly and accurately. The automated nature of the order-taking process makes it possible to capture performance data easily for most customers. The *promptness* attribute, which is the time interval between the delivery of the menu and the taking of the order, can be automatically measured by the system. The interval begins with the activation of the menu screen when the guests are being seated. The system can automatically record the exact time at which this occurs. The times at which the customer approves the order and the waiter completes the validation can also be recorded by the system.

Data on the *knowledge* and *patience* attributes can be collected through a short survey that asks customers to rate various attributes of the service. The survey can be presented on-line at the terminal while customers are waiting for their bill to be settled. During this time, customers are not usually engaged in other activities. A large fraction of customers therefore tends to complete the survey. This results in high response rates for the survey. As shown in Table 9.6, we assume that data on the performance of these attributes are available for 1876 out of 2110 = 89% of the customers. This is typically a very high percentage.

Step 3: Measure the capability of each selected attribute

For the three attributes, the average performance and the variability of performance are chosen as measures of capability. For the promptness attribute, the variability is measured by the mean and standard deviation of the order-taking cycle time. The patience and knowledge attributes are measured on a discrete scale of 1 through 6, with 6 corresponding to exceptional performance. For variables measured on discrete scales, the maximum and minimum rating (or *range*) is a better indicator of variability than the standard deviation. Table 9.7 shows the capability metrics for the three attributes of the order-taking process.

Table 9.7 Capability of order-taking process of Service Edge restaurant

Metric	Average	Variability	No. of observations
Promptness (mins.)	4 minutes	Std. dev. = 0.65 min.	2110
Patience (rating)	5.9	Minimum rating = 5 Maximum rating = 6	1876
Knowledge (rating)	5.99	Minimum rating = 5 Maximum rating = 6	1876

Step 4: Measure the efficiency of key processes

Two measures of efficiency are used. The first is the average utilization of the waiters, which is a measure of resource productivity (and therefore of cost). The second is the percentage of customers who need to reorder items because their first choice was unavailable. This is a measure of rework and of the cost of quality of the process. We will describe how each of these measures is calculated.

1. Average utilization

A sample of the data required for calculating this measure is shown in Table 9.8 for an average waiter station consisting of four tables. Depending on the evening, either four or five waiters work at the station.

The *available minutes* in Table 9.8 measure the *capacity* of the waiter station. Assuming a 5-hour (300-minute) dinner period, the total capacity is given by the number of waiters available for the evening multiplied by 300 minutes. The available minutes are 1200 when four waiters are assigned and 1500 when five waiters are assigned.

The *active minutes* measure the total time during the course of the evening that the waiters at the station are busy. It is assumed that a waiter is busy if a table is occupied. The active time is therefore calculated by tracking the number of minutes during the course of the evening when each table at the waiter station is occupied and adding up this time across the four tables. The *utilization* is given by the number of active minutes divided by the available minutes.

Table 9.8 Sample data for calculating waiter utilization

Date	No. of waiters	Available minutes	Active minutes	Utilization
April 1	4	1200	876	0.73
April 2	5	1500	1145	0.76
April 3	5	1500	1200	0.80
April 4	4	1200	864	0.72
April 5	4	1200	852	0.71
April 6	4	1200	756	0.63
April 7	4	1200	696	0.58

Table 9.9   Efficiency measures for the order-taking subprocess

Metric	Actual value	Design value
Waiter utilization	0.70	0.75
% customers reordering	13%	15%

The service management team should collect a sample of data similar to Table 9.8 at various points during the month. It may not be necessary to track every waiter station every day; rather, tracking a few selected waiter stations several days a month (making sure that at least one data point is collected for every day of the week) and averaging these results should provide an adequate estimate of the average efficiency.

2. *Percentage of customers reordering*

This measure is specific to the order-taking process and is an indicator of the *rework* in the process. If the initial order is not available, the customer needs to place another order. This metric can be automatically measured by the ordering system, which tracks each instance when this takes place.

Table 9.9 shows these two efficiency measures. The values of these measures expected by the design (see Tables 7.2 and 7.3) are also shown in the table.

Step 5: Identify attributes whose performance fails to conform to standards or shows unusual change

The analysis described in this step is conducted in three parts:

A. Effectiveness analysis

B. Capability analysis

C. Efficiency analysis

In *effectiveness analysis*, we examine the effectiveness metrics to identify attributes that do not meet the performance standards, or those that meet them marginally. For these attributes, we examine the run chart of the effectiveness metrics to check whether the poor performance has been encountered in the past.

In *capability analysis*, we examine the capability metrics of selected attributes that may contribute to the poor performance of the attributes identified during the effectiveness analysis. Both current and historical measures are examined.

In *efficiency analysis*, we examine the efficiency metrics of selected attributes that may contribute to the poor performance of the attributes identified during the effectiveness and capability analyses. Both current and historical measures are examined.

We will now describe each analysis for the order-taking process.

A. *Effectiveness analysis*

The first step is to examine the effectiveness measures for each attribute of the process. From this examination, the attributes are divided into three categories:

1. Attributes whose performance does not meet the standards

2. Attributes whose performance meets the standards marginally and may need to be investigated further

3. Attributes whose performance meets the standards comfortably and do not require investigation

The order-taking promptness attribute falls into the first category. Since only 88.5% of the orders are completed in 5 minutes or less, the performance of this attribute does not meet the standards. Further analysis is clearly necessary.

The patience attribute falls into the second category. Since the results for the patience attribute for the given month are only marginally acceptable, the team needs to check whether this performance level is typical, or whether the performance has deteriorated because of some special reason in the past month. This can be done from the *run chart* shown in Figure 9.8. We can see from this figure that the performance in the last month is significantly different from that of the previous four. Since the attribute meets the performance target for the current month, the team decides not to take any action immediately. However, the performance of this attribute needs to be closely monitored in the ensuing months.

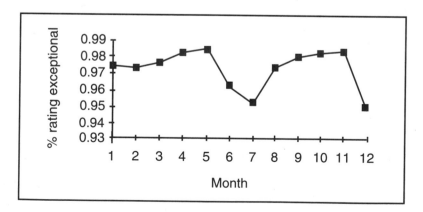

Figure 9.8   Run chart of percentage of customers rating patience "exceptional"

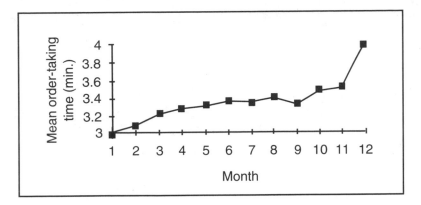

Figure 9.9   Run chart of mean order-taking time

The knowledge rating falls into the third category. For the moment, the process is performing well on this attribute, and there is no reason to examine it any further.

B. *Capability analysis*

Since the order-taking promptness does not meet the performance standards, the service management team decides to examine the *average order-taking time*. From Table 9.7, we can see that the average time is 4 minutes, which is within the performance standards. However, the standard deviation is 0.65 minutes, which means that if the cycle times are normally distributed, we would expect about 20% of the observations to lie beyond the target of 5 minutes. This is clearly not acceptable.

The next step is to ascertain the historical performance of this attribute. Figure 9.9 is a run chart of the average order-taking time for the past twelve months. It can be seen that this measure has slowly increased over time, but the past month shows a sudden sharp increase. It appears, therefore, that the 4-minute average for the current month is unusually high. We need to examine the efficiency metrics to determine if any unusual trends can be seen in reorders or in the utilization level of waiters.

C. *Efficiency analysis*

The results for the current month in Table 9.9 show that the average utilization and reorder percentage are within the design limits, so there appears to be no immediate cause for concern. However, the run charts for the reorder percentage (i.e., percentage of customers reordering items from the menu) and the waiter utilization, shown in Figures 9.10 and 9.11, respectively, indicate a sudden increase in these measures for the current month.

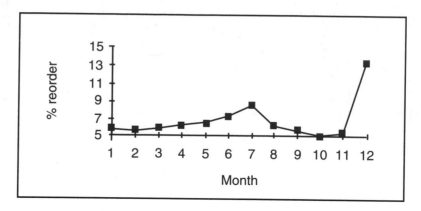

Figure 9.10 Percentage of customers reordering in the past twelve months

Conclusions from analysis

Figures 9.9, 9.10, and 9.11 lead the team to the following hypotheses:

1. The promptness attribute does not meet the performance standard because of the increase in average order-taking time.

2. The increase in average order-taking time may be due to either (a) a change in the percentage of reorders, or (b) an increase in the waiter utilization over the past month.

These hypotheses are investigated in greater detail in the following step.

Step 6: Analyze the attributes identified in Step 5 to determine the cause of poor performance or of unusual change in performance

In this step, we test the hypotheses posed in the previous step through more detailed analysis. Once again, the proposed analysis in this step is carried out in three parts:

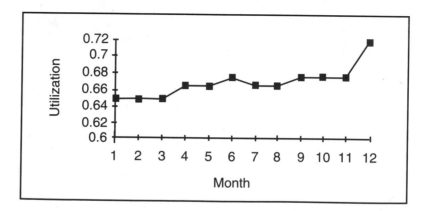

Figure 9.11 Waiter utilization values in the past twelve months

A. Exception analysis

B. Subprocess analysis

C. Root cause analysis

In *exception analysis,* we check whether any unexpected performance changes in a given reporting period can be attributed to any unique, uncontrollable causes or special circumstances. This is usually done by examining *exception reports* that provide details about each service encounter that did not meet the performance standard. In some applications, these exception reports may be generated by sorting on special codes that may have to be entered into a tracking system if there was a problem with a service encounter. If exception reports are not available, the service management team may examine a sample of service encounters in detail (for example, by looking at records of each transaction) to determine whether any unique patterns can be discerned.

The objective of *subprocess analysis* is to isolate the source of a performance problem to a particular subprocess or function. This analysis replicates the process-level analysis at the subprocess level. For each process attribute whose performance needs to be examined, the process/subprocess matrix (see Table 6.7) is used to identify the relevant subprocesses that affect the performance of that attribute. The effectiveness, capability, and efficiency of these subprocesses are analyzed to identify areas of poor performance. This analysis is repeated at the function level if necessary, until the source of the problem is clearly identified.

Finally, once the source of the problem is established and cannot be attributed to a special or unique circumstance, *root cause analysis* is performed to diagnose the reason for the problem. The objective of this analysis is not to settle on the first apparently obvious, superficial reason, but to follow the causal chain all the way until the primary, fundamental source of the problem has been determined. Attempting to solve the problem at this level is more likely to produce a long-term solution than a temporary "quick fix" that attacks only the symptoms.

Let us see how these three types of analysis can be performed for the order-taking process example.

A. *Exception analysis*

The service management team individually analyzed the 242 orders that had order-taking time greater than 5 minutes (11.5% of 2110). As a result of this analysis, it was found that 150 delayed orders took place on a single evening when some unexpected conditions resulted in only half the waiters being available. This is indicated by the histogram of Figure 9.12, which shows the number of days in the past month at which the average utilization was at various levels. The bar on the extreme right of Figure 9.12 shows that on one day, the average utilization was between 0.95 and 1.0. This accounted for the 150 delayed orders.

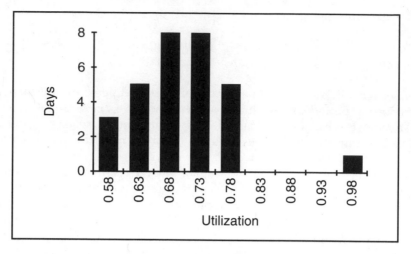

Figure 9.12   Histogram of average utilization levels for a month

The reason for the delay is that the waiter utilization affects the time that customers have to wait for their order to be validated by the waiter (see Section 7.1). This time, called the *order validation wait time,* is a subset of the order-taking interval. Figure 9.13 shows the performance function for the order validation wait time as a function of utilization, repeated from Figure 7.2 (a). It can be seen from Figure 9.13 that the performance function for the order validation wait time is nonlinear and takes on very large values (close to 5 minutes, which is the performance stan-

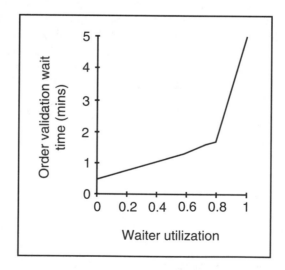

Figure 9.13   Performance function for order validation time [repeat of Figure 7.2(a)]

dard for the *entire* order-taking interval) when the utilization is close to 1. The special circumstances of the single day when the utilization was significantly higher than the design levels led to an exceptionally high order validation wait time, and consequently to a delay in the order-taking interval for 150 orders.

Since the unavailability of waiters was a special circumstance, all the data from this day can be treated as *outliers,* i.e. not representing normal process operations. We can therefore drop these 150 observations and recalculate the effectiveness metrics. These results are shown in Table 9.10.

Conclusions from exception analysis

The following observations can be made from Table 9.10:

- The unavailability of waiters on one day *partially* accounts for the number of delayed orders (150 out of 242).

- The cause of the remaining 92 delayed orders is still unknown, but is suspected to be due to the increased percentage of customers reordering a meal as shown in the run chart of Figure 9.10.

Some additional analysis is therefore necessary to identify the reasons for delays in the remaining orders.

B. *Subprocess analysis*

We now analyze the order-taking process in detail to isolate the particular subprocess or function whose performance is contributing to the delay in the order-

Table 9.10   Recalculated effectiveness of order-taking process of Service Edge restaurant

Metric	Target	Performance	No. of observations
Promptness	100% orders < 5 minutes	95.3% < 5 minutes	1960
Patience	> 95% rating "Exceptional" < 5% rating "Excellent"	97% exceptional 3% excellent	1726
Knowledge	> 95% rating "Exceptional" < 5% rating "Excellent"	99.5% exceptional 0.5% excellent	1726

taking interval. As shown in Table 9.5, the order-taking process has three associated subprocesses:

- Menu reading and ordering
- Availability verification
- Order validation

From the process/subprocess matrix (see Table 6.7), we can also see that the overall order-taking promptness is affected by the performance of all three subprocesses. We now need to identify the subprocesses that are the most likely contributors to the delay in the promptness attribute. We do this by performing effectiveness capability and efficiency analysis (see step 5) on each subprocess of the order-taking process. For purposes of illustration, we will describe the following two analyses:

(a) Effectiveness analysis of the menu reading and ordering subprocess

(b) Capability analysis of the availability verification subprocess

(a) *Effectiveness analysis of menu reading and ordering subprocess:* Recall from Table 9.6 that the design performance target for the promptness attribute was that 100% of the orders should be completed in less than 5 minutes (under 300 seconds). When we evaluated design alternatives for this process in Section 7.1, we saw that approximately half this time was spent in the menu reading and ordering functions. This translates into the *subprocess target* 0 + 150 seconds shown in Table 9.11 for the menu reading and ordering subprocess.

To test whether the subprocess is currently meeting this standard, the performance of the menu reading and ordering subprocess in the past month is shown in the histogram of Figure 9.14. The columns represent the number of orders associated with various ordering intervals. For example, the value "112.5" corresponds to an interval between 100 and 125 seconds.

Figure 9.14 shows that the histogram is *bimodal*, with a large majority of the customers ordering within 150 seconds and a very small number (about 88) ordering in 200–250 seconds. Of the 92 delayed orders still remaining after the exception

Table 9.11   Design standard for the promptness attribute of the menu reading and ordering subprocess

Subprocess	Subprocess design standard for promptness attribute
Menu reading and ordering	100% orders completed within 150 seconds

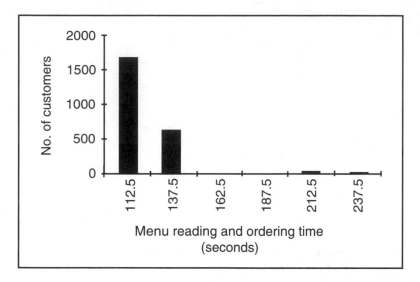

Figure 9.14   Histogram of ordering subprocess cycle time

analysis, it appears that the delay for 88 orders can be attributed to the exceptionally long ordering interval. It now remains to find the root cause for this delay.

(b) *Capability analysis of the availability verification subprocess:* Since the source of the
delay for most of the orders was found to be the ordering subprocess above, we
should not expect any additional delays arising from the availability verification
subprocess. Figure 9.15, which shows a control chart for the average availability
verification time over the past twelve months, indicates that this is indeed the case.
The center line is at 29 seconds, and the control limits are at 28 and 30 seconds. Because this subprocess is entirely automated (the order entry system checks for
availability with no human intervention), its performance variability is low. From
Figure 9.15, it can be seen that the average availability verification time for the past
twelve months is under control.

Conclusions from subprocess analysis

From the subprocess analysis, it can be concluded that the reason that the order-
taking interval does not meet the performance standard for 88 customers is that
these customers take an unusually long time to read the menu and place their order. We now need to investigate the root cause for this.

C. *Root cause analysis*

Now that the source of the delay in the order-taking interval has been identified,
the next step is to investigate its root cause. Further investigation shows that, as
hypothesized at the end of the exception analysis, the reason for the large ordering
time for 88 customers in Figure 9.14 is indeed the fact that some customers are

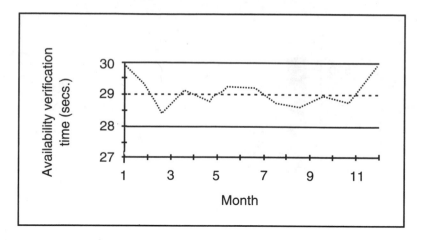

Figure 9.15   Control chart for average availability verification time for past
twelve months

forced to reorder multiple times, and therefore need to browse the menu for a second time to reorder. This causes an increase in the time taken to order the meal, which in turn results in an increased cycle time for the overall process.

However, the increased percentage of reorders is an *effect*, not a *cause*. We need to perform additional analysis to identify the cause. The solution can then be tailored to address this root cause. The service management team investigates two possibilities for the increased reorder percentage:

(a) The popularity and therefore the *demand* for some menu items has increased, resulting in these items being sold out early in the evening.

(b) The *supply* of some menu items has decreased because they are not being prepared by the kitchen any more, or are being prepared in smaller quantities.

Conclusions from root cause analysis

The investigation reveals that the second possibility is the cause of the increased reorder percentage. Over the past few months, the restaurant has reduced the supply of some menu items that require fresh ingredients that are difficult to obtain and store. Customers who ordered these items were often told that they were not available. These customers had to make a different selection. To make matters worse, it turned out that the 88 customers shown in Figure 9.14 had to reorder *multiple times*, because the restaurant had cut back on the production of some closely related menu items that customers would try and order as substitutes for each other. As a result, customers would try to order a whole list of items that were unavailable before trying another menu category. This was the root cause of the problem.

Step 7: Decide whether any corrective action is necessary, and the steps that need to be taken

What corrective steps need to be taken based on the above findings? For any problem, three alternatives are available:

1. Do nothing
2. Correct immediately
3. Correct later as part of a larger plan

In our example, we identified two root causes for the problem of delays in order-taking:

(*a*) *Unavailability of waiters on a particular day:* The delay this caused is an unusual event that is unlikely to be repeated. No action was deemed to be necessary to correct this situation.

(*b*) *Unavailability of closely related menu items:* The delays in ordering caused by the unavailability of menu items is an *operational*, not a *design*, problem. However, this problem can have both a design and an operational solution.

The *operational solution* that can be immediately implemented recommends changing the food preparation strategy so that at least a few of the related menu items are always likely to be available. This increases the probability that customers will find an available item on the first reorder attempt.

The *design solution*, which can be implemented in the future, requires the ordering system to be modified so that unavailable items can temporarily be removed from the menu. This solution should be implemented *in conjunction* with the solution and not as its substitute. Both solutions were recommended by the service management team.

Step 8: Carry out the required steps

An implementation plan is adopted for each recommendation of the service management team. The operational solution is shared with the kitchen managers, who develop a plan for immediately implementing the solution. The design solution is documented and is included as an initiative of a future *service improvement plan*. This plan identifies improvement opportunities and prioritizes them based on their predicted impact on future customer satisfaction and their implementation cost. The most important activities from this plan are then chosen for implementation.

9.6 CONCLUSION

Summary

The following is a step-by-step summary of the activities described in this chapter. The section in the chapter where a particular topic is covered is indicated in parentheses.

Measures for service monitoring and improvement (introduction)

- Service performance measures test whether the service performs as expected by the design.
- Customer measures evaluate how service performance satisfies customers.
- Financial measures determine how the behavior of satisfied customers affects profitability.

Performance monitoring and stabilization process (9.1), (9.5)

- Select the design attributes to be analyzed.
- Measure the performance effectiveness of each selected attribute.
- Measure the capability of each selected attribute.
- Measure the efficiency of key processes.
- Perform effectiveness analysis to identify attributes that do not meet standards.
- Perform capability and efficiency analysis to check for unusual performance changes.
- Perform exception analysis to test whether performance changes can be attributed to unique, uncontrollable causes.
- Perform subprocess analysis to identify subprocesses and functions where the performance changes occur.
- Perform root cause analysis to determine the cause for performance changes in each subprocess or function.
- Decide if any corrective action is necessary.
- Take action immediately or include in service improvement plan for future implementation.

Service performance metrics (9.2)

- Effectiveness metrics measure performance relative to a target or standard.
- Capability metrics measure the intrinsic ability of a process to meet performance standards.

- Efficiency metrics measure the cost of delivering the service and resources utilized.

Data collection and tracking system guidelines (9.3)

- Select a few, critical items for measurement.
- Sample, if necessary.
- Automate, if possible.
- Avoid paper forms.
- Develop easy data access and reporting capabilities.
- Decentralize data analysis.
- Make data collection part of job function.
- Openly communicate the objective of data collection.

Data analysis and reporting (9.4)

- Routine analysis is regular, systematic, and performed in every reporting period.
- Routine analysis procedures should be repeatable, documented, and decentralized.
- Ad hoc analysis is detailed, diagnostic testing.
- Graphical representation enhances ability to interpret data.
- Histograms, run charts, scatter plots and control charts are four versatile graphical tools.
- Reports should be generated appropriate to the level for which they are intended.

Suggested reading

The following texts are recommended for further reading on statistical data analysis and process control. This is not an exhaustive collection, but it provides a good overview of different aspects of these topics.

Kume (1985) provides a detailed description of the analysis tools presented in this chapter and instructions on when to use them. Asaka (1990) is a step-by-step guide to constructing many types of charts. McNeese and Klein (1991), while similar to the previous text, is a little more detailed. It includes descriptions of how to draw different types of control charts. Gukezian (1991) is a more mathematical, statistical approach to process control than the other texts listed.

Chapter
10

Assessing Customer Satisfaction

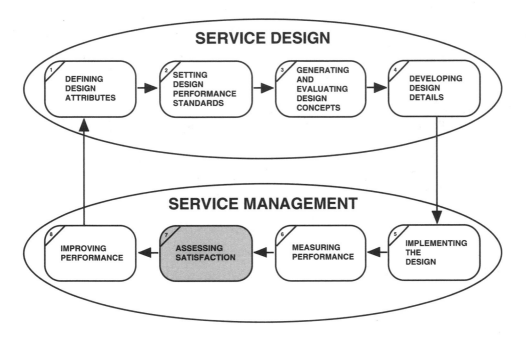

- *Effect of market and customer changes on satisfaction*
- *Defining customer satisfaction—disconfirmation model*
- *Expectations*
- *Other models of satisfaction*
- *Satisfaction and value*
- *Measuring satisfaction*
- *Conclusion*

In Chapter 9, we stated that because the service design standards are customer-generated performance requirements, a service that does not perform to these standards will not satisfy customers. We begin this chapter with the opposite question: *If a service performs reliably at the level expected by the design, can we automatically assume that its customers are satisfied?* If the answer to this question is "yes," then it is enough to measure the performance of the service using the metrics described in Chapter 9, and to take steps to ensure that this performance remains stable over time. However, if the answer to this question is "no," then the service performance measures alone are not enough to determine whether customers are satisfied. We need to define *customer measures* (see Figure 9.1) as well.

To answer this question, recall how the design standards were determined in Chapter 4. We estimated the performance/satisfaction relationship for each design attribute. This relationship predicted overall satisfaction as a function of the performance of the attribute. Based on these relationships, we specified the design standards as initial estimates of the performance needed to maintain a required level of satisfaction. As the design gets implemented and used, if these relationships remain accurate and invariant, then a service that meets the design specifications will continue to deliver the required level of satisfaction. However, if one or more of the following situations takes place:

1. Competitors' service improves

2. Customers' needs change

3. Customers' needs remain the same, but their relative importance changes

then the performance/satisfaction relationship changes, and we can no longer guarantee that meeting the design performance standards will result in an acceptable level of satisfaction. The performance/satisfaction relationship has to be re-estimated, but this time with actual (rather than with hypothetical) satisfaction and performance data. In Chapter 9, we showed how to measure performance. The measurement of satisfaction is the topic of this chapter.

Satisfaction data are usually collected by surveying customers. The design of the satisfaction instrument, the sampling techniques used to select customers, and the methods by which data should be collected to avoid bias are important issues facing practitioners who develop and implement satisfaction surveys. In this chapter, we do not discuss these issues. This is because the problems of questionnaire design and administration are common to all fields in which survey-based data collection is used. The practical details of administering surveys, both within and outside the context of customer satisfaction measurements, is well documented in the literature. However, there is often little discussion in these texts about the different definitions of customer satisfaction, and about the kinds of information that each definition provides, nor is there much discussion about different approaches to measuring satisfaction. To practitioners, this knowledge is as important as knowledge about the mechanics of data collection, since it helps them to create a measurement instrument that is most suitable for their application. Our focus in this chapter will therefore be on these aspects of satisfaction measurement.

In Section 10.1, we describe in detail the impact of changes in customer needs or in competitors' service performance on the performance/satisfaction function. In Sections 10.2 through 10.4, we describe different definitions of satisfaction found in the literature, and discuss the situations in which each definition is applicable. Section 10.5 introduces the concept of value and describes the relationship between satisfaction and value. Section 10.6 describes various approaches for measuring satisfaction and discusses their advantages, limitations, and applicability. Section 10.7 is a summary of this chapter.

10.1 EFFECT OF MARKET AND CUSTOMER CHANGES ON SATISFACTION

In the previous section, we mentioned three factors that cause a change in the performance/satisfaction relationship for an attribute of a service:

1. Competitor's service improves

2. Customers' needs change

3. Customers' needs remain the same, but their relative importance changes

In this section, we will describe the impact of each of these factors on the performance/satisfaction relationship, and the resulting implications for customer satisfaction measurement.

Improvement in a competitor's service

When a competitor offers a higher level of service than what is currently being provided, the satisfaction/performance relationship shifts to a new curve. This is shown in Figure 10.1. In this figure, better performance and higher satisfaction occur in the direction of the arrows on the axes.

Suppose the current satisfaction/performance relationship is given by the line marked "A." The current performance standard is indicated by performance value "STD." Suppose the satisfaction level at this performance has an arbitrary rating of 100, as indicated in Figure 10.1. Also assume that this rating of 100 implies a satisfied customer.

Suppose now that a competitor delivers service at a higher performance level marked "2" in Figure 10.1. Initially, this performance level may not be expected by the customers, and the satisfaction/performance relationship still remains at line "A." On this line, the satisfaction with the new service increases dramatically to a "supersatisfied" or "delighted" rating of 120, while the satisfaction with the current service still receives a rating of 100. Over time, however, customers begin to expect all service providers to perform at the new level. At this time, the satisfaction/performance relationship will shift to the line marked "B." The new performance level "2" will be required to satisfy customers, and, on the new curve, will

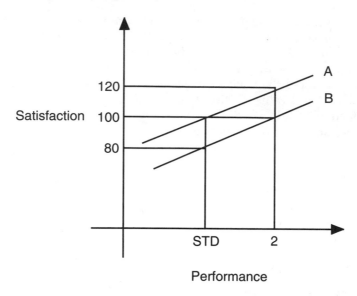

Figure 10.1 Effect of a change in a competitor's performance on satisfaction

correspond to a rating of 100. A service that continues to perform at "STD," the level of the current design standards, will now correspond to a lower satisfaction rating of 80. When this happens, the service clearly no longer satisfies customers merely by performing at the current standards.

Changes in customers' needs

Figure 10.1 also depicts the effect of a change in customers' needs. Consider once again a service that performs at the level "STD" and results in a satisfaction rating of 100 on line "A" in Figure 10.1. As customers' needs change, performance level that is superior to "STD" will be needed for the same satisfaction rating of 100. The satisfaction/performance relationship shifts from the line "A" to the line "B." In order to satisfy the new set of needs, the service has to perform at level "2" which corresponds to the satisfaction rating of 100 on line 8. The current performance of the service, at level "STD," is no longer acceptable.

Changes in relative priority of needs

In some situations, the needs themselves may remain the same, but the relative priority of needs may change. This results in a change in the *slope* of the satisfaction/performance relationship, as shown in Figure 10.2.

Suppose the current satisfaction/performance relationship for a service attribute is given by the line "A." The performance level "STD" corresponds to a satisfaction rating of 100. Since the line does not have a very steep slope, small changes in performance around the standard will not cause significant changes in satisfac-

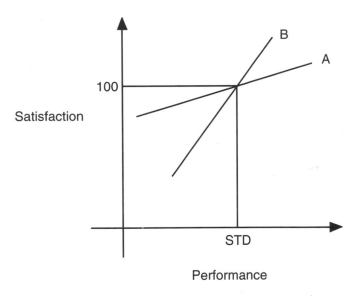

Figure 10.2   Effect of a change in attribute importance on satisfaction

tion. The service management team can therefore exercise some flexibility in managing the performance of this attribute.

Now suppose that the attribute begins to increase in importance over time, and that its performance becomes more and more critical to customers. An example of such an attribute may be the time taken to resolve a problem by the customer service hot line of a software product. Initially, when the product is new or in a trial stage, customers are willing to wait for experts to answer their questions and are less concerned about the amount of time they spend on the telephone trying to get their problem resolved. However, as customers become more experienced with the product, they expect most routine questions to be answered quickly and on their first call, with expert assistance needed only for more complicated problems.

When this occurs, the slope of the satisfaction/performance relationship in Figure 10.2 may change to that of the steeper line "B." Small changes in performance now have a much more serious impact on satisfaction. The performance of the service attribute therefore has to be much more closely controlled. Performance levels slightly inferior to the standards that were considered acceptable in the past may now result in significant dissatisfaction.

Need for customer satisfaction measurements

Figures 10.1 and 10.2 illustrate that it cannot be assumed that a service that meets the performance standards also continues to provide the desired degree of customer satisfaction over time. Measures of customer satisfaction must therefore be independently developed and correlated with performance. These are the

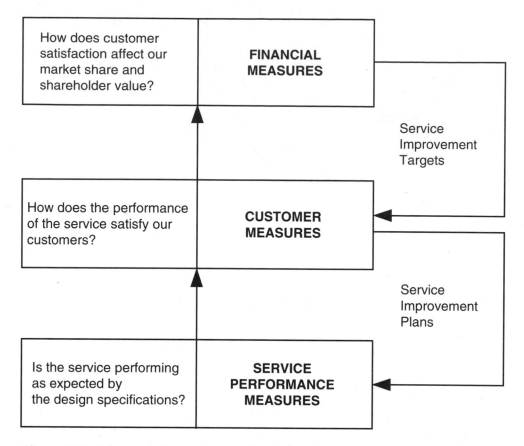

Figure 10.3 Measures for service monitoring and improvement (repeat of Figure 9.1)

customer measures indicated in Figure 10.3 (repeat of Figure 9.1), which answer the question: "How does the performance of the service satisfy our customers?"

If these measures indicate that customers are not satisfied, then service improvements must be made to increase the satisfaction level. Even if the customer satisfaction ratings are currently acceptable, the service management team can proactively develop service improvement plans to maintain superiority in the market. After all, the shift in the satisfaction/performance relationship shown in Figure 10.1 need not be instigated by a competitor; it can be initiated by the organization as part of its strategic plan for growth.

So far in this chapter, we have talked about customer satisfaction as though it had a single, universally understood definition and scale of measurement. This is not the case. There are several definitions and measurement approaches to customer satisfaction in the literature. Each definition carries a different information content and has a different applicability. In the following sections we present several conceptual issues related to the definition and measurement of customer satisfaction. We will discuss these issues in general terms from the viewpoint of the literature on service quality, and where required, clarify how these concepts are applied in the context of this book.

10.2 DEFINING CUSTOMER SATISFACTION— DISCONFIRMATION MODEL

The most commonly used representation of customer satisfaction in the service quality literature is referred to as the *disconfirmation model* (e.g., see Oliver, 1980, 1989, 1993). The elements of this model are shown in Figure 10.4. According to this model, the extent of satisfaction (or lack of satisfaction) that a customer has with a service encounter is determined by the disconfirmation between the customer's expectations of performance and the actual perceived performance of the service.

According to the model, positive disconfirmation occurs when the perceived performance is better than what was expected; it results in a *satisfied* customer. Negative disconfirmation is the result of perceived performance being worse than expectations; it causes *dissatisfaction*. Confirmation (or zero disconfirmation) is a *neutral* state in which the perceived performance just meets the expectations.

Other terminology may also be used to describe the outcomes of the three disconfirmation states. In this book, we assume that a service whose performance meets customers' expectations (as specified by the design standards) with zero disconfirmation will *satisfy* customers, rather than elicit a neutral response. A service encounter that exceeds these expectations (i.e., positive disconfirmation) will *delight*

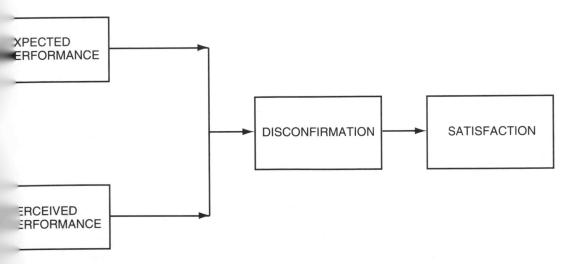

Figure 10.4 Disconfirmation model of customer satisfaction

customers. A service encounter that does not meet the expectations still causes *dis-satisfaction*.

The disconfirmation model has proved to be a robust predictor of satisfaction in many service settings (see Yi, 1991, for a review of applications). It can be seen from Figure 10.4 that in addition to disconfirmation, this model has two other components: the *expected* and the *perceived performance*. We have already described the measurement of perceived performance using service performance metrics in Chapter 9. We have implicitly used the notion of expectations several times in this book without explicitly defining the meaning of the term. We do this in the following section.

10.3   EXPECTATIONS

Types of expectations

What do we mean when we talk about a customer's *expectations* of performance? Do we mean the performance level that a customer would *ideally* expect from a service? Or, do we mean the performance level that the customer would *desire* the service to have, or the level that is *acceptable*? Is it the performance level that the customer would *predict* for a particular service encounter? Or can we think about *comparative* expectations based on the customer's experience with similar services?

Researchers (see Zeithami *et al.*, 1993, for an overview of research) have found evidence for all the types of expectations mentioned above. *Ideal* expectations refer to the performance wished for in a perfect service. *Desired* expectations are the performance levels that customers want the service to meet in practice. If the service provider cannot deliver service at the desired level, customers may be willing to tolerate deviations in performance up to their *acceptable* expectations with relatively small degradation in satisfaction. Dissatisfaction results if the performance falls below this level. Note that the ideal, desired, and acceptable expectations are similar in concept to the ideal, desired, and design performance standards described in Chapter 4.

The *predicted* expectation is the performance level that the customer anticipates will be achieved by a service encounter before this encounter is experienced. This is determined by past experience with the service. If past service encounters have been unsatisfactory, the predicted expectation for the next encounter is likely to be low. For example, a customer who has waited for a long time during previous attempts to make an airline reservation over the telephone is unlikely to expect that the next call will result in a short wait.

Some other types of expectations that have been defined in the literature are *comparative*, *normative*, and *value-based*. *Comparative* expectations refer to the performance levels anticipated for the service derived from experiences with competing services. *Normative* expectations of services are based on brand names—a well-known brand may be expected to perform better than one that is lesser known.

Value-based expectations depend on a "worth what is paid for" analysis—the performance expectations of a service depend on its price.

Selecting the appropriate expectations model

Expectations are used to develop the performance standards to which the service should be designed. Given the range of expectation types presented above, how do we know which type to use for a particular application? The answer depends on the nature of the service and on the objectives of the firm. The *ideal expectations model* is appropriate for services where small imperfections in performance have large consequences. For example, safety inspection procedures for aircraft should be designed to meet ideal, or close to ideal, expectations. Companies that wish to use the quality of their service as a marketing vehicle should attempt to achieve at least the *desired level* of performance and should strive to design and improve their processes to meet the ideal level. Any firm that wants to compete profitably in the market should adopt the *comparative expectations model* and design a service that performs at least as well as the competitors, or, in accordance with *value-based expectations*, should design a service that maximizes the customers' sense of what they get for what they pay. The *normative expectations model* is appropriate for designing a new service for a firm with an already established name or service line. The new service should be designed to match the performance expectations commensurate with the reputation of the firm or of the service line.

Our approach in this book is to simultaneously use several definitions of expectations. Recall the method for specifying the design performance standards in Chapter 4. The data for specifying the design performance levels for each service attribute came from two sources: (a) ideal or desired expectations obtained from interviews with customers and (b) comparative expectations from the customer and technical benchmarks in Rooms 4 and 5 of the QFD matrix. In addition, the design team trades off the benefits of satisfying these expectations with the associated cost. If the cost of meeting the desired expectations is too high for a particular attribute, the team may decide to design the service to meet an acceptable performance level that can be implemented at a lower cost. This is a value-based decision.

In summary, researchers have identified many different kinds of expectations, each of which applies under different circumstances. In practice, there is a need to develop the optimal combination of performance standards that will allow the designed service to satisfy customers, to compare favorably with competitors' services, and to be delivered at a cost that will allow the company to sell the service profitably. Depending on the application, the design or service management team may have to combine different types of expectations in order to define this set of standards.

10.4 OTHER MODELS OF SATISFACTION

The disconfirmation model presented in Section 10.2 can be used to measure the satisfaction resulting from a single individual's experience with a specific service encounter. This is not a useful measure in practice. Our ultimate objective is to predict the impact of customer satisfaction on profitability. In order to do this, we need to know how satisfaction affects the *future purchase decisions* of a *group* of customers. These decisions are not influenced by individual service encounters; rather, they depend on the cumulative effect of *long-term experience* with the service. Also, they depend on who is making the purchase decisions. In order to consider these requirements, we need to define the distinctions among the following:

1. Individual and group satisfaction

2. Transaction-specific and cumulative satisfaction

3. User and decision-maker satisfaction

These are described in this section.

Individual and group satisfaction

The satisfaction of a single individual with a service is easy enough to measure using the disconfirmation model. But in most practical situations, we are interested in measuring the satisfaction of a group, since the service is typically designed to meet the needs of numerous customers. How can we do this?

One approach is to apply the disconfirmation model to each customer in the group. Before each service encounter, we can ask a customer to rate his or her desired performance expectations for the service. After each encounter, we can measure the perceived performance. The difference between these two measures is then correlated with satisfaction.

In practice, this is not a good method. There are several reasons for this. First, because expectations data have to be collected *before* the service encounter and perceptions data *after* the encounter, this would require the customers to be contacted twice to obtain the required information, which is cumbersome and expensive. A less expensive approach is to collect both expectations and performance ratings after the service encounter, but the expectations ratings may be biased by the service experienced during the encounter.

Another problem with collecting expectations data from a written survey is that the absence of a systematic procedure such as QFD that carefully probes for nuances in verbal customer statements may result in a routine documentation of customers' ideal expectations ("I want the best service").

Finally, from a measurement perspective, computing the value of disconfirmation as the difference between expectation and perception rating scores increases the error in its measurement because of the cumulative effect of errors in the measurement of each score. Authors such as Carman (1990) question the psychometric properties of difference scores and the validity of statistical conclusions drawn from models that use these scores.

For these reasons, a better approach is to directly measure *satisfaction*, which is the *output* of the performance/expectations comparison. We survey customers and obtain their satisfaction ratings with the performance of various service attributes. But before we do this, we must segment the population into groups with *homogenous expectations*, so that satisfaction can be measured against a common standard. How do we identify these groups? We are looking here for homogeneity in terms of expectations for service attributes, which may be different from the socioeconomic groupings of age, gender, income, or geographic location often used for market segmentation. Typically, we should look for homogeneities in the *use* of the service. For example, bank customers who conduct most of their service transactions using an ATM will have different performance expectations from customers who prefer to visit the bank in person. Some of the key dimensions along which homogenous groups can be defined are the following:

- Similar needs

- Similar priority ranking of needs

- Similar ratings of the performance of key competitors

- Similar satisfaction ratings of service profiles (i.e., similar satisfaction/performance relationships)

New data are not needed to determine homogenous customer groups along the dimensions mentioned above. This information is available in the customer benchmarks of House of Quality matrix, and in the data used to estimate performance/satisfaction relationships (see Chapter 4). In practice, therefore, identifying customer groups with homogenous expectations simply involves *segmenting the customer population* during the design stage, and setting individual design specification standards for each segment. These segment level design performance standards represent the *collective expectations of the homogenous market segment.*

During the concept generation stage (Chapter 5), the design team should attempt to develop a *single* concept that, with a few modifications, can be robust in meeting the needs of all market segments. If this is not possible, and multiple concepts need to be designed (with associated hardware/software development, staffing, and training) for each segment, then the design team must carefully evaluate the potential profitability of each design. At times, it may be more cost-effective to serve several market segments with a single design, even at the risk of initially dissatisfying some customers in a few segments. It may not always be profitable to attempt to satisfy every customer at any cost.

Once the service is in operation, satisfaction data is collected separately from customers of each group. These ratings are implicitly measured relative to the common expectations of the group. Since these expectations are also the design performance standards, the service performance effectiveness measures in Figure 10.3 are also measured relative to the same set of standards. Satisfaction and service performance for the group are therefore measured on a common basis. This makes it possible to correlate satisfaction with the performance of the service.

Transaction-specific and cumulative satisfaction

In its simplest form, the disconfirmation model predicts *transaction-specific satisfaction,* i.e., the satisfaction of an individual with *each service encounter.* A customer makes an independent evaluation of the perception of performance relative to expectations each time he or she experiences the service, and the satisfaction or dissatisfaction with this experience is measured.

If an organization's objective is to promote long-term loyalty, then it is not necessary to ascertain whether customers are satisfied with each and every service encounter. Rather, the focus should be on how to shift customers to a new satisfaction/performance curve, or how to respond to customers' changing needs. These occur as a result of changes in customers' *attitudes* towards the service, based on their experience and satisfaction with the service over time. We refer to this long-term concept as *cumulative* satisfaction. To measure cumulative satisfaction, we should regularly sample from a pool of customers experienced with the service and who are likely to be able to evaluate the service as a result of this experience.

User and decision-maker satisfaction

Who are the customers whose input is most critical for the strategic management and improvement of the service? Clearly, the occasional user who experiences the service once in a while may not be the best source of information about how his or her behavior is affected by satisfaction with the service. Three types of customers are good targets:

(*a*) *Decision makers:* Their job is to evaluate the quality of service providers and make or influence decisions about the choice of providers for an organization. These customers are valuable sources of information because they are able to objectively articulate the performance requirements for a service that meets their selection criteria. They can therefore help identify the aspects of the service where improvements will generate the greatest benefits.

(*b*) *Regular users of the service:* These customers have maintained a long-term association with the firm, and are therefore able to base their assessment of satisfaction on their cumulative experience with the service rather than on a single encounter.

(*c*) *Customers who leave the service or who complain:* These customers may do so either because of continued dissatisfaction with the service, or because of a specific dissatisfying incident.

The *decision-makers* may or may not have used the service extensively. For a service such as a restaurant, the decision-makers may be diners who travel frequently on business and therefore have eaten in many similar restaurants. In this case, the decision-makers are likely to be the users of the service. On the other hand, for services such as telecommunications or travel, where many service features are available, the decision-makers may be managers in the organization who have not experienced every aspect of the service. They may rely on reports of the satisfaction of the *end users* of the service (i.e., those who interact with the telecommunications company to have service installed and maintained, or those who call up a travel agent to make travel arrangements), on industry reports in trade journals, or on recommendations from peers in other organizations for making their decisions. By contrast, the other two categories of customers described above, i.e., the regular users and customers who complain, have clearly had direct experience with the service.

Because of this difference in personal experience, different measures are necessary to evaluate the satisfaction of each group with the service. Clearly, *transaction-specific satisfaction* is the appropriate measure for customers in group (c) above who have complained about a particular incident. An example of the type of question that measures this is: "Please rate your satisfaction with the service that you received the last time you stayed at the Beauty Sleep motel." In addition to these ratings, detailed qualitative diagnostic information should be collected about the customers' expectations and about how the service failed to fulfill these expectations. Suggestions for improving the performance should also be collected.

Cumulative satisfaction is the appropriate measure for customers in group (b), i.e., regular users. Data should be collected on their overall satisfaction with the service, as well as on their satisfaction with various performance attributes. An example of the type of question that should be asked is: "Based on your experience during your various stays in the Beauty Sleep motel over the past year, please rate your satisfaction with the courtesy of the front desk staff."

Finally, customers in group (a) may not have had direct experience with the service. Clearly, the *satisfaction* of these customers with the service cannot be judged. In this case, we measure their *perceived quality* of the service. These perceptions may be derived from users who have experienced the service, from advertising and other informational material, and from the opinion of experts.

Perceived quality may be different from satisfaction for customers who have experienced the service. For example, a customer may say, " I believe that the service delivered by a particular firm is of high quality, but I was not completely satisfied with my personal experiences with the company." However, for customers who have never experienced the service, the only assumption that can be made is that high perceived quality implies high satisfaction, and that these customers make purchase decisions based on their perception of the quality of the service. A perceived quality measure can therefore be substituted for satisfaction. An example of a question for estimating perceived quality is: "Please rate the cleanliness of the bathrooms at the Beauty Sleep motel."

The three types of customers discussed above, and the associated satisfaction measurements, are presented in Table 10.1.

Our discussion so far has concentrated only on the relationship between satisfaction and the quality of the service. There is another important variable that affects the satisfaction of customers with the service. This is the *price* of the service. Together, quality and price determine the *value* of the service, which is an important predictor of future purchase decisions made by customers. We discuss this concept in the following section.

10.5   SATISFACTION AND VALUE

Value was defined by Zeithami (1988) as "the consumer's overall assessment of the utility of a product based on perceptions of what is received and what is given." In other words, it is the evaluation of whether the quality of service that is received is worth the price that is paid for it. Mathematically, value can be calculated as the ratio of perceived quality to price.

Value is the key determinant of a customer's decision to purchase a service. Even a service whose performance delights customers may not be purchased if it is perceived to cost more than it is worth. Value is therefore the true driver of customer behavior, and the strategic objective of the company should therefore be to *maximize the value* of the service provided to the customer. This is done by providing the customers with the desired level of quality *at the price that they are willing to pay*. For the firm, this means that the service needs to be designed and operated to deliver the desired quality level at a cost that supports this price and keeps the firm profitable.

How is value different from satisfaction? Authors have expressed different theoretical views in the literature (see for example, the paper by Zahorik and Rust,

Table 10.1   Satisfaction measurements for different key customer types

Customer type	Satisfaction measure
Decision-makers	Perceived quality
Regular users	Cumulative satisfaction
Leaving customers	Transaction-specific satisfaction

1991). In this book, when we use the word *value*, we refer explicitly to the customers' assessments of quality/price trade-offs. We use the word *satisfaction* to refer to their assessment of either one or the other variable in the value equation. Depending on the context, the word can mean satisfaction with either the quality of the service, or the price.

In this book, we have primarily talked about satisfaction with the *quality* of the service. This is because the purpose of this book is to demonstrate the use of service quality as a strategic vehicle for maintaining and improving competitiveness in the market. This does not mean that the price part of the value equation is not important. The relative importance of quality and price depends on the type of service, and on the market segment in which the service operates.

Quality and price assumptions for the Service Edge restaurant example

When we introduced the Service Edge restaurant example in Chapter 2 (Section 2.6), we explicitly assumed that the restaurants in the target market segment did not compete on price, but on the quality of the food and the service. We assumed that for the diners who eat at the Service Edge and at other similar restaurants, the price has smaller impact on the perceived value of the service than quality. In the particular market segment chosen for the example, the Service Edge restaurant owner has a greater likelihood of increasing profitability by improving quality and charging for it than by reducing price while maintaining an unremarkable quality level. In other words, we assumed that customers would be willing to pay a little extra for exceptional quality, but would not be willing to pay less for average or mediocre quality.

This assumption was the framework for the design examples shown in Chapters 3 through 7. Since price had less impact than quality, it was not critical to control price to the last dollar during the design process. Price was therefore not expressed as a need in the QFD matrix in Chapter 3, nor did it explicitly enter the design specifications in Chapter 4 (the implicit specification is "charge roughly the same price as the competitors"). This implicit specification was included in the design concept evaluation in Chapter 5 (Section 5.4), when the cost of each concept was used as an evaluation criterion. This served to ensure that the design alternatives adequately provided the required meal at a cost that could meet the unstated price criterion and could maintain an acceptable profit level for the firm. On the other hand, since the service performance attributes were strategically important, more precision was needed in their definition and design. As a result, performance standards were specified for these attributes, and more attention was paid to design a service that could reliably meet these standards.

Price-sensitive services

There are many services where the price side of the value equation is the strategic business driver. An example is the pleasure travelers' market segment in the airline industry. Companies targeting this market segment (such as charter carriers or charter operations on commercial airlines) compete on the price they charge customers, while the service provided is usually basic. The service design problem in this case is the reverse of what was described above for the Service Edge restaurant example. It is important to be precise in designing a service that meets the price criterion (since price differentials of as little as twenty dollars could cause travelers to switch carriers), while some flexibility may be possible in the expected quality of the service (for example, a 30-minute delay may not be significant) as long as a certain threshold quality level is met (safe flights, approximate on-time departures, fairly reliable reservation procedures).

The design methodology described in Chapters 3 through 7 can be used to develop a price-sensitive design, a quality-sensitive design, or any other design in between. The methodology is driven by room 1 (list of needs) in the QFD matrix. The design attributes are generated from this list. If low price requirements drive the list of needs, then the design specifications must focus on the cost of the service. The primary consideration must be to develop a design whose costs allow the company to deliver an acceptable service level at a lower price than the competitors charge. The lower profit margins per customer are balanced by the larger number of customers willing to purchase the service at the lower price.

On the other hand, if performance needs dominate, then performance attributes are emphasized. If price and performance needs must be satisfied, then both quality and cost attributes appear in the columns of the QFD matrix. The service profiles introduced in Chapter 4 will contain both price and performance characteristics, and design standards will be developed for costs and performance. The detailed design will select alternatives that affect both the cost and the performance standards.

10.6 MEASURING SATISFACTION

Like some other attributes we have seen in this book (such as friendliness, responsiveness, or patience), satisfaction is an intangible variable with no obvious measurement scale. An arbitrary scale therefore needs to be created for its measurement. Different measurement approaches result in different scales, each with its own properties and applications. In this section, we describe three methods for measuring satisfaction: *absolute ratings*, *ratings relative to expectations*, and *ratings relative to competition*.

Absolute ratings

This is a very common method of satisfaction measurement that is seen on many customer evaluation forms. Customers are asked questions such as: "Please rate your overall satisfaction with the performance of the installation process on the following scale." The scale values typically range from "extremely dissatisfied" at one end to "extremely satisfied" on the other, with a number of points in between. Five- or seven-point scales are most common, though ten-point and 100-point scales are also used. Five- or seven-point scales take discrete values that translate into descriptions such as:

1—extremely dissatisfied

2—dissatisfied

3—neither satisfied nor dissatisfied

4—satisfied

5—extremely satisfied

The 100-point scales measure the "percent of satisfaction," and so approximate a continuous satisfaction distribution from 0 to 100.

The advantage of the absolute rating methods is that they are easily understandable and therefore simple to administer. However, they suffer from some major limitations. First, as mentioned in Section 10.3, satisfaction ratings are the *outputs* of comparisons between expectations and perceived performance. It is not possible to determine the expectation and perceived performance values that gave rise to a particular satisfaction rating. Each satisfaction rating, especially when measured on a scale with a limited number of points, can be the result of a large number of combinations of expectations and performance. If the group is heterogeneous, and its members have different expectations, then differences in satisfaction ratings may not correlate with differences in the perceived quality of the service. These satisfaction ratings may therefore have limited diagnostic value.

Another limitation of absolute scales is that they are not designed to measure service performance that exceeds expectations. Since expectations are not explicitly included in the scale, it is difficult to differentiate between performance that meets customers' expectations and performance that surpasses them, though it is sometimes possible to estimate this if the ratings cluster around few points on the scale. For example, suppose that on a ten-point scale, most customer ratings cluster around 7 or 8, and a few ratings of 10 are observed. Since a value of 10 (extremely satisfied) is usually only given when customers are delighted, we can assume that the scores of 10 correspond to customers whose expectations have been exceeded, while the scores of 7 or 8 correspond to customers whose expectations are met. On scales with a smaller number of rating points, this distinction in the ratings between satisfied and delighted customers is more likely to be confounded by random measurement errors. This method may not be very accurate in this case.

In summary, absolute satisfaction ratings can be used to measure the satisfaction of a segmented group of customers who are likely to have the similar expectations of the service, and in situations where it is not very important to determine whether performance has exceeded expectations. It is more difficult to make decisions based on these ratings for service where there is variability in expectations across the population of customers, or where significant changes in expectations may take place over time. For these purposes, it is more suitable to adopt an approach that explicitly includes expectations in the satisfaction measurement scale, as shown below.

Ratings relative to expectations

This scale is presented as a response to a question such as the following:

Please rate the performance of the service installation process on the following scale:

1—much worse than expected

2—worse than expected

3—about as good as expected

4—better than expected

5—much better than expected

This method measures disconfirmation, which is closely related to satisfaction. Notice that this scale is anchored at the middle rather than at one end. Satisfactory performance is likely to receive a rating in the middle of the scale ("about as good as expected"). Exceptionally good or exceptionally poor performance will be rated at the top and bottom ends of the scale. This method of measurement is useful for identifying changes in customers' expectations over time, and for determining the performance levels required to design services that exceed customers' expectations. These measurements are oriented towards the future and help to define the strategic improvement and design activities needed to keep the service competitive in the market.

The satisfaction measures need to be used in conjunction with service performance measures (see Figure 10.3) to detect changes in customers' expectations. For example, consider a service attribute that is designed to meet a particular performance standard. Suppose that the performance of this attribute relative to the standard is monitored over time, and the performance measures indicate that the attribute is reliably meeting the standards. On the other hand, suppose that the satisfaction measures are beginning to indicate that the service performance is worse than expected. Clearly, this is a signal that customers' expectations of service performance have changed since the service was designed.

Ratings relative to competition

Recall from Figures 10.1 and 10.2 the discussion at the beginning of this chapter that changes in satisfaction with a service can be caused by two factors: (1) customers' needs and expectations change, or (2) the performance of the competitors' services change. The ratings relative to expectations described above measure the effects of the first factor. The ratings relative to the competition measure the effects of the second. While measuring performance relative to expectations is useful for strategic improvements and planning, satisfaction or performance measured relative to the competition assists in the development of improvement plans that are needed to keep the service competitive in the current market.

One approach for collecting data on this scale is to ask customers to respond to a question such as:

> Please rate your satisfaction with the installation process, compared to "competitor X" on the following scale:
>
> 1—much less satisfied
>
> 2—less satisfied
>
> 3—equally satisfied
>
> 4—more satisfied
>
> 5—much more satisfied

This scale may also be used to measure relative quality or price.

"Competitor X" can be represented in various ways, depending on the application. In industries such as the airlines, where there are a small number of well-known service providers, competitor X may be an explicitly named airline. In industries such as restaurants where the competition differs by geographic region and market, the competitor may be specified as "a similar restaurant you are familiar with." An in-between approach is to first ask customers to identify a similar alternative service provider they are familiar with. This provider is then chosen as the candidate for comparison.

Another approach for measuring the performance or satisfaction of a service relative to competitors is to ask customers to rate the firm and a list of competitors on an absolute satisfaction scale. For example, a question for the airline industry could be: "Please rate your satisfaction with the in-flight service of each of the following airlines (list of airlines). Please rate only the airlines with which you are familiar." If all the passengers who rate the service belong to a homogeneous market segment, then the advantage of this approach is that we can get data on the extent to which each firm satisfies its customers. This information is not available from the relative scale described previously. For example, suppose two firms receive average satisfaction ratings of 6.2 and 6.4 (out of 7), while two other firms receive ratings of 3.2 and 3.4. If each pair of firms is compared to one another, then the relative scale will produce the same ratings for both pairs, masking the difference in their satisfaction ratings. Another advantage of this approach is that it is possible to collect data on a variety of competitors instead of just one.

Once the ratings are obtained for each competitor, a single *aggregate competitor rating* can be calculated by averaging the individual scores or by selecting the highest score ("best competitor"). The firm's satisfaction rating relative to the competition can then be developed by dividing the firm's score by the aggregate competitor rating. Another approach is to take the difference between these two ratings.

The disadvantage of asking customers to evaluate a list of firms is that inexperience or boredom may result in inaccurate ratings. To avoid the limitations of each scale, a hybrid approach that combines both absolute and relative scales may be used. This approach uses two questions. The first asks customers to rate their satisfaction with the service on an absolute scale. The second question asks customers to rate the service relative to a competitor. The disadvantage of this approach is that two questions need to be asked for every attribute. This doubles the survey's size and the effort needed to complete it.

For more details on how to design surveys to measure customer satisfaction, the reader is referred to the text by Rust *et al.* (1994). In the final stage of the Service Design and Management model, these measurements, in conjunction with the financial measures, are used to determine the aspects of the service where strategic improvements are necessary. In Chapter 11, we will describe how this can be done.

10.7   CONCLUSION

Summary

The following is a summary of this chapter. The section in the chapter where a particular topic is covered is indicated in parentheses.

Effect of market and customer changes on satisfaction (10.1)

- A service that meets the design standards does not automatically satisfy customers.
- Changes in the performance of competitors and in customers' needs affect satisfaction.
- Changes in competitors' performance shift the performance/satisfaction function.
- Changes in the relative importance of needs affect the slope of the function.

Defining customer satisfaction—disconfirmation model (10.2)

- The disconfirmation model is a commonly used paradigm of satisfaction.
- Satisfaction is the result of a comparison between expected and perceived performance.
- Positive disconfirmation (performance exceeds expectations) results in satisfaction.
- Negative disconfirmation (performance falls short of expectations) results in dissatisfaction.

Expectations (10.3)

- Many different types of expectations are defined in literature.
- Selecting the appropriate expectations model depends on the nature of the service and on the expectations of the firm.
- The definition of expectations used in this book is a combination of many expectation types.

Individual and group satisfaction (10.4)

- Satisfaction data for groups of customers is needed for managing a service.
- Groups should be segmented to represent customers with homogenous expectations.
- Satisfaction of members of each group should be measured relative to these expectations.

Transaction-specific and cumulative satisfaction (10.4)

- Transaction-specific satisfaction is the satisfaction with each service encounter.
- A customer's long-term attitude about the service is cumulative satisfaction.
- The cumulative satisfaction of key customers should be measured.

User and decision-maker satisfaction (10.4)

- Decision-makers select service providers for an organization.
- Decision-makers may not have direct experience with the service.
- Perceived service performance may be used as a proxy for decision-maker satisfaction.
- Regular users of the service have maintained a long-term association with the firm.
- Cumulative satisfaction of regular users is a good index of attitudes.
- Detailed data about specific incidents should be collected from complaining customers.

Satisfaction and value (10.5)

- Value is the trade-off between what is received and what is given.
- Value can be defined as the ratio of perceived quality to price.
- Both quality and price components should be considered in the design of the service.
- The approach in this book can be applied to both components.

Measuring satisfaction (10.6)

- Different measurement approaches have different properties and applications.

- Absolute scales are not designed to measure performance that exceeds expectations.

- Absolute scales are useful for measuring stable services.

- The performance relative to expectations scale measures changes in customers' expectations.

- These measurements are useful for designing new services.

- Ratings relative to competition can measure either satisfaction or performance.

- Both absolute and relative ratings may be used to measure competitor's performance.

- These measurements are useful for the development of improvement plans for the current market.

Suggested reading

For further reading on survey design and implementation, Emory and Cooper (1991) is a complete and comprehensive survey of topics on data collection, survey design, sampling, and scales. It is an excellent companion text to the topics covered in this chapter.

Chapter
11
Improving Service Performance

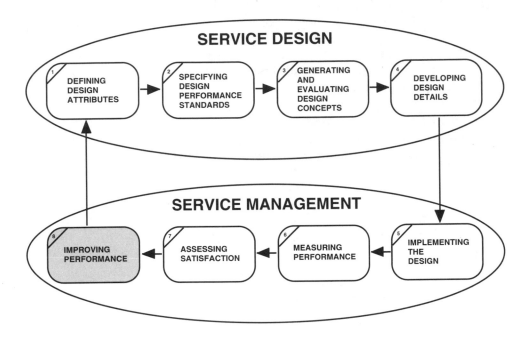

- *Evaluating the financial impact of customer satisfaction*
- *Setting strategic improvement targets*
- *Evaluating the impact of service performance on satisfaction*
- *Selecting attributes for improvement*
- *Specifying improvements at the process level*
- *Developing an optimal process improvement strategy*
- *Conclusion*

This chapter describes the last stage of the service design and management model. At this stage, the service has been in stable operation for some time.

The service management team regularly monitors the performance of the service, and with the help of the analysis methods presented in Chapter 9, ensures that this performance is stable relative to the design standards. The team also measures customers' satisfaction with the quality and price attributes of the service, using one or more of the approaches described in Chapter 10.

The fact that a service is reliably meeting the current design standards does not mean that there is no motivation to further improve the service performance. Improvement initiatives may be motivated by two factors. The first factor may be strategic, with the company wanting to increase its profitability by delighting already-satisfied customers. The second factor may be reactive, in response to market or competitor changes that result in a shift in the performance/satisfaction relationship (see Figures 10.1 and 10.2).

The result of a service improvement effort may be the definition of new standards for the performance of one or more design attributes. The service is then modified to meet these standards. These modifications require the expenditure of time and resources, and it is therefore important for the service management team to carefully evaluate each service improvement initiative to determine the potential returns associated with these expenditures. It is not cost-effective to delight customers if the expenditure required to do so does not produce the returns in terms of enhanced customer loyalty or increased market share. Preferably, an optimal improvement initiative that produces the highest returns for a given investment should be selected.

In this chapter, we describe the analysis required to select an optimal improvement strategy. This analysis involves seven steps:

Step 1: Estimate the relationship between financial objectives and overall satisfaction.

Step 2: Determine the overall satisfaction improvement needed to meet strategic financial objectives.

Step 3: Estimate the relationship between overall satisfaction and attribute performance.

Step 4: Select one or more attributes for improvement, and set their improvement targets.

Step 5: Estimate the relationship between the performance of service-level and process-level attributes.

Step 6: Select candidate processes for improvement.

Step 7: Determine the optimal amount of improvement needed for each process that produces the greatest returns.

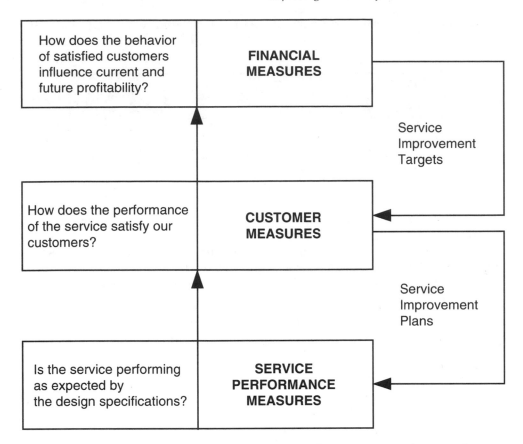

Figure 11.1   Measures for service monitoring and improvement (repeat of Figure 9.1)

Step 1 is discussed in Section 11.1. Step 2 is the topic of Section 11.2. Step 3 is covered in Section 11.3. Step 4 is described in Section 11.4 and Steps 5 and 6 in Section 11.5. Step 7 is presented in Section 11.6. Section 11.7 is a summary of this chapter.

11.1   EVALUATING THE FINANCIAL IMPACT OF CUSTOMER SATISFACTION—STEP 1

Modeling the relationship between profitability and satisfaction

In order to evaluate the financial impact of satisfying customers, we need to develop a model that links the customer measures in Figure 11.1 to some indicator of the company's financial performance, generically referred to as *profitability*. This can be done by a regression equation specified as follows:

$$\text{Profitability} = b_0 + b_1 * \text{overall satisfaction measure} + E \qquad (11.1)$$

where b_0 is a constant term, b_1 is the weight associated with the satisfaction measure, and E is an error term to account for random variability and unmeasurable factors.

The relative magnitudes of b_0 and b_1 indicate the extent to which the customer measures affect the financial performance of the firm. If the value of b_1 is close to zero, then the satisfaction of customers with the service does not influence its performance in the market. The financial health of the company is then purely determined by the baseline specified by the constant term and the random variability associated with the error term.

Specifying the effect of temporal lags between satisfaction and profitability

Time is not included as a variable in Equation 11.1. In this equation, the financial measure at any time period is assumed to be affected by the overall satisfaction during the same time period. This implies that satisfied customers *instantaneously* translate their satisfaction into a change in purchasing behavior.

Intuition tells us that this cannot be a realistic assumption. There should be a *time lag* between a change in attitude and an observed change in customers' behavior. Customers' attitude towards the service today may not affect their buying decisions until several time periods in the future, especially for services (such as telecommunications) which involve a subscription or a large initial monetary investment. The service quality literature indicates that this is indeed the case. Kordupleski *et al.* (1993) report a six- to eight-month time lag between a process improvement and a change in market share for telecommunications.

The lag between a service improvement effort and a change in the financial metrics can be decomposed into three components:

- The time taken for service improvement efforts to be realized by customers
- The time taken for customers' attitudes to change after the new quality is perceived (resulting in greater satisfaction)
- The time taken for customers' behavior to change as a result of this increased satisfaction

Of these components, only the last one is relevant for an equation that links satisfaction and profitability. But how do we incorporate the effect of this time lag into an equation such as 11.1? We do this by the lagged specification shown in Equation 11.2:

$$\text{Profitability } (t) = b_0 + b_1 * \text{overall satisfaction measure} \\ (t - m) + E \tag{11.2}$$

In Equation 11.2, the value of the financial indicator at some time t is affected by the overall satisfaction at time $t - m$. For telecommunications service, the value of m is in the range of 2–3 months. For services such as restaurants where customers can switch from one service provider to another with ease, the lag will be much shorter. If the value of m is zero, then the financial measure is instantaneously affected by satisfaction. Equation 11.2 is then the same model as Equation 11.1.

The lagged model of Equation 11.2 is more realistic than the instantaneous specification of Equation 11.1. However, both specifications are still static snapshots in time, and the effect of *history* is not included in these models. Even in the lagged model of Equation 11.2, the financial performance at time t is affected only by the satisfaction *in a single time period $t - m$*. This represents a *transaction-specific* model for satisfaction (see Section 10.4).

In practice, however, it is more realistic to assume that customers' behavior is influenced by the *cumulative historical effect* of various service experiences over time. A more accurate specification should therefore incorporate this cumulative effect of history. This is done in the model described in the next section.

Specifying the effect of cumulative history—lagged dependent variable model

This model is shown in Equation 11.3:

$$\text{Profitability } (t) = b_0 + b_1 * \text{Profitability } (t - 1) + b_2 * \text{overall} \\ \text{satisfaction } (t - m) + E(t) \tag{11.3}$$

How is Equation 11.3 different from Equation 11.2? The reader can see that Equation 11.3 contains the additional term *profitability* $(t - 1)$. The lagged profitability term represents the cumulative effects of the factors affecting profitability up to and including the previous time period $t - 1$.

To see why this is the case, let us consider a concrete example. Suppose the time scale in Equation 11.3 is expressed in months, and that the current month is July. Also suppose that the value of m is two months. What does Equation 11.3 state about the profitability in July? We can see that the profitability in July is affected by the following:

- The profitability in June (one time period before July)
- The satisfaction with the service in May (two time periods before July)

What affects the profitability in June? From an equation similar to Equation 11.3, we can state that the profitability in June is a function of the following:

- The profitability in May
- The satisfaction with the service in April

The profitability in May and in other preceding months can be broken down in a similar fashion.

The specification of Equation 11.3 therefore represents the profitability in July as the *cumulative* effect of satisfaction with the service in March, April, May, and so on. The relative values of the weights b_1 and b_2 indicate the dominant factor explaining market share. If b_1 is zero for all time periods, then the profitability in July is dependent *only* on the satisfaction with the service in May. This model is identical to the specification of Equation 11.2. On the other hand, if b_2 is close to zero for all time periods, then the attitude toward the service or satisfaction with the service is not a significant predictor of the financial performance. In this case, the market share over time is affected by external factors that have nothing to do with satisfaction and that are collectively represented by the cumulative error term E. Positive values of b_1 and b_2 reflect the effects of both factors.

The model of Equation 11.3 is called a *lagged dependent variable model* because the profitability, which is the dependent variable, appears in its lagged form on the right-hand side of the equation. Of the three models presented in this chapter, this is the most realistic specification of the relationship between profitability and satisfaction. However, it is also the most complicated to estimate. This specification is different from the usual regression equation because of the presence of this dependent variable. If the error terms for each time period can be assumed to be independent, then the model can be treated as an ordinary regression equation and the parameters can be estimated using the standard method (called Ordinary Least Squares, or OLS) found in many spreadsheets and basic statistical packages. In practice, this is unlikely to be the case. The error term reflects unobservable or unmeasurable effects that carry over from one time period to the next. The error terms are therefore likely to be correlated across time periods. In this case, the use of OLS leads to *biased* (i.e., incorrect) estimates. In general, it is preferable to use special estimation techniques such as maximum likelihood techniques (see any econometrics text book, such as Johnston, 1972) for estimating lagged dependent variable models.

In summary, the most accurate model is also the most difficult to estimate. A firm wishing to implement models linking profitability and satisfaction may hire experts to develop the model system. Once the system is developed, it can then be regularly maintained and used by the service management team.

Measuring model variables—overall satisfaction

In Equations 11.1, 11.2, and 11.3, we have used the term *overall satisfaction measure* to refer generically to customers' perceptions of the performance of the service. The actual measure used will depend on the application. Some common measures are:

- Satisfaction rating on an absolute scale

- Performance rating relative to expectations

- Performance or satisfaction rating relative to best (or average) competitor

For example, Rust *et al.* (1994) use a three-point scale to measure performance relative to expectations, with the following values: *much better than expected, about as expected,* and *worse than expected*. The scales described in Gale (1994) and in Ramaswamy and Hafiz (1994) measure performance relative to competing service providers. For services where both price and quality are important to the customer, value (or separate variables for service quality and price) may be the appropriate dependent variable.

For the reasons mentioned in Chapter 10 (Section 10.6), ratings relative to expectations or relative to the competition are preferable to objective satisfaction ratings. Performance measured relative to expectations specifies how the current service is meeting customers' expectations. This measure is useful for the development of new services or for the improvement of existing services so that they exceed customers' current and future expectations. This measure is therefore oriented towards the longer term. Performance measured relative to the competition ensures that the service levels and prices offered by the current service are on par with or better than the competition. These measures assist in the development of shorter-term improvement plans that are needed to keep the service competitive in the current market.

Measuring model variables—profitability

The term *profitability* in Equations 11.1, 11.2, and 11.3 is also a generic term that can represent many different measures. Some examples are the following:

- Shareholder-value–related measures such as return on investment or stock price

- Revenue-related measures such as market share

- Customer-behavior–related measures such as intention to recommend or re-purchase

Shareholder-value–related measures: Anderson *et al.* (1994) use *return on investment* as a measure of profitability. This is clearly a direct measure of economic returns; however, it is an aggregate measure that cannot usually be determined at the level of an individual service if multiple services are offered by the firm. The model of Anderson *et al.* uses published data on return on investments from a cross-section of seventy-seven firms in Sweden. At this broad organizational level, it is possible to find differences in the return on investment between firms that satisfy customers and firms that do not. However, at an individual firm level, many factors affect the ROI, and it may be difficult to isolate the effect of customer satisfaction on this measure. Other disaggregate measures may be more appropriate.

Revenue-related measures: Another indicator of the financial performance of the company in the market is *market share.* If a company has multiple service products oriented towards different market segments, market share data should be available for each product. Market share is an attractive financial measure because it is a direct consequence of customer behavior. Market share increases because customers purchase more of the service, and it can be postulated that this purchasing behavior is linked to the attitudes that customers have about the satisfaction or value provided by the service. However, research (see, for example, Fishbein and Azjen, 1975) shows that attitude and behavior are not directly linked, but are mediated by *intention.* This means that customers' intention or willingness to purchase a service can be predicted by their satisfaction with the service, but other factors may intervene in the actual purchase decision. The effectiveness of using market share as a dependent variable in the specification of Equation 11.1 depends on the extent to which this measure is affected by factors other than service quality. For services that have a stable pool of customers, with changes in share occurring largely because of switching between companies based on price or quality perceptions, the market share may be an appropriate financial measure to correlate with satisfaction. In more volatile markets, dynamics unrelated to service quality may cause customers to enter or leave the market, affecting the share of each service provider. In these markets, the market share may not be a suitable financial measure. In such cases it may be more accurate to directly measure some attribute of customer behavior.

Customer-behavior–related measure: In their Return on Quality model, Rust *et al.* (1994) use satisfaction as a predictor of *repurchase intention,* which is some measure of the probability of the customer's intention to repurchase the service or to continue their association with the service provider in some following time period. Historical customer behavior is then used to adjust this measure to reflect the proportion of customers who follow up on their intent.

11.2 SETTING STRATEGIC IMPROVEMENT TARGETS— STEP 2

Once the relationship between satisfaction and profitability is specified, it can be used to set *strategic improvement targets* for satisfaction. To see how this can be done, consider the example shown in Equation 11.4. In this equation, profitability is measured by market share. For a given time period, satisfaction is measured by the average rating (measured on scale of 1 to 6) of all customers who experience the service in the time period. The parameters b_0, b, and b_2 have values of 0.1, 0.3 and 0.01 respectively.

$$\textbf{Market share } (t) = 0.1 + 0.3 * \textbf{market share } (t - 1) + 0.01 \\ * \textbf{average satisfaction rating } (t - 1)$$

(11.4)

The results from this model for four months are shown in Table 11.1.

Suppose we are currently in the month of February. The market share for this month is 20.8%, and the average satisfaction rating has dropped from 4.8 in January to 4.0 in this month. What impact will that have on the market share for March? The impact can be obtained from Equation 11.4. Since we want to predict the market share for March, the time period t on the left-hand side of Equation 11.4 refers to March, and the time period $t - 1$ on the right-hand side of this equation refers to February. If we substitute 0.208 for *market share* $(t - 1)$ and 4.0 for the *average satisfaction rating* $(t - 1)$ (these are the February values from Table 11.1) in Equation 11.4, then the model tells us that the predicted market share for March will be 20.24%.

Suppose now that we want to increase our market share to 21% in April. Since the April market share is affected by the satisfaction in March, we need to set a target satisfaction level in March to which the service should be improved. What should this target be? The value of this target can also be obtained from Equation 11.4. The

Table 11.1 Results from Equation 11.4

Month	Market share %	Average Satisfaction
January	20	4.8
February	20.8	4.0
March	20.24 (predicted)	5.0 (target)
April	21.0 (target)	

time period *t* now refers to April, and *t* − *1* to March. If we substitute 0.21 for *market share (t)*, and 0.2024 for *market share (t* − *1)* (predicted value for March), the value of *average satisfaction (t* − *1)* is the target satisfaction that must be achieved to meet the April market share target. The model tells us that this value is 5.0. This means that the overall service should improve in March so that the satisfaction rating increases by one point from February. This is the *strategic improvement target* for satisfaction. The service management team needs to identify operational *service improvement opportunities* that will lead to the achievement of the target. The approach for doing this is presented in the following section.

11.3   EVALUATING THE IMPACT OF SERVICE PERFORMANCE ON SATISFACTION—STEP 3

In the last section, we saw how the relationship between the financial and customer metrics allows us to set targets for service improvement. These targets are at the level of the overall service, and are expressed in units of satisfaction (or value). In order to develop a service improvement plan that specifies the activities needed to meet these targets, they need to be translated into the units of the design performance standards at the process level. In this section, we will describe how this can be done.

Modeling the relationship between overall satisfaction and attribute performance

This relationship can be specified by a regression model as shown in Equation 11.5:

$$\text{Overall satisfaction} = b_0 + b_1 * \text{att1 perf.} + b_2 * \text{att2 perf.} + \ldots + b_n * \text{attn perf.} + E \tag{11.5}$$

where att1 perf., att2 perf., etc., refer to the performance of each attribute.

The term *performance* in Equation 11.5 is used generically. The specific measure depends on the application. The following are some examples of performance measures for attributes of the Service Edge restaurant:

- Satisfaction with waiter responsiveness
- Rating of waiter responsiveness relative to expectations
- Time interval between ordering and meal delivery

The *attributes* in Equation 11.5 are usually the service-level design attributes from the columns of the QFD matrix. For example, for the Service Edge restaurant, the

Table 11.2 Attributes for the Service Edge restaurant

Attribute no.	Attribute
att1	Degree of friendliness
att2	Degree of responsiveness
att3	Time between ordering and meal delivery
att4	Degree of patience
att5	Time between seating and menu delivery
att6	Time between menu delivery and order-taking
att7	Degree of knowledge
att8	Percentage of bills produced without errors
att9	Effectiveness in problem resolution
att10	Time between arrival and seating
att11	Percent of meals delivered as ordered
att12	Time between meal completion and bill delivery
att13	Promptness in problem resolution
att14	Time between bill delivery and transaction completion
att15	Average price of restaurant meal

list of possible attributes (obtained from Table 3.9) is shown in Table 11.2. As described in Section 11.1, time lags may be introduced into the specification of Equation 11.5.

The model in Equation 11.5 can be estimated by OLS techniques found in many spreadsheet software packages if the correlation between the independent variables (i.e., the attribute performance variables) is small. This is usually not the case with satisfaction measurements. This is because customers who experience a high degree of overall satisfaction with the service are likely to be satisfied with many of its attributes. All these attributes will receive a high satisfaction or performance rating. Similarly, customers who are dissatisfied with the overall service are likely to be dissatisfied with several attributes, which will all receive a low rating. The attribute ratings will therefore be correlated. This correlation between independent variables in a regression model is referred to as *multicollinearity*. Multicollinearity poses a problem because it is not possible to accurately estimate the parameters of Equation 11.4 using ordinary least squares when there is correlation in the data. Special techniques called "ridge regression" or "equity estimators" (suggested by Rust *et al.*, 1994) must be used. We will not describe these techniques in this book, and refer the reader to the suggested texts cited at the end of this chapter.

Similarity between Equation 11.5 and the performance/satisfaction relationship

The reader should note the similarity between Equation 11.5 and the performance/satisfaction relationships described in Chapter 4. In concept, there is no difference between the two. The difference is that the performance/satisfaction relationship is estimated from *hypothetical* data obtained from the ratings of service profiles. This is because this relationship is estimated in the design stage, when the service does not exist. On the other hand, the parameters of Equation 11.5 are estimated from *actual* performance and satisfaction data collected from a service in operation.

If the service is designed to meet the performance standards derived from the performance/satisfaction relationship, and the relationship is accurate, we would expect the estimates from Equation 11.5 to be approximately equal to those obtained using the conjoint analysis method. If the parameter estimates are different, then this is an indication either that the service profile ratings were inaccurate, or that customers' needs or the market have changed in the period between the design and the implementation of the service. Equation 11.5 therefore provides a validation of the accuracy of the design performance standards.

Estimating the parameters of Equation 11.5—Service Edge restaurant example

Consider Equation 11.6, which links the overall satisfaction with the Service Edge restaurant with the performance of five of its attributes—customer service, promptness, accuracy, problem resolution, and price:

$$\text{Overall satisfaction}(t) = b_1 * \text{Customer Service}(t) + b_2 * \text{Promptness}(t) + b_3 * \text{Accuracy}(t) + b_4 * \text{Problem Resolution}(t) + b_5 * \text{Price}(t) + E(t) \tag{11.6}$$

The five attributes selected are aggregations of the fifteen attributes shown in Table 11.2. The attributes were aggregated because preliminary studies showed that some similar attributes are highly correlated, and so could lead to potential multicollinearity problems during the estimation. The aggregate attributes, and their disaggregate components from Table 11.2, are shown in Table 11.3.

Suppose data on the aggregate attributes are collected through customer ratings for a period of twelve months. These ratings can be averaged for each month to provide a single data point for the month. These are the *independent variables* of Equation 11.6. The *dependent variable* is a satisfaction or value measure, relative to expectations or to the competition. Once again, these ratings are averaged to produce a single data point for each month. Twelve data points are therefore available for the dependent variable and each independent variable to estimate the five parameters ($b_1, b_2, b_3, b_4,$ and b_5) of Equation 11.6.

Twelve fictional data points for the performance of each attribute and for overall satisfaction are shown in Table 11.4. All variables are measured on a scale from 1 to 5 relative to the best competitor. For example, for each attribute, each scale value may correspond to the following:

1—much worse performance than the best competitor

2—worse performance than the best competitor

3—about the same performance as the best competitor

4—better performance than the best competitor

5—much better performance than the best competitor

Table 11.3 Aggregate attributes for regression model

Aggregate attribute	Components from Table 11.2
Customer service	att1, att2, att4, att7
Promptness	att3, att5, att6, att10, att12, att14
Accuracy	att8, att11
Problem resolution	att9, att13
Price	att15

Table 11.4   Input data for the regression model

Month	Overall satisfaction	Customer service	Promptness	Accuracy	Resolution	Price
1	3.82	4.25	4.71	4.12	3.11	3.45
2	3.96	3.86	4.76	3.31	3.43	3.21
3	4.64	4.91	4.69	2.86	4.25	3.69
4	2.87	3.08	4.73	4.14	2.83	4.32
5	2.85	3.41	4.75	4.23	2.36	4.45
6	4.54	4.96	4.76	3.86	1.85	3.67
7	4.01	4.23	4.87	4.86	4.01	4.52
8	3.41	3.31	4.77	4.89	3.42	3.71
9	1.89	2.41	4.68	3.11	2.76	4.45
10	3.02	2.97	4.79	4.31	4.11	4.31
11	3.55	3.86	4.83	4.1	3.39	3.87
12	4.19	4.33	4.85	4.75	2.41	4.11

The parameter estimates and some associated statistics for the model of Equation 11.6 from the data of Table 11.4 are shown in Table 11.5. These results are used to determine which attributes to improve, and to set service improvement targets for the attributes to meet a required increase in satisfaction. We will describe how this is done in the following section.

Table 11.5   Fictional parameter estimates for Equation 11.5   ($R^2 = 0.90$)

Parameter	Estimate	t-statistic
b_1	0.89	10.37
b_2	0.09	0.43
b_3	0.16	1.70
b_4	0.15	1.97
b_5	−0.33	−2.10

11.4   SELECTING ATTRIBUTES FOR IMPROVEMENT—STEP 4

As long as there are enough data points for estimation, the initial specification of the model such as Equation 11.6 should contain all the attributes that can be hypothesized to affect the overall performance. Once the complete model is estimated, it can be further analyzed and fine-tuned. The following measures may be used to analyze the estimation results:

- Overall model fit determined from the R^2 statistic

- The significant parameters determined from the *t-statistics*

- The impact of each independent variable on the dependent variable determined from the *magnitude* of the parameter estimates

- The *elasticity* of satisfaction with respect to the performance of each attribute

- The *performance/importance map* for each attribute

We will now illustrate how each measure can be used to analyze the results from Table 11.5 for the Service Edge restaurant.

Determining overall model fit from the R-squared statistic

The R^2 value is a figure between 0 and 1 that indicates how well the regression model fits the data. If the value is high, then the model has a high *explanatory power*, i.e., the independent variables explain the variation in the dependent variable to a large extent. If the value is low, then any relationship between the dependent and independent variables indicated by the model may only be due to random correlation in the data. An R^2 value of zero indicates that no correlation exists between the dependent and independent variables. A value of 1 indicates a perfect correlation, i.e., the model fits the data with no variability. In this case, the error term in Equation 11.5 is zero and the independent variables exactly predict the dependent variable.

Clearly, 0 and 1 are extreme values. In practice, R^2 values for most models lie somewhere in between. For our model of Equation 11.6, the R^2 value is 0.9, which is close to 1. This is not surprising, because the data that produced the results of Table 11.5 were constructed to produce a good fit. In practical applications, lower R^2 values will be obtained. For perceptual ratings data, a value of 0.5–0.6 can be considered to be an acceptable fit.

If the R^2 for a model is much lower than expected, the following points should be investigated:

- Have all possible independent variables included in the model? Have any important variables been left out?

- Is there enough variability in the dependent variable? If there is very little variability in the dependent variable, then there is no variation to explain. This is a common problem with absolute satisfaction ratings where most observations are clustered around the top of the scale. Variability can be improved by expanding the scale, or by asking more detailed questions that allow customers to better distinguish smaller variations in performance.

- Is a linear model appropriate over the range of data? In some cases, the underlying relationship between the dependent and independent variables may be nonlinear. A linear model will fit the data poorly in this case.

- Is the same model applicable across the entire range of data? Even in cases where a linear model is appropriate, the same straight line may not apply over the entire range of data, because the behavior of different market segments may vary. For example, Rust *et al.* (1994) estimate a different equation for customers who are currently dissatisfied and need to be satisfied, and those who are currently satisfied and need to be delighted. This is because the attributes that are important for the satisfied and the dissatisfied groups may be different.

- Has the appropriate lag structure been included in the model?

- Is the model constrained in some other way? For example, a specification such as equation 11.6 with no constant term may not be appropriate.

If the answer to one or more of these questions is "no," then the model must be re-specified and re-estimated. If no problems are found with the model specification, and the R^2 is still low, then the problem may lie with the data. Measurement errors and random variability may have introduced additional variability in the data that cannot be explained by the model. More careful data collection may be needed.

Testing parameter significance using the *t*-statistics

The *t*-statistic is a measure of the precision of a parameter estimate. This statistic allows us to determine whether an estimated regression weight is significantly different from zero. Such an estimate is referred to as *statistically significant*.

Why do we need to test whether a parameter estimate is different from zero? Recall from Equation 11.6 that the parameters b_1, b_2, b_3, b_4 and b_5 multiply each independent variable. A value of 0 for the parameter of an independent variable implies that no relationship exists between that variable and the dependent variable. The nonsignificant variables therefore do not contribute to the explanation of the dependent variable. Once they are identified, they can be dropped from the model, and the model can be re-estimated using only the significant variables.

The fact that the true value of a parameter is zero does not necessarily mean that the estimated value of the parameter from a particular data set will be zero. Random variability in the input data may produce a nonzero value of the parameter estimate for this data set. How can we determine whether a particular nonzero parameter estimate that we have obtained is truly different from zero? The value of the *t*-statistic gives us a guideline. A parameter estimate is significantly different from zero if the absolute value of the *t*-statistic is larger than a certain *critical value*. This value, tabulated in most statistics textbooks, depends on the confidence level and on the number of observations. The usual rule of thumb is that for a model estimated from 30 or more observations, the *t*-statistic has to be greater than 2 in absolute value for a parameter to be significant at a 95 • 1 significance level. Details about the statistics of significance testing of parameter values can be obtained from the texts referenced at the end of this chapter.

Referring back to Table 11.5, we can see that the customer service and price attributes are significant, and the problem resolution attribute has a *t*-statistic that is close to 2. The promptness and accuracy attributes are not significant. We can now re-estimate the model including only the significant variables. Unless there is no correlation between the independent variables, the model *must* be re-estimated, since the parameter values will change. Table 11.6 shows the re-estimated model for the restaurant attributes. All three variables are now significant.

In general, attributes that have significant nonzero regression weights affect overall service performance and are therefore potential candidates for improvement. However, it must be pointed out that while *t*-statistics below the critical value are generally indicative of nonsignificant variables, this may not always be the case. Multicollinearity between the dependent variables can result in imprecise parameter estimates with low *t*-statistics. In this case, dropping the nonsignificant variables can affect the values of the other correlated variables. Formal testing for multicollinearity is difficult; however, large swings in the estimates and significance levels of one or more parameters when the nonsignificant variables are dropped may be an informal indication of correlation between independent variables. If there is no multicollinearity, then the estimated values of the remaining parameters should not change considerably when the nonsignificant variables are excluded. When multicollinearity is present, the parameter estimates of the correlated variables are highly unstable, and dropping one variable can cause substantial changes in the estimates of the others.

Magnitude of parameter estimates

While *t*-statistics are useful to determine whether the performance of an attribute affects the overall performance, the magnitude of a significant regression weight is

Table 11.6   Revised parameter estimates for Equation 11.6

Variable	Estimate	t-statistic
Customer service	0.95	15.62
Problem resolution	0.16	2.10
Price	−0.14	−2.03

a measure of the importance of the associated attribute. If all attributes are measured on the same scale, then the performance of the attribute with the largest absolute parameter estimate has the highest impact on satisfaction. For example, from Table 11.6, we can see that an increase of one rating point for the customer service attribute results in an increase of 0.95 rating points in overall satisfaction. By comparison, a decrease of one rating point in price only produces an increase of 0.16 rating points in satisfaction. Customer service is clearly a more important determinant of satisfaction than price.

Elasticities

If each attribute is measured on a different scale, then it is not easy to directly compare the attributes based on the magnitude of the estimates. A common measure for evaluating the effect of each independent variable on the dependent variable must be found. The *elasticity* of the overall performance with respect to each attribute is such a measure. (For a detailed discussion of elasticities, see Manheim, 1979.) The elasticity is the percent change in the dependent variable in response to a 1% change in an independent variable, assuming that the other independent variables remain constant. For the regression equation

$$Y = b_0 + b_1 X_1 + b_2 X_2 + b_3 X_3 + E \tag{11.7}$$

the elasticity of Y with respect to X_1 can be calculated from the formula

$$\text{Elasticity } (Y_{X1}) = b_1 X_1 / (b_0 + b_1 X_1 + b_2 X_2 + b_3 X_3) \tag{11.8}$$

where the *b*-values now stand for the estimated parameter values. The elasticities with respect to the other variables can be calculated by appropriate substitutions in the numerator of Equation 11.8. For example, the elasticity of Y with respect to X_2 is obtained by substituting b_2 and X_2 in the numerator of Equation 11.8.

One problem with the above formula is that the elasticity is not constant for all values of the independent variable. This is evident from Equation 11.7, since both the numerator and the denominator depend on X_1. For each variable, we need to select a reasonable value at which to calculate the elasticity. If the model is used for predicting service improvements in a future time period, then the elasticities should be calculated at the most current value of the performance of each attribute. If general, average elasticities are needed, then they can be calculated at the average value of the attributes.

By definition, the larger the absolute value of elasticity associated with an independent variable, the greater its impact on the dependent variable. Attributes with higher elasticities are therefore more desirable candidates for improvement. The elasticity of overall performance with respect to the three attributes of the Service Edge restaurant in Table 11.6 is shown in Table 11.7. The elasticity is calculated using the attribute performance ratings for the most recent month from Table 11.4 (i.e., 4.33 for customer service, 2.41 for problem resolution, and 4.11 for price).

The customer service attribute is the prime candidate for improvement, because a 1% increase in the performance of this attribute will result in a 1.05% increase in overall satisfaction. The elasticity of the price attribute is negative because a 1% *decrease* in price results in a 0.15% *increase* in overall satisfaction.

Performance/importance map

The elasticity is one tool that can be used by the service management team to select one or more attributes for improvement. Another tool is the *performance/importance map*. This is a graph with the *importance* of each attribute (specified by regression estimates or elasticities) on the *x*-axis, and the *performance* of each attribute on the *y*-axis.

Figure 11.2 shows this map for the three Service Edge restaurant attributes from Table 11.7. The absolute value of the parameter estimates is plotted on the importance scale. The performance of each attribute in the most recent month (obtained from the last row of Table 11.4) is plotted on the performance scale. Since the performance of each attribute is measured relative to the best competitor, a rating of 3 indicates that the performance is on par with the competition.

From Figure 11.2, the following kinds of attributes can be identified:

1. *High performance/low importance:* These attributes fall in the *top left corner* of the performance/importance map. The *price* attribute falls in this category. These attributes are clearly not an immediate candidate for improvement, since they are currently performing better than the competition, and additional improvement will not have a large impact on satisfaction.

Table 11.7   Elasticity of satisfaction relative to the three attributes of Table 11.6

Attribute	*Elasticity*
Customer service	1.05
Problem resolution	0.10
Price	−0.15

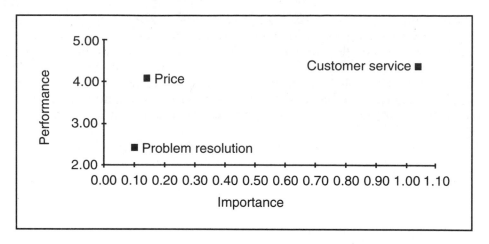

Figure 11.2   Performance/importance map for three Service Edge restaurant
attributes

2. High performance/high importance: These attributes fall in the *top right corner* of
the performance/importance map. The important *customer service* attribute falls in
this category. For the moment, the restaurant is living up to its name of "Service
Edge," by performing better than its competitors on this attribute. However, since
this attribute is a strong predictor of satisfaction, the service management team
should plan to improve the performance of this attribute. Both short-term and
long-term opportunities should be considered.

3. Poor performance/low importance: These attributes fall in the *bottom left corner* of
the performance/importance map. The *problem resolution* attribute falls in this category. The performance of this attribute is below that of the competition. The service management team must investigate the reasons for this performance using
the techniques described in Chapter 9, and determine whether the poor performance was the result of a unique incident that took place in the time period, or
whether a general pattern of poor performance is observed over time. It is possible
that customers' needs regarding this attribute have changed. After the reason for
the poor performance is determined, it should be improved to at least match the
performance provided by the competition.

Notice that we have not listed any attributes that occupy the *bottom right corner* of
the performance/importance map. These attributes fall in a fourth category: *Low
performance/high importance.* This category is not represented in our example. This
is not surprising for a well-designed service. For a carefully planned, well-per-
forming service, we would not expect to find poorly performing service attributes
that have a large impact on satisfaction. The focus of the improvement effort
should be on the forward-looking development of initiatives for better service performance in the future.

In summary, the results from the regression model linking overall performance to attribute performance can be used as the basis for selecting attributes for strategic improvements. However, these results should not be the only consideration for the selection. Other factors should be taken into account, and tools such as the performance/importance map should be used to evaluate the effect of these factors. Some of the key factors that should influence the selection of attributes are the following:

- The amount of improvement effort required and its feasibility and costs
- The current performance of each attribute relative to the competition (it is more important to improve the attributes that perform worse than or at par with the competitors than attributes whose performance is far superior to the competition)
- The number and type of customer complaints about each attribute
- The extent of correlation between the performance of various attributes
- The extent to which each attribute supports the long-term growth plans of the firm

Setting attribute-level service improvement targets

For each candidate attribute, the service improvement targets are derived from Equation 11.6 in the same way that satisfaction improvement targets were obtained from Equation 11.3. For example, suppose a model such as the one shown in Equation 11.3 predicts that the target market share increase in the following quarter will require the average overall satisfaction rating relative to the competition to increase by 0.2 units. From Table 11.7, we can see that this translates into an average improvement of approximately 0.2 units for the customer service attribute. From the last three rows of Table 11.4, we can see that the average performance rating of the customer service attribute in the current quarter is 3.7. The *attribute-level target performance* for customer service in the following quarter is therefore 3.9.

11.5 SPECIFYING IMPROVEMENTS AT THE PROCESS LEVEL—STEP 5 AND STEP 6

The next step is to partition the attribute-level targets to the process level. We do this by identifying the key processes that need to be improved for each attribute, by setting process-level improvement targets, and by developing plans for improving each relevant process. In order to determine the key processes that affect the performance of each attribute, another regression model must be estimated. This model links the performance of each service-level attribute to corresponding performance metrics at the process level. The dependent variable of this regression is the *service-level attribute performance,* and the independent variables are the *process-level performance measures.*

A process-level model for the Service Edge restaurant

Recall from the previous section that the *customer service* attribute was chosen as the best candidate for improvement of the Service Edge restaurant. From Tables 11.2 and 11.3, it can be seen that this attribute consists of the following disaggregate attributes:

- Friendliness
- Responsiveness
- Knowledge
- Patience

The service/process matrix (see Chapter 6, Figure 6.2) can be used to partition these attributes to the appropriate processes. The six process-level attributes, and their associated metrics, are shown in Table 11.8.

A model specification that links the customer service performance to the six process metrics is shown in Equation 11.9. As in the case of Equation 11.6, several months worth of data are needed to estimate the model.

$$\text{Cust Service performance}(t) = b_0 + b_1 * F1(t) + b_2 * F2(t) + b_3 * R1(t) + b_4 * F3(t) + b_5 * P1(t) + b_6 * K1(t) + E(t)$$

(11.9)

Table 11.8 Process level effectiveness metrics for the customer service attribute

Attribute name	Process-level attributes	Effectiveness metric
F1	Degree of friendliness of greeting	% of customers rating "Exceptional"
F2	Degree of friendliness of meal service	% of customers rating "Exceptional"
R1	Degree of responsiveness of meal service	% of customers rating "Exceptional"
F3	Degree of friendliness of leavetaking	% of customers rating "Exceptional"
K1	Degree of knowledge about menu	% of customers rating "Exceptional"
P1	Degree of order-taking patience	% of customers rating "Exceptional"

As before, the *R*-squared value, the *t*-statistics, and the elasticities can be used to determine the process-level attributes that have the greatest impact on the performance of the service. The model is then used to set process-level improvement targets for these attributes.

Estimating an integrated model system

In this chapter, we have described models that specify three relationships:

- Between financial objectives and overall satisfaction
- Between overall satisfaction and service-level attribute performance
- Between service-level and process-level attribute performance

In our discussion, we presented each relationship separately, assuming that the models are unrelated and that each model can be estimated independently. In reality, since the process attributes affect the service attributes, which in turn affect the overall satisfaction and financial measures, the models are likely to be correlated. It is more accurate to estimate all the relationships using a single *multiequation model specification*. This involves estimating the parameters of Equations 11.3, 11.6, and 11.9 *simultaneously*.

An example of such a model system for telecommunications services is presented in the paper by Ramaswamy and Hafiz (1994). Ordinary least squares is not appropriate for estimating models with multiple equations except under some very specific conditions. A commonly used method is called *three-stage least squares*. This method is described in Johnston (1972) and in the other econometrics texts referenced at the end of this chapter.

11.6 DEVELOPING AN OPTIMAL PROCESS IMPROVEMENT STRATEGY—STEP 7

Analyzing the cost-effectiveness of process improvement plans

So far in this chapter, we have demonstrated how satisfaction improvement targets can be specified to meet financial profitability objectives, and how service-level and process-level improvement targets that will deliver the required level of satisfaction can be determined. However, all our discussion of profitability so far has primarily addressed the *revenue* side of the profitability equation. In this section, we discuss the *cost* side of the equation.

We begin by listing the basic steps needed to implement any service improvement plan. They are:

- Generation of improvement alternatives
- Evaluation of alternatives

- Selection of alternatives

- Implementation of alternatives

The reader will notice that these steps are very similar to the *detailed design activities* described in Chapters 6 and 7. Despite this apparent similarity, there is a fundamental difference between selecting process improvements and selecting a design for implementation. The difference lies in the standards that must be met in each case. When a service is being designed, it is mandatory for a firm to offer a service that meets the design standards specified by the customers and the competitors. The company has no option but to design a service that meets these standards if it wishes to stay in business. If the firm is unable to design a service that meets the standards at an acceptable cost, it should reconsider its plans to enter the market.

On the other hand, this obligation to meet prespecified performance targets does not exist in the case of service improvements, unless they are necessary to catch up with the competition. For a well-designed service, the objective of strategic process improvements should not be to improve the process performance to meet some rigidly defined target, but instead should be to enhance the service level to the point where profitability is maximized. The process improvement targets are useful guidelines because they reflect the strategic growth objectives of the firm, but the benefits of achieving these targets should always be compared to the cost and effort required to achieve them. If the costs are too high, then the targets must be reduced to the level at which the greatest net benefit can be achieved. Increasing customer satisfaction through service improvements to enhance market share or revenue is a viable option *only* if the costs of these improvements are low enough to increase the firm's profitability. If the estimated costs of meeting the improvement targets are higher than the projected revenue increase, then it may be more profitable to implement only part of the improvements, or to do nothing at all. A *sensitivity analysis* should be performed for each process to determine if "do nothing" or partial improvement is more effective than meeting the performance target. The improvement level that maximizes the returns should be selected.

This kind of sensitivity analysis is not appropriate when designing the service. This is because there is a base level of performance (specified by the design standards) that needs to be achieved in the design stage, and partial achievement of this level is not an acceptable option.

Sensitivity analysis of service improvement initiatives

How do we perform sensitivity analysis of service improvement initiatives? The foundation for such an analysis lies in the calculation of the costs and benefits of the improvement effort. The analysis itself is relatively simple if costs and benefits are calculated at a *detailed functional level*. All the activities that need to be performed for the process to be improved should be listed in detail. These should include both the activities that will be carried out once (such as training or software development) and those that will be carried out regularly as a result of process changes. The evaluation of costs and benefits should then be done at the level of these activities.

Performing a sensitivity analysis involves the following activities:

1. Identify the benefits and costs of achieving the service improvement target (total improvement).
2. Determine the benefits of doing nothing.
3. Determine the benefits and costs of various partial improvements. This is relatively simple if the costs and benefits are defined at the activity level, since the partial improvements can then be defined as the partial completion of the activities.
4. Compute the net benefits (i.e., benefits − cost) value for each level of improvement.
5. Plot a net benefit curve for each level of improvement.
6. Select the improvement level with the highest net benefit for implementation.

Benefits arising from service improvements are typically realized from two sources:

- Increase in satisfaction resulting from improvements in performance
- Reduction in costs due to increased operating efficiency

These typical costs are associated with process improvements:

- Costs of implementing the improvement effort
- Incremental operating costs due to the process improvements

We will now illustrate how a sensitivity analysis can be performed to determine the optimal improvement level for the *friendliness of the greeting and seating process* of the Service Edge restaurant.

Sensitivity analysis—Service Edge restaurant example

We will describe this analysis under the following headings:

(a) Process activities

(b) Process improvement targets

(c) Proposed process improvements

(d) Benefits of proposed improvements

(e) Costs of proposed improvements

(f) Sensitivity analysis

(a) Process activities: The first step is to list the activities of the greeting and seating process (performed by the host):

1. Greeting the customer upon arrival

2. Escorting the customer to his or her table

3. Signaling the assigned waiter to explain the ordering system

(b) Process improvement target: The target is a 10% increase in the average friendliness rating as a result of the improvements.

(c) Proposed process improvements: In order to determine how best to improve the process, the restaurant conducted a special survey of customers. Customers who participated in the survey indicated that they were generally satisfied with the friendliness level, but that some additional improvements were needed to make the performance of the process exceed their expectations. Based on the results of the survey, the following improvement options are proposed:

Option 1: Ten hours of role-playing training for the hosts to teach poise, pace, and communication skills. The objectives of this training are the following:

- Increased eye contact between the host and the customer

- Better-quality interaction ("improved conversation skills")

Option 2: A change in the process that requires the host to explain the ordering system (instead of the waiter). The objective of this change is to encourage a more relaxed interaction between the hosts and the guests, and to allow guests to get started with the ordering process before the waiter arrives.

(d) Benefits of proposed improvements: Three benefits are predicted as a result of the improvement. The first two result in increased satisfaction, and the third in increased efficiency. The benefits are these:

1. Better-quality interaction as a result of the training

2. More time for relaxed interaction between the host and guests resulting from the process change

3. Increase in waiter capacity (since the host now performs one of the tasks previously performed by a waiter)

These benefits are quantified using experience and judgment. For example, past experiences with the role-playing training have shown that a 10-hour session produces the required 10% increase in the average performance ratings. The increase in waiter capacity is calculated by computing the time normally taken by a waiter to explain the ordering system to a customer and multiplying this time by the number of customers in a month. This is the total amount of additional waiter time that is now available every month.

(e) Costs of proposed improvements: Three costs are predicted:

1. Training delivery costs (one time)

2. Cost of resources to plan and implement improvement (one time)

3. Cost of hiring additional hosts to make up for extra time spent with guests (ongoing)

The cost of hiring new hosts is calculated in the same way that the cost savings for the waiter were calculated above. The additional time spent by a host with each customer is multiplied by the number of customers in a month. The costs for various modules of the training package are obtained from the vendor. The cost of resources to plan and implement the improvement is calculated as a function of the time that is spent on this effort by various members of the organization who are involved in implementing this effort.

(f) Sensitivity analysis: A separate sensitivity analysis should be performed for each proposed improvement option (i.e., training and process change). We will begin with option 2 (process change that requires host to explain ordering system).

First consider the *cost side* for this option. The service management team discovers that the costs of hiring and training new hosts almost exactly balances the savings due to the additional waiter capacity that is generated by the process change. In fact, it seems feasible to retrain the surplus waiters as additional hosts, with minimal training costs and no additional hiring costs. Therefore, *no additional costs will be incurred in implementing the process change.*

On the benefit side, the process change provides the benefit of increased customer satisfaction resulting from the additional time spent by the host with the customer. *Option 2 therefore results in a constant positive net benefit.* Clearly, there can be no argument about implementing this change.

The sensitivity analysis is therefore only necessary for option 1 (special training for hosts). To perform the sensitivity analysis, we calculate the costs and benefits associated with various levels of partial training (i.e., less than 10 hours). This will reduce costs, but also benefits. If the cost or benefit function is nonlinear, then a partial solution may produce a higher net benefit than a total implementation. The costs and benefits of a 90% implementation (9-hour training), 80% implementation (8-hour training), and so on are calculated. Costs are computed at the rate of

$10,000 per hour, and are assumed to decrease linearly up to $50,000, which is the base cost of the training program up to 5 hours. Benefits are quantified as the expected *increase in average performance ratings* as a result of the training. The models described in the previous section linking performance and financial measures are used to translate the expected service improvements into dollars of revenue.

The results of the sensitivity analysis are shown in Figure 11.3. The *y*-axis in Figure 11.3 shows both the net and the total benefits, expressed in units of thousands of dollars per month of additional revenue. The *x*-axis shows the number of hours of training provided. When no training is provided, the costs are zero, and so are the benefits. As more hours are spent on training, the benefits increase. However, since the minimum cost of training is at least $50,000, there is no reason to consider training that is less than 5 hours in duration. As can be seen from Figure 11.3, 5 hours of training produces a slightly larger net benefit than the do-nothing option. Increased expenditure in training beyond this amount produces increasing returns but at a diminishing rate, as is indicated by the flattening slope of the total benefits curve. This means an expenditure of $90,000 or $100,000 does not result in significantly greater satisfaction than a $60,000 or $70,000 expense. The optimal training expenditure is therefore somewhat more than $50,000, but somewhat less than $100,000. Figure 11.3 shows that *maximum returns are obtained for an expenditure of $70,000,* which translates into 7 hours of training.

In summary, the sensitivity analysis leads to the following optimal improvement recommendation for the greeting and seating process of the Service Edge restaurant:

(a) Spend 8 hours in training waiters and hosts on advanced communication skills.

(b) Transfer the task of explaining the ordering system from the waiter to the host.

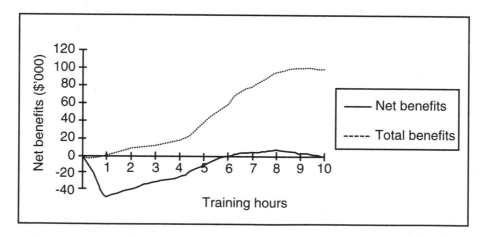

Figure 11.3 Sensitivity analysis of the impact of training on restaurant revenue

Rust *et al.* (1994) refer to this kind of analysis as "Return on Quality." In their text of the same name, which we have cited several times in this chapter, the authors describe their approach to determining optimal improvement expenditures, which is conceptually very similar to what we have discussed here. In their book, the authors also present the details of a software package they have developed to perform the Return on Quality analysis. The reader is referred to this text for another view of the topic of developing and implementing cost-effective service improvements.

11.7 CONCLUSION

Summary

The following is a summary of the topics described in this chapter. The section in the chapter where a particular topic is covered is indicated in parentheses.

Steps for selecting an optimal service improvement strategy (introduction)

- Step 1: Estimate the relationship between financial objectives and overall satisfaction.

- Step 2: Determine the overall satisfaction improvement to meet strategic financial objectives.

- Step 3: Estimate the relationship between overall satisfaction and attribute performance.

- Step 4: Select one or more attributes for improvement, and set their improvement targets.

- Step 5: Estimate the relationship between the performance of service-level and process-level attributes.

- Step 6: Select candidate processes for improvement.

- Step 7: Determine the optimal amount of improvement needed for each process that produces the greatest returns.

Evaluating financial impact of customer satisfaction—Step 1 (11.1)

- Develop a regression model linking the profitability measure to overall satisfaction.

- Use relative satisfaction, performance, or value measures for the independent variable.

- Use shareholder value, revenue, or customer behavior measures for the dependent variable.

- Incorporate the time lag between change in attitude and change in behavior in the model.

- Incorporate the effect of cumulative history by a lagged dependent variable specification.

- Estimate the model using ordinary least squares or another appropriate technique.

Setting strategic improvement targets—Step 2 (11.2)

- Identify the strategic financial objectives to be met by the service.

- Set satisfaction targets required to meet these objectives.

Evaluating impact of service attribute performance on satisfaction— Step 3 (11.3)

- Specify the relationship between overall satisfaction and attribute performance.

- Measure attribute performance relative to expectations for developing new services.

- Measure attribute performance relative to competitors for short-term improvements.

- Estimate parameters using ridge regression or equity estimators if multicollinearity is present.

Selecting attributes for improvement—Step 4 (11.4)

- Use the R^2 statistic to determine the fit of the overall model to data.

- Re-examine the specification of models with poor fit.

- Use the t-statistics to determine significant parameters.

- Calculate the impact of each independent variable from the magnitude of estimated values.

Specifying service level improvement targets (11.4)

- Use elasticities to measure impacts if independent variables are measured on different scales.

- Use performance/importance map to select attributes for immediate and future improvement.

- Partition overall satisfaction targets into attribute-level targets.

Specifying improvements at the process level—Step 5 and Step 6 (11.5)

- Specify the regression equation linking service-level attributes to process-level performance.

- Select key processes that need to be improved and their improvement targets.

- Estimate integrated model system linking process-level performance to financial objectives.

Developing an optimal service improvement strategy—Step 7 (11.6)

- Identify process improvement options to meet the targets.

- Compute the benefits resulting from increased customer satisfaction.

- Compute the benefits resulting from increased operating efficiency.

- Calculate the one-time implementation costs.

- Calculate the ongoing operating costs.

- Perform sensitivity analysis to evaluate the net benefits of partial implementation of the selected approaches.

- Select the approach and the amount of effort that maximizes the returns.

Suggested reading

The following texts are recommended for further reading on regression. This is not an exhaustive collection, but it provides a good overview of different aspects of these topics.

Johnston (1972) is a complete guide to the most important techniques of classical econometrics, for readers with moderate mathematical sophistication. It is a good reference text on econometrics for the practitioner. Cassidy (1981) is a simple text, with do's and don'ts for using regression in many applications. Hung (1970) uses simple mathematics to explain estimation methods mentioned in this chapter. Chatterjee and Price (1991) is a practical introduction to many issues involved in the application of regression models. Finally, Montgomery and Price (1992) provides a mathematical description of all major regression topics, including multicollinearity.

Chapter

12

Conclusion

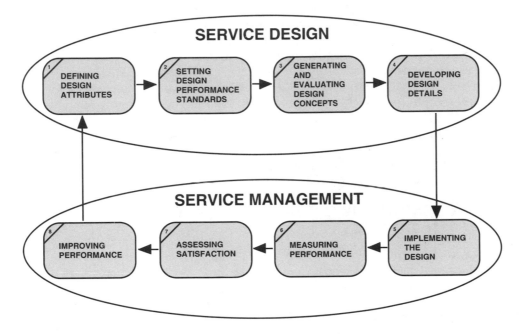

- *Closing the loop—restarting the design cycle*
- *Integrated design of service features, facilities, and processes*
- *Good-bye*

The previous eleven chapters have led the reader through the details of the methodology required to create, engineer, measure, manage, and improve the processes that are used to deliver a service. The *service design and management model* has been used as the framework for the methodology, and we have followed the eight stages of the model sequentially through the chapters of the book. In this final chapter, we conclude our presentation with some suggestions for using and extending the material presented in this book.

Three topics are covered in this chapter. In Section 12.1, we close the loop between the final stage (Stage 8) and the initial stage (Stage 1) of the service design and management model. We describe the conditions that trigger the transition from the management and improvement of an existing service to the implementation of a new service design.

In Section 12.2, we discuss some important extensions to the service design and management model as a preview of future work. In the form presented in this book, the model provides a systematic framework for the design of products, facilities, and processes of a service. However, a service of exceptional quality cannot be created by well-designed processes, products, or facilities alone. Each of these components is independently important, but it is the successful integration of these elements that distinguishes a great service design from a good one. A complete service design approach should therefore systematically incorporate the interactions between the design components. We call such an approach *integrated design*. We show how the service design and management model can be used to formulate a general approach to integrated design.

We end this book with a few concluding remarks to the reader in Section 12.3.

12.1   CLOSING THE LOOP—RESTARTING THE DESIGN CYCLE

In this book, we followed the Service Edge restaurant design and service management teams through the eight stages of the service design and management model. In the first two stages, the design team used the House of Quality matrix to analyze customers' needs and the performance of the competitors. This analysis was used to set specifications for the design of the service processes of the restaurant. In the next two stages (3 and 4), the team developed a design concept for the processes, and evaluated and selected the functions and technologies that would most reliably deliver the required performance specifications.

The last four stages of the model involved the service management team. After the designed processes were implemented in Stage 5, the team measured and stabilized their performance in Stage 6. The team measured the satisfaction of customers with the performance of processes in Stage 7, and selected and implemented strategic improvements to the processes in Stage 8.

Depending on the nature of the industry, the amount of hardware, software, training, and resources that need to be invested in implementing the design, and the strategic objectives of the firm, a service should be designed for a life cycle of at least three to five years to make it worth the effort. The design stages should typically be completed within a year, and the service should be managed and improved for the remainder of its life cycle.

As described in Chapters 10 and 11, the improvement of the service should not be a static process that merely monitors conformance to immutable standards, but should be a strategic vehicle that anticipates and responds to changes in the market. In this sense, the term *life cycle* of a service is a misnomer, since the service should change continuously over time. For a well-managed and continuously improved service, there will be no single point in time when a discrete transition takes place from Stage 8 to Stage 1. Instead, these stages will overlap as part of the everyday process of managing the service.

Rather than define a temporal life cycle for a service, it is more appropriate to state that the point of transition to a new cycle of the service design and management model takes place *when changes to the design concept are necessary.* If a service has been in operation for a while, factors such as innovations in the technology that support the delivery of the service, changes in governmental regulations that allow greater competition, or changes in population demographics and service usage patterns may require a complete rethinking of the way in which a service is provided, and may also give the opportunity for the firm to introduce new services that could not be provided before. Under these circumstances, a totally different design may be appropriate. But even in this case, there should be some temporal overlap between the withdrawal of the existing service and the introduction of the new one. The design team should not wait until the existing design is obsolete to begin the new design. Since the design process can take up to a year, a late start may result in an irrevocable loss of customers before the new service becomes operational. The design team for the new service should be assembled while the existing service is still being used, and improvements to the existing service should be continued during the design period until it becomes more efficient to incorporate service improvements directly into the new design. Finally, if a new design will affect the way in which a customer interacts with the service, then the old and new designs must coexist until customers can make a comfortable transition. As far as possible, customers should experience the introduction of even a radically new service concept as a continuing evolution rather than as an abrupt change.

12.2 INTEGRATED DESIGN OF SERVICE FEATURES, FACILITIES, AND PROCESSES

The approach presented in the eight stages of the service design and management model can be used to design the *features, facilities, and processes* of a service. In this book, we have developed this approach with an emphasis on processes. As mentioned in the preface and in Chapter 1, the reason for this emphasis was that, in our experience, service firms may be methodical while designing the service product and facilities, but very often fail to apply the same discipline to the design of the processes by which the service is provided. This results in unreliable or unmemorable service delivery, leading to dissatisfaction with the entire service. This book presents a systematic approach for designing and managing processes which can be used for service features and facilities as well.

Does this mean that if the approach presented in this text were followed three times: once each for the facilities, features, and processes of the service, we would generate the best possible design for the service? This is not usually the case. A systematic procedure followed for one component of a service may produce an optimal design with respect to that component, but may still be suboptimal for the overall service. The reason for this is the *interaction* between the service components. A design alternative selected for one service component affects the performance of the other components.

For example, consider the Service Edge restaurant. Decisions about the food to be offered at the restaurant (a service *feature*) can affect the design of the restaurant *facilities* (by influencing storage requirements) and the timeliness of the meal delivery *process* (by influencing the meal preparation time). An optimal design for the entire service requires an approach that explicitly incorporates the effect of these interactions into the design evaluation and selection process. Such an approach is called *integrated design*.

In many instances, the method followed by service design teams precludes integration. Most design approaches are *sequential:* the features are designed first, followed by the facilities, followed by the processes. A completely integrated approach is not sequential, but *simultaneous.* Such an approach recognizes that there is no reason to assume an a priori hierarchy among service features, facilities, and processes. Rather, design decisions should be based on an understanding of the customers' overall service requirements and on the trade-offs that customers are willing to make between the various design components. For example, customers may be willing to accept a service without a particular feature if the inclusion of the feature makes the delivery or installation process unreliable. In this case, the optimal design should exclude the feature in favor of a reliable process design. This option will not be considered under a sequential design procedure.

The practical details of an approach for evaluating product/process/facility interactions for designing integrated services is an important topic for future work that is beyond the scope of this book. However, the general framework for integrated design can still be represented by an extended version of the service design and management model. In this version, the service product, process, and facility components are designed together at each stage of the model. An example of how this can be done for one stage of the model is shown in the QFD matrix of Table 3.5 (Chapter 3) for the Service Edge restaurant. In this table, the design attributes for the features, facilities, and process components (called *food design, facilities design,* and *customer service design,* respectively) are developed together in the same matrix from a common set of customer needs.

Since we emphasized process design in this book, we partitioned the matrix of Table 3.5 and only developed the *customer service design* component through the eight stages of the service design and management model. An integrated design approach would not partition the components in this way. Instead, all the attributes of Table 3.5 would be simultaneously considered in each stage of the model.

In an integrated design model, the key design attributes will contain a mix of food, facilities, and service elements. The service profiles described in Chapter 4 for estimating the satisfaction/performance function will also be a combination of these elements. The Pugh concept evaluation procedure described in Chapter 5 will analyze the effects of the design of one component on all other components of the service. For example, the Service Edge restaurant process design concept used throughout this book requires the installation of one or more terminals at each table that the customers use to place their order. Clearly, the implementation of this concept over another that does not require these terminals will affect the layout of tables in the restaurant (facility components). A globally integrated approach will consider both the process and the facility impacts in the evaluation of the concept.

The same principles apply to the other stages of the service design and management model. For example, in the restaurant simulation example described in Chapter 7, attributes such as the type of food ordered or the restaurant layout were not included in the simulation, even though these characteristics can affect process performance attributes such as the meal delivery time. For example, customers may be willing to wait a few minutes beyond the desired meal delivery interval for some special items on the menu. The optimal integrated design will balance the *food considerations* with the *service requirements* and select a combination of dishes and delivery times that meets both sets of customer needs.

Clearly, a service that is designed in an integrated manner should also be managed in the same way. Effectiveness, efficiency, and capability metrics developed in Stage 6 should measure the performance of all service components. For example, the effectiveness metrics for the Service Edge restaurant would include the percentage of customers' ratings that met standards of food quality on a variety of attributes, or ratings of the cleanliness, atmosphere, or decor of the restaurant. The efficiency metrics should calculate the costs of providing a meal as the sum of *all* the resources and materials needed to support the design (e.g., food preparation costs, food material costs, cleaning and facility maintenance costs, resources needed for food preparation and cleaning). Similarly, in Stage 8, the independent variables of the regression models linking overall satisfaction with attribute performance should include food and facility characteristics in addition to process performance attributes.

When managing a service in an integrated manner, improvement decisions should be based on the impact of a change on the entire service. For example, the decision to change some kitchen procedures to improve the taste (or control the temperature, or modify the presentation) of the food may affect the meal preparation times, and therefore the meal delivery interval. Increase in satisfaction resulting from improved food quality may be partially mitigated by unacceptable delivery times. In order to develop an optimal service improvement plan, the *total* benefits resulting from the proposed improvement across all service components should be balanced against the *total* costs of that improvement.

The foregoing discussion should make it clear to the reader that there is no theoretical or methodological difference between the approach taken by this book and integrated design. A practical difference may be that integrated design requires the service design and management model to encompass a larger scope, which may entail more complicated analyses than those presented in this book.

The key difference between component-by-component design and integrated design is one of *philosophy*. In order to design a globally integrated service, the design team must embrace the fundamental principle that the design approach should be driven by a *total set of customer needs*, without any a priori assumptions about the relative importance of the service components. This principle should drive the team members to create a design that includes the attributes most important to customers, irrespective of whether these attributes relate to the features, facilities, or delivery processes of the service. The greatest impediment in practice to implementing a successful integrated design is the inability or unwillingness of design teams to adopt this global service view. As mentioned earlier, design teams typically tend to place a greater emphasis on the service features and facilities than on the delivery processes, and to design the features and facilities before the processes. Future work on integrated design needs to address these perceptual problems as well as methodological issues.

12.3 GOOD-BYE

We began this book with the story of two service firms A and B that used different strategies to compete in the marketplace. Company A used a technology-based strategy, and Company B a service-based strategy. At the end of the story, Company B achieved greater long-term success by being better able to deliver a service that met its customers' needs.

In this book, we have described in detail the activities that are required to successfully implement a service-based strategy. We have presented the steps that our mythical company B needs to follow to achieve a competitive advantage based on service. We had two objectives in writing this book. The first and obvious objective was to introduce the reader to the concepts, approaches, and analysis techniques that are required to develop a service of exceptional quality. The second and more subtle objective was to show the reader the amount of effort, teamwork, skill, and patience that is required to achieve this level of quality. We hope that we have been successful in achieving both objectives.

In our minds, the second objective is no less important than the first. It demonstrates that achieving and sustaining high-quality service is not only a matter of knowing the techniques and understanding how to use them; it also requires a *willingness* to regularly and carefully apply them and to make objective decisions based on the results. The plethora of general books on quality currently available in the market may have created the perception that quality is like spirituality; that somehow, the atmosphere is suffused with the essence of quality that will become visible, in all its glory, to the enlightened. Nothing could be further from the truth. Like everything else, exceptional quality of products and services is achieved by a systematic approach, the right skills, careful analysis, supporting tools—and most of all, hard work, discipline, and an unflagging commitment to satisfying customers. Any team that embarks on the quality journey with these characteristics is likely to succeed, especially with a good, clearly written road map to lead the way. We hope that this book will serve as such a road map. Good luck!

GLOSSARY

Absolute Satisfaction Rating: This refers to the measurement of satisfaction with a service on an absolute scale (for example, from 1 to 10). This scale may not be suitable where there is a wide range of expectations for service performance among the users of the service.

Ad Hoc Analysis: The detailed diagnostic testing that is required to investigate the reasons for unexpected changes in performance for a service in operation.

Affinity Diagrams (or **K-J Diagrams**): A method used to organize and aggregate customer need data into similar groups.

Average (or **Base**) **Performance:** The level of performance expected by a service under a particular, stable set of environmental conditions and operating characteristics.

Brainstorming: A technique, used for design concept generation, in which a team generates design solutions by amassing all the ideas spontaneously contributed by its members.

Capability Metric: A service performance measure of the intrinsic ability of a service attribute to reliably meet its design performance standard. A capability metric specifies the shape and spread of the performance distribution of an attribute.

Common Design Elements (or **Subsystems**): Service elements (features, facilities, or processes) that share common elements that are advantageous to design together.

Commonality Level: A measure of the extent of commonality among two or more service elements. Commonality levels vary from 1 to 4. A design common to all processes corresponds to commonality level 1; independent designs for each process or service activity correspond to commonality level 4.

Communications Plan: A plan that lists, schedules, and coordinates the activities needed to disseminate information about the new service design and the progress of the implementation. The plan specifies who should be kept informed, how often, and by what means.

Concept Generation: A facilitated, imaginative activity whose objective is to develop innovative design solutions for service features, facilities, and processes.

Contingency Plan: A plan that specifies the steps that need to be taken if a new service fails after implementation.

Control Chart: A chart that compares the performance of a variable against statistically computed control limits. These limits represent the expected variation in the performance of the variable if the only source of variability is random variability. The performance of a variable is deemed to be out of control if more points than expected in a sample of observations fall outside the control limits.

Cumulative Satisfaction: This is the satisfaction with the service that occurs as the result of multiple experiences with the service over a period of time. Cumulative satisfaction is an indicator of a customer's attitude towards the service.

Customer Benchmarks: The customers' assessment of the ability of the competitors' services to satisfy their needs.

Customer Measure: This measure determines the customer satisfaction associated with the performance of an attribute of a service in operation. Customer measures and service performance measures can be used together to develop performance/satisfaction relationships for existing services from historical data.

Customer Service Activity: An activity that reflects the personal interaction between the customer and the service provider during the course of service delivery. The quality of a customer service activity is generally evaluated by attributes that are not objectively measurable.

Design Alternative: A detailed design solution that satisfies a particular concept. Several design alternatives may exist for a concept, each with different performance and cost implications. The detailed design procedure requires the evaluation of these alternatives to select the one that delivers the best performance at the lowest cost.

Design Attribute (also called **Design Characteristic**): A design solution that meets a customer need identified in the QFD matrix. A design attribute can be either a specific service feature, or a quantifiable characteristic of the service that can measure the ability of a design solution to meet the need.

Design Capability: The ability of a design to meet the design standards. A design attribute that is capable is characterized by a mean performance value that is located centrally between the upper and lower bounds of the design standards for the attribute and shows low performance variability around this mean. Capability is measured at a particular value of operating characteristics and environmental conditions and is therefore a weaker property than robustness, which refers to performance invariance over an operating range.

Design Concept: An innovative high-level design solution to meet customers' needs for service.

Design Dimension: A characteristic of a design unit that can be manipulated to influence the performance of a design. Each specific manipulation produces a design alternative. For example, the training level of customer service associates may be a design dimension for a customer service process design. Each training method is a design alternative.

Design Factor: The performance characteristic of a design alternative that determines how the service will perform if the particular alternative is implemented. Design factors are properties of a design and are therefore controllable. For example, the ability of a customer service associate to search a database for solutions as the result of a particular training program (design alternative) is a design factor that affects the performance of the customer service process.

Design Implementation Plan: A "plan of plans" that oversees the implementation and integration of all aspects of the design. It serves as the framework for managing the entire implementation, and at any time it provides a high-level overview of the status of the implementation.

Design Performance Standard (or **Design Standard**): The performance level that a design attribute is required to achieve for the design to be acceptable.

Design Specifications: The design attributes and design standards for a service together make up the specifications for the design.

Design Unit: The level of detail at which a design alternative should be created and analyzed. Depending on the application, a set of processes, a single process, a subprocess, or even an individual activity can be treated as a design unit.

Desired Performance Standard (or **Desired Standard**): The performance level for a design attribute desired by the customers. The desired standard may not be the same as the design standard if technology or cost constraints do not permit the service to be designed to meet the desired performance level.

Detailed Design: A systematic approach for designing the elements of a design concept so that the overall service meets the design performance standards for all attributes. Detailed design starts with the idea specified by the concept and develops the service through the addition of successive levels of detail.

Disconfirmation Model: A model from the service quality literature that explains the determinants of customer satisfaction. According to this model, satisfaction is correlated with disconfirmation, which is a measure of how well the perceived performance of a service meets the expected performance. Positive disconfirmation occurs when the perceived performance is better than a customer's expectations, and results in satisfaction. Negative disconfirmation results when the perceived performance is worse than a customer's expectation, and results in dissatisfaction.

Discrete Event Simulation Model: A model that simulates process activities in discrete events of time.

Effectiveness Metric: A service performance measure that indicates the extent to which a service attribute meets the design performance standards.

Efficiency Metric: The cost of delivering a service and the resources utilized in delivery are determined by this service performance measure.

Elasticity: A unit-independent measure of the effect of one variable on another. The elasticity of a variable Y with respect to another variable X is the percent change that occurs in Y as the result of a 1% change in X.

Environmental Condition: A characteristic of the surroundings in which the service operates that contributes to variability in performance. Location and weather are two examples of environmental conditions. Environmental conditions affect the operating characteristics of the service in uncontrollable ways.

Event: An occurrence in a simulation model that triggers a change in the state of the system.

Exception Analysis: Analysis performed to test whether any unexpected changes in service performance in a given reporting period can be attributed to unique, uncontrollable causes or to special circumstances.

Experimental Design: The methodology for combining performance values of design attributes to create a set of service profiles to be rated by customers so that the impact of each attribute on satisfaction can be independently estimated.

Failure point: The value of an operating characteristic at which the performance of an associated design attribute fails to meet the design specifications.

Financial Measure: This measure evaluates the impact of satisfying customers on the current and future profitability of the firm.

Flow unit: The entity that flows through a simulation model. Depending on the application, customers, orders, projects, etc., are examples of flow units.

Fractional Factorial Design: A set of service profiles that is a fraction of a full factorial design. Only selected combinations of attributes are included in a fractional factorial design, making the profile rating task more manageable.

Full Factorial Design: A set of service profiles in which all possible combinations of the design attributes are included. For example, for two attributes each at two levels, the full factorial design is made up of a total of four profiles. For services with more than two or three attributes, the number of service profiles to be rated under a full factorial design becomes unmanageably large.

Functional Analysis System Technique (FAST): A tool for visually representing the activities that must be completed for delivering a service and the interactions among them. The FAST diagram is used as an interactive visual aid when designing the processes for a new service.

Histogram: A pictorial description of the frequency distribution of a variable. It shows the number of times each value of the variable occurs in a set of observations.

House of Quality (HOQ): The first matrix in the QFD hierarchy used to translate customer needs into service design characteristics.

Ideal Standard (or **Ideal Performance Level**): The optimal, but possibly unattainable, performance level for a design attribute. The ideal performance level may be different from the design and desired standards, but the service must be improved over time in the direction of the ideal performance level.

Integrated Design: A design that simultaneously designs the features, facilities, and processes of a service and explicitly considers interactions between the design alternatives available for each of these elements. Under this approach, design decisions are based on an understanding of the customers' overall service requirements and on the trade-offs that customers are willing to make between the performance of various design elements. The service design is therefore simultaneously optimized across all design elements.

Interaction: The dependence of one design attribute on the performance level of another design attribute for its contribution to satisfaction. Interaction effects can only be picked up by a conjoint analysis approach.

Kano Model: A conceptual model, attributed to Noriaki Kano, that maps three types of needs (basic, satisfiers, and delighters), and the level of customer satisfaction achieved with their fulfillment.

Lagged Dependent Variable Model: A regression model where the dependent variable lagged by one or more time periods appears as an independent variable in the regression equation. Such a model is used to model the cumulative effect of experience with a service on profitability or satisfaction.

Lagged Variable: A variable in a regression model that takes a value from one or more time periods in the past.

Level: The discrete performance value of a design attribute chosen for inclusion in a service profile. Typically, two or three levels are chosen for each attribute.

Line of Visibility: A line on a service blueprint that separates the activities that are visible to the customer from those that are invisible.

Minimum Acceptable Satisfaction Threshold: The base level of customer satisfaction that the service provided by the film should achieve in order to meets its strategic market share or revenue objectives.

Moment of Truth: A point in a process at which the output of the internal workings of the process becomes visible to the customer. These points present opportunities for delighting customers through exceptional service.

Needs: The desires, or wishes, that a customer has for a service. These include customers' expectations of what the service should contain, as well as how the service should be delivered. Needs may be stated or unstated, and a design that delights customers is one that can address the unstated needs.

Operating Characteristic: A factor of the operations of a service that contributes to variability in performance of a design attribute. For example, the number of requests received by a customer service facility may affect the time taken to answer the telephone. Operating characteristics depend on the environmental conditions under which the service operates, and on the design of the service.

Operating Range: The range of operating characteristics within which a design should deliver a required level of performance. This would be the normal range of operating conditions (present and future) that the design may experience. As far as possible, the performance of all attributes of the design should be robust within this range.

Operational Activity: A process step that needs to be performed to deliver a service to the customer. The quality of an operational activity is generally evaluated by objectively measurable attributes.

Operational Solution: An attempt to correct flaws in a service design by making changes to the operations of the service. An operational solution may be acceptable in the short term, but will prove to be ineffective or expensive in the long term. A design solution is always better than an operational solution.

Parameter of a Distribution: A set of measures that allow the selection of a particular curve from a family of curves characterizing a distribution. The mean and standard deviation are parameters of a normal distribution.

Pareto Chart: A histogram in which the frequency distribution of the occurrence of different values of a variable is sorted in decreasing order. The Pareto chart is used to identify the values or categories of a variable that occur most frequently. If the variable is a performance attribute such as causes for defects, improvement initiatives may be launched to address the top few causes indicated on the Pareto chart.

Performance Function: A function that expresses the average relationship between the value of a design factor or operating characteristic and the performance of a design attribute. Performance functions are used to predict the average performance of a design alternative under a range of realistic operating characteristics or design factors.

Performance/Importance Map: A graph that lists the importance of a service on the *y*-axis and the performance of the attribute on the *x*-axis. This map is used to select attributes for improvement.

Performance/Satisfaction Function: The function that expresses the relationship between various levels of performance of a design attribute and customer satisfaction.

Pilot Implementation: A limited operation of a design under controlled conditions, usually for testing the design before it is deployed.

Probability Distribution: A probability distribution is used to represent the random variability in the performance of a design attribute. The normal (Gaussian) distribution is a common example of a probability distribution.

Process/Subprocess Matrix: The third matrix in the QFD hierarchy, used to translate process design specifications into subprocess design specifications.

Process Flow Chart: A visual representation of a process that indicates how the process activities are connected to each other.

Pugh Method: A method developed by Prof. Stuart Pugh for evaluating design concepts that allows the selection of the best concept from among several alternatives. The method allows the concepts to be enhanced continuously during the evaluation procedure by using quantitative comparison and qualitative discussion of the candidate concepts.

Quality Function Deployment (QFD): A systematic, matrix-based visual approach for designing high-quality products and services. The technique uses a series of interconnected matrices to translate customer needs into service, process, and functional requirements for the design of the service.

R-squared: A measure of the percentage of the total variation in the dependent variable that is explained by the independent variables of a regression model. It is a measure of how well the model fits the data.

Random Variability: The spread or scatter around the base performance of a service as a result of unpredictable or unmeasurable environmental or operating effects.

Relationship Matrix: The QFD matrix that specifies the correlation between the customer needs and the design attributes.

Robust Design: A service design whose performance is insensitive to a range of variability in operating characteristics and environmental conditions. Robustness is a desirable property of any design.

Rollout and Transition Plan: A rollout plan addresses the logistics of the deployment of the new service in the organization. The transition plan spells out how a smooth transition from the old to the new design can be effected when existing operations are being replaced.

Root Cause Analysis: A form of analysis intended to identify the real, underlying reason for a problem. By finding the root cause of a service performance problem and fixing it, we ensure that we are not merely resolving some symptom of the problem, allowing the problem itself to recur later.

Routine Analysis: The service performance data that must be regularly and systematically analyzed in every reporting period to evaluate the performance of a service on the effectiveness, capability, and efficiency metrics.

Run Chart: A graph that shows the performance of a variable over time.

Satisfaction Rating Relative to Competition: This is a scale that measures customers' satisfaction with a service relative to the best or average competitor in the market. This comparison can be used to identify areas where the service must be immediately improved to keep up with or catch up to the competition.

Satisfaction Rating Relative to Expectations: This is a scale that measures customers' satisfaction with the performance of a service relative to their expectations. This scale is a measure of disconfirmation, which is correlated with satisfaction; it can be used to determine service attributes that can be improved over time by new design or reengineering efforts.

Scatter Plot: A graph that shows the relationship between two variables. The values of the dependent variable (whose value is predicted) are on the y-axis, and those of the predictor or independent variable (which predicts the value of the dependent variable) are on the x-axis. Each point on the graph represents a pair of values of the dependent and predictor variables. The amount of scatter and the shape of the scatter plot indicate the strength and form of the relationship between the variables.

Service: A business transaction that takes place between a service provider and a customer in order to produce an outcome that satisfactorily meets the customer's needs.

Service-Based Competitive Strategy: An approach taken by a firm to increase its profitability by developing a reputation for excellence in its interactions with customers, and by designing the processes that are needed to support these interactions.

Service Blueprinting: A process of flow-charting techniques that places process activities above or below a line of visibility. All activities above the line are visible to the customer, while those below the line are invisible.

Service Construction Plan: A plan that details the activities that are needed to build the functional components of the design, and their scheduling and coordination requirements. These include the documentation of the procedures needed to operate the service, the development of systems supporting the delivery of the service, and the training of personnel.

Service Delivery: The manner in which the service is offered to the customer during a service encounter. Delivery is influenced by the individuality and heterogeneity of the service encounter.

Service Design: The systematic, analytical methodology to construct service products, facilities, and processes that will reliably deliver the expected level of performance to satisfy or delight customers. The design affects the stability and reproducibility of service performance.

Service Facility: The location where the service is provided. This includes both front-room (visible to the customer) and back-room (invisible to the customer) locations. For some services, the facility may not correspond to a physical location.

Service Management Plan: A plan for the management and improvement of a service after the design is implemented and the new service is a stable operation. Service management activities involve the systematic and regular monitoring of service performance to confirm that the design is continuing to meet the performance standards, and to identify areas where improvement may be necessary.

Service Performance Measure: This measure evaluates the performance of an attribute of a service in operation. It ensures that the attribute is continuing to reliably meet the design specifications.

Service/Process Matrix: The second matrix in the QFD hierarchy, used to translate service design specifications into process design specifications.

Service Process: The sequence of activities that need to be performed to deliver the service.

Service Product: The tangible, physical attributes of a service.

Service Profile: A hypothetical descriptor of the service, consisting of a combination of design attributes at various prespecified performance levels.

Standard Deviation: Measure of variability around a mean value.

Status Metric: Metric used in a simulation model to provide instantaneous information on the current state of various process performance parameters. Status metrics are reset as often as necessary during the simulation.

Strategic Service Culture: An organizational culture that supports a service-based competitive strategy by being sensitive to customers' service requirements, but at the same time recognizes the need for the firm to remain profitable while satisfying these requirements. An organization with such a culture constantly seeks innovative design and improvement methods to meet customers' needs and its profitability objectives.

Subprocess/Function Matrix: The fourth matrix in the QFD hierarchy, used to translate subprocess design specifications into detailed hardware, software, documentation, and training requirements.

t-Statistic: A measure of the precision of an estimated parameter of a regression model that can be used to determine whether the parameter is significantly different from zero. A parameter is "significant" when its t-statistic is larger in absolute value than a "critical value" obtained from statistical charts. Independent variables with significant parameters have a relationship with the dependent variable.

Technical Benchmarks: The design team's technical assessment of the performance of key competitors on important design attributes. As far as possible, these benchmarks should be objective, engineering evaluations of competitors' performance.

Total Service Design: A multidisciplinary, iterative activity that integrates engineering methodology with marketing and management principles to transform an idea or market need into a successful service.

Transaction-Specific Satisfaction: The satisfaction from a single service encounter. It may influence, but may be different from, a customer's attitude towards the service provider.

Value: A customer's measure of the overall worth of the service, based on perceptions of how well it meets the customer's needs relative to its price. Value is a key determinant of a customer's decision to purchase a service.

BIBLIOGRAPHY

Akao, Yoji, Editor-in-Chief (1990). *Quality Function Deployment: Integrating Customer Requirements into Product Design,* translated by Glenn H. Mazur and Japan Business Consultants, Ltd. Productivity Press, Cambridge, MA.

Anderson, E. W., C. Fornell, and D. R. Lehmann (1994). "Customer satisfaction, market share and profitability: Findings from Sweden," *Journal of Marketing* **58**, 53–66.

Asaka, T., Editor (1990). *Handbook of Quality Tools: The Japanese Approach,* Productivity Press, Cambridge, MA.

Barker, T. B. (1994). *Quality by Experimental Design.* Marcel Dekker, New York.

Belasco, J. A. (1990). *Teaching the Elephant to Dance: The Manager's Guide to Empowering Change.* Crown Publishing, New York, NY.

Bicknell, Barbara A., and Kris D. Bicknell (1995). *The Road Map to Repeatable Success: Using QFD to Implement Change.* CRC Press, Boca Raton, FL.

Brassard, M. (1989). *The Memory Jogger Plus.* Goal/QPC, Methuen, MA.

Carman, J. M. (1990). "Consumer perceptions of service quality: An assessment of the SERVQUAL dimensions," *Journal of Retailing* **66**, 33–55.

Carter, Don E., and Barbara Stillwell Baker (1992). *Concurrent Engineering: The Product Development Environment for the 1990s.* Addison-Wesley Publishing Company, Reading, MA.

Cassidy, H. J. (1981). *Using Econometrics: A Beginner's Guide.* Reston Publishing Company, Reston, VA.

Chatterjee, S., and B. Price (1991). *Regression Analysis by Example.* Wiley, New York.

Clausing, Don P. (1994). *Total Quality Development: A Step-by-Step Guide to World-Class Concurrent Engineering.* ASME Press, New York.

Cohen, Lou (1995). *Quality Function Deployment: How to Make QFD Work for You.* Addison-Wesley Publishing Company, Reading, MA.

Condra, L. W. (1993). *Reliability Improvement with Design of Experiments.* Marcel Dekker, New York.

Cross, Nigel (1989). *Engineering Design Methods.* John Wiley and Sons, New York.

de Brentani, U. (1993). "The new product process in financial services: Strategy for success," *International Journal of Bank Marketing* **11**(3), 15–22.

DeSarbo, W. S., L. Huff, M. M. Rolandelli, and J. Choi (1994). "On the measure of perceived service quality: A conjoint analysis approach," in R. T. Rust and R. L. Oliver (Eds.), *Service Quality: New Dimensions in Theory and Practice.* SAGE Publications, Thousand Oaks, CA.

Dubé, L., L. M. Renaghan, and J. M. Miller (1994). "Measuring customer satisfaction for strategic management," *Cornell H.R.A. Quarterly*, February.

Emory, C. W., and D. R. Cooper (1991). *Business Research Methods*, 4th Ed. Irwin, Homewood, IL.

Fishbein, M., and I. Azjen (1975). *Belief, Attitude, Intention and Behavior.* Addison-Wesley Publishing Company, Reading, MA.

Fisher, K. K. (1993). *Leading Self-Directed Work Teams: A Guide to Developing New Team Leadership.* McGraw-Hill, New York.

Fowlkes, W. Y., and C. M. Creveling (1995). *Engineering Methods for Robust Design: Using Taguchi Methods in Technology and Product Development.* Addison-Wesley Publishing Company, Reading, MA.

Gale, B. T. (1994). *Managing Customer Value: Creating Quality and Service That Customers Can See.* Free Press, New York.

Green, P. E., and V. Srinivasan (1978). "Conjoint analysis in consumer research: Issues and outlook," *Journal of Consumer Research* **5**, 103–123.

Green, P. E., and V. Srinivasan (1990). "Conjoint analysis in marketing research: new developments and directions," *Journal of Marketing* **54**, 3–19.

Griffin, A., and J. R. Hauser (1993). "The Voice of the Customer," *Marketing Science* **12**(1).

Grove, D. M., and T. P. Davis (1992). *Engineering, Quality and Experimental Design.* John Wiley and Sons, New York.

Gukezian, R. C. (1991). *Process Control: Statistical Principles and Tools.* QualityAlert Institute, Inc., New York.

Hartley, J. R. (1992). *Concurrent Engineering: Shortening Lead Times, Raising Quality and Lowering Costs.* Productivity Press, Cambridge, MA.

Hauser, J. R., and Don P. Clausing (1988). "The House of Quality," *Harvard Business Review* **66**(3) (May–June), 63–73.

Hicks, C. R. (1993). *Fundamental Concepts in the Design of Experiments*, 4th Ed. Saunders College Publishing, New York.

Hildebrand, D. K., and L. Ott (1987). *Statistical Theory for Managers.* Duxbury Press, Boston.

Hung, D. S. (1970). *Regression and Econometric Methods.* Wiley, New York.

Jick, Todd D. (1993). *Managing Change: Cases and Concepts.* Richard D. Irwin, Inc., Homewood, IL.

Johnston, J. (1972). *Econometric Methods*, 2nd Ed. McGraw-Hill, New York.

Juran, J. M., and Frank M. Gyrna (1990). *Quality Planning and Analysis*, 3rd Ed. McGraw-Hill, New York.

Kacker, R. N. (1985). "Taguchi's quality philosophy: analysis and commentary," in Khosrow Dehnad (Editor), *Quality Control, Robust Design and the Taguchi Method.* Wadsworth & Brooks/Cole, Pacific Grove, CA.

Kordupleski, R., R. T. Rust, and A. J. Zahorik (1993). "Why improving quality doesn't improve quality," *California Management Review* **35** (Spring), 82–95.

Kume, H. (1985). *Statistical Methods for Quality Improvement*. The Association for Overseas Technical Scholarship, Tokyo.

LaMarsh, Jeanenne (1995). *Changing the Way We Change: Gaining Control of Major Operational Change*. Addison-Wesley Publishing Company, Reading, MA.

Larsen, R. J., and M. L. Marx (1986). *An Introduction to Mathematical Statistics and Its Applications*, 2nd Ed. Prentice-Hall, Englewood Cliffs, NJ.

Law, A. M., and W. D. Kelton (1991). *Simulation Modeling and Analysis*, 2nd Ed. McGraw-Hill, New York.

Manheim, M. L. (1979). *Fundamentals of Transportation System Analysis*, Vol. 1, MIT Press, Cambridge, MA.

Masson, R. D. (1986). *Statistical Techniques in Business and Economics*, 6th Ed. Irwin, Homewood, IL.

McNeese, W. H., and R. A. Klein (1991). *Statistical Methods for the Process Industries*. ASQC Press, Milwaukee.

Montgomery, D. C., and E. A. Price (1992). *Introduction to Linear Regression Analysis*. Wiley and Sons, New York.

Nelson, L. S. (1984). "The Shewhart control chart—tests for special causes," *Journal of Quality Technology* **16**(4), 237–239.

Normann, R., and R. Ramirez (1993). "From value chain to value constellation: designing interactive strategy," *Harvard Business Review*, July–August.

Oliver, R. L. (1980). "A cognitive model of the antecedents and consequences of satisfaction decisions," *Journal of Marketing Research* **17**, 460–469.

Oliver, R. L. (1989). "Processing of the satisfaction response in consumption: A suggested framework and research propositions," *Journal of Consumer Satisfaction, Dissatisfaction and Complaining Behavior* **2**, 1–16.

Oliver, R. L. (1993). "A conceptual model of service quality and service satisfaction: Compatible goals, different concepts," in T. A. Swartz, D. E. Bowen, and S. W. Brown (Eds.), *Advances in Services Marketing and Management: Research and Practice*, Vol. 2, pp. 65–85. JAI Press, Greenwich, CT.

Osborn, A. (1957). *Applied Imagination—Principles and Practices of Creative Thinking*. Charles Scribners Sons, New York.

Peace, G. S. (1993). *Taguchi Methods*. Addison-Wesley Publishing Company, Reading, MA.

Phadke, M. S. (1985). "Quality engineering using design of experiments," in Khosrow Dehnad (Editor), *Quality Control, Robust Design and the Taguchi Method*. Wadsworth & Brooks/Cole, Pacific Grove, CA.

Pidd, M. (1992). *Computer Simulation in Management Science*. Wiley, New York.

Pindyck, R. S., and D. L. Rubinfeld (1981). *Econometric Models and Economic Forecasts.* Mc-Graw-Hill, New York.

Pugh, S. (1991). *Total Design: Integrated Methods for Successful Product Engineering.* Addison-Wesley Publishing Company, Reading, MA.

Quirke, Bill (1995). *Communicating Change.* McGraw-Hill, New York.

Ramaswamy, R., and K. Hafiz (1994). "Estimating a customer focused service process improvement model," AT&T paper.

Rust, R. T., A. J. Zahorik, and T. L. Keiningham (1994). *Return on Quality: Measuring the Financial Impact of Your Company's Quest for Quality.* Probus Publishing Company, Chicago.

Shiba, S., A. Graham, and D. Walden (1993). *A New American TQM: Four Practical Revolutions in Management.* Productivity Press/Center for Quality Management.

Shina, S. G., Editor (1994). *Successful Implementation of Concurrent Engineering Products and Processes.* Van Nostrand Reinhold, New York.

Shostack, L. G. (1984). "Designing services that deliver," *Harvard Business Review* **62**(1) (January–February), 133–139.

Sontow, K., and Don P. Clausing (1993). "Integration of Quality Function Deployment with further methods of quality planning." Working paper, Laboratory of Manufacturing and Productivity, Massachusetts Institute of Technology, Cambridge, MA.

Stalk, G., Jr., and A. M. Webber (1993). "Japan's dark side of time," *Harvard Business Review,* July–August.

Taguchi, G., and Y. Wu (1979). *Introduction to Off-line Quality Control.* Central Japan Quality Control Association.

Turtle, Q. C. (1994). *Implementing Concurrent Project Management.* Prentice-Hall, Englewood Cliffs, NJ.

Wesner, J. W., J. M. Hiatt, and D. C. Trimble (1995). *Winning with Quality: Applying Quality Principles in Product Development.* Addison-Wesley Publishing Company, Reading, MA.

Yi, Youjae (1991). "A critical review of consumer satisfaction," in V. A. Zeithami (Ed.), *Review of Marketing 1990,* pp. 68–123. American Marketing Association, Chicago.

Zahorik, A. J., and R. T. Rust (1991). "Modeling the impact of service quality on profitability: A review," in T. A. Swartz, D. E. Bowen, and S. W. Brown (Eds.), *Advances in Services Marketing and Management: Research and Practice,* Vol. 1, pp. 247–276. JAI Press, Greenwich, CT.

Zeithami, V. A. (1988). "Consumer perceptions of price, quality and value: A means–end model and synthesis of evidence," *Journal of Marketing* **52**, 2–22.

Zeithami, V. A., L. L. Berry, and A. Parasuraman (1993). "The nature and determinants of customer expectations of service," *Journal of the Academy of Marketing Science* **21**(1), 1–12.

INDEX